THE WORLD OF WORK
Readings for Writers

John W. Presley
Norman Prinsky

Augusta College

Prentice-Hall, Inc., Englewood Cliffs, N.J. 07632

Library of Congress Cataloging-in-Publication Data

The World of work.

1. Readers—Work.   2. Work.   3. Work ethic.
4. Vocation.   5. College readers.   6. English language—
Rhetoric.   I. Presley, John W.   II. Prinsky, Norman
PE1127.W65W57   1987   808'.0427   86-12307
ISBN   0-13-966169-7

Editorial/production supervision and
   interior design: Sylvia Moore
Cover design: Lundgren Graphics, Ltd.
Manufacturing buyer: Ray Keating

©1987 by Prentice-Hall, Inc.
A Division of Simon & Schuster
Englewood Cliffs, New Jersey 07632

Printed in the United States of America

10 9 8 7 6 5 4 3 2 1

ISBN   0-13-966169-7   01

Prentice-Hall International (UK) Limited, *London*
Prentice-Hall of Australia Pty. Limited, *Sydney*
Prentice-Hall Canada Inc., *Toronto*
Prentice-Hall Hispanoamericana, S.A., *Mexico*
Prentice-Hall of India Private Limited, *New Delhi*
Prentice-Hall of Japan, Inc., *Tokyo*
Prentice-Hall of Southeast Asia Pte. Ltd., *Singapore*
Editora Prentice-Hall do Brasil, Ltda., *Rio de Janeiro*

CONTENTS

WORK AND MORALITY   43

WORK AND EDUCATION   74

CAREERS FOR THE 1990'S   104

MONEY   147

TO THE INSTRUCTOR

No teacher would argue that a student should not take a serious view of career, work, and finance; however, teachers often feel that students choose majors and occupational goals that will result in a job at the end of four years, with too little consideration given to how work, studies, and self-realization may be blended. In other words, not often enough do students heed how the full development of their abilities, minds, and sensitivities may be matched with fulfilling careers.

The essays collected here, the questions, and the writing assignments all encourage students to explore their choice of career, or their choice of major, both to see whether that choice reflects their sense of self and to arrive at a broader, humanistic notion of work.

Our anthology contains selections from many of the world's great authors and thinkers—Hesiod, Montaigne, Calvin, Samuel Johnson. These are only a few of many important writers for whom the questions of work and money—how to make a living—were subjects of intense concern. Such renowned essayists as Addison, Emerson, Carlyle, and Lamb (selections by all of whom could not be included because of space considerations) have treated them. The students in American colleges and universities today are by no means unique in their concern with choosing a career and their occupational goals. Though this focus on the working life is often decried as "mere vocationalism," the great writers of the past found the idea of *vocation* certainly worthy of their pens, as exemplified by essays in this anthology.

Together with his practical advice about saving and working, Benjamin Franklin dispensed sound moral and psychological advice. In the preface to his *Poor Richard's Almanack,* we find Franklin arguing that true economy and success stem from one's ethics and personality. For Thoreau, the essential question was not "How to make a living?" so much as "Why make a living as people now do?" John Calvin was even more direct in seeing spiritual dimensions in one's choice of vocation. Likewise, important authors like Samuel Johnson and Thomas Fuller found larger, philosophical issues to consider when exploring the world of work and finance.

These beliefs, that work has an ethical dimension and is profoundly interrelated to one's sense of self and the world, continue in the writings of modern authors like Patrick Fenton, who find that the modern workplace alienates the worker from the larger dimensions of work. Those writers who, like Richard Selzer, do find satisfaction in the workplace, have discovered that an occupation may enhance one's sensitivity to self and the surrounding world.

Even in one of the most recent and most practical essays in this collection, Davidyne Mayleas says that finding a job can be "a valuable personal adventure" and that taking stock of abilities and prospects can help you "develop new ideas about yourself."

In sum, the student's need for practical advice need not conflict with the teacher's charge to explore vital areas of the liberal arts curriculum while presenting the student with rhetorical models for analysis and selections to improve reading comprehension.

The World of Work: Readings for Writers includes forty-two essays from thirty-eight writers, ranging from Hesiod and Francis Bacon to Adam Smith, Samuel Clemens, and several contemporary authors. These essays are divided into nine thematic categories:

Job Choice and Self-fulfillment
Work and Morality
Work and Education
Careers for the 1990s
Money
Job Opportunities and Other Practical Matters
Varieties of Work
Efficiency and Success on the Job
The Work Environment

Essays written by authors prominent in either the worlds of business or belles-lettres are preceded by introductions that are designed to inform students about the author's standing, as well as to provide various "pre-reading" and "post-reading" aids. All essays have some pre-reading apparatus, designed to alert the student to such things as an essay's original place of publication, date, or intended audience, which will help explain the form, style, and level of difficulty of the selection.

We have followed all selections with full vocabulary lists, believing, after having taught a wide range of students at several post-secondary institutions of various kinds, that improvement in vocabulary recognition is one of the quickest (though all too often ignored) routes to improving reading comprehension. The teacher should apprise students that common words such as "want," "embarrassed," "peculiar," and "rude"— all in our twentieth selection, by Adam Smith—are listed when used to convey a different sense or meaning from an average reader's first expectation.

Four kinds of questions follow each essay. Questions on "Ideas and Aims" are intended to develop literal and inferential comprehension. "Organization and Form" questions stress rhetorical structures of both the overall essay and individual paragraphs, while also emphasizing the topics of coherence and transition. "Words and Style" questions point out rhetorical devices, figurative language, and the writer's control of denotation and connotation. The questions listed under "Discussion and Writing" provide impetus for classroom discussion of larger or personal issues and application of the author's ideas to contemporary student concerns. Topics for writing often involve comparing or contrasting the ideas in several selections, and the topics frequently suggest that the student use a particular selection as a rhetorical model.

At the end of each of the nine sections of this book are additional questions, which may by used for discussion or writing or both. As the heading for these questions suggests ("Taking Stock: Comparing and Contrasting the Selections"), they are aimed at providing further linkages between and among the various readings. Sometimes in these questions the student is invited to compare or contrast readings from different sections of the book; our hope is to give this anthology a more unified feeling than is usually derived from anthologies.

For some selections our apparatus is rather detailed. We have provided numerous specific questions, knowing from experience that generality in a question often becomes vagueness or obscurity to the freshman (or even the sophomore or junior) reader. Further, some questions will work better for a particular class or class section or teacher, while different questions will be more effective for another class, class section, or teacher. Also, an instructor for variety may well want to vary the questions asked from one term to the next. Of course, not all questions need by any means be assigned for class discussion or writing.

The World of Work, we believe, provides a sound apparatus for introducing students to a variety of prose models and to the long tradition of essay literature treating a subject of deep—and real—importance to college students.

We wish to thank the small conglomerate who have contributed to the final incorporation of our enterprise: our editor, Phil Miller, stalwart steering committee of one; Sylvia Moore, our production editor and in all the best senses book-keeper, cheerful and meticulous; and finally, our several scrupulous auditors—our copy editor and reviewers—for helpful comments and suggestions: Ilene McGrath, copy editor; Douglas Butturff, formerly University of Central Arkansas; Lucas Carpenter, Oxford College of Emory University; Kenneth Davis, University of Kentucky; Stanley J. Kozikowski, Bryant College; Paul Lizotte, Rivier College; and Twila Yates Papay, Rollins College. Lastly, thanks to those models of productivity on several levels: Ruth and Arnold Prinsky.

JOB CHOICE AND SELF-FULFILLMENT

DULL WORK

Eric Hoffer

Eric Hoffer was born in New York City in 1902 and died in 1983. He was, in his own words, "practically blind up to the age of fifteen. When my eyesight came back, I was seized with an enormous hunger for the printed word." He read voraciously. During his early years as a migrant worker, a dishwasher, a gold miner, and a longshoreman, Hoffer took advantage of every opportunity to read and to write. During one long winter, snowed in, he read all of Montaigne's Essays *six times. (See Section 2, "Work and Morality," for a short essay by Montaigne.)*

Hoffer migrated to California early. He said, "I knew several things: one, that I didn't want to work in a factory; two, that I couldn't stand being dependent upon the good graces of a boss; three, that I was going to stay poor." While waiting for trains, or at noon, or during rest periods in the fields, he wrote his early works, among them The True Believer *(1951),* The Passionate State of Mind *(1955), and* The Ordeal of Change *(1963). Among his later works,* Reflections on the Human Condition *(1972) is probably the most notable. Hoffer was famous for his clarity and logic. Self-educated philosopher, controversialist, and author of six books, he has been called "a born generalizer, with a mind that inclines to the wry epigram and the icy aphorism."*

1 There seems to be a general assumption that brilliant people cannot stand routine; that they need a varied, exciting life in order to do their best. It is also assumed that dull people are particularly suited for dull work. We are told that the reason the present-day young protest so loudly against the dullness of factory jobs is that they are better educated and brighter than the young of the past.

2 Actually, there is no evidence that people who achieve much crave for, let alone live, eventful lives. The opposite is nearer the truth. One thinks of Amos the sheepherder, Socrates the stonemason, Omar the tentmaker. Jesus probably had his first revelations while doing humdrum carpentry work. Einstein worked out his theory of relativity while serving as a clerk in a Swiss patent office. Machiavelli wrote *The Prince* and the *Discourses* while immersed in the dull life of a small country town where the only excitement he knew was playing cards with muleteers at the inn. Immanuel Kant's daily life was an unalterable routine. The housewives of Königsberg set their clocks when they saw him pass on his way to the university. He took the same walk each morning, rain or shine. The greatest distance Kant ever traveled was sixty miles from Königsberg.

3 The outstanding characteristic of man's creativeness is the ability to transmute trivial impulses into momentous consequences. The greatness of man is in what he can do with petty grievances and joys, and with common physiological pressures and hungers. "When I have a little vexation," wrote Keats, "it grows in five minutes into a theme for Sophocles." To a creative individual all experience is seminal—all events are equidistant from new ideas and insights—and his inordinate humanness shows itself in the ability to make the trivial and common reach an enormous way.

4 An eventful life exhausts rather than stimulates. Milton, who in 1640 was a poet of great promise, spent twenty sterile years in the eventful atmosphere of the Puritan revolution. He fulfilled his great promise when the revolution was dead, and he in solitary disgrace. Cellini's exciting life kept him from becoming the great artist he could have been. It is

legitimate to doubt whether Machiavelli would have written his great books had he been allowed to continue in the diplomatic service of Florence and had he gone on interesting missions. It is usually the mediocre poets, writers, etc., who go in search of stimulating events to release their creative flow.

5   It may be true that work on the assembly line dulls the faculties and empties the mind, the cure only being fewer hours of work at higher pay. But during fifty years as a workingman, I have found dull routine compatible with an active mind. I can still savor the joy I used to derive from the fact that while doing dull, repetitive work on the waterfront, I could talk with my partners and compose sentences in the back of my mind, all at the same time. Life seemed glorious. Chances are that had my work been of absorbing interest I could not have done any thinking and composing on the company's time or even on my own time after returning from work.

6   People who find dull jobs unendurable are often dull people who do not know what to do with themselves when at leisure. Children and mature people thrive on dull routine, while the adolescent, who has lost the child's capacity for concentration and is without the inner resources of the mature, needs excitement and novelty to stave off boredom.

Editors' note: We have included definitions and notes where they make a selection more easily understood. Other than these aids and some necessary elision, we have not altered the original texts, and this has left some language that may now be considered sexist, such as Hoffer's use, in paragraph 3, of "man" and "he." We trust that modern readers will consider such usage in its historic context.

VOCABULARY

crave (P2), *eventful* (P2), *Amos* (P2), *Socrates* (P2), *Omar* (P2), *humdrum* (P2), *Machiavelli* (P2), *immersed* (P2), *muleteers* (P2), *Kant* (P2), *unalterable* (P2), *transmute* (P3), *momentous* (P3), *petty* (P3), *physiological* (P3), *vexation* (P3), *Keats* (P3), *Sophocles* (P3), *seminal* (P3), *equidistant* (P3), *inordinate* (P3), *Milton* (P4), *Cellini* (P4), *mediocre* (P4), *faculties* (P5), *compatible* (P5), *savor* (P5), *thrive* (P6), *novelty* (P6), *stave off* (P6)

IDEAS AND AIMS

1. What does Hoffer mean by "dull" work?
2. What kinds of examples does Hoffer use to illustrate his idea that brilliant people do not require exciting lives? In what categories are these people famous?
3. What is the outstanding characteristic of human creativity, according to

Hoffer? How do human beings, in other words, make dull circumstances eventful?

4. What is the danger of an eventful life, for the creative person?
5. How does Hoffer illustrate this danger?
6. How did Hoffer busy his mind while performing routine work?
7. According to Hoffer, then, must "dull" work be dull? What kinds of people, according to Hoffer, find dull jobs unendurable?
8. Hoffer's overall aim in this essay is to argue and persuade, rather than to explain. What from the essay makes this clear?
9. Hoffer's essay depends on two key concepts and terms, "dull" and "creative." What does he mean by each, judging from how he uses the terms in the essay?
10. What implicit distinction is there in the essay between "dull people" (P6) and the mind of a person being dulled by work (P5)?

ORGANIZATION AND FORM

1. Hoffer's argument is primarily inductive rather than deductive. (Look up these as well as other such technical terms in your collegiate dictionary or composition handbook.) How is the inductive method used in P2, P3, P4, and P5?
2. What sentence in Hoffer's essay comes closest to stating his overall thesis?
3. How does P1 function to state the con side that Hoffer will argue against?
4. How is Hoffer's inductive example in P5 different from the preceding examples in PP2–4? Is it effectively used for an argumentative or persuasive essay? Why or why not?
5. How does Hoffer's conclusion, P5, extend or develop his main idea rather than merely repeating or restating it?

WORDS AND STYLE

1. Hoffer very successfully uses clear abstract words to convey his ideas. How are the first sentence of P2, the first sentence of P3, and the first sentence of P4 effective in this respect? What other examples would you add?
2. How does Hoffer use parallelism effectively in P2?
3. Which is the shortest sentence of P5 (and, indeed, of the whole essay)? How does its length work rhetorically—that is, how does it help Hoffer convey his idea and mood (tone) at this point in the essay?

DISCUSSION AND WRITING

1. Weak spots in the argument based on induction are that the examples used as evidence may be too few or not representative. Are enough individuals from enough fields cited to convince you? Why or why not?

2. On the issue of representativeness (see question 1), what might an opponent argue against Hoffer's example used for evidence in P5?

3. Compose an inductive argumentative essay, countering Hoffer's, based on "creative" or "brilliant" people whose work was seriously retarded or hindered by dull jobs.

4. Have you ever held a dull, routine job? What did you do to occupy your mental capacities while you did the work demanded of you?

5. Compare or contrast Hoffer's essay with Patrick Fenton's in Section 7, "Varieties of Work: Professions and Blue Collar." After reading both of these essays, do you find yourself more on Hoffer's side or Fenton's? Why?

THE WORKAHOLIC IN YOU

Warren Boroson

☐

Born and raised in New York, Warren Boroson was educated at Columbia University and has worked mostly in journalism, as both an editor and a writer. Our selection, published in Money *magazine, has a journalistic style. Generally, paragraphs are short, making them suitable for a narrow-column format; likewise, blocks of text are broken up by teaser headings ("Billiards to Him," "Murderous Tennis"). In line with good magazine writing, Boroson uses some erudite words where appropriate ("recondite," "frenetically"), and, most importantly, many facts, figures, and quotations from experts.*

1 ● *"When things slow down at the hospital, I get unhappy, morose," says Dr. Denton Cooley, the Houston heart surgeon. "I like to see how much more I can do than the next fellow. And the next fellow happens to be Dr. [Michael] DeBakey."*

2 ● *A few years ago, when friends told Ralph Nader they had spent a week-end lying on the beach, going for walks and reading the newspapers, Nader exclaimed in disbelief, "That takes all weekend?"*

3 ● *When somebody recently joshed George Allen, the hard-working coach of the Washington Redskins football team, about allowing himself five or six hours of sleep a night, he answered seriously, "Everybody needs some leisure."*

4   Lots of Americans work hard and play hard. But some just work, either from the unquenchable love of it or from a compulsion beyond their control. Work lovers—the unquenchables—provide society with many leaders in business, politics, science and the arts. Those who overwork out of compulsion—the work addicts, or workaholics, of this world—are in trouble. Their addiction can lead to dead-end careers, to poor health, even to early death. They are so emotionally dependent on work that without it they start coming unglued. Though the purebred workaholic is rare, there is a little of him in almost everyone. It is well to know the warning signals and how to cope with them.

Billiards to Him

5   Confusing workaholics with work lovers is a bit like confusing winos with oenophiles. Mark Twain was a work lover. In 1908, when he was nearly 73, he said he hadn't done a lick of work in over 50 years. Wrote Twain: "I have always been able to gain my living without doing any work; for the writing of books and magazine matter was always play, not work. I enjoyed it; it was merely billiards to me."

6   Psychiatrist Carl Jung once said that the difference between the recondite prose of James Joyce and the poetry of Joyce's insane daughter was that he was diving and she was falling. The work lover is diving. He works hard and long by choice. When he wants to, he can stop without suffering acute withdrawal pains. When work addicts go on vacation, however, it is not the natives but the tourists who are restless.

7   The work lover's work is also his play. The work addict's motives are mixed. In many cases, he is seeking the admiration of other people because he doesn't approve of himself. As Dr. Alan McLean, an IBM psychiatrist, points out, the healthiest people usually have various sources of satisfaction: they are lawyers, say, but they are also spouses, parents, friends, citizens, churchgoers, art lovers, stamp collectors, golf- ers and so forth. If such people lose their jobs, or if their work becomes less satisfying or its quality starts deteriorating, they have not lost their sole interest in life, the only prop to their self-esteem. Many compulsive workers, according to cardiologist Meyer Friedman of San Francisco, co- author of the bestselling book *Type A Behavior and Your Heart* (1974), "want status, and their status depends on what other people think of them." Eventually, many addicts manage to labor under the delusion that they are indispensable.

8   Guilt propels some workaholics. Several years ago, a theological seminary in the East had a problem with guilt-ridden students who kept working even when the school closed for vacations. To get them out, the school was finally forced to turn off the electricity and water and change all the locks during vacation periods.

9   Because of their diligence, work addicts in corporations tend to keep

getting promoted; but a lack of imagination keeps them from reaching the top rungs. They make great salesmen and terrible corporation presidents. "Workaholics rarely become famous," says Dr. Frederic Flach, a New York psychiatrist who has treated many people with work problems. "Because they lack creativity, they rarely make an original contribution to the welfare of mankind. They usually end up in upper-middle management, giving grief to everyone around them."

Murderous Tennis

10 Continual work, Dr. Flach notes, "violates one of the basic rules for coming up with original solutions—to move into another area and let the problem simmer." He adds that one reason workaholics work ten to twelve hours a day is that "they are not good at finding ways to think about something in a new fashion." Work addicts, says Robert F. Medina, an industrial psychologist in Chicago, like "the sureness and safety of processing endless details. Creativity is a little too scary. It looks like idleness to them."

11   As employees of large corporations, work addicts can have a hard time of it. The staff psychiatrist at a huge national manufacturing firm tells of an executive in the New York headquarters who came to him for help. Discussion brought out that the executive felt best when things were "impossible"—when he was being seriously tested and overworked. Free time made him uneasy and anxious. Many addicts like him end up self-employed so they can have expandable working time. (But even blue-collar workers can manage to become work addicts by taking second jobs or constantly volunteering for overtime.)

12   Wherever he earns his living, the workaholic is likely to work hard not just on the job but off duty too. "When his back is to the wall," says Dr. Howard Hess, a Western Electric corporate psychiatrist, "he may cut the lawn with a vengeance or play a murderous game of tennis." A Chicago psychiatrist, Dr. Saul M. Siegel, recalls a work addict who had an extramarital affair. He kept working as hard as ever, though, and "wound up with both a nagging wife and a nagging mistress."

13   While work addicts work hard, they tend to die easily. Time and again, researchers have found that the compulsively hard-working person is particularly prone to heart disease in middle age. Dr. Friedman and his cardiologist co-author, Dr. Ray H. Rosenman, divide the world into two working types. Hard-driving people are classified as Type A and low-pressure people as Type B. Both types can become workaholics, but in different ways. The Type-A person is excessively ambitious and competitive, and frequently hostile; he feels pressured by deadlines. Cardiologists have found that he is two to three times as likely to have a

premature heart attack as a Type B, who is not so competitive and hard driving.

14   Type-B workaholics are civil service types who lose themselves in dull paperwork or other routine activities. Wayne Oates, a Louisville psychologist, thinks that a Type-B work addict, unlike the individualistic Type A, tends to identify with the company he works for and "not have any selfhood of his own. The company is a flat earth to him. Everything beyond it is dragons and disaster."

15   The domestic life of the workaholic is likely to be troubled. In some cases, addicts marry each other and go their own unmerry ways. More typically, the wife is a nonaddict, resentful that her husband has so little time and energy to expend on the family. The addict himself may nonetheless expect his wife and children to be robotlike perfectionists. Although the typical work addict doesn't like to help around the house, he "may be a busybody poking into his wife's household affairs and telling her how inefficient she is with the cooking and the housecleaning," reports Dr. Nelson J. Bradley, a psychiatrist in Park Ridge, Ill. "He's too preoccupied with his own work goals to be sensitive to the needs of others" in the family.

16   Going on a family vacation with a workaholic can be a hellish ordeal. Robert Medina, the Chicago psychologist, tells of the president of a midwestern company whose wife and daughter shanghaied him to Hawaii for three weeks on the beach. The man hadn't taken a vacation in 13 years. He made everybody so miserable by his compulsion to keep phoning the office that after four days his family was as frantic to get home as he was.

17   A housewife can be a workaholic too. She may insist on doing so much that her children never learn everyday household skills. The daughters of such women "often grow up without knowing how to cook, sew, clean and decorate the home," says psychologist Wayne Oates.

18   Sometimes a work addict can persuade himself as well as other people that he is really a work lover, the way an alcoholic can persuade himself and others that he doesn't have a drinking problem because all he drinks is vintage cognac. Reading someone's basic motives can be difficult. But it's very likely that a work lover—unlike a work addict—has a job that offers freedom and diversity; he is well recognized and amply rewarded for his efforts. An obscure middle-aged heart surgeon or social reformer who works as hard as Dr. Denton Cooley or Ralph Nader is more likely to be a self-destructive work addict than those two men are. Nader scoffs at the notion that his ceaseless toil makes him a workaholic. "You wouldn't ask an Olympic swimmer or chess player why he works 20 hours a day," Nader says. People don't understand Nader "because we haven't a tradition which explains me."

Like Giving Birth

19 Without being workaholics, most people experience the addict's symptoms from time to time. "Anyone who's been busy and active," says Dr. Flach, the New York psychiatrist, "has a tendency to get locked in, to become dependent on his work." Examples are accountants in March and April, salesclerks during the Christmas rush, air traffic controllers all the time. When they are no longer so busy, they may suffer from a mild version of "postpartum depression," like women who have just given birth.

20   Some people work too long and hard at times because they fear being fired or are bucking for promotion or cannot do their jobs as well as they know they should. Other people sometimes lose themselves in work to escape emotional problems—the loss of a loved one, a financial setback or some other worry. They use work to keep from breaking down completely. Occupational therapy is, after all, one of the very best painkillers and tranquilizers.

21   These people differ from chronic addicts in that once they have stopped working for a while, their pain begins to ebb, their spirits perk up, and they are back to normal. But someone who has been temporarily habituated to hard work would be best advised to unwind slowly. People who suddenly switch from hard work to idleness tend to develop a variety of physical and psychological illnesses, heart disease in particular. Social psychologist Jerome E. Singer of the National Research Council in Washington, D.C., mentions how people often die shortly after retiring from important posts.

22   For some work addicts, the realization that something is amiss comes only when they develop health problems. For Wayne Oates, author of *Confessions of a Workaholic* (1971), recognition came when his five-year-old son asked for an appointment to see him. (Oates probably coined the term "workaholic," though the editors of the Merriam-Webster dictionaries give the *Wall Street Journal* of Feb. 2, 1971, as the first source.) Someone who suspects he may be growing psychologically dependent on work should ask himself whether he can unwind readily over a weekend or during a vacation.

23   Jerome Singer recommends that hard-working people generally avoid making abrupt major changes in their work habits. People who work frenetically all year long may suffer if they suddenly flop down on a beach in Hawaii for a few weeks. Instead, Singer suggests that hard workers would be better off taking frequent short vacations or easing into long vacations by cutting down gradually on their work.

24   Recognizing the value of vacations, many companies (General Motors, for one) now require all employees to take the vacations they are entitled to instead of accumulating them from year to year. Dr. Nicholas

A WORKAHOLIC'S SOBRIETY TEST

When psychologists interview patients for symptoms of compulsive work habits, they often ask questions like these. Well-adjusted people may give the same answers as work addicts to some of the questions, but a true workaholic will probably answer nearly all of them as indicated at the bottom of the page.

1. Do you frequently telephone friends in the evening just to chat?
2. Do you generally keep your office door closed?
3. If you had to choose, would you rather be admired than liked by friends and co-workers?
4. Do you usually let people finish what they're saying to you?
5. Does your spouse (or closest friend) think of you as relaxed and easygoing?
6. a) Do you get upset when the car ahead is driving too slowly and you can't pass? b) If so, do you keep your annoyance to yourself rather than expressing it to others in your car?
7. Do you like to help with household chores such as dishwashing?
8. Do you often bring work into the bathroom?
9. Are you punctual for appointments?
10. Are you usually much annoyed when your spouse (or a friend) keeps you waiting?
11. While you're in a meeting or busy with someone in your office, do you usually refuse to take phone calls?
12. When someone is talking to you, do you often let your mind stray to other lines of thought?

A. Pace, medical director of GM's New York executive offices, adds that employees who try not to take vacations "don't get brownie points any more. They're just looked upon as damn fools." But a vacation need not be long to be therapeutic. Dr. John P. McCann of the Life Extension Institute in New York, which gives physicals to executives, points out that for many people even a one-day vacation may constitute a refreshing change of pace.

25   The ideal vacation, in the opinion of Dr. Ari Kiev, a New York psychiatrist and author of *A Strategy for Handling Executive Stress* (1974), is a foil to a person's occupation. Someone who does close, detailed work all year long, like an accountant, might take up something less exacting, like sailing. (Says Dr. Howard Hess: "A Caribbean vacation is

ANSWERS 1. No, 2. No, 3. Yes, 4. No, 5. No, 6. a) Yes, b) No, 7. No, 8. Yes, 9. Yes, 10. Yes, 11. No, 12. Yes.

not the solution to everyone's problems. Just mine and yours.") A person who sees in himself symptoms of workaholism should try developing interests outside of his job. Dr. Flach recommends returning to the hobbies of your adolescence—photography, stamp collecting or what have you. "Your early interests," he believes, "are perhaps the closest expression of you as a person." Wayne Oates suggests renewing old acquaintances, making new friends and reading books you don't have to read, like mysteries. It may be easier for those further along the path to addiction to switch to hobbies that, like work, have well-defined goals, such as woodworking or sports.

26   To suppress temptations to expand your work load, Oates cautions, take a wary look at offers of promotions that would keep you from doing the things you like best about your present job. Lest he try to do two jobs at once, a salesman who enjoys selling might be best off turning down a promotion to sales manager; a teacher who loves teaching might refuse a department chairmanship. In his own case, to keep from taking on so much extra work, Oates put a ceiling on the extra income he wanted each month, and he has stuck to it—with periodic adjustments for inflation.

27   Sometimes workaholism is thrust on people. There are workaholic companies, which may expect everyone to be at work early, to skip lunch, to work late and to think about office problems on weekends. Work addicts tend to wind up in such places; incipient addicts should escape while they easily can. Dr. Flach, for one, doesn't think the workaholic organization has a special edge over its competitors. Like work addicts themselves, such outfits may lack imagination. "The typical workaholic organization," he says, "may set up the most carefully thought-out way to distribute money into a project, for example, and miss the obvious point— like how all that money is going to get ripped off."

28   The incipient addict with the hard-driving personality of a Type A should consider slowing down the general pace of his life. Dr. Friedman, a Type A himself (complete with heart attack), deliberately began dressing informally. He spent lunch hours examining the stained glass windows in a nearby cathedral; he began rereading the seven parts of Marcel Proust's interminable *Remembrance of Things Past*. He now avoids cocktail parties: "I found that all you do at them is shout, and no one cares whether you leave or stay." And he keeps away from "people who readily bring out my free-floating hostility, because I've never been able to convince those sons of bitches about anything and they've never been able to convince me."

Out to Tee

29   To get advice from other well-known people who are reputed to work very hard, I wrote Harold S. Geneen, president of ITT, actor Elliot Gould, film director Robert Altman, Governor Jerry Brown of California and Dr.

DeBakey, among others. A spokesman for ITT apologetically reported that Geneen could not reply because he had been very busy with management meetings recently and was out on the golf course. The others did not respond at all. Presumably they were too busy working.

VOCABULARY

morose (P1), *joshed* (P3), *unquenchable* (P4), *compulsion* (P4), *purebred* (P4), *oenophiles* (P5), *billiards* (P5), *Carl Jung* (P6), *recondite* (P6), *James Joyce* (P6), *acute* (P6), *cardiologist* (P7), *seminary* (P8), *simmer* (P10), *prone* (P13), *shanghaied* (P16), *cognac* (P18), *amply* (P18), *postpartum* (P19), *chronic* (P21), *ebb* (P21), *habituated* (P21), *amiss* (P22), *frenetically* (P23), *therapeutic* (P24), *foil* (P25), *incipient* (P27), *interminable* (P28), *Marcel Proust* (P28)

IDEAS AND AIMS

1. What are the essential differences between the work lover and work addict? Why are the terms Boroson chooses for these differing classes so alike?
2. Why do work addicts' careers generally stall in the middle levels? Why or how do they wind up causing trouble at these levels?
3. Why do work addicts have difficulties in solving problems?
4. Are workaholics necessarily executives? Who or what else may be a workaholic?
5. How do Type A and Type B workaholics contrast?
6. What is life outside work like for most workaholics?
7. What does Nader mean when he says "we don't have a tradition which explains me" (P18)?
8. Why is an obscure person more likely to be a work addict than a famous person?
9. Why is there a pattern of sudden death for many people who have just retired, according to this essay?
10. How should someone who fears that he or she is a workaholic set about changing?

ORGANIZATION AND FORM

1. How does Boroson use comparison and contrast as a technique of defining in the essay? Cite some examples. What other techniques of definition does he use?
2. In what way do PP4-15, PP16-21, and PP22-28 form main units of the essay?

3. What function do the quotations that open the essay (PP1–3) serve for the reader?
4. Where is the central idea of this essay stated?
5. What is the organizing principle of P4 and P7?
6. How does the conclusion of Boroson's essay extend or develop his thesis, rather than merely restate or repeat it?
7. What function does the last paragraph have as part of the conclusion of Boroson's essay?

WORDS AND STYLE

1. How does Boroson's prose style range between fancy, polysyllabic words and plain and colloquial ones? Cite some examples.
2. What does the use of words such as "symptoms" (P19), "acute" (P6), and "therapeutic" (P24) suggest about the subject of workaholics, and about the author's attitude toward the subject? How might this relate to the kind of medical specialist Boroson quotes most often in the essay?
3. How are Boroson's words "unglued" (P4) and "propels" (P8) vivid, striking, or active? What similar words can you find in the essay?
4. How does Boroson use clichés effectively by putting new twists on them in the last sentence of P6 and the second sentence of P15?
5. When Oates claims life beyond the company is "dragons and disasters" (P14) for the workaholic, what implicit comparison is being made? How does it characterize the workaholic?
6. What word is negatively "slanted" in Boroson's phrase "robotlike perfectionists" (P15)? What differentiation is Boroson suggesting here between perfection and "robotlike perfectionists"? What defect does it reveal in the workaholic?

DISCUSSION AND WRITING

1. Are you a workaholic? A work lover? In what ways do you match or not match the definitions given by Boroson in his essay?
2. Do you know any work addicts or work lovers? How do they fit the definition as given in the essay?
3. Are there student workaholics ("schoolaholics") or work lovers? Describe them in an essay, defining their essential characteristics. Use comparison and contrast to other students, taking care not to have traits from the ordinary student overlap those of the special class you are attempting to define.
4. Do you think that the world needs some workaholics? Do you think we need a

tradition of workaholism or "work-loverism," as Nader implies in his remark (P18)?

5. Is workaholism necessarily bad? How? For whom?

6. Compare what Boroson reports in PP9–10 as good advice for completing a task with what Robert Benchley suggests in "How to Get Things Done" in Section 5, "Efficiency and Success on the Job." Have you found this to be true in your own experience? How so?

OPPORTUNITIES FOR YOUNG AMERICANS

Malcolm N. Carter

□

Published in Money *magazine, which, like newsmagazines such as* Time *and* Newsweek, *is directed to a relatively educated and upwardly mobile readership, Carter's essay is written in a journalistic style. It makes use of some erudite words ("plaintively," "confluence," "antipathy"), but in the main sticks to a simpler vocabulary and the short paragraph designed to be printed in a narrow-column format. Like most good journalists, Carter uses many facts, figures, and quotations from experts. To accommodate this last element, the author, like many a journalist before him, avails himself of the time-honored journalistic inversion: "Says Robert Theobald" (P7), "Says Alexander Astin" (P10), "Said he" (P14).*

1 From the limited perspective of today's high school and college students, the masses of people just ahead of them have clouded the future. Never has the U.S. had to absorb so many births as in the baby-boom years 1946 through 1964. Some 76 million Americans born in those 19 years are dominating the consumer market, imprinting their taste and values on the culture, swamping the labor force and generally overwhelming the economy. On demographic charts, they look collectively like an enormous pig progressing through a python.

2   Small wonder that the current crop of adolescents looks ahead and

sees only that pig blocking its way. At a time when the nation's growth has slowed and the American dream seems to have lost its focus, young people envision themselves having to scramble for a smaller share of a sharply limited pie. Indeed, 85% of the young people sampled last year by the market research firm of Yankelovich Skelly & White said they didn't take it for granted that they'll be able to improve on their parents' standard of living. Compared with the youth of the '70s, whose search for "self-fulfillment" and "meaning" earned them the "me generation" label, young people today worry less about their psyches and more about their pocketbooks. Sensing narrower horizons, they grab for economic security. Plaintively, they perceive themselves as the "Why me?" generation.

3   In cold economic terms, it's a fair question. High inflation endures in the face of a stubborn rate of unemployment. But further ahead in this decade, the outlook should improve. "What young people are doing now is extrapolating the past, the immediate past," says Roy Amara, president of a Menlo Park, Calif. business consulting group called the Institute for the Future. "The situation is going to look a lot better in the late 1980s."

4   Such economic predictions necessarily depend on a host of imponderables—chief among them the effectiveness of President Reagan's tax and spending cuts. The Administration forecasts a rise in the gross national product, starting next year, at a robust 4% to 5% a year through 1986, up from an estimated 1.1% in 1981—and over the same period a decline in the inflation rate from 11.1% to 4.2%. Michael Evans, a conservative economic consultant in Washington, estimates that unemployment will decline from 7.3% now to roughly 5% by the end of 1983 and stay near that level for the rest of the decade.

5   Allen Sinai, senior economist of the Lexington, Mass., research firm Data Resources Inc., is optimistic too. "By the second half of the decade," he says, "we may be back to some really good economic times." Although many economists don't see that rosy a future, even skeptical Joseph Pechman of the Brookings Institution believes that opportunities should be better in the late '80s, when fewer people will be entering the labor force.

6   If only because of technological and social changes already under way, the coming decade holds the promise of successful careers for young people who chart a calculated course. They need simply examine the major matters on the national agenda to pinpoint opportunity. For example:

- The need to develop new energy supplies.
- The challenge of preserving natural resources.
- The aging of the population and its drift to the sunbelt.
- The displacement of workers by technological and scientific advances.
- Insufficient productivity.
- A new social order, evolving from two-income families on the one hand and reduced government spending on the other.

• The pervasiveness of the computer.

7   What the new generation will find is a confluence of profound technological and social developments, many of them springing from those computers. People now producing goods will lose their jobs on assembly lines to robots that can handle tedious, exhausting or hazardous tasks. In a decade or so, computers could also take over 40% of the tasks now performed by clerical workers, according to SRI International, a research firm in California. Says Robert Theobald, an Arizona business consultant and futurist: "We're going to have to find jobs that only humans can do." People in Theobald's forward-looking line of work like to say that the U.S. is in transition from an industrial society to an information society. In this new world, man and computer will work as a team. Dartmouth College president John Kemeny contends: "It's as unforgivable to let a student graduate without knowing how to use a computer as it was in the past to let him graduate without knowing how to use a library."

8   Familiarity with computer technology is just one of a variety of skills necessary for success in an information society. Humanists had better be able to communicate with technicians. Engineers should know how to read a balance sheet and understand regional economies, population shifts, interest rates and tax structures. Businessmen in a world of expanded trade will be well advised to speak one or two foreign languages as an aid to grasping hidden implications in seemingly unrelated world events—for instance, that a new labor minister in one country could cause strikes that affect a second country's balance of payments and thus its ability to close a deal.

9   Young people arriving at maturity in the next 10 years may be surprised to discover that they will have greater control of their lives than their predecessors did. Many companies have discovered that management by executive edict is no longer effective. Consequently, they have begun to involve subordinates as well as supervisors in decision-making. The employee who might have resented the boss's directives can more cheerfully follow orders that he's helped to frame.

10   Americans will also have more of a chance to set their own hours, work at home and function with reduced supervision. Some members of the preceding generation felt it necessary to declare their independence by dropping out of the economy. The present generation, however, has an excellent chance to achieve independence by plunging into entrepreneurial ventures. That's just as well, because more than anything the desire for financial success drives today's young people—especially those in their college years. Says Alexander Astin, a UCLA education professor who annually polls 200,000 college freshmen: "For the past six or seven years, we've seen a steady rise in what I can only call materialism—an interest in money, power and status." In 1967, only 43.5% of the freshmen said being "very well-off" financially was "very important" to them; in 1980 it was 63.3%.

11   The University of Michigan's Institute for Social Research has detected a similar shift in attitude among high school seniors. Jerald Bachman, a psychologist at the institute, finds that the importance attached to advancement and prestige has risen, while antipathy to business has waned. "Obviously the work ethic is far from dead in this generation," he says.

12   To bring the statistics to life, *Money* asked Patricia Gurin, a University of Michigan social psychologist, to hand-pick a small but fairly representative sampling of students willing to assess themselves and their prospects. In late April, *Money* met in Ann Arbor with nine students, aged 19 to 22, from middle- and upper-middle-income families in the East and Midwest.

13   Through the discussion ran a strong current of uncertainty and chastened expectations. Nobody thought the government would create opportunities for them. Few anticipated attaining a luxurious standard of living. Most felt the generational odds were stacked against them. Some said they would sacrifice parenthood if that was the price of success in a career; others spoke of wanting "meaningful" work.

14   The 1960s echoed in comments by Daniel Olshansky deploring the military-industrial establishment and yearning for the old days of social activism. Said he: "I kind of wish I were born back then to be part of that." Marc Jacobs typified the other extreme. Headed for law school and perhaps a political career, he stressed academic achievement: "We're going to have to remain competitive every step of the way. If we come out of college doing well, then we'll be able to start a little bit higher."

15   The two blacks in the group, Gale Graves and Rhonda Cozart, expressed an intense desire to help out the less advantaged of their race. Mike Zartman, who graduated from Oberlin College last year and became a research assistant at Ann Arbor with plans to study economics and law, spoke of wanting to influence public policy from the inside— because he has worked with "a lot of people from the government who don't seem to know what they're doing."

16   Young people like these, who don't feel that the world owes them a living, have a leg up on reality. Observes Paul Wachtel, an economist at New York University's Graduate School of Business Administration: "The future for that generation is complicated and uncertain. Life will be more difficult and yet more fun and challenging. The chances of success are there—just harder to find."

VOCABULARY

swamping (P1), *demographic* (P1), *psyches* (P2), *plaintively* (P2), *extrapolating* (P3), *imponderables* (P4), *robust* (P4), *skeptical* (P5), *sunbelt* (P6), *productivity* (P6), *pervasiveness*(P6), *confluence* (P7), *tedious* (P7), *futurist* (P7), *contends* (P7), *balance sheet* (P8), *balance of payments* (P8), *edict* (P9), *entrepreneurial* (P10), *ventures* (P10), *materialism* (P10), *antipathy* (P11), *waned* (P11), *chastened* (P13), *deploring* (P14), *yearning* (P14), *typified* (P14), *research assistant* (P15)

IDEAS AND AIMS

1. What evidence is there for optimism about the rest of the 1980s for young people looking toward the job market?
2. What evidence is there for pessimism about the rest of the 1980s for young people looking toward the job market?
3. What have polling organizations discovered about the values of college freshmen?
4. According to the essay, what might be responsible for the shift in attitude of the young people polled?
5. Are students still in high school likely to have different values when they reach college?

ORGANIZATION AND FORM

1. How might PP1–5, PP6–10, and PP10–16 be seen as the main parts of the essay?
2. Where does the central idea of the essay appear?
3. In the last paragraph (P16) how does Carter circle around to his thesis? P16 is thus linked to what preceding paragraph?

WORDS AND STYLE

1. This essay is, essentially, an organized presentation of attitudes and possibilities. Is the vocabulary specialized? What sort of audience does this author have in mind, to judge from his style?
2. How does Carter's simile in the last sentence of P1 (". . . like an enormous . . .") help express the ideas of retardation, feeling trapped, helplessness, and unpleasantness that young people might feel at the prospects for work in the coming decade?
3. How does Carter's play on words in the contrast between the phrases "me generation" and "'Why me?' generation" (P2) very well capture the difference between the two generations?
4. How does parallelism help bind up the diverse observations or examples of P13?

5. Where and how does Carter, like many journalists and others who have to explain background details to their reader, repeatedly use the appositive construction? (Look up this term in your composition handbook or collegiate dictionary.)

DISCUSSION AND WRITING

1. Reread the essay's listing of "matters on the national agenda" (P6). What careers or businesses may prosper, with these influences at work in society?
2. How do you and your friends feel about your own future prospects? Do you find the information presented in the essay encouraging or discouraging?
3. Would you place yourself as part of the new trend toward materialism, mentioned in the essay? Why or why not?
4. How does Carter's advice correspond with that given by Marlys Harris in her essay in Section 6, "Job Opportunities and Other Practical Matters"?

EVERY VOCATION IS A POST ASSIGNED BY THE LORD

John Calvin

□

Born in France, educated at the University of Paris (where he earned an M.A.) and then law school, Jean Cauvin (1509–1564), who later was known as John Calvin from the translation of the Latin version of his name, was trained in theology, logic, law, Latin, Greek, and Hebrew. After he settled in Switzerland, where he fled to escape persecution for his religious views, he published his Institutes of Christian Religion. *Probably the most important of his works, which take up 48 volumes in the standard English translation, the* Institutes *were first published in Latin (1536) and then expanded and translated into French by Calvin himself (1541). A repository of Calvinism (ideas such as man's fundamentally corrupt nature, salvation possible only through grace, and so on), the* Institutes, *because of their clear, precise, and compact style as well as the forcefulness of their logic and supporting proof texts, were very influential. They affected the beliefs of the common people in both Europe and America (especially the beliefs of the Puritans), as well as those of such well-known writers as John Milton, John Bunyan, and Jonathan Edwards.*

In the following selection from the Institutes *(Book III, Chapter 10, Part 6), Calvin shows how work fits into his theological scheme of things.*

1 Lastly, it is to be remarked that the Lord commands every one of us, in all the actions of life, to regard his vocation. For he knows with what great

inquietude the human mind is inflamed, with what desultory levity it is hurried hither and thither, and how insatiable is its ambition to grasp different things at once. Therefore, to prevent universal confusion being produced by our folly and temerity, he has appointed to all their particular duties in different spheres of life. And that no one might rashly transgress the limits prescribed, he has styled such spheres of life *vocations,* or *callings.* Every individual's line of life, therefore, is, as it were, a post assigned him by the Lord, that he may not wander about in uncertainty all his days.

2   And so necessary is this distinction that in his sight all our actions are estimated according to it, and often very differently from the sentence of human reason and philosophy. There is no exploit esteemed more honorable, even among philosophers, than to deliver our country from tyranny; but the voice of the celestial Judge openly condemns the private man who lays violent hands on a tyrant. It is not my design, however, to stay to enumerate examples. It is sufficient if we know that the principle and foundation of right conduct in every case is the vocation of the Lord, and that he who disregards it will never keep the right way in the duties of his station. He may sometimes, perhaps, achieve something apparently laudable; but however it may appear in the eyes of men, it will be rejected at the throne of God; besides which, there will be no consistency between the various parts of his life.

3   Our life, therefore, will then be best regulated, when it is directed to this mark; since no one will be impelled by his own temerity to attempt more than is compatible with his calling, because he will know that it is unlawful to transgress the bounds assigned him. He that is in obscurity will lead a private life without discontent, so as not to desert the station in which God has placed him. It will also be no small alleviation of his cares, labors, troubles, and other burdens, when a man knows that in all these things he has God for his guide. The magistrate will execute his office with greater pleasure, the father of a family will confine himself to his duty with more satisfaction, and all, in their respective spheres of life, will bear and surmount the inconveniences, cares, disappointments, and anxieties which befall them, when they shall be persuaded that every individual has his burden laid upon him by God. Hence also will arise peculiar consolation, since there will be no employment so mean and sordid (provided we follow our vocation) as not to appear truly respectable, and be deemed highly important in the sight of God.

VOCABULARY

vocation (P1), *inquietude* (P1), *desultory* (P1), *levity* (P1), *hither* (P1), *thither* (P1), *insatiable* (P1), *temerity* (P1), *rashly* (P1), *transgress* (P1), *styled* (P1), *post* (P1), *sentence [archaic sense]* (P2), *exploit* (P2), *station*

(P2), *laudable* (P2), *impelled* (P3), *alleviation* (P3), *surmount* (P3), *peculiar* (P3), *mean* (P3), *sordid* (P3)

IDEAS AND AIMS

1. What is the primary reason for the importance of one's calling?
2. Why is each of us, according to Calvin, assigned a vocation?
3. Why does "the celestial Judge" condemn a man attempting to overthrow a tyrant? How does this differ from the human view of "reason and philosophy"?
4. Why, according to Calvin, will happiness result from understanding that every vocation is a post assigned by the Lord?
5. Is Calvin's purpose here basically expository or argumentative? How can you tell?
6. How can Calvin's celebrated disparaging view of human nature be seen throughout the essay? How does it provide one of the essay's basic premises?
7. The Puritans, known for strictures and strictness, were influenced heavily by Calvin's line of thinking. Where does one find strictness and restrictions as ingredients in Calvin's view of human vocation?

ORGANIZATION AND FORM

1. How do the three paragraphs of this section of the *Institutes* in fact form a complete unit or sort of miniature essay?
2. Point out examples and explain how Calvin uses deductive reasoning—that is, how he states some premise and then shows what must follow logically from it.
3. Why does Calvin stop with one example in P2? How is this related to the organizational principle or method of the whole excerpt?
4. What transitional devices (words, pronouns, repetition of key terms) does Calvin use, and where?

WORDS AND STYLE

1. How are Calvin's word choice and sentence structure appropriate for his subject, purpose, and audience?
2. Despite the essay's being at a high level of abstraction, and despite Calvin's explicit rejection of examples (P2), how does the author still work in concrete words and images to help keep his essay stirring and vivid?
3. How does Calvin's use of parallelism and series, a favorite stylistic device, help clarify his ideas in any particular instance?
4. What is the "distinction" referred to in P2?

5. How is Calvin's term (technically, a *periphrasis*) for God, "the celestial Judge," particularly appropriate in the context of P2, where it is used?

6. In P3 Calvin refers to vocation with the word "burden." What does this say about his attitude toward the work of one's life?

DISCUSSION AND WRITING

1. Contrast the modern view of choosing a vocation with Calvin's view.

2. Does Calvin mean by "vocation" or "calling" the same thing a modern writer would take those words to mean? Explain Calvin's idea of vocation.

3. Can you provide examples to illustrate Calvin's ideas as he states them in the last sentences of P2?

4. Does Calvin convince you that happiness will result from realizing that every vocation is a post assigned by the Lord?

5. What modern attitudes toward work and toward social class contrast strikingly with Calvin's ideas?

6. Calvin seems to assume and to suggest that finding one's right occupation is relatively easy and straightforward. Contrast Clemens' "Jack of All Trades" (in Section 8, "Efficiency and Success on the Job") on this point. Which author is closer to the truth, in your view? Provide specific examples for support.

"THEY WON'T WORK":
The End of the Protestant
Ethic and All That

Ivar Berg

□

The following essay was written for an academically oriented journal, The
Columbia Forum, *by the George E. Warren Professor of Business at Columbia University. Though in places his word choice is sophisticated
("opprobrium," "adduced," "juxtapose"), in others Berg uses colloquialism or
cliché, as with humor and irony he turns the tables on the opposition. The
business community and government, says Berg, are accustomed to blaming
labor and employees for not following the pronouncements of Calvinism (see
the preceding essay, by Calvin) and thus bringing on the woes of companies,
commerce, and the economy. But Berg, himself an expert on business, asks
wryly and authoritatively whether Calvin is really dead among the work
force and whether the blame for our woes doesn't verily belong elsewhere.*

1 Dissimilar and divided as they have often appeared on other counts, it
has been a long-standing commonplace about Americans that thrift, diligence in work, an instinct for craftsmanship, and a capacity for deferring
gratification were traits they both exhibited and commended to the
world. Such traits made us economically productive, and in being so we
served our consciences no less than our pocketbooks; it is no wonder that
the "Protestant ethic" in America has found adherents among Catholics
and Jews and Muslims no less than among Presbyterians and Lutherans.

The philosophical gap in this way of life—between personal worth and market value—we early and conveniently bridged by adorning economic necessity with all the medals of moral virtue. The net effect was to impart a high order of legitimacy to an economic system whose individual members could be credited or blamed for their own circumstances according to the degree of their prosperity.

2   Since the system is seen as the very vehicle of moral behavior, we have tinkered with it only occasionally—through homestead laws, antitrust statutes, selected regulatory measures, more benign collective bargaining laws, and, in recent times, provisions to broaden access to education. By these adjustments we have sought to compensate for gross inequalities at the starting lines of the competitive race. That all but a very few citizens tried to enter the race was not remarkable. Poor Richard's aphorisms about the rewards of self-discipline, diligence, and the alert pursuit of opportunity are with us yet, in the inelegant but expressive slogan: "You can't get something for nothing." Few contest it.

3   But who has not recently heard the news, in one form or another, that after nearly two hundred years Americans are renouncing the Protestant ethic for new and spreading heresies? Decades ago a similar alarm was raised by persons who overestimated (long before Joe McCarthy and Whittaker Chambers) the allure of the European doctrines of "collectivism." In our own time, however, the news is passed among many more than that small contingent of witch-hunters of other times, and troubles those never seriously worried by the radical Left. Thoughtful parents, for example, who can abide their offspring's clothes and music and coiffure— even their questioning of marriage—are troubled by their insistence on "personal authenticity," by their attraction to communal values, and by their calling into question the worth of competition, of status seeking, and of material consumption. The impact of the so-called youth culture is threatening not because it has borrowed occasional terms of opprobrium from the orthodox Left—dependably, "people outgrow that"—but because questions are asked that have little to do with the state and ownership.

4   Additional evidence that stock in the Protestant ethic is low is readily inferred by some from the behavior of the working classes. We are told, for example, that workers are more independent, less attentive to their obligations, more prone to absenteeism, and generally less accepting of supervisory and managerial authority—and this despite the fact that unemployment rates have become uncommonly high. It is even more remarkable, perhaps, that absenteeism and other indicators of loose industrial discipline have allegedly risen among the hitherto well-behaved white-collar workers, whose own unemployment rates have also increased dramatically.

5   No one is accustomed to seeing such evidence of workers' deficiencies side by side with high unemployment statistics, and their rubbing together has produced heat. Thus one hears annoyance expressed over

the fact that blacks are proportionately represented among the absentees from relatively high-paying auto factories. Surely when their own leaders deplore the blacks' unemployment rate, employed black workers should be happy with jobs and weekly paychecks; surely they ought not to tempt their employers by negligent attendance.

6   And when one looks at the unions, what should one make of, say, the rules requiring duplicative work in printing shops; the firemen who famously tend no fires on diesel locomotives; the work rules which prescribe the width of paint brushes, the size of crews, the number of plumbing vents to be installed in which houses by construction workers? Nor is there much sign of guilty feeling among workers over these (as Veblen dubbed them) "strategies of independence," an omission that amazes observers to whom the "withdrawal of efficiency" (as labor calls it) seems thoroughly shameful. All is insouciance and euphemism, apparently.

7   But beyond doubt the most inflammatory evidence offered for the end of the ethic is the testimony of the public welfare rolls, statistics rarely mentioned in editorials, summer cottages, seminars, or corporate boardrooms without the word "scandalous" appended. Indeed, so famous are the welfare figures now that they need no rehearsal here. It suffices to say that they are favored above all other demonstrations that "people don't want to work."

Another Diagnosis

8 The condition of the Protestant ethic may, however, be too glibly stated. "For instance" is notoriously not proof, and not all observers will infer the same conclusions from a given statistic or set of facts. Thus it is at least possible that the ethic is alive though not entirely well, and that a very different diagnosis can be made. That diagnosis suggests that work does occupy a central place in the lives of most Americans but that the legitimacy of "the system"—what and whom one works for—is much in doubt. Among the faithful who work in the old imperative way, this widening doubt can easily inspire resentment, for it could imply that they themselves are naive at the best, downright foolish at worst. This explains the censorious tone so often taken toward defectors, who might otherwise be seen only as deficient or self-damaging.

9   One could argue, first off, that the young are at least as interested in work as any generation has been at the school-leaving age. (Consider that even the so-called social dropouts who turn to communes enter into social compacts requiring individual contributions of labor the magnitude of which never fails to surprise the visiting journalists from the Sunday supplements.) But within the conventional labor markets and the jobs they offer, the skeptical young complain of, among other things, educational requirements that increasingly exceed what employers can actually use, a criticism which can be sustained in an extraordinarily

large number and variety of work settings. The demonstrable consequence for those employed, of any age, is dissatisfaction with the work, frustration of talents, and turnover—whose statistics are more often cited as proof of a widespread indifference toward work than as signs of managerial irrationality. No one can accurately assess how much of business and industry's rates of mental illness and alcoholism begin with thwarted abilities. It should surprise no one, least of all modern employers spending vast sums on "morale" and "human relations" programs, that the dissatisfaction of underutilized workers can reflect itself in expensive personnel and production problems.

10   Nor is the "withdrawal of efficiency" news. Sociologists have been reporting for more than forty years, even before the pioneering studies of workers in Western Electric's Hawthorne works, that employees will "bank" work, will invent concealed timesaving improvements on their own machines, and, in general and wherever possible, seek their own ratio of monetary-to-nonmonetary satisfactions in their shops, offices, and factory lines. In other days, it was the rare top-level manager who would not, in unemotional moments, acknowledge that workers were no less rational for making the most of every comfort possible to them. That younger, bolder, and better-educated workers may have elaborated the preferences of older immigrant and depression-scarred workers should not puzzle us.

11   It may of course be true that workers' independence is on the rise. But it is not necessarily clear that workers' motivations have changed from those long ago adduced in social science studies of informal groups. Many of these studies, in their assessments of productivity, pointed specifically to the crucial work of managers. It may well be that we overlook that work in our assertions about employees.

12   Take the matter of featherbedding, about which publicists, managers, trade-association spokesmen, and others regularly remind us. The term is applied to work rules covering an enormous number of practices in innumerable work settings. The history of the most celebrated work rules, including those mentioned earlier, shows that they were formulated within the bargaining process, with employers obtaining something of great value in return for an "arrangement" managers never thought would be problematic. Railroad managers, for example, simply did not expect that diesel engines would revolutionize railroad technology, and traded a seat for firemen in these engines for a favorable wage settlement. The seat could of course be bought back in a reversal of the bargain: workers, no less than management, conform to that article of our creed which encourages us to husband our capital, whatever it might be.

13   The responsibility for nonwork can be similarly redistributed in other industries. Plumbing vents, for example, are typically required by building codes, whose terms most often reflect, not the sinful "makework" instincts of construction workers acting unilaterally, but the effec-

tiveness and ethics of municipal governments, contractors, and supporting union officials. Indeed, in much recent muttering about the devalua-
tion of work, one might suppose that management had nothing to *do* with
work.

Facts about Welfare Recipients

14 Even the shockingly large number of people receiving welfare payments
—solely or in addition to wages—can be seen in more than one light.
Those persons who suppose that the welfare increases in the nation's
largest cities provide statistical indices of the ethic's demise must con-
front some inconvenient facts. For example, among heads of families who
work full-time, about 7 percent earn an income at what has come to be
called the poverty level. Among persons who are fully employed but without spouses or family, fully 30 percent are impoverished.[1] "In fact," wrote
two sociologists recently, "about a third of all impoverished families (2.4
million in 1967) are headed by a fully employed person. Another million
'unrelated individuals' are in the same situation—fully employed but
poor. Millions more live at the margins of poverty."[2] These millions may
have something to tell us about the state of work in America. At the very
least, they are Protestant ethic loyalists like none that we have imagined—or lately heard from.

15 If a sizable number of actual welfare recipients are fully employed,
another sizable number are underemployed; and a very significant
number of eligible underemployed, unemployed, and impoverished workers are not beneficiaries of welfare at all. A survey of low-income families
in Detroit in 1965, for example, showed that 43 percent of eligible recipients in that city were not on the welfare rolls. In New York City in 1968,
approximately 150,000 families were eligible for wage subsidies, according to the city welfare department's estimates, but only about 15,000
families were claiming them.[3]

16 The total of the ineligible but poor, plus the eligible nonrecipients,
plus the eligible but fully employed recipients, is large. One can juxtapose it with the number of able-bodied, unemployed recipients—after
subtracting from the latter figure all the dependent children and aged
persons it includes—and arrive at figures most unhelpful to the argument that welfare programs cosset a mob of lazy apostates who mock the
Protestant ethic.

1. Patricia Cayo Sexton and Brendan Sexton, *Blue Collars and Hard Hats: The Working Class and the Future of American Politics* (New York: Random House, 1971), p. 68.

2. Ibid., p. 69.

3. Frances Piven and Richard A. Cloward, *Regulating the Poor: The Functions of Public Welfare* (New York: Pantheon Books, 1971), p. 74.

17   Meantime, the facts available on the attitudes toward work of typical welfare recipients—man, woman, or even dependent child—suggest that President Nixon's formulation last September of a "welfare ethic" is seriously flawed. A 1972 study by the staid Brookings Institution of the "work orientations" of the poor demonstrates that the poor as a body share with more prosperous Americans all those beliefs in employment, incentives, and rewards which the President claimed, in his celebrated Labor Day speech, help "build strong people" while "the welfare ethic breeds weak people." Welfare recipients, according to the Brookings study, viewed public assistance with favor—with *mild* favor—only *after* they had experienced serious occupational failures; these failures the researchers found attributable to labor market conditions, not to the inadequacies of those who had become public charges.[4] There is simply no evidence in this competent investigation (which took account of possible disparities between what respondents said and what they actually did about work) that we shelter from the chill winds of the marketplace large numbers of poor people who subscribe to what the President knows is out there: ". . . the new 'welfare ethic' that could cause the American character to weaken."

18   Some observers might even argue that our welfare policies tell a far sadder story about the values of the architects of these policies, and about the constituencies who encourage them, than about attitudes toward work in the larger population. Others might add, with Calvin Coolidge, that "the reason we have such high unemployment rates is that there aren't enough jobs." And carrying a suspicion of current policy a bit further, what should we make of the "workfare" concept? Does this considerable effort to get poor mothers of young children off the "aid-to-dependent-children" rolls serve the ethic? Or do our national income accounts, which assign no economic value at all to child-rearing, give testimony to an enduringly narrow and highly selective application of the ethic's prescriptions?

Corporate Morale

19 Our several logics, and our tendency to infer favored conclusions from selective facts, may suit our continuing need to equate necessity with morality. Can that be why no one suggests that the tenets of the faith have been toyed with by its own most ardent—and its most powerful—followers? Corporations, in whose corridors march the most articulate proponents of the ethic, face "the worst attitude climate in a decade,"[5]

4. Leonard Goodwin, *A Study of Work Orientation of Welfare Recipients Participating in the Work Incentive Program* (Washington, D.C.: Brookings Institution, 1971).

5. "America's Growing Antibusiness Mood," *Business Week*, June 17, 1972, p. 100.

according to the Opinion Research Corporation, a subsidiary of the McGraw-Hill Company, whose own journal, *Business Week,* editorializes on the facts of a survey: "[Reversal of public disaffection with business] will take management that thinks in terms of long-run objectives rather than short-run profits. Much of the trouble that business has got into during the past five years has developed because executives were watching the security analyst and playing for a quick flash in the stock market instead of building for the future. Now the future they did not prepare for is here."[6] Deferred gratification? Saving for growth? The *Business Week* data on public attitudes toward business might well unsettle the *Business Week* editors. These data show that the "staunchest supporters" of business have an increasingly low opinion of extant businesses; the proportion of respondents reporting "low approval of companies" is 60 percent, up nearly 15 percentage points since 1965. In the same issue, *Business Week* provides a handy if incomplete summary of the reasons for this. It is a grim litany of rapacious conglomerates, "humiliating miscalculations" in aerospace, I.T.T. in the Justice Department, junk in the environment, and plain shoddy merchandise.

20   Try as they will to be objective about an important matter, however, *Business Week* cannot resist pronouncing a curse on the other house—a comfort to those executive subscribers who brood upon workers and the Protestant ethic. Thus, two tables purport to show that of late "people want more for less." These same tables are captioned: "They will not work harder to increase their standard of living, but they say they could produce more if they tried." Sure enough, the proportion of worker-respondents who "say they could produce more if they tried" can be seen to have risen appreciably since the late 1940s. From this, *Business Week* concludes that more and more workers want a higher standard of living but refuse to work harder for it. But a careful inspection of the tables and the several captions could as easily support the interpretation that larger numbers of respondents are content with their standard of living, thanks all the same, and in that respect see no purpose in working harder.

21   Indeed, in not yearning after new feats of consumption these workers seem well within the ethic, which never did put much stock in consuming but urged, instead, deferred gratification. Poor Richard could not have envisioned Miami Beach, and Horatio Alger knew not Neiman-Marcus. Conversely, of course, any society whose citizens consistently deferred their pleasures in the interests of security, liquidity, and growth would find little place for, say, credit-granting institutions and advertising agencies.

22   All in all, it seems a waste of good elbow grease for the executive classes to wring their hands unduly over the apostasy of workers from the

6. "Why the Public Has Lost Faith in Business," *Business Week,* June 17, 1972, p. 116.

ethic. Perhaps the least consolable have read the April 1972 Gallup poll, to which 57 percent of the "total public" admitted that ". . . they could produce more each day if they tried." But did those same executives notice that the figure for professional people and businessmen was *70 percent*? Only one group felt less productive still: 72 percent of young people between eighteen and twenty-nine years old.[7]

23   These last statistics suggest (though they do not prove; "for instance" is not proof) that the question of legitimacy higher up is an important one. Corporate shenanigans, political deceptions, and a professional-executive class avowedly and conspicuously underworked, may simply not inspire the larger population to seek "success" in the old way. One wonders if all of Madison Avenue's capacities for persuasion could blot out what millions see in their workaday lives: basic industries that turn tidy profits while great portions of their productive capacity stand idle through business-cycle swings; huge, unearned subsidies for inefficient aerospace firms; expense-account juggling, rapid corporate tax write-offs, and oil depletion allowances; railroads managed into bankruptcy; industrial wastes managed into rivers and lakes. It is naive to believe that the nonexecutive population is unaware of these things. Even *Playboy* has presented its readers with a compendium of bare facts on the subject of malpractices. In a recent article Senator Philip A. Hart reviewed case after depressing case of mismanagement, managerial skullduggery, and breach of faith. Among the items: the nation's seventy largest corporations have run afoul of antitrust, false advertising, patent, copyright, and labor laws 980 times in a forty-five-year period; of the 980, "779 indicated that crimes had been committed."

24   Nor does it please earners to be told, most often by their elected leaders, that it is their wages and salaries which are to blame for an inflationary spiral that has very nearly consumed the economic gains of many years. Wage earners know that war is simultaneously expensive and unproductive, and many are also mindful of the spiraling costs of government. James W. Kuhn has pointed out that "Philadelphia pays its clerical employees a third more than the average paid in private industry, and in both Houston and Buffalo clerks' pay is a fifth larger; municipal data processors earn salaries about a fifth larger than those employed by private firms in Philadelphia, Newark, and Los Angeles; and maintenance workers in New York and Newark average 42 percent larger salaries than those in private industry."[8] Government is expensive in other ways: wage earners in New Jersey must read that their Secretary of State has been indicted for exploiting his office to line his pockets on the very eve of his predecessor's incarceration for the same behavior;

7. "America's Growing Antibusiness Mood," pp. 100-101.

8. James Kuhn, "The Middle of Inflation: A New Answer," *The Public Interest,* no. 27 (spring 1972), p. 66.

this, only months after Newark's former mayor and some other public servants had been jailed for similar violations of the public trust.

25   Yet we are continually warned that the wage earners subvert the work ethic. The journalist recently published in *Reader's Digest* who spent "much of 1971 . . . interviewing 500 representatives of construction companies" so as to inveigh against work rules unaccountably missed the wholesale corruption, involving builders and New York City inspectors, documented in the *New York Times* in the same month that *Reader's Digest* exposed the workers.[9]

Conclusion

26 To put it judiciously, evidence that workers are misbehaving as never before is less than abundant. All the recently fashionable conferences on "work alienation" and "the changing work ethic" would have us believe that there is a new crisis and that productivity has suddenly given way to job turnover, industrial conflict, and worse. Yet the "quit rate" per 100 workers in manufacturing went *down* from 2.7 in 1969 to 1.8 in 1971, the last full year for which data are available. (Data on other employees are not recorded by the Bureau of Labor Statistics; exceedingly few managers have trend data on white-collar workers or consider them if they have them.) And President Nixon reminded us, in his Labor Day speech, that "today, we have achieved an era of relative calm on the labor-management front, with work stoppages at a six-year low."

27   Now it would be quite wrong to suppose that there are not some complex difficulties connected with work in contemporary American society. There are organizations in which absenteeism, turnover, conflict, and other offenses against productivity are of some moment and the causes of these and other problems deserve systematic study. But it is well to view with skepticism all simplified explanations that focus only and owlishly on the worker's philosophy and to examine a number of the currently popular prescriptive solutions with care.

28   Consider, for example, that E. Daniel Grady, division traffic manager for Michigan Bell Telephone Company, reduced the absenteeism of Detroit operators from 7.5 percent to 4.5 percent in one quarter by keeping attendance records on a weekly rather than a monthly basis. Mr. Grady, after digging into the matter, discovered that telephone operators felt that a month's record had already been marred if they were absent early in that month; in for a penny, they went in for a pound. By recording in a shorter unit, he removed that easy rationale for multiple absences. And Edward J. Feeny, a vice-president of Emery Air Freight Corporation, was able to increase his employees' care and skill at packing cargo containers to capacity by the staggeringly simple expedient of *tell-*

9. Sexton and Sexton, pp. 103-104.

ing the workers the difference in profits between filling to 45 percent and filling to the 90 percent they quickly achieved. The result: a $520,000 annual cost reduction. These illustrations could be multiplied to a degree that is dumbfounding; they may be found in any second-rate textbook on "human relations."

29   The plain truth is that the overriding majority of Americans are not lazy malcontents who soldier on the job at every opportunity. Even auto workers, universally famous for having the best reasons to be unhappy with their work, *act* upon their disenchantments with surprising inconsistency. Only about half of the production workers employed by the Big Three retire before reaching sixty-five, according to Melvin Glasser, director of the UAW's Social Security Department. This, despite a "thirty and out" retirement plan for workers fifty-eight or older with thirty years service. Many keep working for financial reasons—to maintain preretirement pay and to benefit, ultimately, from any expansion in retirement benefits. The indication, says Mr. Glasser, is that the retirement age will be lowered, but he does not believe it will be lowered much.

30   We have dissatisfied workers in America, but work dissatisfaction is not laziness or historicocultural sabotage. One might expect management, at so late a date, to know that. But that is another matter—for, as some of the observations in these paragraphs suggest, there are grounds for doubt about *managers'* willingness, in any sector of the economy, to get on with it. Dissatisfied workers may well become less productive in the face of evidence that managers don't know what they are doing themselves; evidence that employers are so protected from market pressures that they can afford to be inefficient; evidence that they will blame employees for their own miscalculations; or evidence that managers will seek to deceive the workers.

31   It is interesting to note in this regard that the single most frequent complaint listed by employees in a University of Michigan study was over the difficulty of getting their jobs done and done properly amid faulty materials, badly scheduled deliveries, and other manifestations of mismanagement. The second largest category of job dissatisfactions involved health and safety hazards, the overriding majority of which are wholly under management's control.[10]

32   Readers unfamiliar with life in the basic industries might contemplate the experience of workers with avoidable occupational accidents and illnesses. In 1968, a total of 14,300 people died in industrial accidents—about the equivalent of American fatalities in Vietnam that year. "In the same year," report Patricia Cayo Sexton and Brendan Sexton, "90,000 workers suffered *permanent impairment* from industrial accidents, and a total of 2,100,000 suffered total but temporary disability. . . .

10. Neal Q. Herrick and Robert P. Quinn, "The Working Conditions Survey as a Source of Social Indicators," *Monthly Labor Review* 94, no. 4 (April 1971): 15-24.

In 1969 [exposures to industrial pollutants in the workplace] caused one million new cases of occupational disease. Among the casualties were 3,600 dead and over 800,000 cases of burns, lung and eye damage, dermatitis, and brain damage."[11] It is simply fatuous to believe that managers whose employees have an intimate, daily association with unnecessary risks to life and limb should be thought competent, never mind "legitimate," by those same employees. The "staunchest supporters" of industry questioned by *Business Week* may consult the front page of the *Wall Street Journal* for August 5, 1969, where an executive pronounced, "When you come right down to it, a lot of our safety decisions are really cost decisions. We give our workers safety glasses because they cost just $3.50. Safety shoes, which they also need, cost $14. . . ."

33   It is equally fatuous to believe that the current rash of experiments in "work enlargement" or "work enrichment" will fool workers anywhere when these programs are only ostensibly designed to enhance satisfaction in work. Well-intentioned social scientists who lecture managers on the currently favored techniques for elevating the "self-actualization" of workers may be in deeper than they know. Edwin Mills, director of the "Quality of Work Program" of the much touted National Commission on Productivity, told a Chicago business audience, just before the turn of the year, that 80 percent of 150 firms currently conducting experiments designed to "enlarge" and "enrich" work were nonunion. Their managers reported in a private poll, according to Mr. Mills, that these experiments were part of such firms' overall antiunion policy. It is doubtful, on historical grounds, that the dissatisfactions and needs which move workers to collective bargaining will be dissipated by "self-actualization." And deceptions will not help; employees will not be blinded to management incompetence by such strategies.

34   The fact is that management has lately become far more visible to the American employee, and the close-up is not flattering. The sociologist Fred Goldner has argued compellingly that the growing ranks of managers have themselves become a work force of extraordinary magnitude. Managers' habits, their technical competence, and their dedication to work are on display as never before, and are as open to interpretation as their workers'. Particularly in a "service economy," in which so many of us "work with our heads," it is not difficult to justify visits to the barber shop or the hairdresser as being, so to speak, continuing work toward the same end. After all, "the mind doesn't punch in and out," and "we're really working all the time." To the extent that we believe and act on that premise we will be observed doing so. That is, we will ourselves be judged by the rest of our countrymen who have brought their ascetic heritage into a convenient—a necessary—synthesis with the impulse toward comfort.

11. Sexton and Sexton, p. 103.

35   It was Max Weber, the German sociologist and economic historian, who explored most fully the role of the Protestant ethic in the genesis of capitalism. And it was Weber who examined at length, in his studies of authority, the concept of legitimacy. He concluded that in large, complex organizations, technical competence was a central inducement to the acceptance of authority by subordinates. Weber might see in those facts of contemporary American life I have touched on signs of damage, not to the ethic that stimulates workers under legitimate conditions, but to management's claim to the loyalty and industrious output of its millions of charges.

VOCABULARY

dissimilar (P1), *commonplace* (P1), *deferring* (P1), *gratification* (P1), *commended* (P1), *adherents* (P1), *legitimacy* (P1), *benign* (P2), *aphorisms* (P2), *renouncing* (P3), *heresies* (P3), *allure* (P3), *collectivism* (P3), *contingent* (P3), *abide* (P3), *coiffure* (P3), *authenticity* (P3), *communal* (P3), *opprobrium* (P3), *(Thorsten) Veblen* (P6), *insouciance* (P6), *euphemism* (P6), *inflammatory* (P7), *appended* (P7), *glibly* (P8), *imperative* (P8), *naive* (P8), *censorious* (P8), *compacts* (P9), *Sunday supplements* (P9), *thwarted* (P9), *elaborated* (P10), *adduced* (P11), *featherbedding* (P12), *publicists* (P12), *husband* (P12), *unilaterally* (P13), *indices* (P14), *demise* (P14), *subsidies* (P15), *juxtapose* (P16), *cosset* (P16), *apostates* (P16), *staid* (P17), *disparities* (P17), *architects* (P18), *constituencies* (P18), *tenets* (P19), *ardent* (P19), *articulate* (P19), *proponents* (P19), *extant* (P19), *litany* (P19), *rapacious* (P19), *conglomerates* (P19), *purport* (P20), *consumption* (P21), *consolable* (P22), *shenanigans* (P23), *avowedly* (P23), *compendium* (P23), *skullduggery* (P23), *predecessor* (P24), *incarceration* (P24), *subvert* (P25), *inveigh* (P25), *judiciously* (P26), *moment* (P27), *owlishly* (P27), *expedient* (P28), *malcontents* (P29), *soldier* (P29), *impairment* (P32), *fatuous* (P32), *ostensibly* (P33), *actualization* (P33), *touted* (P33), *ascetic* (P34), *synthesis* (P34), *inducement* (P35), *charges* (P35)

IDEAS AND AIMS

1. What *is* "the Protestant Ethic"? Who is concerned about it?
2. Why is a person who is fully employed, yet still poor, a "Protestant ethic loyalist"?
3. What has been the role of management, according to Berg, in the advance of "make work" rules?
4. In contrast to other authors you have read, what reasons does Berg advance for the dissatisfaction of workers today?

5. Is there, according to Berg, a "welfare ethic"? What are the attitudes of welfare recipients toward work?
6. What is Berg's view of the ethic of American workers?
7. If there is a deterioration of the work ethic in America, where does Berg's evidence suggest it is to be found?
8. What is Berg's overall opinion of management?
9. Why, according to Berg, are most companies concerned about "work enrichment" for their employees?
10. How is Berg's overall purpose or aim in the essay argumentative or persuasive? How does he attempt to accomplish this purpose calmly and authoritatively?
11. Several minor points in the essay call for inference: (a) why Calvinism forces the union of necessity and morality (P1, P9); (b) the meaning of the statement "'For instance' is notoriously not proof" (P8)—cf. P23; (c) the meaning of the phrase "the faithful who work in the old imperative way" (P8); (d) the referent of "the other house" in the first sentence of P20.

ORGANIZATION AND FORM

1. Where does Berg introduce the central idea of his essay?
2. What functions are served by the first seven paragraphs of the essay?
3. The essay is divided into parts by its headings. How is each of these parts a separate unit? What main idea or topic is advanced by Berg in each of these parts?
4. In which paragraphs does Berg bring up the assertions of the opposing side of the issue about which he is writing? How does he deal with these assertions—by limiting them, conceding to them (or parts of them), arguing against their logic, citing facts in rebuttal, or assembling authorities to refute the other side? List examples of each of these tactics, noting in which paragraphs they occur.
5. How does Berg use repetition of a key word for transition in the first sentences of P4 and P5? Where else (e.g., PP32–33) does he use this device? Where (as in the second sentence of P5) does the essayist use transitional words? List examples of Berg's use of transitional devices within and between paragraphs. Explain one or two instances of how these work to help effect the transition from one idea to the next in the essay.

WORDS AND STYLE

1. Berg repeatedly uses words with religious connotations or denotations in this essay, as in P6 ("guilty," "shameful"), P8 ("the faithful"), P13 ("sinful"), P16 ("apostates"), P19 ("litany"), P20 ("curse on the other house"), P22 ("apos-

tasy"), and P23 ("breach of faith"). How does this vocabulary help Berg to illustrate any of his main points, and how does it help him to show how people think and feel about the subjects he is discussing?

2. Berg modulates through a variety of tones in this essay—humorous and ironic, reasonable, earnest, scholarly. The following questions all deal with the first of these strands. (a) How is Berg's word "coiffure" in P3 (fourth sentence) humorously overformal? Whom and what does it gently mock? (b) How is the underlying metaphor in the first sentence of P5 (equating one kind of friction with another kind) funny? What pun—play on at least two different definitions of a word—is Berg making on "heat"? (c) How is the contradiction in the last sentence of P17—between Berg's citation of an expert study and his use of the word "knows"—ironic? Whom and what does it mock? (d) Of what is Berg's inverted word order in P21 ("knew not") reminiscent? How does this create a humorous or ironic effect in the sentence? (e) How does Berg in the first sentence of P22 nearly create a mixed metaphor by piling one cliché expression or dead metaphor on top of another? (Look up "mixed metaphor," "cliché," and "dead metaphor" in your composition handbook or collegiate dictionary.) How are the two dead metaphors related, revivified, and then barbed, enabling the mockery of management's spending time on one thing when it should be spending it on something else? (f) What is the pun on "bare" in the fifth sentence of P23? What two kinds of exposure does it humorously juxtapose?

3. How does Berg use the colloquial level of style effectively—how does it help him express or convey his point—in the last sentence of P3, the last sentence of P20, the second sentence of P23 ("shenanigans"), the second sentence of P28, or the third sentence of P30? How might Berg's use of colloquial language relate to his overall contrast in the essay between management or government and employees or the public?

4. Which of the main strands of the essay's tones (see question 2 of this section) are the following examples connected to? (a) Berg's use of "may" or "may well _____" in P8 and P11, "might" in P18, and "could . . . support" (P20)—all, technically, instances of the "modal auxiliary verb." (b) Berg's use of litotes or understatement in "nor is . . . news" (first sentence of P10), "least" or "at least" (P8, P9, P14), "no less" (P12), and "less than abundant" (first sentence of P26). How does the tone created by these examples help Berg accomplish his main aim or purpose of the essay (see Ideas and Aims, question 10)?

5. What point does Berg try to hammer home through the repetition of the word "evidence" (as well as the parallelism) in P30? To which of the essay's main tones does this paragraph contribute?

6. What is structurally unusual about the third sentence of P2 and the last sentence of P10? To which of the essay's main tones do they contribute?

7. How does Berg's use of the interrogative sentence in P3, P6, P18, and P19 help him accomplish his main aim or purpose of the essay? (See question 10 of Ideas and Aims.)

8. How does Berg use the shortness of the last sentence of P2 to help convey an idea or point in that paragraph? How does he use the lengthiness of the third sentence of P23 to convey an idea or point in that paragraph?

DISCUSSION AND WRITING

1. If all that Berg says about welfare programs is true, then why do we have welfare programs? Is there a connection between wages and welfare programs?
2. Why does Berg repeat (in P8 and P23) the sentence "'For instance' is not proof"? Does Berg adhere to this tenet of logic and argumentation better than his opposition? How so?
3. Do you agree or disagree with Berg? Why?
4. Much of Berg's essay centers on reinterpretation of facts that others have used to blame American workers. Can you reinterpret any of Berg's facts?
5. How do P9 and other remarks about managers and white-collar workers in Berg's essay compare or contrast with what Drucker says about these groups in his essay "Evolution of the Knowledge Worker" (Section 4, "Careers for the 1990s")?
6. Benjamin Franklin's essay "The Way to Wealth" (see Section 5, "Money") is alluded to by Berg several times (P1, P2, and P21), as are Calvin's ideas (see his essay in Section 1, "Job Choices and Self-Fulfillment"), every time "the Protestant ethic" is mentioned. What basis can you find in Franklin's and Calvin's essays for the notions that Berg says have been derived from these two authors?
7. For a class report, go to a library and look through some recent issues of *Business Week* magazine. In the magazine's editorials and articles is the bias that Berg claims still to be found? Explain.

TAKING STOCK: COMPARING AND CONTRASTING THE SELECTIONS

1. Compare or contrast the attitudes toward work expressed in Eric Hoffer's essay "Dull Work" with those in Henry David Thoreau's "Getting a Living" (Section 2, "Work and Morality").
2. Compare or contrast Hoffer's essay with Patrick Fenton's "Confessions of a Working Stiff" (Section 7, "Varieties of Work: Professions and Blue Collar") on the topic of boredom and other unpleasant features of work.
3. Compare or contrast what Eric Hoffer says about the benefits of dull work with what effects exciting work seems to have had on Richard Selzer in "The Knife" (Section 7, "Varieties of Work: Professions and Blue Collar").
4. Apply what Boroson says about the work addict's or workaholic's off-the-job behavior to boss B. J. Winfall's conduct in his Chicago "vacation," as described in James Thurber's "How to Adjust Yourself to Your Work" (Section 9, "The Work Environment").

5. Could anyone with Eric Hoffer's attitude toward work, especially dull work, become a workaholic or work addict (to use the concepts of Warren Boroson's essay)? Why or why not?

6. Are the workers described in Adam Smith's "High Wages and Overwork" (Section 5, "Money") by and large work lovers or work addicts (workaholics)? How so?

7. From his essay (Section 7, "Varieties of Work: Professions and Blue Collar"), do you suppose Richard Selzer is a work lover or a work addict? What is your evidence from Selzer's essay, as well as from Warren Boroson's article?

8. Do the students sampled by Malcolm Carter for his essay seem to agree with Hoffer or with Thoreau in "Getting a Living" (Section 2, "Work and Morality")? Explain your answer, citing evidence and examples from the essays.

9. How do PP6-8 of Carter's essay suggest the utility of academic liberal arts courses in areas like history, political science, and sociology? In his implied view of education, how does Carter compare with Perelman's dry cleaner (pages 234-36) or with any of the authors from the section entitled "Work and Education"?

10. Could any of Calvin's ideas in his essay turn a worker into what Warren Boroson would call a "work addict" or "workaholic"? Into a "work lover"? How?

11. Are the essays by Davidyne Mayleas (Section 6, "Job Opportunities and Other Practical Matters"), Marlys Harris (Section 6), and Malcolm Carter based on the main assumption or principle of Calvin's essay, or some other assumption or principle? Explain.

12. Do you side with Patrick Fenton (Section 7, "The Varieties of Work: Professions and Blue Collar") or John Calvin regarding one's contentment with a particular job? Why?

13. Many of our questions on other essays have asked for comparison with Calvin's essay. See Taking Stock question 2 (from the section "Money"), comparing Calvin and several authors on the issue of acquiring money; also from Taking Stock at the end of the section "Varieties of Work: Professions and Blue Collar," see questions asking for comparison or contrast of Calvin's essay with the selections by Richard Selzer, Samuel Johnson, Thomas Fuller, and Studs Terkel.

14. Ivar Berg's "They Won't Work" has a number of affinities with Henry David Thoreau's "Getting a Living" (Section 2, "Work and Morality"). How do Berg's main ideas echo Thoreau's?

15. How does Berg's view of the motivations and values of today's workers compare or contrast with the views expressed in the essays by Studs Terkel (Section 7, "The Varieties of Work: Professions and Blue Collar") and Patrick Fenton (Section 7)?

16. In the essays by James Thurber (Section 9, "The Work Environment"), William Ouchi (Section 9), C. Northcote Parkinson (Section 9), and John L. McCaffrey (Section 3, "Work and Education"), there are various portraits of managers and white-collar workers. Select one or more of these essays to compare or contrast with that of Ivar Berg on the topic of the credits or debits of today's corporate manager.

Note: See also Discussion and Writing question 6 of Warren Boroson's "The Workaholic in You," question 4 of Malcolm Carter's "Opportunities for Young Americans," question 6 of John Calvin's "Every Vocation Is a Post Assigned by the Lord," and questions 5 and 6 of Ivar Berg's "'They Won't Work': The End of the Protestant Ethic and All That."

WORK
AND MORALITY

CONFESSIONS OF A ROOF SELLER

Art Buchwald

☐

Journalist, comic lecturer, writer of travelogues (e.g., Paris After Dark*), novelist (*A Gift from the Boys *[1958],* Irving's Delight *[1975]), and dramatist (*Sheep on the Runway *[1970]), Art Buchwald is best known as America's premier humorous newspaper columnist. Born in 1925 in Mount Vernon, New York, and educated on the G.I. Bill at the University of Southern California, Buchwald left school without his degree to travel to Paris. There, following up on his journalism experience in college, he worked in a variety of writing departments of the* New York Herald Tribune *(Paris Edition). The books gathering his columns from this period reflect his European* *residence:* Art Buchwald's Paris *(1953)*, More Caviar *(1957)*, Don't Forget to Write *(1960)*, How Much Is That in Dollars? *(1961)*, and Is It Safe to Drink the Water? *(1962)*. *In 1961 he returned to the United States with his family, settling in Washington, D.C. Like Russell Baker, Buchwald is the inheritor of an admirable tradition of the humorous columnist focusing on American customs, manners, and institutions, particularly, for Buchwald, as they are to be found in the nation's capital. (See Section 4, "Careers for the 1990s," for a selection by Russell Baker.) Among the dozen books collecting Buchwald's essays about the American scene are* I Chose Capitol Punishment *(1963)*, Have I Ever Lied to You? *(1968)*, Getting High in Government Circles *(1971)*, I Never Danced at the White House *(1973)*, Washington Is Leaking *(1976)*, Down the Seine and Up the Potomac *(1977)*, The Buchwald Stops Here *(1978)*, Laid Back in Washington *(1981)*, and While Reagan Slept *(1983)*.

Inevitably, some of Buchwald's essays deal with work and money in each of his books; from one of his most recent, Laid Back in Washington, *there are "The Medicine Flackers," "The New Retailers," "How to Buy a Car," "What Do You Do?" and "My Bendix Problem," among others. Though his essays are humorous, they often have serious and moral points. The following essay is an example of expository narration. Rather than purely telling a story, Buchwald gives the essay an explanatory framework by suggesting in both introductory and concluding paragraphs what its overall points—its main ideas—are.*

1   Everyone has a skeleton in his closet that he lives in deathly fear a *Time* magazine researcher may uncover. My skeleton is that I used to sell roofs in Los Angeles. Now I know this doesn't sound like something I should be ashamed of, but that's because nobody really knows the roofing situation in Los Angeles, or at least how it was in the days when I was in the business. I'm sure now it's all different and very much aboveboard.

2   My life as a roofing salesman began one warm day in 1946, when, as a student at the University of Southern California, I was hitchhiking along Vermont Avenue and was picked up by a man who introduced himself as Johnny B.

3   Johnny asked me if I was interested in making extra money, and I said it was possible. He told me he was in the roofing business, and he needed a young, clean-cut-looking fellow like myself to act as a legman for him.

4   I said I didn't know anything about roofs, and Johnny said it didn't matter. He then gave me a fast course in roofmanship.

5   "The war is over, and everyone needs a new roof," Johnny said. "But if you just go out and ask people if they want a new roof, they're bound to say no. So you have to have a story they're willing to listen to."

6   "What's the story?" I asked.

7   "The story is that you are a representative of the Rumraw and Zingoff advertising agency. You are looking for a home in the neighborhood to put on a new asbestos-type shingle. If the homeowner will permit you to put this new roof on, your agency will photograph it, advertise it, and bring around people to look at it. In exchange for any inconvenience caused to the homeowner by all the publicity, Rumraw and Zingoff will arrange to have the roof put on at absolute rockbottom wholesale cost."

8   "Which," I said brightly, "is probably the same price that any roof would cost."

9   "You catch on fast for a college kid," Johnny B. said. "Now I don't want you to think we're doing anything dishonest. The people do get a good roof, and besides, they have something to tell the neighbors. It gives them status on their street."

10   "What am I supposed to do?"

11   "You give your story to the wife and the husband. If they are *both* interested, you tell them your advertising manager will come by and talk to them, and you set up an appointment. Then I go in with the sales pitch. If they buy a roof, you get ten percent on the sale."

12   "It sounds easy," I admitted.

13   The next afternoon I was out ringing doorbells in Los Angeles. It took a week before I made a sale, but the commission was $30, and when Johnny paid me, I was so excited I decided I might make the roofing business my lifework.

14   My job was quite simple, and I didn't have too much trouble getting someone to listen to my story. I discovered Los Angeles is made up of a lot of lonely people, and they're delighted to have their day interrupted by anybody who has an interesting tale to tell.

15   I remember once I rang a doorbell and a man answered the door with a fiddle in his hand. He asked me to come in. There was no furniture in the house except for several wooden grocery crates. He told me to sit down, and then he proceeded to play the fiddle. He played for two straight hours without stopping, and every time I attempted to leave, he became very agitated.

16   Another time a large-bosomed blond lady listened to me make my pitch, and then she said, "What does your advertising manager look like?"

17   I described him, and she said, "Send him over tonight around eight o'clock."

18   "Will your husband be home?"

19   "I'm divorced," she said.

20   I told Johnny the story, and he said he'd look into it, just on the off-chance that the lady really did want a roof.

21   The next day I called. "Did you make a sale?"

22   "What are you talking about?" Johnny wanted to know.

23   "Didn't she want a roof?"

24   "Damn," said Johnny, "I knew there was something I wanted to ask her."

25   Being my age and involved in the type of work I was doing, I must say I was always looking for an "adventure" similar to those all the other salesmen seemed to claim they were having.

26   There was one fellow—a short, squat, fat, greasy man—whom I used to go out doorbell ringing with at times. He worked one side of the street and I worked the other.

27   It never failed that sooner or later he would disappear into a house and I'd have to wait an hour for him on the corner. When he finally came out he had a big grin on his face.

28   "Tell me everything that happened," I'd say excitedly, and for the next two hours, while I gnashed my teeth, he went into every detail about the conquest.

29   "Why doesn't it ever happen to me?" I cried.

30   "Your trouble, boy," he said softly, "is all you really want to do is sell roofs."

31   Johnny B. was fantastic when he went into his sales pitch, and it was rare that he would fluff a sale after I got him into the house.

32   I went with him on several occasions just to see the master at work.

33   He walked in with a blowtorch, a beautiful presentation of photographs in a leather-bound, looseleaf folder, samples of the shingle, and, of course, the contract.

34   Johnny never behaved like a salesman. He always acted as if he were the city health inspector and he were just about to give the homeowners a summons.

35   He never talked about the roof. He started off by demanding background on the wife and husband. He pointed out his agency had to make absolutely sure that they were upstanding citizens of good moral character. He demanded to know how much money they made, what books they read, whom their children played with. Johnny would find some fault with the construction of the house which made it look as though there were no chance of the agency using the home for display purposes.

36   In less than an hour both husband and wife were pleading with Johnny to put a roof on the house, no matter what it cost. As a clincher Johnny always asked the people if they had a Bible in the house. They usually did. He then told the couple to place their hands on it and swear to him that neither one had lied to him.

37   Johnny was beautiful and could have been one of the great actors of our time, if he hadn't discovered early in life there was so much more money in selling roofs.

38   Occasionally after a roof was put on a house, someone would call in and complain that all the publicity and advertising that they were promised never came to them.

39   I remember once when I was sitting in the roofing contractor's office on a Saturday afternoon and a call came in. The lady told the boss he had promised to photograph her house and he never had.

40   "We'll do it this afternoon."

41   The boss tossed me a Brownie camera and said, "Go out to the house and take some pictures of her damn roof."

42   "There's no film in the camera," I said.

43   "Get out of here," he snarled.

44   I went out and for more than an hour pretended I was taking photos of the lady's roof.

45   I retired from the roofing business when Johnny decided to expand into barbecue pits. There seemed to be some moral justification in conning someone into a roof, but it was hard to feel I was doing the right thing when it came to barbecue pits, particularly since many of the people Johnny was selling barbecue pits to could hardly pay for their roofs.

46   It was more than twenty years ago, but every time I fly into Los Angeles, I look down over the roofs trying to see if the ones I sold are still in good condition. And you know something? Despite Johnny and our crooked sales pitch, a lot of them are.

VOCABULARY

aboveboard (P1), *legman* (P3), *agitated* (P15), *squat* (P26), *gnashed* (P28), *fluff* (P31), *looseleaf* (P33), *conning* (P45)

IDEAS AND AIMS

1. Part of the lightly ironic tone in this essay is due to the lighthearted attitudes expressed in the narrative. For example, what is Johnny B.'s attitude toward the roofing business? What is his attitude toward education?

2. What is the logic of Johnny B.'s statement "'The war is over, and everyone needs a new roof'" (P5)? What do these two things have to do with each other? What intervening connecting steps have been left out in Johnny B.'s reasoning? What is Buchwald suggesting here about the principles and rationality of this particular business enterprise?

3. (a) What do both Johnny B. and his other salesmen value more than the money in the roofing business? (b) What is the humor or irony of Buchwald's double hedging or qualification in P25—his words "seemed" and "claim"? What typ-

ical male verbal behavior, on the part of the salesmen other than Buchwald, seems to be suggested here?

4. (a) Is the young Buchwald a very good salesman? Why or why not? (b) What is the underlying idea or logic in the following italicized phrase: "Being my age *and involved in the type of work I was doing,* I . . . was always looking for an 'adventure' similar to those . . . the other salesmen . . . were having" (P25)? What has the "type of work" got to do with what Buchwald is talking about here?

5. (a) Why does Johnny B.'s sales pitch work so well? (b) What is the function, do you think, of each item of Johnny B.'s paraphernalia, detailed by Buchwald in P33? Why a blowtorch? Why a *leather-bound* looseleaf folder? (c) What are the components of Johnny B.'s sales pitch, as detailed by Buchwald in PP34–36? How is each one effective in selling? What psychology of persuasion is involved in each one?

6. What view of customers is expressed in the essay? What other recollections in the essay confirm the truth of this view for Buchwald?

7. Why are customers interested in the publicity and advertising even after they've already received and paid for the new roof?

8. In light of the rest of the essay and its revelation of the workings of human nature, how is Buchwald's disclaimer in P1 ironic?

ORGANIZATION AND FORM

1. What is the time structure of this essay? Which paragraphs might be said to be in present time? Which in past time?

2. The essay consists of several anecdotes (brief narratives) about roof selling linked together. How are the anecdotes organized? Which ones appear first? Why?

3. Which anecdotes does Buchwald put later? Why?

4. What are the overall parts of the essay?

5. In what paragraph or paragraphs does Buchwald come closest to stating his central thesis?

WORDS AND STYLE

1. How do words like "aboveboard" (P1), "legman" (P3), "conning" (P45), and "story" (PP6, 7, 11) establish the tone of Buchwald's essay? Why are they effective?

2. Where does Buchwald use slang or colloquialism effectively? Explain how in a few instances.

3. Why might Buchwald use the word "seller" rather than "salesman" in the title? Why "roof seller" rather than "roof salesman"?

4. In what way is the word "roofmanship" in P4 funny? What ideas does it help to suggest about the whole enterprise?
5. How are the names of the owners of the advertising agency in P7 amusing?

DISCUSSION AND WRITING

1. How does the narrator *really* feel about his roof selling days?
2. Do you think the methods used to sell roofs as described in this essay are unethical? Why or why not?
3. Have you ever engaged in, or would you engage in, business practices less than totally ethical? Why or why not?
4. Have you or an acquaintance ever made a foolish purchase because of being sold by one or more of the sales techniques used by Johnny B.? Explain.
5. How might this essay by Buchwald be seen as conflicting with Adam Smith's "High Wages and Overwork" (Section 5, "Money") in its view of wage earners as well as what workers value most as compensation from the job (money or something else)? (See question 3 of **Ideas and Aims** above.) Which author is correct, or are both? What is *your* view on this subject?

TWO KINDS
OF COMPETITION
(from *Works and Days*)

Hesiod

Hesiod, who lived in the eighth century B.C., *was, along with epic poet Homer, a founding father of Greek poetry and classical literature. In addition, his writings were of enormous importance in molding the very influential body of stories about heroes and gods that today we refer to as Greek mythology. His extant poetic works are* The Theogony, *an account of the origins of the universe and gods, and* Works and Days, *basically a discussion of agriculture and the value of work. Hesiod opens the latter poem with a brief comment on competition, which is reprinted in our selection.*

Strife is no only child. Upon the earth
Two Strifes exist; the one is praised by those
Who come to know her, and the other blamed.
Their natures differ: for the cruel one
Makes battles thrive, and war; she wins no love
But men are forced, by the immortals' will,
To pay the grievous goddess due respect.
The other, first-born child of blackest Night,
Was set by Zeus, who lives in air, on high,

Set in the roots of earth, an aid to men.
She urges even lazy men to work:
A man grows eager, seeing another rich
From ploughing, planting, ordering his house;
So neighbour vies with neighbour in the rush
For wealth: this Strife is good for mortal men—
Potter hates potter, carpenters compete,
And beggar strives with beggar, bard with bard.

VOCABULARY

strife, thrive, immortals, grievous, Zeus, vies, potter, bard

IDEAS AND AIMS

1. What is the function of the first kind of "strife," according to Hesiod?
2. What is the function of the second kind of strife?
3. According to Hesiod, in what and how many fundamental ways do the two kinds of competition or "strife" differ?
4. How are the two kinds of competition comparable?
5. How is the second kind of strife or competition "an aid to men"?
6. What may Hesiod be suggesting about the second kind of competition by identifying it as the first-born child of blackest Night, considering that Night (Nyx or Nox) was among the eldest of the gods, immensely powerful, and both reverenced and feared?
7. How does Hesiod include *himself* in the second strife through the last example he cites of this striving (in the last line of the selection)? What might this inclusion indicate about his attitude toward competition? How so?

ORGANIZATION AND FORM

1. Poetry is often—wrongly—considered to be less organized or thoughtful than prose. What quite logical outline can be made of this passage of poetry, showing a quite rational layout of its points and parts?
2. Why might Hesiod discuss the kinds of competition in the order that he does?
3. What rationale or rationales might there be for the order or sequence of examples Hesiod gives for the individuals or groups in which the second kind of competition is manifested?

WORDS AND STYLE

1. In what way is the form of Hesiod's opening assertion—"strife is no only child"—unusual? (Technically it uses the devices of litotes and metaphor, terms you will find in your collegiate dictionary.) Why might Hesiod not want to begin "strife is one of many children" or "strife is a set of twins"?
2. With what slanted or highly connotative words does Hesiod characterize the first kind of "strife" he discusses? In what ways are these words applicable?
3. What may Hesiod be suggesting about competition by his metaphor when he says that Zeus has set strife "in the roots of earth"?

DISCUSSION AND WRITING

1. Do you agree that there are two kinds of competition and that "their natures differ"? Why or why not?
2. Do you agree that the second kind of competition is "an aid to men"? Is it always? Why or why not? In what circumstances?
3. Have you ever found in school or an off-campus job that the second kind of competition was helpful (or harmful) to you, your co-workers, or productivity?
4. Find Adam Smith's remark in "High Wages and Overwork" (Section 5, "Money") about "mutual emulation" (in the sentence beginning "Till this stipulation was made, mutual emulation . . .") and compare it with Hesiod's view.

THE GOOD MERCHANT

Thomas Fuller

☐

Thomas Fuller (1608–1661) was a writer greatly admired by celebrated authors Samuel Pepys, Charles Lamb, and Samuel Taylor Coleridge. Coleridge considered him one of the "uniques" in British literature, ranking him with Shakespeare, Milton, and Defoe; and the distinguished modern scholar George Lyman Kittredge pronounced him "one of the wittiest . . . authors of the seventeenth century." Born in Northhamptonshire and educated at Cambridge University (B.A., 1625; M.A., 1628; B.D., 1635), Fuller became an Anglican clergyman, holding various church posts throughout his life. He was prolific, publishing more than 38 books in his lifetime, with one important title coming out the year after his death.

Although Fuller tried his hand at poetry (e.g., David's Heinous Sin, Hearty Repentance, Heavy Punishment *[1631]) and political satire (*Andronicus, or the Unfortunate Politician *[1646]), he is remembered for his superior nonfiction, which includes works of biography and history, as well as collections of sermons and of essays. In these, Fuller shows himself a stylist of sharp insight, using epigrams, anecdotes, puns, and pithy sentences—overall a blend of the whimsical and the profound. In his work overall, Fuller shows his skills as antiquarian, historian, scholar, preacher (Fuller was one of the most popular in his day), biographer, and essayist.*

Fuller's main works are The History of the Holy War *(1639), an account of the Crusades;* Joseph's Parti-colored Coat *(1640), one of more than fourteen books of sermons;* The Holy and the Profane State *(1642), a blend of characters (short model biographies of good and bad human "types"), essays, and biographies;* Good Thoughts in Bad Times *(1645), a small book of meditations, observations on scriptural passages, and applica-tion of historical incidents and anecdotes to current events;* Good Thoughts in Worse Times *(1647);* A Pisgah-Sight of Palestine *(1650), a large historical work about the Holy Land;* Abel Redevivus: or the Dead Yet Speaking *(1651), a collection of clerical biographies;* The Church History of Britain *(1655), an account from the birth of Jesus to the execution of King Charles I;* The History of the University of Cambridge *(1655);* Mixed Contemplations in Better Times *(1660); and* The History of the Worthies of England *(1662), Fuller's most famous work, an encyclopedic account of the people, history, proverbs, geography, and physical resources of all the counties in Britain.*

In our selection, from The Holy and the Profane State *(1642), Fuller is composing a "character," a kind of definition of a certain type or class of human being. Fuller's humor, prose style, and clerical background all come through in his discussion of business and the business professional.*

1 The good merchant is one who by his trading claspeth the island to the continent, and one country to another; an excellent gardener, who makes England bear wine, and oil, and spices; yea, herein goes beyond nature, in causing that *omnis fert omnia tellus* [the globe bears all things to all its peoples]. He wrongs neither himself nor the commonwealth, nor private chapmen which buy commodities of him. As for his behavior towards the commonwealth, it far surpasses my skill to give any rules thereof; only this I know, that to export things of necessity, and to bring in foreign needless toys, makes a rich merchant, and a poor kingdom. For the state loseth her radical moisture, and gets little better than sweat in exchange, except the necessaries which are exported be exceeding plentiful; which then, though necessary in their own nature, become superfluous through their abundance. We will content ourselves to give some general adver-tisements concerning his behavior towards his chapmen, whom he uses well in the quantity, quality, and price of the commodities he sells them.

2   1. He wrongs not the buyer in number, weight, or measure. These are the landmarks of all trading, which must not be removed; for such cozenage were worse than open felony. First, because they rob a man of his purse, and never bid him stand. Secondly, because highway thieves defy, but these pretend justice. Thirdly, as much as lies in their power, they endeavor to make God accessory to their cozenage, deceiving by pretending his weights. For God is the principal clerk of the market. "All the weights of the bag are his work."[1]

3   2. He never warrants any ware for good but what is so indeed. Otherwise he is a thief, and may be a murderer, if selling such things as

1. Proverbs 16:11. [Fuller's note.]

are applied inwardly. Besides, in such a case he counts himself guilty if he selleth such wares as are bad, though without his knowledge, if avouching them for good; because he may, professeth, and is bound to be master in his own mystery [trade], and therefore in conscience must recompense the buyer's loss, except he gives him an item to buy it at his own adventure.

4   3. He either tells the faults in his ware, or abates proportionably in the price he demands; for then the low value shows the viciousness of it. Yet commonly when merchants depart with their commodities, we hear (as in funeral orations) all the virtues but none of the faults thereof.

5   4. He never demands out of distance of the price he intends to take; if not always within the touch, yet within the reach of what he means to sell for. Now we must know there be four several prices of vendible things. First, the price of the market, which ebbs and flows according to the plenty or scarcity of coin, commodities, and chapmen. Secondly, the price of friendship, which perchance is more giving than selling, and, therefore not so proper at this time. Thirdly, the price of fancy, as twenty pounds or more for a dog or hawk, when no such inherent worth can naturally be in them, but by the buyer's and seller's fancy reflecting on them. Yet I believe the money may be lawfully taken. First, because the seller sometimes on those terms is as loth to forego it as the buyer is willing to have it. And I know no standard herein whereby men's affections may be measured. Secondly, it being a matter of pleasure, and men able and willing, let them pay for it, *volenti non fit injuria* [no injury is done to a consenting party]. Lastly, there is the price of the cozenage, which our merchant from his heart detests and abhors.

6   5. He makes not advantage of his chapman's ignorance, chiefly if referring himself to his honesty, where the seller's conscience is all the buyer's skill, who makes him both seller and judge, so that he doth not so much ask as order, what he must pay. When one told old Bishop Latimer that the cutler had cozened him, in making him pay twopence for a knife not (in those days) worth a penny, "No," quoth Latimer, "he cozened not me but his own conscience." On the other side St. Augustine tells us of a seller, who out of ignorance asked for a book far less than it was worth, and the buyer (conceive himself to be the man if you please) of his own accord gave him the full value thereof.

7   6. He makes not the buyer pay the shot for his prodigality; as when the merchant through his own ignorance or ill husbandry hath bought dear, he will not bring in his unnecessary expenses on the buyer's score; and in such a case he is bound to sell cheaper than he bought.

8   7. Selling by retail, he may justify the taking of greater gain; because of his care, pains, and cost of fetching those wares from the fountain, and in parceling and dividing them. Yet because retailers trade commonly with those who have least skill what they buy, and commonly

sell to the poorer sort of people, they must be careful not to grate on their necessity.

9   But how long shall I be retailing out rules to this merchant? It would employ a casuist an apprenticeship of years; take our Saviour's wholesale rule, "Whatsoever ye would have men do unto you, do you unto them; for this is the law and the prophets."[2]

VOCABULARY

claspeth (P1), *commonwealth* (P1), *chapmen* (P1), *commodities* (P1), *superfluous* (P1), *advertisements* (archaic sense) (P1), *cozenage* (P2), *bid* (P2), *stand* (archaic sense, from the phrase, "stand and deliver!") (P2), *accessory* (P2), *warrants* (P3), *ware* (P3), *avouching* (P3), *mystery* (archaic sense) (P3), *recompense* (P3), *adventure* (P3), *abates* (P4), *viciousness* (archaic sense) (P4), *depart with* (P4), *vendible* (P5), *ebbs* (P5), *perchance* (P5), *fancy* (P5), *pounds* (P5), *inherent* (P5), *loth* (P5), *affections* (P5), *detests* (P5), *abhors* (P5), *cutler* (P6), *St. Augustine* (P6), *shot* (P7), *prodigality* (P7), *husbandry* (P7), *dear* (P7), *score* (P7), *fountain* (P8), *grate* (P8), *retailing* (P9), *casuist* (P9), *apprenticeship* (P9).

IDEAS AND AIMS

1. What does Fuller mean by saying that the merchant "claspeth" the island (Britain) to the continent (Europe), or one country to another? How does the merchant's activity result in this?

2. How may an irresponsible merchant "make a poor kingdom"?

3. Why is a dishonest merchant worse than a highwayman?

4. How might a dishonest merchant be a murderer?

5. How may an amoral merchant's sales pitch be like a funeral oration?

6. What does Fuller mean by "the price of cozenage," the fourth of the "four several prices of vendible things," which the good merchant "detests and abhors" (P5)?

7. Explain Fuller's fifth point in your own words.

8. How may the Christianity and Christian values of the Anglican clergyman author be seen pervading his essay, up to and including its concluding paragraph?

9. Overall, the aim of this essay is to define something: the good merchant. Usually, definition is a particular mode or form of exposition. How is it used in this essay more for a persuasive or argumentative purpose?

---

2. Matthew 7:12.

ORGANIZATION AND FORM

1. How does Fuller define the good merchant using comparison and contrast as a defining technique? Where and how does he use it for definition?
2. How does Fuller define the good merchant using illustration and example? Where and how does he use this technique for the purpose of definition?
3. In what way do P1, PP2–8, and P9 form the introduction, body, and conclusion, respectively, of Fuller's essay?
4. If Fuller's seven enumerated points (PP2–8) are not merely a random list, how are they in fact organized? What underlying organizational principle or principles seem to order them in some meaningful sequence?
5. How is the organizational principle of the points in P2 one of climax (ascending order; lesser to greater)?
6. How does Fuller's seventh point (P8) lead naturally into his concluding paragraph (P9)?
7. How does Fuller's concluding paragraph gather the main idea or point underlying the introductory paragraph and seven enumerated specific points of the entire essay?

WORDS AND STYLE

1. Some of the punning that Fuller is known for, and that appealed to the renowned essayist Charles Lamb, may be found in the first and second sentences of P9. What pun does Fuller make on "retailing"—that is, in what two different senses does he use the word simultaneously? Through this pun, in the context of the whole sentence, how does Fuller equate himself as writer to a kind of merchant? How does this equation suggest Fuller's sympathy for the subject of his essay?
2. What pun does Fuller make on "wholesale" in the second sentence of P9? How does Fuller thus equate Christian principle and business dealing?
3. On account of (as one might say) the punning context set up in P9, what pun may there be in the very last word of the essay? How might it also work like Fuller's pun on "wholesale" (see the preceding question)?
4. Fuller uses a good deal of figurative language in his essay—principally metaphor, simile, and analogy. These figures may be found in (a) the first sentence of P1 ("claspeth"; the good merchant as gardener), (b) the fourth sentence of P1 (the carelessly exporting merchant draining the "radical moisture"—that is, one of the four fluids thought to be necessary for the health of a human body—of the state in exchange for "sweat"), (c) the second sentence of P2 (the dishonest merchant removing the "landmarks" of trading), (d) the third sentence of P2 (the immoral merchant as a robber not bidding his victim "to stand"—that is, "stand and deliver," or "halt and turn over your goods"), (e) the fifth sentence of P2 (the immoral merchant attempting to make God an "accessory" to

theft), (f) the sixth sentence of P2 (God as the "principal clerk" of the marketplace), (g) the last sentence of P4 (the bad merchant's sales talk as like a funeral oration), (h) the first sentence of P5 (the "touch" and "reach" of selling price), (i) the first sentence of P6 (the good merchant as a court judge), (j) the first sentence of P8 ("fountain"), (k) the second sentence of P9 (the implied metaphor of Jesus as a kind of merchant). How do any of these help Fuller to express and clarify his ideas?

5. How do the metaphors in the sixth sentence of P2 and second sentence of P9 relate to Fuller's concept of the interrelation of Christianity and business?

6. How does Fuller use antithesis (look up this term in your collegiate dictionary or composition handbook) effectively in the third sentence of P1, the fourth sentence of P1, and the fourth sentence of P2?

DISCUSSION AND WRITING

1. Is Fuller's description similar to or different from the modern idea of a "good merchant"?

2. Can you give examples of your own which illustrate Fuller's four kinds of prices?

3. Can someone stay in business and follow Fuller's explicit and implicit advice to merchants?

4. Is Fuller's idea of good business practice similar to the ideas of the modern consumer movement?

5. "The low value shows the viciousness of it." Do you get what you pay for?

6. Using Fuller's essay as a model, write a description of the qualities necessary to be a good member of your chosen profession (or define "the good student").

GETTING A LIVING

Henry David Thoreau

□

In this selection, "Getting a Living" (an excerpt from a longer essay, "Life Without Principle"), Henry David Thoreau (1817-1862) several times alludes to various jobs he has had. Indeed, Thoreau tried a wide variety: he was variously a schoolteacher, proprietor (with his brother) of his own private school, tutor, general handyman for Ralph Waldo Emerson (he lived with the Emersons for several years), lecturer, mason, painter, carpenter, day laborer, and worker in his father's pencil factory (he helped this business by inventing a process for making graphite superior). This diversity in many respects accords with the ideas of "Getting a Living."

Born in Concord, Massachusetts, Thoreau was educated at Harvard University, where he was much influenced by Edward T. Channing's teaching about English composition as well as by his own study of classical Greek (especially its economy of style and propensity for ringing phrases). While always his own man, a believer in individualism and the need to get back to the essentials of life, Thoreau was influenced by the Transcendentalism of friends Orestes Brownson and Ralph Waldo Emerson, the philosophy advocating a quest for reality beyond the mere physical world through the use of intuition. At Emerson's suggestion, Thoreau faithfully recorded his feelings, observations, and ideas in journals that eventually ran to two million words and were the basis of all his books; they account for fourteen of the twenty volumes of his collected works, which were published posthumously (like most of Thoreau's writing) in 1906.

Thoreau was also an avid traveler, and accounts of these trips along with general observations were the subjects of several of his books. Among his books and essays are A Week on the Concord and Merrimack Rivers *(1849);* "Civil Disobedience" *(1849), a famous call for not obeying a government in the wrong—resulting from Thoreau's one-day jailing for not paying the poll tax levied for the Mexican War, which Thoreau thought unjust;* "Slavery in Massachusetts" *(1854), one of several speeches Thoreau made on behalf of the abolitionist cause;* Walden: Or, Life in the Woods *(1854), a discussion of nature, man, society, and government, emerging from a solitary stay in a cabin at Walden Pond in woods owned by Emerson;* "A Plea for Captain John Brown" *(1859), one of three published speeches on behalf of the famous abolitionist;* "Life Without Principle" *(1863);* Excursions (1863); The Maine Woods *(1864);* Cape Cod *(1865); and* A Yankee in Canada *(1866). Thoreau was also an estimable poet, influenced, not surprisingly, by the Metaphysicals, seventeenth-century British writers who combined feeling, philosophy, and ingenuity; his poems were collected in 1895 and again in 1943.*

Our selection represents only about half of the essay "Life Without Principle," which takes up 48 paragraphs or 22 pages of relatively dense print in its unabridged form. (Specifically, our selection consists of paragraphs 3 through 21.) Originally it was delivered as a lecture in the 1850s, sometimes with the title "Getting a Living" and other times with the title "What Shall It Profit?" (an allusion to the Biblical verse "What shall it profit a man if he gain the whole world but lose his own soul?"). A moral and Biblical dimension are threaded through the essay, in fact. One scholar has summarized the piece as follows: "[Thoreau] asks us to get down to fundamental principles in life and not be led astray by our neighbors, our nation, our churches, public opinion, the desire for wealth, or any other diverting influence. [The essay] is pure transcendentalism, advocating that the good life be discovered within oneself."

1 Let us consider the way in which we spend our lives.

2   This world is a place of business. What an infinite bustle! I am awaked almost every night by the panting of the locomotive. It interrupts my dreams. There is no sabbath. It would be glorious to see mankind at leisure for once. It is nothing but work, work, work. I cannot easily buy a blank-book to write thoughts in; they are commonly ruled for dollars and cents. An Irishman, seeing me making a minute in the fields, took it for granted that I was calculating my wages. If a man was tossed out of a window when an infant, and so made a cripple for life, or scared out of his wits by the Indians, it is regretted chiefly because he was thus incapacitated for—business! I think that there is nothing, not even crime, more opposed to poetry, to philosophy, ay, to life itself, than this incessant business.

3   There is a coarse and boisterous money-making fellow in the outskirts of our town, who is going to build a bank-wall under the hill along the edge of his meadow. The powers have put this into his head to keep

him out of mischief, and he wishes me to spend three weeks digging there with him. The result will be that he will perhaps get some more money to hoard, and leave for his heirs to spend foolishly. If I do this, most will commend me as an industrious and hard-working man; but if I choose to devote myself to certain labors which yield more real profit, though but little money, they may be inclined to look on me as an idler. Nevertheless, as I do not need the police of meaningless labor to regulate me, and do not see anything absolutely praiseworthy in this fellow's undertaking, any more than in many an enterprise of our own or foreign governments, however amusing it may be to him or them, I prefer to finish my education at a different school.

4   If a man walk in the woods for love of them half of each day, he is in danger of being regarded as a loafer; but if he spends his whole day as a speculator, shearing off those woods and making earth bald before her time, he is esteemed an industrious and enterprising citizen. As if a town had no interest in its forests but to cut them down!

5   Most men would feel insulted, if it were proposed to employ them in throwing stones over a wall, and then in throwing them back, merely that they might earn their wages. But many are no more worthily employed now. For instance: just after sunrise, one summer morning, I noticed one of my neighbors walking beside his team, which was slowly drawing a heavy hewn stone swung under the axle, surrounded by an atmosphere of industry—his day's work begun,—his brow commenced to sweat—a reproach to all sluggards and idlers—pausing abreast the shoulders of his oxen, and half turning round with a flourish of his merciful whip, while they gained their length on him. And I thought, Such is the labor which the American Congress exists to protect—honest, manly toil,—honest as the day is long—that makes his bread taste sweet, and keeps society sweet—which all men respect and have consecrated: one of the sacred band, doing the needful, but irksome drudgery. Indeed, I felt a slight reproach, because I observed this from the window, and was not abroad and stirring about a similar business. The day went by, and at evening I passed the yard of another neighbor, who keeps many servants, and spends much money foolishly, while he adds nothing to the common stock, and there I saw the stone of the morning lying beside a whimsical structure intended to adorn this Lord Timothy Dexter's premises,[1] and the dignity forthwith departed from the teamster's labor, in my eyes. In my opinion, the sun was made to light worthier toil than this. I may add, that his employer has since run off, in debt to a good part of the town, and, after passing through Chancery, has settled somewhere else, there to become once more a patron of the arts.

6   The ways by which you may get money almost without exception

---

1. Dexter *called* himself a lord. He had used his wealth to build a mansion featuring statues of himself, George Washington, and classical gods.

lead downward. To have done anything by which you earned money *merely* is to have been truly idle or worse. If the laborer gets no more than the wages which his employer pays him, he is cheated, he cheats himself. If you would get money as a writer or lecturer, you must be popular, which is to go down perpendicularly. Those services which the community will most readily pay for it is most disagreeable to render. You are paid for being something less than a man. The State does not commonly reward a genius any more wisely. Even the poet-laureate would rather not have to celebrate the accidents of royalty. He must be bribed with a pipe of wine; and perhaps another poet is called away from his muse to gauge that very pipe. As for my own business, even that kind of surveying which I could do with most satisfaction my employers do not want. They would prefer that I should do my work coarsely and not too well, ay, not well enough. When I observe that there are different ways of surveying, my employer commonly asks which will give him the most land, not which is most correct. I once invented a rule for measuring cordwood, and tried to introduce it in Boston; but the measurer there told me that the sellers did not wish to have their wood measured correctly—that he was already too accurate for them, and therefore they commonly got their wood measured in Charlestown before crossing the bridge.

7   The aim of the laborer should be, not to get his living, to get "a good job," but to perform well a certain work; and, even in a pecuniary sense, it would be economy for a town to pay its laborers so well that they would not feel that they were working for low ends, as for a livelihood merely, but for scientific, or even moral ends. Do not hire a man who does your work for money, but him who does it for love of it.

8   It is remarkable that there are few men so well employed, so much to their minds, but that a little money or fame would commonly buy them off from their present pursuit. I see advertisements for *active* young men, as if activity were the whole of a young man's capital. Yet I have been surprised when one has with confidence proposed to me, a grown man, to embark in some enterprise of his, as if I had absolutely nothing to do, my life having been a complete failure hitherto. What a doubtful compliment this is to pay me! As if he had met me half-way across the ocean beating up against the wind, but bound nowhere, and proposed to me to go along with him! If I did, what do you think the underwriters would say? No, no! I am not without employment at this stage of the voyage. To tell the truth, I saw an advertisement for able-bodied seamen, when I was a boy, sauntering in my native port, and as soon as I came of age I embarked.

9   The community has no bribe that will tempt a wise man. You may raise money enough to tunnel a mountain, but you cannot raise money enough to hire a man who is minding *his own* business. An efficient and valuable man does what he can, whether the community pay him for it or not. The inefficient offer their inefficiency to the highest bidder, and are

forever expecting to be put into office. One would suppose that they were rarely disappointed.

10   Perhaps I am more than usually jealous with respect to my freedom. I feel that my connection with and obligation to society are still very slight and transient. Those slight labors which afford me a livelihood, and by which it is allowed that I am to some extent serviceable to my contemporaries, are as yet commonly a pleasure to me, and I am not often reminded that they are a necessity. So far I am successful. But I foresee, that, if my wants should be much increased, the labor required to supply them would become a drudgery. If I should sell both my forenoons and afternoons to society, as most appear to do, I am sure, that, for me, there would be nothing left worth living for. I trust that I shall never thus sell my birthright for a mess of pottage.[2] I wish to suggest that a man may be very industrious, and yet not spend his time well. There is no more fatal blunderer than he who consumes the greater part of his life getting his living. All great enterprises are self-supporting. The poet, for instance, must sustain his body by his poetry, as a steam planing-mill feeds its boilers with the shavings it makes. You must get your living by loving. But as it is said of the merchants that ninety-seven in a hundred fail, so the life of men generally, tried by this standard, is a failure, and bankruptcy may be surely prophesied.

11   Merely to come into the world the heir of a fortune is not to be born, but to be still-born, rather. To be supported by the charity of friends, or a government-pension—provided you continue to breathe—by whatever fine synonyms you describe these relations, is to go into the almshouse. On Sundays the poor debtor goes to church to take an account of stock, and finds, of course, that his outgoes have been greater than his income. In the Catholic Church, especially, they go into Chancery, make a clean confession, give up all, and think to start again. Thus men will lie on their backs, talking about the fall of man, and never make an effort to get up.

12   As for the comparative demand which men make on life, it is an important difference between two, that the one is satisfied with a level success, that his marks can all be hit by point-blank shots, but the other, however low and unsuccessful his life may be, constantly elevates his aim, though at a very slight angle to the horizon. I should much rather be the last man,—though, as the Orientals say, "Greatness doth not approach him who is forever looking down; and all those who are looking high are growing poor."

13   It is remarkable that there is little or nothing to be remembered written on the subject of getting a living: how to make getting a living not merely honest and honorable, but altogether inviting and glorious; for if

2. Thoreau refers here to the story of Jacob and Esau in Genesis 25:30-34.

getting a living is not so, then living is not. One would think, from looking at literature, that this question had never disturbed a solitary individual's musings. Is it that men are too much disgusted with their experience to speak of it? The lesson of value which money teaches, which the Author of the Universe has taken so much pains to teach us, we are inclined to skip altogether. As for the means of living, it is wonderful how indifferent men of all classes are about it, even reformers, so called—whether they inherit, or earn, or steal it. I think that society has done nothing for us in this respect, or at least has undone what she has done. Cold and hunger seem more friendly to my nature than those methods which men have adopted and advise to ward them off.

14   The title *wise* is, for the most part, falsely applied. How can one be a wise man, if he does not know any better how to live than other men?—if he is only more cunning and intellectually subtle? Does Wisdom work in a tread-mill? or does she teach how to succeed *by her example*? Is there any such thing as wisdom not applied to life? Is she merely the miller who grinds the finest logic? It is pertinent to ask if Plato got his *living* in a better way or more successfully than his contemporaries—or did he succumb to the difficulties of life like other men? Did he seem to prevail over some of them merely by indifference, or by assuming grand airs? or find it easier to live, because his aunt remembered him in her will? The ways in which most men get their living, that is, live, are mere make-shifts, and a shirking of the real business of life,—chiefly because they do not know, but partly because they do not mean, any better.

15   The rush to California,[3] for instance, and the attitude, not merely of merchants, but of philosophers and prophets, so called, in relation to it, reflect the greatest disgrace on mankind. That so many are ready to live by luck, and so get the means of commanding the labor of others less lucky, without contributing any value to society! And that is called enterprise! I know of no more startling development of the immorality of trade, and all the common modes of getting a living. The philosophy and poetry and religion of such a mankind are not worth the dust of a puff-ball. The hog that gets his living by rooting, stirring up the soil so, would be ashamed of such company. If I could command the wealth of all the worlds by lifting my finger, I would not pay *such* a price for it. Even Mahomet knew that God did not make this world in jest. It makes God to be a moneyed gentleman who scatters a handful of pennies in order to see mankind scramble for them. The world's raffle! A subsistence in the domains of Nature a thing to be raffled for! What a comment, what a satire on our institutions! The conclusion will be, that mankind will hang itself upon a tree. And have all the precepts in all the Bibles taught men only this? and is the last and most admirable invention of the human race only an improved muck-rake? Is this the ground on which Orientals and Occidentals meet? Did God direct us so to get our living, digging where

---

3. Thoreau refers here to the Gold Rush in 1849.

we never planted—and He would, perchance, reward us with lumps of gold?

16   God gave the righteous man a certificate entitling him to food and raiment, but the unrighteous man found a *facsimile* of the same in God's coffers, and appropriated it, and obtained food and raiment like the former. It is one of the most extensive systems of counterfeiting that the world has seen. I did not know that mankind were suffering for want of gold. I have seen a little of it. I know that it is very malleable, but not so malleable as wit. A grain of gold will gild a great surface, but not so much as a grain of wisdom.

17   The gold-digger in the ravines of the mountains is as much a gambler as his fellow in the saloons of San Francisco. What difference does it make, whether you shake dirt or shake dice? If you win, society is the loser. The gold-digger is the enemy of the honest laborer, whatever checks and compensations there may be. It is not enough to tell me that you worked hard to get your gold. So does the Devil work hard. The way of transgressors may be hard in many respects. The humblest observer who goes to the mines sees and says that gold-digging is of the character of a lottery; the gold thus obtained is not the same thing with the wages of honest toil. But, practically, he forgets what he has seen, for he has seen only the fact, not the principle, and goes into trade there, that is, buys a ticket in what commonly proves another lottery, where the fact is not so obvious.

18   After reading Howitt's account of the Australian gold-diggings one evening, I had in my mind's eye, all night, the numerous valleys, with their streams, all cut up with foul pits, from ten to one hundred feet deep, and half a dozen feet across, as close as they can be dug, and partly filled with water—the locality to which men furiously rush to probe for their fortunes—uncertain where they shall break ground—not knowing but the gold is under their camp itself—sometimes digging one hundred and sixty feet before they strike the vein, or then missing it by a foot—turned into demons, and regardless of each other's rights, in their thirst for riches—whole valleys, for thirty miles, suddenly honey-combed by the pits of the miners, so that even hundreds are drowned in them—standing in water, and covered with mud and clay, they work night and day, dying of exposure and disease. Having read this, and partly forgotten it, I was thinking, accidentally, of my own unsatisfactory life, doing as others do; and with that vision of the diggings still before me, I asked myself, why *I* might not be washing some gold daily, though it were only the finest particles—why *I* might not sink a shaft down to the gold within me, and work that mine. *There* is a Ballarat, a Bendigo for you—what though it were a Sulky Gully?[4] At any rate, I might pursue some path, however

---

4. Ballarat and Bendigo are towns in Australia where in 1851 gold was discovered, and "Sulky Gully" is a prosaic name for contrast, used much as a modern writer might use "Podunk."

solitary and narrow and crooked, in which I could walk with love and reverence. Wherever a man separates from the multitude, and goes his own way in this mood, there indeed is a fork in the road, though ordinary travellers may see only a gap in the paling. His solitary path across-lots will turn out the *higher way* of the two.

19   Men rush to California and Australia as if the true gold were to be found in that direction; but that is to go to the very opposite extreme to where it lies. They go prospecting farther and farther away from the true lead, and are most unfortunate when they think themselves most successful. Is not our *native* soil auriferous? Does not a stream from the golden mountains flow through our native valley? and has not this for more than geologic ages been bringing down the shining particles and forming the nuggets for us? Yet, strange to tell, if a digger steal away, prospecting for this true gold, into the unexplored solitudes around us, there is no danger that any will dog his steps, and endeavor to supplant him. He may claim and undermine the whole valley even, both the cultivated and the uncultivated portions, his whole life long in peace, for no one will ever dispute his claim. They will not mind his cradles or his toms.[5] He is not confined to a claim twelve feet square, as at Ballarat, but may mine anywhere, and wash the whole wide world in his tom.

VOCABULARY

incapacitated (P2), *incessant* (P2), *coarse* (P3), *boisterous* (P3), *bank-wall* (P3), *hoard* (P3), *industrious* (P3), *police* (P3), *speculator* (P4), *esteemed* (P4), *hewn* (P5), *sluggards* (P5), *flourish* (P5), *consecrated* (P5), *irksome* (P5), *reproach* (P5), *common stock* (P5), *whimsical* (P5), *teamster* (P5), *Chancery* (P5), *perpendicularly* (P6), *render* (P6), *poet-laureate* (P6), *accidents* (P6), *pipe* (P6), *rule* (P6), *cord-wood* (P6), *pecuniary* (P7), *capital* (P8), *hitherto* (P8), *underwriters* (P8), *sauntering* (P8), *embarked* (P8), *transient* (P10), *birthright* (P10), *synonyms* (P11), *almshouse* (P11), *point-blank* (P12), *musings* (P13), *wonderful* (P13), *advise* (P13), *ward off* (P13), *miller* (P14), *Plato* (P14), *succumb* (P14), *puff-ball* (P15), *Mahomet* (P15), *precepts* (P15), *muck-rake* (P15), *Occidentals* (P15), *raiment* (P16), *facsimile* (P16), *coffers* (P16), *malleable* (P16), *checks* (P17), *compensations* (P17), *transgressors* (P17), *paling* (P18), *lead* (P19), *auriferous* (P19), *geologic ages* (P19), *solitudes* (P19), *dog* (P19), *supplant* (P19), *undermine* (P19), *cradles* (P19), *toms* (P19)

IDEAS AND AIMS

1. Is Thoreau's aim in this essay primarily expository or argumentative (persuasive)? Is it meant to advocate a certain point of view and course of action?

---

5. Cradles and toms are used in panning for gold.

2. Thoreau examines several important concepts and terms, repeating them constantly and attempting to define them, such as "idle(ness)," "business," "living," and "getting a living." How does Thoreau define "idleness" in contrast to how the everyday world defines it, and how does he define truly "getting a living" in contrast to how the everyday world defines it?

3. For what reasons does Thoreau criticize the man building the bank-wall?

4. Why does he criticize the teamster and the teamster's employer?

5. Why should a town pay its laborers almost too well, according to Thoreau?

6. On what grounds does Thoreau disapprove equally of inheriting money and of grubbing for it?

7. In his concluding paragraphs, why does the author criticize the prospectors at the Gold Rush so harshly?

8. Why does Thoreau maintain that a merchant—that is, someone who "goes into trade"—at the gold rush site is also involved in a kind of lottery? What is the "gold" that Thoreau resolves to mine for?

ORGANIZATION AND FORM

1. What are the main parts of the selection?

2. How does Thoreau define various words and concepts by using comparison and contrast? Cite examples.

3. How does Thoreau's analytical and developmental tool of comparison and contrast affect the structure of some of his paragraphs? Cite examples.

4. In what paragraphs does Thoreau use illustrations and examples to explain and substantiate his points? Cite instances of examples that are mostly anecdotal or narrative. In what paragraphs are these used, and how do they help Thoreau explain and substantiate his ideas?

5. Where and how does figurative language (imagery, simile, metaphor) have an organizational function of making a single paragraph coherent (e.g., P18 or P19)? Where and how does metaphor link parts of the essay together (e.g., the wayfaring metaphors of P8 and P18, or the monetary metaphors of P10, P11, P15, and P16)? (Look up the specialized literary terms in your collegiate dictionary or composition handbook.)

WORDS AND STYLE

1. One of the most colorful and distinctive features of Thoreau's prose style in the essay is his use of figures of speech, especially metaphors, similes, and analogies. Choose one or two you find especially striking and explain how they help Thoreau say what he wants to say (e.g., the postural metaphor in P11 or the firearms metaphor of P12).

2. A recurrent feature of Thoreau's prose style in the essay is antithesis. (Look up this term in your collegiate dictionary or composition handbook.) It can be found, for example, in P3 ("profit" vs. "money"), P4 ("loafer" vs. "speculator"),

the second sentence of P9, first sentence of P12, first sentence of P13, and second sentence of P19. In any of these instances, how does it help Thoreau make precise discriminations or differentiations? How is this stylistic feature in accord with the principal method by which Thoreau manages definition in the essay (see question 2 of Organization and Form)?

3. What is the effect of all of Thoreau's interrogative sentences and rhetorical questions on the tone of the essay? In what paragraphs do they occur? In what paragraph are there the most interrogative sentences of the selection? What might be reasons for this particular accumulation?

4. What is the effect of all of Thoreau's exclamatory sentences on the tone of the essay? In what paragraphs do they occur? In what paragraph are there the most of these sentences? What might be the reasons for this particular accumulation?

5. How does Thoreau use short sentences effectively to express his ideas in P10?

6. How does the lengthiness of the first sentence of P18 help Thoreau convey what he wants to at this point?

7. Thoreau engages in a good deal of word play and punning in this essay. Comment on how this element of style helps him make his point in one or more of the following instances: play on "business" and "busy-ness" in the first sentence of P2; play on "minding his own business" in the second sentence of P9; "life" vs. "living" in the ninth sentence of P10; "living" vs. "loving" in the next to last sentence of P10; "shake . . . dice" in the second sentence of P17.

8. How is Thoreau's word choice revealing in the word "lumps" (rather than, say, "nuggets") in the last sentence of P15? What connotations does "lumps" have that Thoreau prefers over "nuggets" in this paragraph? Why does Thoreau reverse this word choice when talking about mental or intellectual gold panning in P19, where we now have "shining particles" and "nuggets" (and *not* "lumps")?

9. How is Thoreau's tone ironic in P2 and P3? Where else is Thoreau ironic in the essay?

DISCUSSION AND WRITING

1. Do you see work around you that you consider as meaningless as the work Thoreau describes?

2. Do you think Thoreau's analysis of work is correct? Why or why not?

3. Given Thoreau's analysis of work, how do you think he would feel about modern education? What college courses would he criticize, and which would he endorse?

4. Do you agree or disagree with Thoreau's contention that "if *getting* a living is not [inviting and glorious], then living is not" (P13)? Why?

ONE MAN'S PROFIT IS ANOTHER MAN'S HARM

Michel de Montaigne

□

Born in southwestern France to an aristocratic family, Michel de Montaigne (1533–1592) was tutored at home in classical languages and went on to study law. After holding important political posts, he decided at age 37 to retire to his chateau to read, think, and write.

For the rest of his life he devoted himself to these tasks and, in the process, he originated, in the opinion of most scholars, the personal or familiar essay. While short and long nonfiction prose may be found in ancient Greek and Roman literature, Montaigne's form was new, as was the word essai *(French) he invented for it. Meaning something like "assay," Montaigne's* essai *was a relaxed, frankly speculative attempt to explore himself and the world around him. The first two editions of his book, called simply* Essays, *were published in 1580 and 1582. By the third edition of the book in 1588, as a result of Montaigne's ceaseless speculative striving the number of his essays had grown to 94 and some of the early ones had been considerably altered. They were divided into three "books" or sections. Philosophy, education, politics, psychology, autobiography—all subjects came within Montaigne's purview. The titles reveal an amazing range of topics, from large to small: "Of Experience," "Of Fear," "Of Liars," "Of Smells," "Of Cannibals," "Of Thumbs." Many later writers were influenced by Montaigne's form, style, and thought, including Francis Bacon (see Section 8, "Efficiency and Success on the Job," for a selection by Bacon) and Charles Lamb.*

Frequently notes of skepticism and pessimism sound in Montaigne's shrewd assays into human and external nature. In our selection, essay xxii from Book I, hints of Montaigne's skeptical view of life, and business affairs within life, may be glimpsed.

1 Demades the Athenian condemned a man of his city whose trade was to sell things necessary for burials, on the ground that he demanded too much profit, and that this profit could not come to him without the death of many people. This judgment seems to be badly taken, inasmuch as no profit is made except at the expense of others, and by this reckoning you would have to condemn every sort of gain.

2 The merchant does good business only by the extravagance of youth; the plowman by the high cost of grain; the architect by the ruin of houses; officers of justice by men's lawsuits and quarrels; the very honor and function of ministers of religion is derived from our death and our vices. No doctor takes pleasure in the health even of his friends, says the ancient Greek comic writer, no soldier in the peace of his city; and so for the rest. And what is worse, let each man sound himself within, and he will find that our private wishes are for the most part born and nourished at the expense of others.

3 Considering which, it strikes me how nature in this does not belie her general policy. For students of natural law hold that the birth, nourishment, and growth of each thing is the alteration and corruption of another:

Whenever anything is changed and leaves its bounds,
Instantly this brings death to that which was before.

LUCRETIUS

VOCABULARY

Athenian (P1), *condemned* (P1), *extravagance* (P2), *plowman* (P2), *vices* (P2), *sound* (P2), *expense* (P2), *belie* (P3), *natural law* (P3), *hold* (P3), *alteration* (P3), *corruption* (P3), *bounds* (P3), *Lucretius* (P3)

IDEAS AND AIMS

1. Is Montaigne's main purpose in this essay to explain or to argue and persuade? What in the essay reveals his main purpose?

2. Explain Demades' basis for condemning the merchant referred to in P1. Is the merchant condemned for making too much profit, or for the source of his profits?
3. Does the author agree with Demades? Why?
4. State in your own words the point being made in P3. How far does the principle of "profit" extend in human affairs? Does the author intend to refer only to profit in business when he uses the word "profit"?

ORGANIZATION AND FORM

1. How is the structure of P1, with the illustration preceding the main point and topic sentence rather than the reverse order, effective in catching the reader's attention?
2. In P2 does the author support his main contention by the inductive or deductive method? (Look up these terms in your collegiate dictionary or composition handbook.)
3. What kind of proof or evidence does Montaigne use in P3 with his reference to "students of natural law" and his quoting from Lucretius? (Look up in your composition handbook the kinds of evidence or support available in argument.)
4. How does Montaigne's conclusion (P3) develop or extend his general point in P1 rather than merely repeating or restating it?

WORDS AND STYLE

1. How do Montaigne's words "and what is worse" in the last sentence of P2 reveal something of his attitude toward his subject?
2. How is the language of P3 more abstract or general than that of the preceding two paragraphs? How might this greater abstractness or generality be appropriate for the concluding paragraph of the essay?

DISCUSSION AND WRITING

1. Do you agree that "our private wishes are for the most part born and nourished at the expense of others"? Can you provide examples, as the author does, to support your point of view?
2. Do you agree that in nature "the birth, nourishment, and growth of each thing is the alteration and corruption of another"? Provide examples to support your point of view.
3. Compare and contrast Montaigne's ideas with those of Hesiod in "Two Kinds of Competition" (also in Section 2, "Work and Morality").

TAKING STOCK: COMPARING AND CONTRASTING
THE SELECTIONS

1. Compare or contrast (or both) Buchwald's depiction of sales and salesmen in "Confessions of a Roof Seller" with George Ade's exploration of the same subject in his character Mr. Hailfellow in "The Fable of the Divided Concern That Was Reunited Under a New Management" (Section 9, "The Work Environment").

2. How does Buchwald's view of business in "Confessions of a Roof Seller" compare or contrast with his view in "Before the Ax Falls" (Section 6, "Job Opportunities and Other Practical Matters")?

3. Compare Buchwald's "Confessions of a Roof Seller" with Samuel Clemens' "Jack of All Trades" (Section 8, "Efficiency and Success on the Job") on the subject of ethics. See also question 6 of Discussion and Writing for the Clemens essay, as well as question 3 of Discussion and Writing for the Buchwald essay.

4. Compare and contrast Hesiod's ideas in "Two Kinds of Competition" with those of Montaigne in "One Man's Profit Is Another Man's Harm."

5. How does Art Buchwald show in "Confessions of a Roof Seller" that Hesiod's "strife" plays a part not only in workers and merchants but also in *customers* or the buying public? That is, how does Buchwald's roof salesman use customers' "strife" with their neighbors as a sales device?

6. In what way can the concept of Hesiod's "strife" be seen operating in how Americans run or want to run business in William Ouchi's "Japanese and American Workers: Two Casts of Mind" (Section 9, "The Work Environment")—such as the incentive system in PP1–2 or the cost accounting system in PP8–9? Compare and contrast Hesiod's and Ouchi's views of "strife," particularly, for Ouchi "strife" within the corporation.

7. Is Hesiod's "strife" as depicted in C. Northcote Parkinson's "Crabbed Youth" (Section 9, "The Work Environment")—between old and young, between 35-year-olds and 37-year-olds, and between Mrs. A and Mrs. B, Mrs. C, and Mrs. D—the good thing that it is for Hesiod in "Two Kinds of Competition"? Why or why not?

8. How is Thomas Fuller similar to Samuel Johnson (Section 7, "The Varieties of Work: Professions and Blue Collar") or John Calvin (Section 1, "Job Choice and Self-Fulfillment") about the relationship between work and human dignity?

9. Merchants are depicted in the essays by Ilene Kantrov (Section 6, "Job Opportunities and Other Practical Matters"), Samuel Johnson (Section 7, "The Varieties of Work"), and George Ade (Section 9, "The

Work Environment"). Are they fundamentally like or unlike Fuller's "good merchant"? Explain.

10. How would Thomas Fuller have regarded Art Buchwald's and Johnny B.'s business enterprise, as described in "Confessions of a Roof Seller"? Why? Do you think Fuller could sell roofs in Los Angeles?

11. Does competition—"strife," to use Hesiod's term—figure in the personality or behavior of the good merchant as defined by Thomas Fuller?

12. Many of the questions on other essays have asked for comparisons with Fuller's essay. See Taking Stock question 2 in the section "Money," comparing Fuller and several authors on the topic of money; Taking Stock question 5 in the section "Job Opportunities and Other Practical Matters," comparing Fuller and several authors on ethics in various businesses; Taking Stock questions 1, 3, 4, 7, and 13 in the section "Varieties of Work: Professions and Blue Collar"; and Taking Stock question 2 from the section "Efficiency and Success on the Job."

13. How does Thoreau compare or contrast with Hesiod in the way each views "strife" or competition, either in the workplace or in general?

14. How does Thoreau compare with Thomas Fuller, George Ade (Section 9, "The Work Environment"), Samuel Johnson (Section 7, "The Varieties of Work: Professions and Blue Collar"), or Ilene Kantrov (Section 6, "Job Opportunities and Other Practical Matters") on the subject of merchants?

15. Compare or contrast Thoreau with any of the authors in the section "Money" about that subject.

16. Compare and contrast Montaigne's ideas in "One Man's Profit Is Another Man's Harm" with those of Hesiod.

17. Contrast Montaigne's ideas with those of Thomas Fuller.

18. How may Montaigne's concept be applied in W. H. Auden's "The Almighty Dollar" (Section 5, "Money"), Art Buchwald's "Before the Ax Falls" (Section 6, "Job Opportunities and Other Practical Matters"), Samuel Clemens' "Jack of All Trades" (Section 8, "Efficiency and Success on the Job"), C. Northcote Parkinson's "Crabbed Youth" (Section 9, "The Work Environment"), or Art Buchwald's "Confessions of a Roof Seller"?

Note: See also Discussion and Writing question 5 on Buchwald's "Confessions of a Roof Seller," questions 4 and 5 on Hesiod's "Two Kinds of Competition," and question 5 on Thoreau's "Getting a Living."

WORK AND EDUCATION

SEND YOUR CHILDREN
TO THE LIBRARIES

Arthur Ashe

☐

In the following essay Arthur Ashe (born in 1943) speaks with authority about professional sports. After having won many amateur titles in tennis, Ashe entered the professional ranks in 1969, maintaining his pioneer status as one of the few black athletes in this sport. Not only has he won several professional tournaments, including what is perhaps the most prestigious, Wimbledon (in 1975), but he has also served as coach for the United States Davis Cup team.

Ashe's advocacy of acquiring other life skills besides prowess in athletics is supported by his own example: his ability with verbal expression is evident not only in the following essay but also in his television sports commentary and capably delivered television commercials for athletic products.

1   Since my sophomore year at University of California, Los Angeles, I have become convinced that we blacks spend too much time on the playing fields and too little time in the libraries.

2   Please don't think of this attitude as being pretentious just because I am a black, single, professional athlete.

3   I don't have children, but I can make observations. I strongly believe the black culture expends too much time, energy and effort raising, praising and teasing our black children as to the dubious glories of professional sport.

4   All children need models to emulate—parents, relatives or friends. But when the child starts school, the influence of the parent is shared by teachers and classmates, by the lure of books, movies, ministers and newspapers, but most of all by television.

5   Which televised events have the greatest number of viewers?— Sports—The Olympics, Super Bowl, Masters, World Series, pro basketball playoffs, Forest Hills. ABC-TV even has sports on Monday night prime time from April to December.

6   So your child gets a massive dose of O. J. Simpson, Kareem Abdul-Jabbar, Muhammad Ali, Reggie Jackson, Dr. J. and Lee Elder and other pro athletes. And it is only natural that your child will dream of being a pro athlete himself.

7   But consider these facts: For the major professional sports of hockey, football, basketball, baseball, golf, tennis and boxing, there are roughly only 3,170 major league positions available (attributing 200 positions to golf, 200 to tennis and 100 to boxing). And the annual turnover is small.

8   We blacks are a subculture of about 28 million. Of the 13½ million men, 5 to 6 million are under 20 years of age, so your son has less than one chance in 1,000 of becoming a pro. Less than one in a thousand. Would you bet your son's future on something with odds of 999 to 1 against you? I wouldn't.

9   Unless a child is exceptionally gifted, you should know by the time he enters high school whether he has a future as an athlete. But what is more important is what happens if he doesn't graduate or doesn't land a college scholarship and doesn't have a viable alternative job career. Our high school dropout rate is several times the national average, which contributes to our unemployment rate of roughly twice the national average.

10   And how do you fight the figures in the newspapers every day? Ali has earned more than $30 million boxing. O. J. just signed for $2½ million, Dr. J. for almost $3 million, Reggie Jackson for $2.8 million, Nate Archibald for $400,000 a year. All that money, recognition, attention, free cars, girls, jobs in the offseason—no wonder there is Pop Warner football, Little League baseball, National Junior Tennis League tennis, hockey practice at 5 A.M. and pickup basketball games in any center city at any hour.

11   There must be some way to assure that the 999 who try but don't make it to pro sports don't wind up on the street corners or in the unemployment lines. Unfortunately, our most widely recognized role models are athletes and entertainers—"runnin'" and "jumpin'" and "singin'" and "dancin.'" While we are 60 percent of the National Basketball Association, we are less than 4 percent of the doctors and lawyers. While we are about 35 percent of major league baseball, we are less than 2 percent of the engineers. While we are about 40 percent of the National Football League, we are less than 11 percent of construction workers such as carpenters and bricklayers.

12   Our greatest heroes of the century have been athletes—Jack Johnson, Joe Louis and Muhammad Ali. Racial and economic discrimination forced us to channel our energies into athletics and entertainment. These were the ways out of the ghetto, the ways to get that Cadillac, those alligator shoes, that cashmere sport coat.

13   Somehow, parents must instill a desire for learning alongside the desire to be Walt Frazier. Why not start by sending black professional athletes into high schools to explain the facts of life?

14   I have often addressed high school audiences and my message is always the same. For every hour you spend on the athletic field, spend two in the library. Even if you make it as a pro athlete, your career will be over by the time you are 35. So you will need that diploma.

15   Have these pro athletes explain what happens if you break a leg, get a sore arm, have one bad year or don't make the cut for five or six tournaments. Explain to them the star system, wherein for every O. J. earning millions there are six or seven others making $15,000 or $20,000 or $30,000 a year.

16   But don't just have Walt Frazier or O. J. or Abdul-Jabbar address your class. Invite a benchwarmer or a guy who didn't make it. Ask him if he sleeps every night. Ask him whether he was graduated. Ask him what he would do if he became disabled tomorrow. Ask him where his old high school athletic buddies are.

17   We have been on the same roads—sports and entertainment—too long. We need to pull over, fill up at the library and speed away to Congress and the Supreme Court, the unions and the business world. We

need more Barbara Jordans, Andrew Youngs, union card-holders, Nikki Giovannis and Earl Graveses. Don't worry: we will still be able to sing and dance and run and jump better than anybody else.

18   I'll never forget how proud my grandmother was when I graduated from U.C.L.A. in 1966. Never mind the Davis Cup in 1968, 1969, and 1970. Never mind the Wimbledon title, Forest Hills, etc. To this day, she still doesn't know what those names mean.

19   What mattered to her was that of her more than 30 children and grandchildren, I was the first to be graduated from college, and a famous college at that. Somehow, that made up for all those floors she scrubbed all those years.

VOCABULARY

expends (P3), *dubious* (P3), *emulate* (P4), *turnover* (P7), *subculture* (P8), *viable* (P9), *pickup basketball games* (P10), *Jack Johnson* (P12), *cashmere* (P12), *instill* (P13), *benchwarmer* (P16)

IDEAS AND AIMS

1. Is Ashe's main purpose in this essay narration, description, exposition, or argumentation? What evidence can you find to support your choice?
2. Where does Ashe state his main idea? Where does he refer to it elsewhere in the essay?
3. Twice Ashe refers to his own qualifications to write on this subject. Where are those places in the essay? Why is he an authoritative writer on this subject?
4. What group is Ashe's audience? Whom does he mean, mainly, by "we," and how is he particularly qualified to speak to this group? How do his ideas apply to most Americans?
5. What two role models for black children are advanced by television, according to Ashe? Which of these roles does Ashe emphasize most? Why?
6. Ashe discussed three problems that await any child who hopes for a career as a professional athlete. What is the first problem in preparing solely for a career as a professional athlete? The second? The third?
7. How or in what way might parents be "teasing" their children "as to the dubious glories of professional sport" (P3)?
8. Why, exactly, should the benchwarmer be asked if he sleeps every night (P16)? Why wouldn't he?
9. In what way, by implication, did Ashe's college graduation "make up" for the floors his grandmother scrubbed "all those years" (P19)?

ORGANIZATION AND FORM

1. How do PP1–6, PP7–12, and PP13–19 each form main units or blocks of the essay?
2. Explain where and how in the essay Ashe carefully balances points for and against the case for a career in professional sports.
3. How does Ashe use parallelism to bind up or make more coherent P11?
4. How does Ashe's automobile metaphor in P17 link to the last sentence in P12? What might the point of this linkage be?
5. Point out instances of Ashe's effective use of transitional words and phrases.
6. How does Ashe make the conclusion of his essay particularly moving and effective?

WORDS AND STYLE

1. Where does Ashe use sentences with series in them to provide facts and concrete examples?
2. Citing examples, explain how Ashe's constant use of concrete examples and illustrations helps lend an authoritative tone to his essay.
3. Point out instances where Ashe uses interrogative sentences effectively.
4. How does Ashe use parallelism effectively in the second sentence of P3, the first sentence of P11, and the third sentence of P12?
5. How does Ashe use colloquial contractions in the second sentence of P11 to help vividly characterize the activities that have defined success for black people in the past?

DISCUSSION AND WRITING

1. Do you think Ashe is against athletics in general? What is his advice to high school audiences? Do you agree? Why or why not?
2. What other job fields—art, for example—are there in which the odds against success are so overwhelmingly negative? What would be your advice to beginners in those fields?
3. What have been the traditional alternatives for athletes who fail or whose careers as athletes are cut short by injury or retirement? Are these still viable possibilities?
4. Do you know of any athletes or people in other occupations who developed second careers or educated themselves for alternate careers and whom you particularly admire?
5. One problem with athletics Ashe does not mention in his essay is the high percentage of students on athletic scholarships who fail to graduate from college. Research this topic for a written or oral report to the class.

WHAT CORPORATION PRESIDENTS THINK ABOUT AT NIGHT

John L. McCaffrey

The following essay was reprinted in Fortune *magazine (September 1953) after being delivered as a speech to a group of business executives completing the University of Chicago's two-year Executive Program. Its author ought to know what corporation presidents think about, having been for several years President and Chief Executive Officer (CEO) of the International Harvester Company, whose annual sales were estimated in the 1960s to be over a billion dollars. (Recently this giant corporation has been renamed Navistar.) Vividly and humorously, the company CEO discusses the corporate value of a broad-based liberal arts education.*

1 The mechanics of running a business are really not very complicated, when you get down to essentials. You have to make some stuff and sell it to somebody for more than it cost you. That's about all there is to it, except for a few million details. I saw a play recently in which one of the characters summed up the fundamental problem of business pretty well. He said he'd been trying for two years to think of something that would cost a dime, sell for a dollar—and be habit-forming.

2 So it isn't hard to run a business, from the standpoint of business operations. And a President doesn't usually worry too much about the things that most people expect to bother him. For example, he seldom lies

awake very long thinking about finances or lawsuits or sales or production or engineering or accounting problems. He is pretty well able to take care of those during regular business hours.

3   Furthermore, when he approaches such problems the President can bring to bear on them all the energy and the trained judgment and past experience of his whole organization. He has a lot of help with problems of that kind.

4   There are other problems, however, that he has to sweat and struggle with, largely by himself. They are the problems he thinks about at night. They all arise out of one simple fact. I can sum up this situation in one sentence:

5   The biggest trouble with industry is that it is full of human beings.

6   The longer you are a President, the more firmly that fact will be riveted in your mind. That is why you will lose sleep. That is why your hair will first turn gray, then get thin, and then fall out altogether, unless you are lucky.

7   You will learn to your sorrow that, while a drill press never sulks and a drop hammer never gets jealous of other drop hammers, the same cannot be said for people. You will learn that a turret lathe may run one part for ten years without affecting its ability or its willingness to be switched at any time to another part. But men are not that way. They develop habits and likes and dislikes.

8   You will learn that you have with people the same general problems of preventive maintenance, premature obsolescence, or complete operational failure that you have with machines. Only they are much harder to solve.

9   You will discover that problems change rapidly, techniques change rapidly, products can be transformed in a period of months; but, unfortunately, people change slowly if at all. And you cannot rearrange or retool the human organization of your business with the same ease and frequency as you rearrange or retool the plant.

10   We have constructed in this country an economic system which is marvelously complicated. In the last forty years or so, this system has developed from what the football coaches call in their trade a one-platoon system to something that approximates a thirty- or forty-platoon system in industry.

11   All this is because we have applied to its uttermost limits the principle of the division of labor which was first described by the classical economists. We have come from the age when a product was made in its entirety by one craftsman, performing all operations, to the present age where nearly every small operation on every part of every product is performed by different men. We have reached a form of production so specialized that frequently the machine does all the work and the man merely nurses and feeds it, as in the case of the boltmaker or the auto-

matic screw machine. The division of labor has gone so far, here in America, as it affects the factory worker, that labor has been atomized rather than just divided.

12   The sociologists and psychologists, as well as the practical operating men in industry, have recognized some of the problems this extreme specialization creates. There is the problem of loss of versatility. There is the problem of loss of pride in personal accomplishment and skill. There is the problem of boredom from repetitive operations, and many others, as they affect the worker at the machine or on the assembly line.

13   The thing I want to point out to you is this: We are only now beginning to understand that the effects of this atomizing of labor are not limited to production employees. As management, too, has become extremely specialized, these same problems have spread over into the management group, and even into the executive group. The specialization of management at all levels, including the executive, has lagged somewhat behind the specialization of equipment and employees, but it is following exactly the same course, and giving rise to the same problems.

"A Good Old-Fashioned Jackknife"

14 The President of a modern company often seems to me like the ringmaster of a thirty-ring circus. We sit at our desks all day, while around us whiz and gyrate a vast number of special activities, some of which we only dimly understand. And for each of these activities there is a specialist.

15   We have engineers of assorted kinds. We have lawyers of many breeds, from patents to admiralty. We have market analysts and sales engineers and industrial-relations experts and credit men and research metallurgists and time-study engineers. We have accountants and economists and statisticians, purchasing agents and traffic men and chemists.

16   All of them, no doubt, are good to have. All seem to be necessary. All are useful on frequent occasions. But it has reached the point where the greatest task of the President is to understand enough of all these specialties so that when a problem comes up he can assign the right team of experts to work on it. We have a lot of people like Ed Wynn's famous painter who only painted boats and not horses, and when a customer insisted that he do a picture of his horse, the painter said: "Well, all right. But it's gonna look like a boat."

17   The President is like a man confronted by an enormous tool bench, who only hopes that he can pick the right screw driver for a particular special job. There must be others like me, who sometimes wish for a good old-fashioned jackknife, with twelve blades and a corkscrew, that could handle almost any job in passable fashion.

18   Because business has wanted these specialists, the colleges and uni-

versities have produced them by the thousands. If we need a good cost accountant, one is available. If we want an industrial psychologist, he can be had. If a man is needed to estimate a market potential with the latest scientific methods, he will be on tap.

19   And that's fine, as far as it goes, but it still doesn't let the President sleep at night. The President has no great problem in finding men to run a section or a department, where one line of work is followed. But he tosses plenty over the problem of finding executives who have wider knowledge, more general savvy, and enough background of the right kind to run a whole group of things.

20   What are the plus and minus factors in specialization, as it applies to management men? On the plus side, the great advantage is that by limiting his work to a relatively small area, the man becomes a genuine expert in that area. Many detailed improvements are possible as a result. By specializing from the start, in education and in work, he greatly reduces the time and expense which his employer would otherwise have to devote to his training. By coming as a ready-made specialist he is more useful at an earlier time, and this tends to give him a larger income at a younger age than the average man. That's an attraction to him, and is one of the reasons why he specializes.

21   What are the disadvantages? The great disadvantage, of course, is that specialization produces a man with limited knowledge and limited interests and experience, except in rare instances. The world of the specialist is a narrow one and it tends to produce narrow human beings. The specialist usually does not see overall effects on the business. And so he tends to judge good and evil, right and wrong, by the sole standard of his own specialty.

22   We have all seen the credit man whose big interest in life is not the making of good sales under variable conditions, but simply the ratio of past-due paper, and the possibility that at some future time, on a particular deal, he might be criticized.

23   We have seen the time-study man who clings so firmly to what he regards as a principle that he just doesn't care whether it meets ordinary human standards of fairness, or whether his actions shut down a 3,000-man plant.

24   We have seen the salesman who expects complicated machines to be redesigned in a week whenever one of his customers has a whim, and who bitterly blames engineering if it doesn't happen that way. Or the engineer who knows what is good for the customer, even if the customer doesn't like it. Or the manufacturing man who can't see why we won't pour more millions into his plant, even though the product is already losing money.

25   We have seen the industrial-relations man for whom life begins and ends with a legalistic interpretation of the union contract, and who never

looks past the grievance committee, gathered around his desk, to catch a glimpse of the human individuals who work in his plant.

Middle-Management Morale

26 This narrowness of view, this judgment of all events by the peculiar standards of his own specialty, is the curse of the specialist from the standpoint of top-management consideration for advancement. Except in unusual cases, it tends to put a road block ahead of him after he reaches a certain level.

27 This presents a problem to the President in building his top organization. Because of the trend of the times, he finds that he has more and more specialists and fewer and fewer general executives just below the top level. Some of these specialists he simply cannot promote. And even with the others, if he does promote them, he has to ask them to make a sudden and radical change in the thinking and acting habits of a lifetime.

28 This may or may not present a problem to the specialist himself. In most cases I believe it does. There are men, of course, who, after achieving reasonable eminence in their specialty, ask nothing more of life. But among men of real ability, specialists or no, we usually find ambition to advance. And in such cases, specialization can produce a considerable degree of frustration.

29 So we have a two-horned problem. There are many specialists whom the President simply cannot promote. And because they are not promoted there is a natural tendency for the mature specialist to become somewhat sour.

30 There is another fact about the specialist which is a problem to him and therefore to the organization. It arises from the very fact that he knows more about his specialty than his superiors or anyone else in the business. This situation frequently arises: a problem comes up related to his special field. He produces a solution which is entirely satisfactory from the standpoint of good practice in his specialty. But then the higher management won't buy it. They do something else instead.

31 This can happen either because the specialist has failed to explain and sell his solution adequately, or because he did not take into account other factors of the problem which might lie outside his special field. To put it bluntly, such a situation can occur either because top management knows more than he does or because it knows less. In either case, the result for him is the same. His advice has been disregarded and his judgment overruled. That will seldom make him happy.

High-Priced Office Boys

32 In this area probably lies a good part of the cause for a new note which has begun to creep into some of the studies of corporate management—

the beginning of concern about the morale of what is called "middle management," which includes nearly all the specialists and is largely composed of them.

33   The top men operate high, wide, and handsome. The decisions are theirs, so their attitudes are usually good. In spite of frequently expressed concern about attitudes of foremen and other first-line management men, it is a fact that the first-line men have specific duties and responsibilities, and they are at the point where things happen. In spite of their normal griping, they have the relief of taking personal part in action.

34   The man in the middle of the management pyramid, however, neither makes the decisions nor carries them out. He finds it easy to feel that his judgment is neither sought nor honored, that his training and experience are ignored, and that he does not participate to any real degree in the management of the corporation. He often feels, and he frequently says, that he is just a high-priced office boy.

35   Now, those are some of the reasons why many a President lies awake at night. How can he maintain the interest of and get full advantage from the specialists who are too specialized to be promoted? On the one hand, the company absolutely requires the skills of the specialists in order to carry on its complicated operations. On the other hand, he has to get future top management from somewhere. And that somewhere has to be largely within the existing company, if he is to have any management morale at all.

Sheep with Goat's Blood

36   The problems are easy to describe. But the ground becomes uncertain and the atmosphere cloudy when someone raises the simple question: What will we do about it?

37   One answer that has been offered is to start with the educational processes that take place before the man goes to work. Recently we have seen, as an example, some attempts made by engineering and other technical schools to give a larger part in their courses to the liberal-arts subjects, to try to produce an educated man as well as a trained engineer or doctor or what not. I think that is a hopeful trend.

38   We have also seen in recent months a number of speeches by corporation officials, pointing out the necessity for rounded education and underlining the importance of the liberal-arts college for the future, not only for the future of business but also of this country. The nation, like the corporation, suffers from this problem of too much specialization.

39   Unhappily, it appears that we company Presidents are not practicing what we preach in this regard. True, some of us have been giving money to support liberal-arts colleges, but we have not been offering jobs to such graduates.

40   *Fortune* Magazine [in April 1953] recounted some of the actual experiences of educational institutions with business recruiters who came to the campus looking for talent. At Yale University, for example, in 1950, only 18 out of 66 corporation talent scouts were willing to talk to arts college graduates. In 1951 it was 15 out of 91. And in 1952 it was 16 out of 117. At Johns Hopkins University this year only 16 out of 200 scouts had any interest in the liberal-arts man as compared with the engineer, the chemist, or other specialists.

41   So we are obviously not making progress in that field and will have to change our approach before we do. These graduates are bright young men with a natural desire to eat. They see what is happening. And however much we may cry about overspecialization, we'll get more and more of it so long as our hiring policies are not in tune with top management's thinking and talking.

42   Another answer which has been proposed is to catch the specialist after he is in industry but while he is still young enough to respond and try to give him a wider training, a broader outlook—to take him away from his tree and show him the forest.

43   This has sometimes been attempted by means of coaching, as it is called. Coaching consists basically of selecting promising young men and moving them around through different functions of a business, letting them stay long enough in each to get a real feel of it. Its advantage is that it teaches through experience and not just through precept.

44   One of the difficulties, however, is that it soon becomes obvious to everyone that certain people are on the coaching list while others are not. You create a sheep-and-goat division among your younger men and the goats don't like it a bit. Mistakes are also made, of course, and sometimes a sheep turns out to have goat's blood in him.

Back to College

45 Still another answer to the same problem has been the training of executives at a university. The theory is something like this. The employer says: "Here's a younger man who has a record of accomplishment up to now. There may be something wrong with him that we don't yet know, but, as matters stand, he looks as if he had the possibility for future development. Maybe he has. Maybe he hasn't. Training can't hurt and it may help a lot. So we'll give him the training, give him the chance to grow, and then wait and see what happens."

46   My personal view happens to be that this is the most promising of the approaches to the problem and that results so far have justified it in the case of my own company.

47   By one means or another, we need to produce a type of business executive who, after carefully learning that all balls are round, will not

be completely flabbergasted the first time he meets one that has a square side. And he will meet them, for we live in a complicated world—a world that has spiritual and moral problems even greater than its economic and technical problems. If the kind of business system we now have is to survive, it must be staffed by men who can deal with problems of both kinds.

48   Businessmen today and in the visible tomorrows will need to know how to earn a profit and why it is good for everyone that a profit should be earned. That's obvious. They also need to know how to get along with, and direct the efforts of, other human beings, both individuals and groups. And, finally, every businessman needs to know enough about the society in which he lives and operates so that he can follow its changes intelligently, adjusting himself and his enterprise to changing conditions, and making sure that his business serves its most useful purpose for society.

49   Those are some of the problems you will think about at night, when you are President. I sincerely hope you will find better answers—and get more sleep—than I have.

VOCABULARY

riveted (P6), *sulks* (P7), *drop hammer* (P7), *lathe* (P7), *premature* (P8), *obsolescence* (P8), *retool* (P9), *platoon system* (P10), *uttermost* (P11), *atomized* (P11), *gyrate* (P14), *admiralty* (P15), *metallurgists* (P15), *Ed Wynn* (P16), *paper* (P22), *whim* (P24), *grievance* (P25), *eminence* (P28), *bluntly* (P31), *morale* (P32), *recounted* (P40), *precept* (P43), *flabbergasted* (P47)

IDEAS AND AIMS

1. Carefully considering the conclusion of his essay, explain whether McCaffrey's overall purpose is exposition, argument, or a blend of the two. Cite specifics from the essay in your answer.
2. What, according to McCaffrey, is the root of all the most serious problems in business?
3. What are some of the disadvantages of an extreme division of labor?
4. Overspecialization in a particular branch of business concerns McCaffrey most. What is that branch? Why should it concern McCaffrey the most?
5. What are the advantages to a business of hiring specialists? What are the disadvantages?
6. What are the disadvantages *personally* for the specialist?

7. What forces in business tend to "sour" the specialist?

8. Does McCaffrey believe it is always an advantage to know your specialty better than others do?

9. Why are first-line managers likely to be happier than middle managers? Does the same hold true for top managers, according to McCaffrey?

ORGANIZATION AND FORM

1. In what sentence does McCaffrey state the central idea of his essay?

2. How does the conclusion of his essay extend or develop McCaffrey's main idea rather than merely repeating or restating it?

3. What are the main parts of the essay?

4. Does McCaffrey prove his point that "the specialist does not see overall effects on the business" using induction or deduction, primarily? (Look up these terms in your collegiate dictionary or composition handbook.)

5. Where does McCaffrey vividly and forcefully use parallelism to bind up single paragraphs? To bind up several paragraphs with each other? (Look up parallelism in your composition handbook.) How does this parallelism help hammer home his points in one or two of these instances?

6. This essay was originally a speech delivered to a group of business executives completing the University of Chicago's two-year Executive Program. How are McCaffrey's word choice and humor frequently appropriate to a speech or a talk? Cite specifics in your answer.

WORDS AND STYLE

1. One of the outstanding traits of McCaffrey's essay is its humor. How does McCaffrey's word choice in the second sentence of P1 (especially "stuff") create that humor, as well as make a basic point? How do the self-contradictory words in the third sentence of P1 create humor, as well as make a basic point? How does the dash (and the delay it causes) in the last sentence of P1 help create humor and make a basic point?

2. Cite other instances of McCaffrey's humor in the essay, and explain how his sentence structure or choice of words creates that humor. Give one or two instances of how McCaffrey's humor helps him make his point effectively.

3. McCaffrey repeatedly uses analogies, metaphors, or similes in the essay, such as in PP7–8, P14, P17, and P44. Comment on how these comparisons accurately apply to what McCaffrey seeks to identify as part of the job, effectively help him express his point (particularly to a group of business executives, to whom this essay was first delivered as a speech), and also often have a touch of humor. How is McCaffrey's specificity helpful in PP7–8 (particular machines mentioned)? To what in the Bible does McCaffrey allude in P44?

4. What careful distinction is McCaffrey making in the last sentence of P11 by his contrast between the words "atomized" and "divided"? How does this differentiation help him make his point here?

5. The third and fourth sentences of P15 use a device known as polysyndeton, the repetition of the connective "and" or "or" between items in a series (as opposed to just using commas between the items). How does polysyndeton help McCaffrey get across the idea of abundance in these sentences more effectively than would routine series punctuated with commas?

6. How do the short, repetitive sentences that open P16 help McCaffrey express his point?

7. How is the phrase set off with dashes in the second sentence of P49 an ironic qualification, making it a rhetorical use of parenthesis? How does it help conclude the essay on a note of poignant humor?

DISCUSSION AND WRITING

1. Do you agree with McCaffrey that division of labor has gone too far? Why?

2. Do McCaffrey's remarks on specialization seem relevant to your own planned career? Why or why not?

3. What should be the response of colleges and universities to the problems McCaffrey notes?

4. The statistics in P40 are for the early 1950s. Have these figures changed in recent years? What does such evidence say about the longevity of the principle of specialization?

5. How, specifically, can certain courses from a liberal arts curriculum broaden the perspective of a specialist? Explain how courses in history, sociology, literature or humanities, and so on could help such an individual see the "forest" at the company rather than just his or her particular "tree."

6. In P23, P25, and P48 McCaffrey focuses on the ethical or moral concerns of business. How do his ideas in these paragraphs compare with those of the writers in the section "Work and Morality"? How do his ideas in these paragraphs compare with what William Ouchi has to say about Japanese and American businesses (Section 9, "The Work Environment")?

7. How might what McCaffrey says in PP20–21 be connected to C. Northcote Parkinson's remarks in PP8–9 of his essay (Section 9, "The Work Environment")? How might these same paragraphs by McCaffrey be applied to what goes wrong with the meeting to discuss a new advertising campaign in PP21–27 of Robert Benchley's "From Nine to Five" (Section 8, "Efficiency and Success on the Job")?

WHAT EMPLOYEES
NEED MOST

Peter F. Drucker

☐

Peter F. Drucker (born in 1909) is an acknowledged expert on business who has published well over twenty books on the subject, most of them required reading for those interested in this area. Born in Austria and educated at the University of Hamburg and the University of Frankfurt, where he earned an LL.D. degree, Drucker emigrated to the United States in 1937 and became a citizen in 1943. He has been a journalist, foreign and finance editor for a German newspaper, economist for a London international banking house, American adviser to a group of British banks and investment trusts, private consultant on business, and professor at several colleges and universities (most recently Clarke Professor of Social Science and Management at Clare-mont Graduate School in California).

Among Drucker's books (most of them in print, and several in paper-back editions) are The Future of Industrial Man *(1942; new ed., 1965),* Concept of the Corporation *(1946; new ed., 1972),* The New Society: The Anatomy of the Industrial Order *(1950),* The Practice of Management *(1954),* Managing for Results: Economic Tasks and Risk-Taking Decisions *(1964),* The Effective Executive *(1967),* The Age of Discontinuity: Guidelines to Our Changing Society *(1969),* Management: Tasks, Practices, Responsibilities *(1974),* An Introductory View of Management *(1978),* Adventures of a Bystander *(1979),* Toward the Next Economics and Other Essays *(1981), and* The Changing World of the Executive *(1982).*

Because of his background in law, education, the social sciences, and business, Drucker is able to see the interaction of various forces in our civilization and their impact on society and the world of work. His background in journalism enables him to communicate his ideas clearly and to appreciate the importance of this clarity of communication both in and out of the business world.

1   Most of you . . . will be employees all your working life, working for somebody else and for a pay check. And so will most, if not all, of the thousands of other young Americans . . . in all the other schools and colleges across the country.

2   Ours has become a society of employees. A hundred years or so ago only one out of every five Americans at work was employed, i.e., worked for somebody else. Today only one out of five is not employed but working for himself. And where fifty years ago "being employed" meant working as a factory laborer or as a farmhand, the employee of today is increasingly a middle-class person with a substantial formal education, holding a professional or management job requiring intellectual and technical skills. Indeed, two things have characterized American society during these last fifty years: the middle and upper classes have become employees; and middle-class and upper-class employees have been the fastest-growing groups in our working population—growing so fast that the industrial worker, that oldest child of the Industrial Revolution, has been losing in numerical importance despite the expansion of industrial production.

3   This is one of the most profound social changes any country has ever undergone. It is, however, a perhaps even greater change for the individual young person about to start. Whatever he does, in all likelihood he will do it as an employee; wherever he aims, he will have to try to reach it through being an employee.

4   Yet you will find little if anything written on what it is to be an employee. You can find a great deal of very dubious advice on how to get a job or how to get a promotion. You can also find a good deal on work in a chosen field, whether it be metallurgy or salesmanship, the machinist's trade or bookkeeping. Every one of these trades requires different skills, sets different standards, and requires a different preparation. Yet they all have employeeship in common. And increasingly, especially in the large business or in government, employeeship is more important to success than the special professional knowledge or skill. Certainly more people fail because they do not know the requirements of being an employee than because they do not adequately possess the skills of their trade; the higher you climb the ladder, the more you get into administrative or executive work, the greater the emphasis on ability to work

within the organization rather than on technical competence or professional knowledge.

5   Being an employee is thus the one common characteristic of most careers today. The special profession or skill is visible and clearly defined; and a well-laid-out sequence of courses, degrees, and jobs leads into it. But being an employee is the foundation. And it is much more difficult to prepare for it. Yet there is no recorded information on the art of being an employee.

6   The first question we might ask is: what can you learn in college that will help you in being an employee? The schools teach a great many things of value to the future accountant, the future doctor, or the future electrician. Do they also teach anything of value to the future employee? The answer is: "Yes—they teach the one thing that it is perhaps most valuable for the future employee to know. But very few students bother to learn it."

7   This one basic skill is the ability to organize and express ideas in writing and in speaking.

8   As an employee you work with and through other people. This means that your success as an employee—and I am talking of much more here than getting promoted—will depend on your ability to communicate with people and to present your own thoughts and ideas to them so they will both understand what you are driving at and be persuaded. The letter, the report or memorandum, the ten-minute spoken "presentation" to a committee are basic tools of the employee.

9   Of course . . . if you work on a machine your ability to express yourself will be of little importance. But as soon as you move one step up from the bottom, your effectiveness depends on your ability to reach others through the spoken or the written word. And the further away your job is from manual work, the larger the organization of which you are an employee, the more important it will be that you know how to convey your thoughts in writing or speaking. In the very large organization, whether it is the government, the large business corporation, or the military, this ability to express oneself is perhaps the most important of all the skills a [person] can possess.

10   Of course, skill in expression is not enough by itself. You must have something to say in the first place. The popular picture of the engineer, for instance, is that of a man who works with a slide rule, T square, and compass. And engineering students reflect this picture in their attitude toward the written word as something quite irrelevant to their jobs. But the effectiveness of the engineer—and with it his usefulness—depends as much on his ability to make other people understand his work as it does on the quality of the work itself.

11   Expressing one's thoughts is one skill that the school can really teach, especially to people born without natural writing or speaking tal-

ent. Many other skills can be learned later—in this country there are literally thousands of places that offer training to adult people at work. But the foundations for skill in expression have to be laid early: an interest in and an ear for language; experience in organizing ideas and data, in brushing aside the irrelevant, in wedding outward form and inner content into one structure; and above all, the habit of verbal expression. If you do not lay these foundations during your school years, you may never have an opportunity again.

12   If you were to ask me what strictly vocational courses there are in the typical college curriculum, my answer—now that the good old habit of the "theme a day" has virtually disappeared—would be: the writing of poetry and the writing of short stories. Not that I expect many of you to become poets or short-story writers—far from it. But these two courses offer the easiest way to obtain some skill in expression. They force one to be economical with language. They force one to organize thought. They demand of one that he give meaning to every word. They train the ear for language, its meaning, its precision, its overtones—and its pitfalls. Above all they force one to write.

13   I know very well that the typical employer does not understand this as yet, and that he may look with suspicion on a young college graduate who has majored, let us say, in short-story writing. But the same employer will complain—and with good reason—that the young [people] whom he hires when they get out of college do not know how to write a simple report, do not know how to tell a simple story, and are in fact virtually illiterate. And he will conclude—rightly—that the young [people] are not really effective, and certainly not employees who are likely to go very far.

VOCABULARY

i.e. (P2), *Industrial Revolution* (P2), *profound* (P3), *dubious* (P4), *metallurgy* (P4), *manual* (P9), *T square* (P10), *compass* (P10), *wedding* (P11), *overtones* (P12), *illiterate* (P13)

IDEAS AND AIMS

1. According to Drucker, what did it mean to be an employee one hundred years ago?
2. How has the ratio of employees to self-employed workers changed in a hundred years?
3. What have been the social consequences of this shift?

4. Where does one go to learn what Drucker calls "the special profession or skill"?

5. What is the one common trait or characteristic of most careers today?

6. What is the one skill most valuable in the "art of being an employee"? Why?

7. What academic courses for the future employee are recommended by Drucker? Why?

8. Who is Drucker's main intended audience, the "you" he repeatedly addresses in the essay? How do we get our first clear idea of who this "you" is in P6?

9. Drucker says in P8 that communication is the key to "success as an employee" and that he is "talking of much more here than getting promoted." What, then, does Drucker mean by "success as an employee," if not mainly promotion?

10. What does Drucker mean by his phrase "wedding outward form and inner content into one structure" in P11?

11. What does Drucker mean by the importance, "above all," of "the *habit* of verbal expression" in P11?

ORGANIZATION AND FORM

1. Is Drucker's argument largely inductive or deductive? (Look up these terms in your collegiate dictionary or composition handbook.) What are his premises, and what logical inferences does he draw from them?

2. How may PP1–5, PP6–10, and PP11–13 be seen as the main parts of the essay?

3. Point out examples of Drucker's use of transitional words and expressions, especially at the beginnings of sentences.

4. How is the extreme shortness of P7 effective?

5. How is the conclusion of Drucker's essay an extension or development of his introduction, not merely a repetition or restatement of it?

WORDS AND STYLE

1. What effect do all the transition words at beginnings of sentences (especially "and" and "this") have on the ease of reading the essay? How so?

2. Drucker is fond of parenthetical statements (often punctuated by commas or dashes). List several examples. How do some of these help Drucker explain his ideas more clearly in specific instances?

3. Point out examples of Drucker's effective use of the series to convey much information in a single sentence.

4. Cite examples of Drucker's balancing of long against short sentences in a paragraph. In which paragraphs does he do this? In a few instances, explain how this mixture is effective in emphasizing or clarifying specific points Drucker wants to make.

DISCUSSION AND WRITING

1. Does Drucker prove his point that almost all nonmanual work involves speaking and writing skills? Why or why not?

2. What do you think are the causes of the social change in employment Drucker describes in the first three paragraphs of his essay?

3. What are some other skills that are important to "employeeship" that Drucker doesn't discuss? How important are these skills? Where does one learn them?

4. Are there other college courses, besides short-story and poetry writing, in which one can learn the kinds of skills Drucker is describing? Which ones? How?

5. How important will speaking and writing be in your career? Research this topic, if you can, by contacting local employees and employers and asking about communication (oral and written) on the job.

6. Write an essay describing professions in which speaking and writing skills are important. Can you think of any vocations, other than manual labor, in which these skills are not important?

7. Has "the good old habit of the 'theme a day' . . . virtually disappeared" (P12) in the introductory English courses at your school? Why or why not? Does Drucker's essay make you feel any better about the continuance or disappearance of "the good old habit"?

ON THE COMPATIBILITY OF INTELLECTUAL IMPROVEMENT WITH THE SUCCESSFUL PROSECUTION OF BUSINESS

G. M. Bell

☐

G. M. Bell was a prominent nineteenth-century British banker. The following essay, which he wrote in 1849 for The Banker's Magazine, *a British publication, has the flavor of an earlier era, with its introductory "Nay . . ." (second sentence of the first paragraph), slightly archaic "mere animal labor" (sixth sentence of the second paragraph), and the oratorical flourishes of the two sentences whose elaboration requires Bell to restart them (first sentence of the third paragraph, first sentence of the ninth paragraph).*

In his clear tones and ringing style, Bell proves a worthy successor to essayist Joseph Addison, whom he quotes, and shows himself a model of the main point he argues in the essay: that business and a liberal education do chime.

1 It is not unusual to meet with men, otherwise considered intelligent, who are ready to maintain that the cultivation of the mind for any purposes beyond the mere business or occupation which an individual may pursue, is a waste of time and of money; that, in point of fact, to be a good man of business, or a successful tradesman, it is enough to know the principles

and routine of the business that is followed. Nay, they go farther than this, and assert, that the pursuit of literary and scientific knowledge is detrimental to those qualities which are necessary to the successful prosecution of the business life. As these opinions are by no means confined to a few individuals, but are more generally prevalent than might at first be imagined, it may be worth the trouble to examine upon what they are founded, and how far they are supported by history and daily experience.

2   It may be confidently asserted that no literary or scientific man, no man who has enjoyed what is generally understood by a liberal education, will hazard the remark, or for one moment give place to the opinion, that the cultivation of the mind is inconsistent with or injurious to the successful prosecution of business. There is no calling in life which does not require the exercise of some degree of intelligence. The very humblest and most ordinary occupation in which men can engage cannot be followed without some portion of mental exercise. And if we take any one single occupation, and suppose several persons to be engaged in carrying it on, which of these, I may take the liberty to ask, would be most likely to gain your patronage? Assuredly, the man who displayed the greatest shrewdness, the greatest skill in his work. In the exercise of mere animal labor, how often is the man of the strongest sinew, and the most powerful bodily faculties, completely outwitted and beaten at his own work, by the man of small bodily strength, but of superior ingenuity and intelligence? We witness cases of this kind daily. We know that an intelligent workman is at all times to be preferred, and is preferred, before the man who has nothing to recommend him but his brawny arm and unwieldy person. Let us gradually rise in the scale of employment, and it will be found to be the invariable practice, that employers will search out and prefer men of some knowledge, ingenuity, and ability, to others who know merely the routine of their duties, and nothing more. Why is this? Simply because intelligent men are found to be more useful, and to give more satisfaction to their employers, than men who are devoid of all knowledge.

3   Among the instances, and they are innumerable, of persons who have raised themselves from obscurity to distinction, by persevering in the acquisition of knowledge, and remembering that they had minds to cultivate as well as bodies to cherish, and that it is only by the cultivation of those natural abilities which our bountiful Creator has given to every man, that even worldly distinction can be obtained—among innumerable instances of this kind, I may be allowed to mention a very few . . . .

4   You have all heard of the celebrated brothers Lords Eldon and Stowell . . . . They were the sons of a poor barge-maker and small coal-dealer in Newcastle-upon-Tyne. Lord Stowell borrowed £40 to go to the circuit; and both supported themselves for a time by their talents as private tutors. The one rose to be Lord Chancellor, and the other to be one of the judges of the land.

5   Lord Tenterden was the son of a barber at Canterbury. He received

an eleemosynary education, but obtained the means to go to college. While there, he enjoyed from a company in the city of London an exhibition [allowance] of £ 3 per annum, until he took his degree. Some years since, in dining with that company, he alluded to the circumstance, and expressed his gratitude . . . .

6 Sir John Williams, one of the Judges of the Queen's Bench, was son of a horse-dealer in Yorkshire . . . . Mr. Serjeant Talfourd is the son of a brewer at Reading; received the rudiments of his education at the Protestant Dissenters' Grammar School, at Mill-hill near Hendon . . . .

7 Sir Frederick Pollock, now Chief Baron of the Exchequer, and his brother Mr. David Pollock, are the sons of a saddler near Charing Cross. The mother of Mr. Baron Gurney kept a small book shop in a court in the city . . . .

8 There is no station in life in which a man may be placed, where he may not, by proper application, qualify himself for some position still higher. A remarkable instance of this has just occurred at Edinburgh. Among the numerous candidates for the office of librarian to the Advocates' Library, vacant by the resignation of Dr. Irving, was Mr. Samuel Halkett. This gentleman has acquired an extensive knowledge of philology, and cannot only read all, and speak most of the living languages of Europe, but has a profound acquaintance with the Eastern tongues, including Hebrew and Arabic; while his translations of scientific papers, in Swedish, Norwegian, and Danish, have been much appreciated. The most singular circumstance connected with the history of Mr. Halkett is, his application to a business, during the whole period of his life, that might be considered uncongenial to his literary pursuits, being of the firm of Harrison and Halkett, woolen drapers, North Bridge. This gentleman might well be called an accomplished woolen draper. It is gratifying to be able to add that the vacancy in the office of librarian to the Advocates' Library has been filled up by the appointment of Mr. Halkett, who has thus obtained to some extent the end of his ambition, and the reward of his industry.

9 The profession to which I have myself the honor to belong (banking), boasts of many names eminent in general literature; not merely writers upon that most entangled and indigestible of all subjects, the currency— men who rack their brains in vain attempts to solve that mysterious question, "What is a pound?" I say they are not mere writers upon the currency, but men eminent in general literature and science. Among the London bankers are the names of Grote, author of a valuable history of Greece; the venerable Samuel Rogers, author of *The Pleasures of Memory*; Bosanquet, author of different works, and a Fellow of the Royal Society; Gilbart, author of *Lectures on Ancient Commerce*, and a Fellow of the Royal Society; Samuel Jones Loyd, a man of acknowledged learning, and also an author; John Horsley Palmer, Mr. Norman, Mr. Salomons, and several others, directors of the Bank of England. In the provinces

there are many names of considerable note, among whom may be mentioned the late Mr. Leatham, of Wakefield; Bernard Barton; Wright, of Nottingham; Bailey, of Sheffield; Coulthart, of Ashton. The number of banking authors has been considered a striking feature in the intellectual character of the age.

10   I think there can be no difference of opinion upon the point that, other things being equal, the chances of success in any trade or business are infinitely in favor of an intelligent man over an ignorant and illiterate one; and I may add that we have the authority of Addison for the observation that men of learning who take to business, discharge it generally with greater honesty than men of the world. And I may as well give you the reason why he thinks so: "Because," says he, "a man that has spent his youth in reading has been used to find virtue extolled, and vice stigmatized. A man that has passed his time in the world, has often seen vice triumphant and virtue discountenanced. Extortion, rapine, and injustice, which are branded with infamy in books, often give a man a figure in the world; while several qualities which are celebrated in authors, as generosity, ingenuity, and good nature, impoverish and ruin him. This cannot but have a proportionate effect upon men whose tempers and principles are equally good and vicious."

11   You will observe that I have said nothing regarding the abstract pleasures which arise to an individual from the cultivation of his mind, from the increase of his knowledge of men and of manners, of nations, and of people; their laws, governments, customs; the various arts and sciences which are prosecuted in different parts of the world; and the laws of matter and of motion; the principles of light, heat, and electricity; of attraction and gravitation; of the order of the universe, of which the earth upon which we dwell is only one small planet—one infinitesimal part, amidst the thousands of other worlds which revolve above and around us, obedient to the will of that Great First Cause, that Infinite Wisdom, whose power, goodness, and glory are displayed throughout the whole. I have said nothing of the pleasures and delights which may arise to the soul of man in the pursuit of such knowledge, nor of the moral obligation under which he lies to acquire knowledge, for these have scarcely come within the scope of my subject. I may, however, be allowed to remark that by employing his leisure in reading and reflection, he creates for himself a paradise of intellectual enjoyment, to which he can at all times resort without fear of interruption from others, and which will often prove a solace to his spirit under all the afflictions and the evils of life.

VOCABULARY

tradesman (P1), *detrimental* (P1), *prosecution* (P1), *prevalent* (P1), *hazard* (P2), *patronage* (P2), *sinew* (P2), *ingenuity* (P2), *brawny* (P2), *unwieldy*

(P2), *devoid* (P2), *persevering* (P3), *bountiful* (P3), *Lord Chancellor* (P4), *eleemosynary* (P5), *brewer* (P6), *rudiments* (P6), *saddler* (P7), *philology* (P8), *singular* (P8), *drapers* (P8), *industry* (P8), *eminent* (P9), *Royal Society* (P9), *extolled* (P10), *stigmatized* (P10), *discountenanced* (P10), *rapine* (P10), *infamy* (P10), *impoverish* (P10), *vicious* (archaic sense) (P10), *infinitesimal* (P11), *First Cause* (P11), *solace* (P11)

IDEAS AND AIMS

1. Basically, what are the two sides of the argument about the value of a liberal education in the occupations, according to Bell?
2. What, according to Bell, are the primary reasons why everyone should pursue a general or liberal education?
3. According to Bell, how will education improve one's "station in life" and make a businessman more honest?
4. Are there flaws in Bell's logic or argument in P2?
5. P10 has a hidden—and very Victorian—assumption about the relationship of honesty to success. What is this hidden assumption?
6. If, as Bell claims in P11, pursuit of the liberal arts will make a person happier in private life, how, by implication, might this make a person a better worker as well?
7. What might Bell mean in P11 by the "moral obligation . . . to acquire knowledge"? Why or how would acquiring knowledge be a "moral obligation"?
8. In P3, P10, and P11, how does Bell use or imply a religious or moral dimension in his argument? That is, how does he suggest that his view is not merely practical but also morally or spiritually correct? How does Bell's metaphor in P11 of a "paradise of intellectual enjoyment" fit in this strand of Bell's reasoning?

ORGANIZATION AND FORM

1. Each of the first three paragraphs of Bell's essay serves a different function. How does the first paragraph serve as an overall introduction, stating the con side of the argument and implying its opposite?
2. The second paragraph offers a sort of general, logical proof for the importance of liberal education in business on the basis of three components: Liberal education trains minds and improves intelligence; the more intelligent the worker, the better job he will do; employers look for whoever can do the best job. What is Bell's chain of reasoning using these three components?
3. How does the third paragraph move from the abstraction or generality of the first two paragraphs to the concrete, and serve as an introduction to the following several paragraphs? How is Bell's proof inductive rather than deductive here? (Look up these terms, including *abstract* and *concrete*, in your dictionary or composition handbook.) Where else does Bell use inductive proof?

4. In what way is the category of workers who have improved their station in P8 somewhat different from that in PP3–7?
5. In P10 Bell introduces a new idea about the value of a liberal education to the prospective businessman or worker; what is it? Is his proof basically inductive or deductive in this paragraph?
6. How is Bell's introduction of his own profession into the discussion (P9) a persuasive tactic or strategy?

WORDS AND STYLE

1. What sort of audience is Bell aiming at in this essay, judging from the kinds of words and sentences he uses? Cite examples to support your answer.
2. Find examples of Bell's use of the expletive construction (the use of "it" or "there" as anticipatory subjects in sentences beginning "it is . . ." or "it seems . . ." or "there is . . ."). (For further information, look up these terms in your collegiate dictionary or composition handbook.) What tone do they lend to the essay?
3. Bell repeatedly uses the words "may" and "allow" in the essay. In what paragraphs? What tone do they create, and what relationship do they imply between Bell and his reader?
4. In what paragraph do interrogative sentences bulk the largest? What is their function in that paragraph?
5. Where does Bell use short sentences, contrasting with the longer sentences elsewhere in a particular paragraph? Choose a few examples and explain how the short sentence effectively does its job in each instance.
6. A very distinctive feature of Bell's prose style is parallelism, especially the parallelism of pairs. (Look up this term in your composition handbook or collegiate dictionary.) Examples may be found in the first sentence of P2 ("inconsistent . . . to"), the third sentence of P2 ("humblest . . . occupation"), the sixth sentence of P2 ("strongest . . . work"), the eighth sentence of P2 ("brawny . . . person"), the last sentence of P2 ("to be . . . employers"), and the last sentence of P8 ("end . . . industry"). Bell also uses the constructions "not (only) . . . but (also) . . ." and "as well as" for a similar purpose. What feeling or tone does this parallelism impart to the essay? Explain how it helps Bell convey his ideas in some specific instance.

DISCUSSION AND WRITING

1. Is there *really* "no calling in life that does not require the exercise of some degree of intelligence"?
2. Do you think Addison's idea (quoted by Bell) that "Extortion, rapine, and injustice . . . often give a man a figure in the world" is still true? Are Addison's ideas about the ethics of literature, referred to by Bell, still relevant?

3. Bell severely limits his remarks about the "abstract pleasures" of reading. Can you provide examples that will illustrate his point?

4. After some research in the library, write a paper about famous modern authors who have been active or successful in occupations other than writing or literature (some starting points might be William Carlos Williams and Wallace Stevens).

5. Trying to use inductive or deductive logic wherever applicable, attack Bell's essay by pointing out various artists and intellectuals who have been terribly unhappy in various occupations.

6. Although Bell cites Addison for support in P10 of the essay, how does Addison seem to be at odds with Bell on education in PP8–9 of his *Spectator* 21 (available in your library)? What answer would Bell make to Addison about the usefulness of a liberal arts education to a silk merchant (one of Addison's examples)?

TAKING STOCK: COMPARING AND CONTRASTING THE SELECTIONS

1. Given the ideas expressed in the essays in this section, what do you think college students should be sure to learn?

2. Do you get the impression, from these essays or others in this book, that there is such a thing as an "ideal education"? If so, what is it? What are your own thoughts on the subject?

3. Arthur Ashe in his essay advises acquiring education to ensure work. Do the job opportunities that Marlys Harris (Section 6, "Job Opportunities and Other Practical Matters") and Malcolm Carter (Section 1, "Job Choice and Self-Fulfillment") discuss require such education, such "time in the library"? Does Ashe seem to be correct, to judge from these essays?

4. Arthur Ashe advises parents particularly; what would be the advice to parents by Calvin (Section 1, "Job Choices and Self-Fulfillment"), Fuller (Section 2, "Work and Morality"), or Thoreau (Section 2)? How would this advice to parents compare or contrast with Ashe's?

5. John L. McCaffrey, Robert Benchley in "From Nine to Five" (Section 8, "Efficiency and Success on the Job"), James Thurber (Section 9, "The Work Environment"), William Ouchi (Section 9), C. Northcote Parkinson (Section 9), and Ivar Berg (Section 1, "Job Choice and Self-Fulfillment"), all offer views of management or managers. How do these views concur or differ?

6. Would John L. McCaffrey agree with C. Northcote Parkinson that the young shouldn't be promoted too early or rapidly in a company? Why? (See especially PP42–46 of McCaffrey's essay.)

7. How does Marlys Harris' article in "Job Opportunities and Other Practical Matters" (Section 6) seem to call for specialization? What, according to McCaffrey, is the danger in this?

8. In PP26–34 of his essay, McCaffrey analyzes and details the causes of frustration among white-collar workers and management in a corporation. How do McCaffrey's views compare with those of Peter Drucker (Section 4, "Careers for the 1990s") on this subject?

9. Though they are writing about would-be executives and would-be athletes, John McCaffrey and Arthur Ashe make similar observations about both groups. What characteristics do these groups have in common? Do Ashe and McCaffrey make similar points about over-specialized training? By implication, what should the schools be doing, according to these authors?

10. How do the ideas of Peter Drucker's essay combine with those in P5 and PP14–16 of Davidyne Mayleas' essay (Section 6, "Job Opportunities and Other Practical Matters") to suggest the importance of writing skills in all phases of the employment cycle?

11. How do PP8–11 of Benchley's "From Nine to Five" (Section 8, "Efficiency and Success on the Job") illustrate Drucker's points about writing on the job?

12. What different audiences are being addressed by Peter Drucker, Arthur Ashe, and John McCaffrey? How does this difference in audience affect their ideas about education and preparation for careers? How does this difference in audience affect the style and tone of their essays?

13. In what way does the emphasis on education in Drucker's essay differ from the emphasis in Ashe's or McCaffrey's?

14. How do these three authors both concur in and differ about what they seem to understand by success or how they define it?

15. In P3, P10, and P11 of his essay, G. M. Bell introduces the consideration of religion or morality into the issue of work and education. How do Bell's views compare with those of John Calvin (Section 1, "Job Choice or Self-Fulfillment"), Thomas Fuller (Section 2, "Work and Morality"), or Michel de Montaigne (Section 2)?

16. How do Bell's views coincide with those of the other writers in the section "Work and Education"? How do these ideas differ in some respects or in their emphasis?

17. Many college students expect their education to help train them for a better job. The relationship between work and education may be seen in three areas: *training* for a job, *getting* or *finding* a job, and *doing* the job (or *doing better work* on the job). Which aspects does each of

the essays in "Work and Education" explore? What answers does each suggest about the value of education in relation to work and career?

Note: See also Discussion and Writing question 6 on Arthur Ashe's "Send Your Children to the Libraries," questions 6 and 7 on John McCaffrey's "What Corporation Presidents Think About at Night," and question 6 on G. M. Bell's "On the Compatibility of Intellectual Improvement with the Successful Prosecution of Business."

CAREERS FOR THE 1990s

THE FUTURE FOR WORKING WOMEN

Juanita Kreps

□

Juanita Morris Kreps was born in Lynch, Kentucky, in 1921. She was educated at Berea College and at Duke University. Before serving as Secretary of Commerce from 1977 to 1979, Kreps taught economics at Denison University and at Duke. She has also served on the boards of several national corporations and as a member of several government task forces, such as the Presidential Commission on a National Agenda for the '80s. She is the author of Sex in the Marketplace: American Women at Work *(1971);* Women and the American Economy *(1976); and* Sex, Age, and Work *(1975); as well as college economics textbooks.*

1 Women have been stereotyped in the marketplace, just as they have been stereotyped in their home work. More than one third of the married women in the work force are clerical workers. One fifth are service workers. One sixth are professionals, and one sixth are operatives. Most of the remainder are in the retail trade. The working woman is a typist, maid, teacher, nurse, cashier, or saleswoman. Despite their education, women have failed to make significant inroads into the most valuable market occupations. Women have been hampered in their choice of occupation not by the level, but by the type of education they receive. Indeed, women have had impressive levels of educational attainment which, until recently, men have not matched. In 1952, the average number of years of school completed by all men in the work force was 10.4; the average for women was 12.0. Not until 1974 did the educational attainment of men catch up to that of women in the work force, at 12.5 years each.

2 But on entering the work force most women have had to rely on the vocational training they had in high school. Apart from training for non-market activities through courses such as home economics, women have been encouraged to concentrate on learning the market skills of shorthand and typing. Their market careers have been viewed as temporary, covering a short period in the work force before their children are born. Little thought has been given to that significant period of a woman's labor-force activity in the quarter century or more after children have reached school age. Even when post-high school vocational training has been undertaken by women, it has followed closely the traditional patterns of sex segregation. Ninety-five percent of the health courses and 79 percent of the business and commercial courses in vocational and technical schools are taken by women. Ninety-eight percent of technical, industrial, and trade subjects are taken by men. Without a range of education and training programs leading to different vocations, women will continue to face similar occupational limitations.

3 When a wife shifts from home to market work, it is generally assumed that her earnings improve the family's economic well-being; accordingly the national income accounts show that the Gross National Product is increased by the amount of her earnings. But the family's gains from the additional market work might be revealed as illusory if precise estimates were available. The gains are illusory if work is undertaken purely for increased income which, although apparently forthcoming, is actually offset by the costs of forgone services when a woman works outside the home.

4 The fact that labor done in the marketplace—but not that carried on in the home—is rewarded by pay that presumably bears some relation to its value makes it difficult to calculate the net gain from women's growing contribution to market work. However, the important consideration is not the failure to measure the value of home work, but the tendency to impute a low market value to those services which, being customarily

performed in the home, have commanded no price at all. Cleaning, laundry, and cooking have brought low wages in the labor market, reflecting the fact that in most instances these services bear no price tags. Not only has the buyer been conditioned to view these services as cheap; the women who do the work are conditioned to think of them in the same way.

5   The low value imputed to women's domestic work may help to explain the similarly low appraisal of the work she does for pay. From the "free" services offered in the home, low-priced services in the labor market called for only a comfortably short step. Any work done by a woman came to be regarded as of less value than that done by a man. The narrow range of jobs available to women, moreover, has led frequently to conditions of oversupply and a pushing down of wages paid for "female" jobs. The limitations on market work set by the demands of dual careers reinforce the traditional view of women's work.

6   Even with the growing attachment of women to the work force, a substantial difference in male–female earnings remains. Part-time employment reduces average female earnings, but even when allowance is made for this, female earnings fall well short of those of males. Currently, median earnings of year-round full-time women workers are only 58 percent of those of men, having fallen from 64 percent two decades ago. Attempts to explain the earnings gap between men and women have been made by adjusting for such factors as occupation, education, and work experience. Various studies have produced remaining "unexplained" differences in earnings of approximately one third. There is a strong implication that this remaining difference in earnings is the result of sex discrimination and that even further differences in earnings are the result of role differentiation based on sex rather than the requirements of individual occupations.

7   The loss of free time has seldom been protested by married women when they enter the labor market; indeed, they have seemed eager to demonstrate that they can manage both home and market work without making heavy demands on the rest of the family. This position is understandable, given the traditional view that women should stay in the home, which has led them to feel they had to justify an assumption of market work. Yet in the allocation of time between market and nonmarket work, the value of the third dimension of choice—free time—has received little explicit consideration.

8   Studies of family time allocation before and after women have taken market jobs have revealed different patterns of redistribution. An increase in the amount of market work done by the adult members of a family may be accompanied by some reduction in the amount and quality of home services, but it appears that working wives and their families continue to perform most of their own household work. The big trade-off

for the woman's market work is not a reduction in her home work, but a reduction in her free time. In one study, the total work load for the wife rose by an average of 13 hours per week as a result of her move into market work, while that of her husband actually dropped by an average of 1.5 hours per week.

9   One of the major explanations for the lack of male involvement in home work has been the widely accepted practice of packaging market work in eight-hour days and five-day weeks. Such workweeks, when added to commuting time and other work-related duties, make the market work commitment extremely time-consuming. The prevalence of part-time work among working wives attests to the need for a reexamination of working hours. More than two thirds of all part-time workers are women and three fifths of them are married. The two industry groups dominated by women—the finance and service industries—employ nearly half of all part-time workers.

10   With a continued growth of the service sector of the economy, part-time work is likely to increase. In addition, the length of the full-time work package will probably continue to decline, narrowing the difference between full-time and part-time employment. In some instances 40-hour workweeks have been compressed into four or even three days instead of the usual five. Surprisingly, many women have found these arrangements advantageous since they allow much of the nonmarket production to be done in three-day weekends. A more promising suggestion for the long-term reallocation of work roles and time, however, appears to be an approach which has been called "flexitime." Rather than compressing the workweek, it would extend the period of time during which the usual full-time work load could be completed. Workers could choose within a given range of starting and finishing times, as long as they were present during a short period of "core" time each day, and as long as they completed a set number of hours within a given time period—usually a month.

11   If such arrangements came to be widespread, it would be possible for male workers to take on increased responsibility for nonmarket production that often involves irregular hours and sometimes conflicts with full-time market schedules. In a period when the level of economic activity is expected to slow, some rescheduling of work would be particularly appropriate. Work-sharing arrangements could further redefine full-time work responsibilities. Temporary work-force withdrawals may also offer new sources of flexibility. To current practices such as postponed labor-force entry, extended vacations, leave without pay, and early retirements, which have changed male working lives dramatically, it would be possible, for example, to add maternity and paternity leaves. Arrangements for phasing in and out of full-time work, or assuming a reduced work load permanently, would open possibilities for improvements in time allocation and ultimately in the quality of life available to American families.

VOCABULARY

stereotyped, (P1), *operatives* (P1), *inroads* (P1), *attainment* (P1), *Gross National Product* (P3), *illusory* (P3), *forgone* (P3), *net* (P4), *impute* (P4), *appraisal* (P5), *implication* (P6), *allocation* (P7), *explicit* (P7), *redistribution* (P8), *prevalence* (P9), *attests* (P9), *service industries* (P9), *paternity* (P11), *phasing* (P11)

IDEAS AND AIMS

1. List the principal ideas presented in this essay.
2. As more and more women have entered the nation's work force, what has happened to their families, according to Kreps?
3. What are the relations between the work that women have traditionally performed in the home and the kinds of jobs traditionally taken by women, according to Kreps?
4. According to Kreps' statistics, what happens to the work done around the home when a woman takes a job? Why?
5. Is Kreps enthusiastic about working women and their future?
6. What is the meaning of the last sentence of P3? Put it in your own words.
7. Although the title of this essay is "The Future for Working Women," PP1–9 actually focus on the past and the present, rather than the future. If this essay isn't mistitled, what *do* these paragraphs have to do with the future? What do we learn about how Kreps, and some economists, try to deal with the future and with predictions?
8. Although her aim in the essay is primarily objective exposition, Kreps does have a rather clear point of view about her material. What is this point of view, and what are the details or clues from which it may be inferred? How does Kreps shift, in PP9–11, from mostly exposition to a blend of exposition and argument or persuasion?

ORGANIZATION AND FORM

1. What are the main parts of the essay?
2. How does the rest of the essay explain and clarify rather than merely repeat the general thesis sentence of the essay (first sentence of P1)?
3. How does Kreps use cause and effect as a method of analysis and paragraph development in P4 and P5? Where else does she use it?
4. Where does Kreps use comparison and contrast as a method of analysis and paragraph development in her essay?
5. In what paragraphs does Kreps use example and illustration as a principal method of development?

6. How does Kreps' conclusion (P11) develop from the preceding essay rather than merely restating or repeating its main points?

WORDS AND STYLE

1. How would you characterize the tone of this essay? Why do you think Kreps has adopted this tone? What words help convey it?
2. How does Kreps' use of specifics, facts, and figures contribute to the tone of the essay?
3. Defects in some of the writing of the social sciences are overuse of jargon and nominalization (piling up nouns on nouns or using nouns where adjectives would be preferable). Rewrite and try to improve the clarity of "nonmarket production" (P10), "family time allocation" (P8), and "temporary work-force withdrawals" (P11). What similar examples can you find whose clarity could be improved?
4. The last two sentences of P10 are written at such a high level of abstraction that they really need examples and illustrations to clarify them. Provide such illustrations in your own sentences to explain those of Kreps.

DISCUSSION AND WRITING

1. What are the "proper roles" for men and women living together, if both work? Who should pay all debts? How should household work be allocated? Can statistics adequately illustrate these problems?
2. Should mothers work?
3. Many Americans are trying to fulfill even more responsibilities than Kreps lists. What difficulties are faced by a working woman or man who is also attending college classes?
4. From your own experience and knowledge, do you agree or disagree with Kreps' assessment of what has happened to families as more and more women have entered the nation's work force?
5. As an option for any essay written about the preceding topics, use specifics, facts, and figures, drawing from materials at the library.

THE DECLINE
OF THE MACHINE

John Kenneth Galbraith

□

J. K. Galbraith was born in Ontario, Canada, in 1908. He was educated at the University of Toronto, the University of California, and Cambridge University. There followed a career striking in its variety: Galbraith has held numerous government posts, academic posts, and at least one journalistic post. His career in government began with advising presidents and culminated in Galbraith's being named ambassador to India.

He is a prolific writer, having produced dozens of works on economics, along with novels, diaries, and satires. Having decided early that he wished to write for a wide audience, Galbraith became the "noneconomist's economist." His major work, The Affluent Society *(1958), is a key reference for those interested in "political economics." In this book and in* The New Industrial State *(1967) Galbraith widened the concerns of economists—past politics—into moral issues. Galbraith addresses himself to the educational and scientific estate; in his work he urges educators and scientists to a new understanding of their society and economic system. His insights are sometimes startling, but always based upon his central criticism of the American economic system: that it is based upon blind consumption of goods produced merely to be consumed, suppressing individuality.*

Galbraith is noted for the conversational clarity of his prose style, which some people claim is a rarity among members of Galbraith's profession. He suggests that it may be due to his composing habits: four drafts to get everything correct, then a fifth draft "to add the touch of spontaneity." In the essay printed here, notice all the ironic touches that create the particular

Galbraith tone, as Galbraith thoughtfully weighs the relative commercial worth of money (capital), technology, and people in the workplace. To the exponents of technology, the computer, and "the market" (Wall Street), Galbraith offers educational, sharp-eyed, and wry qualifications.

1 Those who guide our worries on large issues regularly ask us to ponder man's losing competition with the machine. On the assembly lines he is being replaced by automatic machinery which is regulated and instructed by electronic controls. If the resulting product is a consumer item it has almost certainly been designed to minimize both the effort and intelligence required of its user. Not even the question of whether people will want it has been left entirely to judgment. This has been ascertained by market surveys and insured by advertising and both, perhaps, were analyzed with the aid of an electronic computer, sometimes too ambitiously called an electronic brain.

2 The tendency to dispense with men and intelligence is held to go far beyond the consumer gadgets. The unmanned missile is about to replace the old-fashioned hand-operated bomber. In the near future, according to enthusiasts, unmanned missiles will take flight to intercept other unmanned missiles which will prevent these from intercepting other automated missiles. The operation will be handled under contract by IBM. If the globe were larger or the explosions smaller the prospect would not be unattractive. The machines having taken over, men would all be noncombatants. The charm of war has always been greatest for those whose role was to guide it from a certain distance.

3 These visions of the triumph of the machine can be multiplied endlessly. We do not take them quite seriously for we do not really believe that we are being replaced, and our instinct is sound. If there is a competition between man and machine, man is winning it—not for at least two centuries has his position been so strong as compared with the apparatus with which he works.

4 And the fact that this is the age of ascendant man, not triumphant machine, has practical consequences. If machines are the decisive thing, then the social arrangements by which we increase our physical plant and equipment will be of first importance. But if it is men that count, then our first concern must be with arrangements for conserving and developing personal talents. It will be these on which progress will depend. Should it happen, moreover, that for reasons of antiquated design our society does well in supplying itself with machines and badly in providing itself with highly improved manpower, there would be cause for concern. There is such cause, for that, precisely, is our situation.

5 But first, what is the evidence that men have been gaining on machines—that skill and intelligence have become more important in what we call economic progress than capital plant and equipment?

2

6 The change is most prominently reflected in the changed position of the owner or supplier of physical capital. For a half century he has been a man of steadily declining prestige and importance. Once it was taken for granted that ownership of an industrial enterprise—the ownership of the capital assets or a substantial share of them—gave a man a decisive voice in its direction. So it was with Ford, Carnegie, the elder Rockefeller, Commodore Vanderbilt, and John Jacob Astor. And to be a source of capital, as in the case of the elder Morgan, insured an almost equal power over the enterprise. It also insured a considerable position in the community. Indeed, it was because the provision of capital conveyed such power that the system was called capitalism.

7   Now the ownership of capital, or the capacity to supply it, accords no such power. Few large corporations are now run by their owners; those like Du Pont where, for many generations, a talented family has had a decisive influence on the enterprise it owns, are becoming a rarity. Typically the power lies with the professional managers. These make elaborate obeisance to the stockholders. But they select the Board of Directors, which the stockholders then dutifully elect, and in equally solemn ritual the Board then selects the management that selected it. In some cases, for example the Standard Oil Company of New Jersey, once dominated by the first Rockefeller, the Board consists exclusively of managers selected by the managers who were selected by the Board.

8   There are a number of reasons for the rise of the professional manager, but by far the most important is that ownership of capital has come to count for much less than ownership of ability, knowledge, and brains. The man of ability could get the capital; the man who had capital and was devoid of other qualification had become pretty much a hopeless case. (Even to give away his money would eventually require the services of a professional.) The relatively impecunious but better-trained, more intelligent, more determined, or politically more adept managers have almost everywhere taken over. Once in office it is only rarely that the owners of capital can dislodge them.

9   Nor is this a misfortune for the companies in question. Some of the worst cases of corporate misfortune in recent times have been those in which the owners of the capital have managed to use their power to keep the professionals out. In the thirties and early forties the elder Henry Ford used his power as the sole owner of the Ford Motor Company to remain in command. It is now freely acknowledged that the company suffered severely as a result. Following his death the management was professionalized and much improved. The great merchandising house of Montgomery Ward under Sewell Avery provided a parallel example. Control and direction of a large company by a capitalist has become, indeed, a

rather risky affair. He may try to do what can only be done well by a professionally qualified group of diverse and specialized talent.

3

10 But though it is most visible at the top, the shift in the comparative importance of men and capital is perceptible throughout the modern industrial enterprise. The procedures by which the large and successful enterprise raises funds for new plant and equipment are orderly and predictable. And, depending on circumstances, there is a considerable range of choice—earnings can be withheld, there can be resort to banks, or securities can be sold. A great deal of pompous ritual attends this process, but for the large and successful firm this signifies neither uncertainty nor difficulty but only that we have considerable respect for money and expect large sums to be handled with decent ceremony.

11   There is no similar certainty in the procedures by which even the most successful concern supplies itself with talent. It must send its emissaries to participate in the annual talent hunt, and if the most imposing men still go to the money markets, the most eloquent go to the colleges. The bag is always uncertain and frequently inadequate. If a successful firm is contemplating a considerable expansion it will almost certainly worry more about where to find the men than where to get the money.

12   And the change is reflected in the fears and apprehensions of the community at large. We wonder whether we are investing as much as we should in physical capital; we hear that the Soviets, who in our time have largely replaced conscience as the stern small voice of duty, are doing much more. But there is more everyday concern about the state of our schools and colleges. Are they doing properly by our children? Where can we find the resources to enable them to do better? Increasingly we are wondering about the adequacy of our output of highly trained and educated people.

13   This shows itself in a very practical way. Every family knows that the automobile industry is equipped to supply it with a new car almost on a moment's notice. Such is the admirable condition of our physical plant. But it cannot be at all sure there will be a place for all the children in a good college. Even the automobile executive may wonder where he can get his boy in. Such is the contrasting state of our facilities for human development.

4

14 The forces back of the change in the relative position of man as compared with capital are not new. Some of them, curiously enough, are those which, at first glance, seem to suggest the ascendancy of the machine.

15   The classical trinity of productive factors were land (including natural resources), labor (broadly defined to include both physical and intellectual effort), and capital. All production was seen as resulting from the combination of these factors in one form or another and in one proportion or another. Some economists have questioned whether there was much difference between land and capital goods—both support man's efforts to produce things, and many economists have insisted on adding as a fourth factor of production entrepreneurship or the human effort which was devoted to organizing and managing the other three factors. Subject to these modifications and a few quibbles, the classical delineation of productive agents is still accepted and, indeed, is deeply imbedded in economic thought.

16   All production requires all three (or all four) factors and in this sense all are equally vital. But the importance attached to the different factors has changed remarkably in the last hundred and fifty years. At the beginning of the last century—the formative years of modern economics—land seemed peculiarly important. Population was growing. Europe and Asia seemed very crowded. The vast fertile spaces of the Americas, Australia, and Africa were but slightly appreciated. The effect of modern agricultural techniques on production per acre was, of course, beyond view. Both Ricardo and Malthus, two of the towering figures in the history of economic ideas, concluded that, in different ways, man's fate would be largely decided by the relentless pressure of population on limited land. Labor being abundant, perhaps excessively so, it seemed far less important than land. Capital, though important, also lacked the life-and-death significance of the land supply. Land was the factor of greatest prestige.

17   As the nineteenth century passed, capital gained rapidly to a position of dominance in the trinity. The new world added enormously to the supply of land. The decisive question was its development and for this ports, steamships, roads, railroads, farmsteads, and farm equipment were needed. The land was there; the labor came almost automatically; but the more capital the greater the pace of progress.

18   This emphasis on capital was reinforced by the nature of industrial advance during the last century. It consisted not of the invention of a great number of new techniques but the spread of a relatively small number of spectacularly important ones. Thus, textile manufacture became a factory industry. Steam power was applied to manufacturing, transport, and mining to replace power from men, animals, falling water, or wind. Iron and steel became plentiful and cheap and thus available for many new uses.

19   These inventions resulted, so far as anyone could tell, from a combination of accident, inspiration, and genius. Men like James Watt, Ben-

jamin Franklin, and Eli Whitney could not be cultivated, and while they might under some circumstances be protected by the patent office, that was about all that could be done to foster technological progress.

20　　But if little could be done to stimulate inventions, much could be done about putting them to use. Savings could be stimulated by exhortations to thrift—and even more by a system of ethics and religion which assured the diligent, abstemious, and self-denying man esteem in this world and salvation in the next. Investment could be encouraged by stable government and laws which assured investors that profits would be theirs to enjoy. Looking rationally at the thing that was subject to wise policy, economists came to measure progress by the proportion of the nation's income that, each year, was saved and invested.

5

21　Investment in physical capital is still a prime measure of progress but it is an obsolescent one. More and more progress is coming to depend on the quality rather than the quantity of the capital equipment in use and on the intelligence and skill of those who use it.

22　　There are reasonably good figures to go on. Between the early seventies of the last century and the decade 1944–53, according to calculations made under the auspices of the National Bureau of Economic Research, the net output of the American economy increased by an average of 3.5 percent a year. Less than half of this (1.7 percent) is explained by increases in the supply of capital and labor.[1] The rest was the result of improvements in capital equipment—technological advance—and improvements in the working force, including, of course, its leadership and direction. The *share* in the advance attributable to technological improvement and to the improved skill and ability of workers, technicians, and managers has been increasing.

23　　But both technological advance and improved skills and abilities are the product of personal development. Machines do not improve themselves; this is still the work of highly improved men. And most technological advance is now the result not of the accident of inspiration or genius but of highly purposeful effort. Once we had to wait for the accidental appearance of Edisons and Wrights. Now through education and organized effort in a laboratory or experimental shop we get something approaching the same results from much more common clay.

24　　So it comes to this. We now get the larger part of our industrial growth not from more capital investment but from improvements in men

1. These figures have been most thoughtfully interpreted by Professor Theodore Schultz, to whom all who discuss these matters are in debt. See his "Investment in Man: An Economist's View," *Social Service Review*, XXXIII, No. 2, June 1959.

and improvements brought about by highly improved men. And this process of technological advance has become fairly predictable. We get from men pretty much what we invest in them. So now in its turn, after land and after capital, labor—highly improved labor to be sure—has come to the center of the stage. Investment in personal development is therefore at least as useful as an index of progress as investment in physical capital. It could be more valuable. This is the kind of change which solemn men of self-confessed soundness of judgment will continue to resist; the familiar is always defended with much more moral fervor just before it becomes foolish.

25   What then of our practical accommodation to this new urgency of investment in personal development?

6

26 At first glance our position would seem to be quite good. We have been reaping large gains from the application of trained intelligence to our economic life. This is the fruit of one of the world's pioneer experiments in public education. Surely our advantage will continue.

27   We cannot be so optimistic. Until the last century learning and even literacy were the badges of privilege. They had always been reserved to the favored few. Accordingly learning was a symbol of equality—a symbol that our grandparents, determined to establish their claim to full equality, were not disposed to overlook. Hence the free elementary schools, high schools, the Land Grant College system, and the remarkable number and variety of other institutions of higher (and not excessively high) learning.

28   This system was adequate, even admirable, so long as education was a socially provided service designed to insure (though it had other purposes too) rough equality of opportunity. It has ceased to be sufficient as education has become a form of investment.

29   The test of what a community should spend on a social service is what it can afford—what it believes it can spare from other forms of consumption. The test of investment, by contrast, is what will pay for itself. We apply the investment test as a matter of course to physical capital and even the commonplace terminology reflects the different attitudes; while we "invest" in physical capital, we "spend" for education.

30   The investment test is far the more generous of the two—that is to say, it sanctions much larger outlays. It implies an aggressive canvass of all possible uses of funds to see what will pay off at a profit. To find new ways of investing at a profit is to prove one's enterprise. One of the most familiar theorems of accepted economics is that, subject to some lags and irregularities, investment in physical capital will occur whenever marginal return exceeds the marginal cost; that is, whenever the return to

additional investment is sufficient to cover the added cost including interest and some allowance for risk.

31   The test of what can be afforded, by contrast, invokes far more frugal attitudes. The outlay, even if it is for education, is vaguely self-indulgent. If we wish it—if we wish our children to have the prestige and satisfactions and opportunities from learning—we must measure the cost against other important alternatives. Virtue resides not in finding ways of investing more but in finding ways of spending less. The community honors the man who is identified with economy. These attitudes remain even though, as we have seen, the outlays economized may yield as large a return (perhaps larger) as those for physical capital.

32   Investment in personal development is also handicapped by the lack of a close relationship of outlay with the resulting benefit. A chemical company invests in a new plant because it knows it will get the higher earnings. If it invests in the education of a young chemist it has no similar assurance that it will get a return from its outlay. The fellow may decide to become an artist or a farmer, or he may go faithlessly to work for a competitor.

33   One can see by a simple illustration what the kind of firm relationship of cost to benefit that exists for physical capital would do for investment in personal development if it existed there. Imagine an arrangement by which promising youngsters, when halfway through high school, were indentured for life to a corporation. The corporation would then be responsible for all further education and would be assured of their services for life. Performance of the companies tomorrow, it would soon be evident, would depend on the quality of the postulant executives, scientists, and other specialists being selected and trained today. The quality of this group would become a matter of major concern. It would be under the eye of accomplished educators. Money would start flowing into it. Investment fund managers would send scouts to seek information on its quality. If one of the larger oil companies found that the schools and colleges available for training its oncoming geologists and engineers were inadequate, it would obviously have to take steps to remedy the situation—perhaps by establishing its own. Otherwise, in a few years, it would be outclassed by the companies with better talent. One can easily imagine bond issues by backward companies to develop stronger technical echelons. The result would be a substantial and possibly an astronomical increase in outlays for personal development—all justified by the resulting profit. All this would be the result of giving the corporation a firm lien on the individual's services and thus on the return on the money it spends on him. It has such a lien on a machine; the example only makes human beings as privileged, for purposes of investment, as are machines.

34   The final reason for thinking that our arrangements for investing in personal development are deficient is that the Soviets have, technically

speaking, superior ones. They begin with all resources under public control; hence, there is no problem in transferring those to be devoted to personal development from private to public use. And outlays for physical capital and those for personal development are items in the same huge budget. The returns from one type of investment can be measured against the returns from the other. There is no inherent reason why physical capital should have a preference as in our case. The result is that the U.S.S.R., by our standards still a comparatively poor country, treats its schools, research and training institutes, universities, and adult and worker education with a generosity which impresses all Western visitors. These outlays, needless to say, not old-fashioned expansion of physical capital, were decisive for launching the Sputniks and for landing their successor on the moon.

7

35   We cannot solve the problem of personal investment by indenturing our youngsters at a tender age to a corporation. And we should not expect the kindly corporation to rise to the rescue with large voluntary grants for education. Time has already been wasted on this notion. The problem is far too serious to be left to the conscience of those with a particular willingness to spend the stockholder's money.

36   Most likely we will solve the problem by making fuller and better use of the familiar instruments of public finance. We must see spending for personal development not as a cost but as an opportunity. Then we must make sure that we are taxing ourselves sufficiently to exploit this opportunity. That the Federal Government must play a role is elementary. It has access to fiscal resources that are inherently far greater than those of states and localities; now that education has become an investment rather than a social service, these resources are indispensable. It is also the unit of government with responsibility for national development and growth. There is at least a likelihood that investment in personal development is a better guarantee of national power than some of our military expenditures.[2]

37   We need also to review our attitudes toward state and local taxation. In a poor country there are sound reasons for reluctance in taxing objects of everday consumption in order to have more public services and amenities. But we are not a poor country and personal development has become not a service but an investment. So states and localities should no longer hesitate to use sales and excise taxes (as an addition to and not as a substitute for others) to pay for schools and universities. And liberals, in particular, should not be too indignant when this is proposed.

2. We must see too that waste, including that of the athletic circuses, is brought under control. It is not only indefensible in itself; it brings investment in human development into disrepute.

38   There is another way of putting provision for personal development on a par with capital development that we should consider. We assume that a corporation, either by withholding from earnings or by resort to the capital market, will take responsibility for improving and expanding its own physical plant. The pressure for voluntary contributions by corporations to education reflects, no doubt, a feeling that there is a similar responsibility for personal development. Corporations are the largest employers of trained talent. They reap the rewards from employing such people. Why shouldn't they pay a part of the cost of training this talent?

39   Perhaps they should. Voluntary contributions will always be inequitable as well as inadequate. Conscience can readily be assuaged by a small contribution and the levy falls only on those with a social view of the corporation. But a special tax for education and training would encounter no similar objection. Levied as a percentage of total payroll— executive, scientific, skilled and unskilled—it would be roughly proportioned to the quantity and quality of the people employed. Thus it would be related to benefit from past investment in personal development; and it would mean that the company was assuming its rough share of the cost of replacing with improved talent the skilled workers, technicians, scientists, and executives that it employs. Initially the tax would presumably be borne in the form of higher prices by the consumers of the product. Ultimately the better talent would bring better methods, improved efficiency, and hence lower prices. It would be self-liquidating for it supports a profitable investment.

40   Corporations are now at great pains to explain that their prices must include provision for earnings sufficient to replace and expand their physical capital. This, they regularly assure their public, means that production will continue and be more efficient in the future. But, as the National Bureau figures show, we have more to gain from improving the quality of people. So a levy for this purpose would be an even better bargain.

41   Maybe there are other ways of augmenting the flow of resources into personal development. In a society that is changing we dare not assume that we have thought the last thoughts on any such subject. For man has not retreated before the machine; rather the machine has become desperately dependent on the improvement of man. And our economy is still arranged to supply machines rather than to improve men.

VOCABULARY

ascertained (P1), *dispense* (P2), *noncombatants* (P2), *ascendant* (P4), *antiquated* (P4), *capital assets* (P6), *Commodore Vanderbilt* (P6), *John Jacob Astor* (P6), *rarity* (P7), *obeisance* (P7), *devoid* (P8), *impecunious* (P8), *adept* (P8), *dislodge* (P8), *securities* (P10), *pompous* (P10), *emissaries*

(P11), *trinity* (P15), *entrepreneurship* (P15), *quibbles* (P15), *delineation* (P15), *imbedded* (P15), *James Watt* (P19), *Eli Whitney* (P19), *cultivated* (P19), *foster* (P19), *exhortations* (P20), *diligent* (P20), *abstemious* (P20), *obsolescent* (P21), *auspices* (P22), *net* (P22), *fervor* (P24), *disposed* (P27), *sanctions* (P30), *canvass* (P30), *frugal* (P31), *indentured* (P33), *postulant* (P33), *echelons* (P33), *lien* (P33), *inherent* (P34), *Sputniks* (P34), *exploit* (P36), *fiscal* (P36), *amenities* (P37), *excise taxes* (P37), *indignant* (P37), *inequitable* (P39), *assuaged* (P39), *levy* (P39), *borne* (P39), *self-liquidating* (P39), *augmenting* (P41)

IDEAS AND AIMS

1. In what way is Galbraith's overall aim or purpose in this essay to argue or persuade, as much as to explain? What evidence from the essay can you find to support this conclusion?
2. In past generations, what was the role of the capitalists? What has happened to their roles now?
3. Why have professional managers become so important?
4. How does Galbraith contrast the way a modern company raises the money with the way it "raises" talented employees?
5. What exactly does Galbraith mean in P12 that the "Soviets . . . in our time have largely replaced conscience as the stern small voice of duty"? What ironic criticism of contemporary Americans is Galbraith making here?
6. Why was land so important in 1800, according to the essay?
7. What happened which then caused capital to replace land as the more important agent of productivity?
8. What reasons have now made talented employees more important than either land or capital, in Galbraith's view?
9. How does Galbraith contrast the idea of education as an investment with the notion of education as a social service?
10. What forces hamper the perception of education as an investment?
11. List the author's proposals for funding better schools.

ORGANIZATION AND FORM

1. Where does the author state his central idea? What are the functions of the paragraphs that precede it?
2. What main units of thought or structural parts do Galbraith's numbered sections mark off?
3. In an argumentative or persuasive essay, an author should offer evidence to support his or her assertions. Does Galbraith offer such evidence? Where? What kind?
4. List Galbraith's effective use of transition words to link parts of a paragraph,

one paragraph to another, and one section of the essay to another. Choose one example and explain how it works.

5. Where and how does Galbraith use comparison and contrast to develop his points?

6. How do PP11–13 function as a unit? What do they illustrate about the importance of educated employees? How do they relate to the central thesis of the essay?

7. What is the overall pattern of organization in PP14–25?

8. What function does the extreme brevity of P25 help serve?

WORDS AND STYLE

1. Where does Galbraith effectively use common, ordinary words? Where does he effectively use long, polysyllabic words? Explain the reasons for some of your choices.

2. A trademark (so to speak) of Galbraith's prose style is its witty, understated irony. How can it be seen in the last sentence of P1, the fifth sentence of P2, and the last sentence of P2 (especially in the word "charm")? List other examples of Galbraith's irony in the essay. How might this irony be helpful for an argumentative or persuasive essay?

3. How does Galbraith's repetition of the word "select" and related forms of the verb in P7 help him express or convey the tautology of corporate operations?

4. How do Galbraith's words "trinity" (P15), which he repeats, and "postulant" (P33) have religious overtones? What is Galbraith urbanely mocking here about the business world and economic theorists? How is this vocabulary with religious overtones to be found in PP 7, 10, 12, 24, 35, and 39?

5. Where does Galbraith use short sentences effectively? Choose some examples and explain how these sentences are set off and how they help Galbraith make or underline a point.

DISCUSSION AND WRITING

1. This essay was written well before the most recent developments in machines and computers. Have any of the most recent developments made the author's overall argument incorrect? How about specific parts of it?

2. How do most Americans view education, as a service or as an investment? How do you, your parents, and your friends view it?

3. Has the author convinced you? Which are more important to our economy, human beings or machines?

4. Which of the author's proposals for funding education do you think may have the best chances of being adopted? Why? Can you think of other ways of funding education?

5. Who benefits from an education? The individual, his employer, or society in general?

6. Compare what Galbraith says in Section 2 about the rise of the managerial class with the comments on this group by Ivar Berg (Section 1, "Job Choice and Self-Fulfillment"), John L. McCaffrey (Section 3, "Work and Education"), and Peter Drucker in "Evolution of the Knowledge Worker" (Section 4, "Careers for the 1990s").

7. Compare Galbraith's analysis of the historical development of business and wealth in PP14–17 with that of W. H. Auden in the opening of his essay (Section 5, "Money"). How does Auden's analysis have a psychological and moral slant? How does Galbraith keep his analysis generally neutral or objective?

WORK IN CORPORATE AMERICA

Russell Baker

☐

Born in Virginia (in 1925) and educated at Johns Hopkins University, Russell Baker has worked as a journalist on the Baltimore Sun *and* New York Times, *from 1947 to 1962, as well as having contributed to magazines such as* Ladies' Home Journal, McCall's, Sports Illustrated, *and* Saturday Evening Post. *With his syndicated newspaper column, Baker, together with Art Buchwald, is the inheritor of the tradition of the humorous newspaper columnist running from Mark Twain to "Kin" Hubbard, Eugene Field, George Ade, Don Marquis, Franklin P. Adams, and Heywood Broun.*

Both Baker and Buchwald zero in on the panoply of foibles to be found in the American scene, which seem to supply them with material for an unending number of columns. Among Baker's several books collecting his essays are An American in Washington *(1961),* No Cause for Panic *(1964),* All Things Considered *(1965),* Poor Russell's Almanac *(1972),* The Upside Down Man *(1977), and* So This Is Depravity *(1980). Inevitably, several other essays by Baker focus on work and money, from "Ben [Franklin] Was Swell, But He's Out" (*All Things Considered*) to "Lost Labor Love" (*So This Is Depravity*). These subjects also come to the fore when Baker begins his moving and amusing autobiography,* Growing Up *(1982), by promising to explain how he happened to choose writing as his career. As a consequence of this focus, he touches many times in a personal and fascinating way on work and money in their several manifestations, both in his life and in all the lives around him.*

1 It is not surprising that modern children tend to look blank and dispirited when informed that they will someday have to "go to work and make a living." The problem is that they cannot visualize what work is in corporate America.

2 Not so long ago, when a parent said he was off to work, the child knew very well what was about to happen. His parent was going to make something or fix something. The parent could take his offspring to his place of business and let him watch while he repaired a buggy or built a table.

3 When a child asked, "What kind of work do you do, Daddy?" his father could answer in terms that a child could come to grips with. "I fix steam engines." "I make horse collars."

4 Well, a few fathers still fix steam engines and build tables, but most do not. Nowadays, most fathers sit in glass buildings doing things that are absolutely incomprehensible to children. The answers they give when asked, "What kind of work do you do, Daddy?" are likely to be utterly mystifying to a child.

5 "I sell space." "I do market research." "I am a data processor." "I am in public relations." "I am a systems analyst." Such explanations must seem nonsense to a child. How can he possibly envision anyone analyzing a system or researching a market?

6 Even grown men who do market research have trouble visualizing what a public relations man does with his day, and it is a safe bet that the average systems analyst is as baffled about what a space salesman does at the shop as the average space salesman is about the tools needed to analyze a system.

7 In the common everyday job, nothing is made any more. Things are now made by machines. Very little is repaired. The machines that make things make them in such a fashion that they will quickly fall apart in such a way that repairs will be prohibitively expensive. Thus the buyer is encouraged to throw the thing away and buy a new one. In effect, the machines are making junk.

8 The handful of people remotely associated with these machines can, of course, tell their inquisitive children "Daddy makes junk." Most of the work force, however, is too remote from junk production to sense any contribution to the industry. What do these people do?

9 Consider the typical twelve-story glass building in the typical American city. Nothing is being made in this building and nothing is being repaired, including the building itself. Constructed as a piece of junk, the building will be discarded when it wears out, and another piece of junk will be set in its place.

10 Still, the building is filled with people who think of themselves as working. At any given moment during the day perhaps one-third of them will be talking into telephones. Most of these conversations will be about paper, for paper is what occupies nearly everyone in this building.

11   Some jobs in the building require men to fill paper with words. There are persons who type neatly on paper and persons who read paper and jot notes in the margins. Some persons make copies of paper and other persons deliver paper. There are persons who file paper and persons who unfile paper.

12   Some persons mail paper. Some persons telephone other persons and ask that paper be sent to them. Others telephone to ascertain the whereabouts of paper. Some persons confer about paper. In the grandest offices, men approve of some paper and disapprove of other paper.

13   The elevators are filled throughout the day with young men carrying paper from floor to floor and with vital men carrying paper to be discussed with other vital men.

14   What is a child to make of all this? His father may be so eminent that he lunches with other men about paper. Suppose he brings his son to work to give the boy some idea of what work is all about. What does the boy see happening?

15   His father calls for paper. He reads paper. Perhaps he scowls at paper. Perhaps he makes an angry red mark on paper. He telephones another man and says they had better lunch over paper.

16   At lunch they talk about paper. Back at the office, the father orders the paper retyped and reproduced in quintuplicate, and then sent to another man for comparison with paper that was reproduced in triplicate last year.

17   Imagine his poor son afterwards mulling over the mysteries of work with a friend, who asks him, "What's your father do?" What can the boy reply? "It beats me," perhaps, if he is not very observant. Or if he is, "Something that has to do with making junk, I think. Same as everybody else."

VOCABULARY

dispirited (P1), *incomprehensible* (P4), *systems analyst* (P5), *prohibitively* (P7), *inquisitive* (P8), *ascertain* (P12), *confer* (P12), *eminent* (P14), *scowls* (P15), *quintuplicate* (P16), *mulling over* (P17)

IDEAS AND AIMS

1. Is Baker exaggerating?
2. What in his essay reveals that Baker's main purpose is the humorous criticism of work in corporate America? Where does Baker use comparison and contrast, and what does he compare or contrast? What process or techniques does Baker use to define what he means by "work in corporate America"?

3. According to Baker, why are previous notions of work no longer tenable?
4. According to Baker, are children the only people confused about what kinds of work adults do?
5. Baker emphasizes the word "paper," reducing the work done in corporations down to its physical record. What might a corporation executive argue that this paper really is?
6. What does "corporate America" mean? Are there "other Americas" to which Baker's ideas do not apply?
7. What joke does Baker imply about the progressive waste of a paper-producing society in P16? How does he convey this joke?

ORGANIZATION AND FORM

1. Explain how Baker's essay is divided into two main parts, PP1–9 and PP10–17.
2. How is each of the two main parts of the essay subdivided?
3. How does Baker use the repetition of such key terms as "junk" and "paper" to help make parts of his essay cohere? In which paragraphs are the words "junk" and "paper" used?
4. How is Baker's last use of the word "junk" unexpected? How does this surprise help create irony?
5. In what paragraphs does Baker use comparison and contrast, and in what paragraphs does he use definition, as modes of development or analysis of his subject? (See question 2 of Ideas and Aims.)

WORDS AND STYLE

1. In what ways is Baker's style a blend of the standard and colloquial levels of usage? What are examples of each? How does Baker use this blend for effective expression of his points?
2. What is Baker's tone? What specific words illustrate his point of view about work?
3. How does Baker use verbal repetition as in the last sentence of P9 and elsewhere to create an ironic impact for his ideas?
4. In what way is Baker's style so simple as to be almost childish in P11? Why is such a style appropriate for this paragraph?

DISCUSSION AND WRITING

1. What readers can you imagine who would not find Baker's essay humorous? Why?

2. Write an essay similar to Baker's, defining the work of college students for their parents or for others who may not know what college students really *do*.

3. Baker rather quickly dismisses that very large section of the work force that "makes junk." Write an essay explaining, in more detail, the workday of this kind of worker.

4. Try to turn the tables on Baker, and explain in a humorous essay why many of today's goods and services are actually superior to those of the good old days.

5. How does Peter Drucker's discussion of primary and secondary industries in P9 and elsewhere of "Evolution of the Knowledge Worker" (Section 4, "Careers for the 1990s"), together with similar analysis by Robert Heilbroner (Section 4), in part provide a reply to Russell Baker's droll criticism of a paper-shuffling rather than goods-producing society?

EVOLUTION OF THE KNOWLEDGE WORKER

Peter F. Drucker

□

See the introduction to Peter Drucker's "What Employees Need Most," on pages 89-90 of this book. Unlike the other selection by Drucker, this one was not written as a kind of speech or exhortation to high school graduates, to be published in a newsmagazine. Rather, it is part of Professor Drucker's book The Age of Discontinuity: Guidelines to Our Changing Society. *The book explores how the continuities in four areas (technology, the world economy, political institutions, and education or knowledge) from the nineteenth century through the Second World War have been, recently, interrupted or changed, making our time an "age of discontinuity." Containing seventeen chapters, the book is divided into four parts: "The Knowledge Technologies" (Drucker refers to this part in paragraph 7 of our selection), "From International to World Economy," "A Society of Organizations," and "The Knowledge Society."*

This selection is from Chapter 12, "The Knowledge Society," in Part 4 (specifically, paragraphs 1–4, 6–7, 13–14, 16, 18–20, 32–35, 39, 43–44, 47–48, 50–51, and 53 of the 54 paragraphs of the main section of the chapter). The more substantial paragraphs and abundance of facts and figures in this second selection by Drucker clearly show that this analysis of the impact on the workplace of the change from a "goods economy" to a "knowledge economy" is scholarly writing. However, Professor Drucker, true to his experience as a journalist, conscientiously aims to make his material and analysis clear to the general reader.

1   The "knowledge industries,"[1] which produce and distribute ideas and information rather than goods and services, accounted in 1955 for one-quarter of the U.S. gross national product. This was already three times the proportion of the national product that the country had spent on the "knowledge sector" in 1900. Yet by 1965, ten years later, the knowledge sector was taking one-third of a much bigger national product. In the late 1970's it will account for one-half of the total national product. Every other dollar earned and spent in the American economy will be earned by producing and distributing ideas and information, and will be spent on procuring ideas and information.

2   From an economy of goods, which America was as recently as World War II, we have changed into a knowledge economy.

3   The figures are impressive enough. Ninety per cent of all scientists and technologists who ever lived are alive and at work today. In the first five hundred years since Gutenberg, from 1450 to 1950, some thirty million printed books were published in the world. In the last twenty-five years alone an equal number has appeared. Thirty years ago, on the eve of World War II, semiskilled machine operators, the men on the assembly line, were the center of the American work force. Today the center is the knowledge worker, the man or woman who applies to productive work ideas, concepts, and information rather than manual skill or brawn. Our largest single occupation is teaching, that is, the systematic supply of knowledge and systematic training in applying it.

4   In 1900 the largest single group, indeed still the majority, of the American people, were rural and made a living on the farm. By 1940, the largest single group, by far, were industrial workers, especially semi-skilled (in fact, essentially unskilled) machine operators. By 1960, the largest single group were what the census called "professional, managerial, and technical people," that is, knowledge workers. By 1975, or, at the latest by 1980, this group will embrace the majority of Americans at work in the civilian labor force. . . .

5   But the statistics, impressive though they are, do not reveal the important thing. What matters is that knowledge has become the central "factor of production" in an advanced, developed economy.

6   Economists still tend to classify the "knowledge industries" as "services." As such, they contrast them with the "primary" industries—agriculture, mining, forestry, and fishing, which make available to man the products of nature—and with the "secondary" industries—that is, manufacturing. But knowledge has actually become the "primary" industry, the industry that supplies to the economy the essential and central resource of production. The economic history of the last hundred years in

1. The term was coined by the Princeton economist Fritz Machlup in his book *Production and Distribution of Knowledge in the United States* (Princeton: Princeton University Press, 1962).

the advanced and developed countries could be called "from agriculture to knowledge." Where the farmer was the backbone of any economy a century or two ago—not only in numbers of people employed, but in importance and value of what he produced—knowledge is now the main cost, the main investment, and the main product of the advanced economy and the livelihood of the largest group in the population. . . .

7   "Knowledge" rather than "science" has become the foundation of the modern economy. This has already been mentioned in Part One, but it needs to be said again. To be sure, science and scientists have suddenly moved into the center of the political, military, and economic stage. But so have practically all other knowledge people. It is not just the chemists, the physicists, and the engineers who get fat on consulting assignments—to the point where they may have a larger income from consulting outside the university than from teaching and research inside. Geographers, geologists, and mathematicians, economists and linguists, psychologists, anthropologists, and marketing men are all busy consulting with governments, with industry, with the foreign aid program, and so on. Few areas of learning are not in demand by the organizations of our pluralist society. There is, I admit, little call for the consulting services of the classics faculty.[2] But there is more demand for the theologians than most people realize. Altogether it is the exceptional area of knowledge which is not today being brought into play in business and industry, in government and the military, in the hospital and in international relations.

8   This demand, in turn, reflects the basic fact that knowledge has become productive. The systematic and purposeful acquisition of information and its systematic application, rather than "science" or "technology," are emerging as the new foundation for work, productivity, and effort throughout the world. . . .

9   The demand ahead for knowledge workers seems insatiable. In addition to a million computer programmers, the information industry in the United States will need in the next fifteen years another half-million systems engineers, systems designers, and information specialists. We will need, perhaps, two million health care professionals—nurses, dietitians, medical and X-ray technologists, social and psychiatric case workers, physical therapists, and so on. These people are both highly trained, well beyond secondary school, and highly skilled. They are fully the equivalent of the skilled machinist or the skilled carpenter with his years of apprenticeship. But their skill is founded on knowledge. . . .

10   These examples bring out some fundamentals of the knowledge economy.

11   1. Knowledge work does not lead to a "disappearance of work." Emi-

---

2. Though Bible scholars are highly prized by both Israeli and Arab armies as consultants on topography, hidden water resources, and so forth.

nent doctors tell us today that work is on its deathbed in the rich, industrially advanced countries, such as the United States, Western Europe, or Japan. The trends are actually running in the opposite direction. The typical "worker" of the advanced economy, the knowledge worker, is working more and more, and there is demand for more and more knowledge workers. The manual worker, the typical worker of yesterday, may have more leisure. He may go home at five in the evening, but the knowledge worker everywhere works increasingly longer hours. The young engineer, the accountant, the medical technologist, and the teacher take work home with them when they leave the office. Knowledge work, like all productive work, creates its own demand. And the demand is apparently unlimited.

12   2. Knowledge does not eliminate skill. On the contrary, knowledge is fast becoming the foundation for skill. We are using knowledge more and more to enable people to acquire skills of a very advanced kind fast and successfully. Knowledge without skill is unproductive. Only when knowledge is used as a foundation for skill does it become productive. Then it enables us to acquire in less time and with less effort what it took years of apprenticeship to learn. It enables us to acquire new skills, i.e., computer programming, which could never be acquired through apprenticeship alone. Knowledge, that is, the systematic organization of information and concepts, is therefore making apprenticeship obsolete. Knowledge substitutes systematic learning for exposure to experience. . . .

13   The man or woman who has once acquired skill on a knowledge foundation has learned to learn. He can acquire rapidly new and different skills. Unlike apprenticeship, which prepares for one specific purpose, a knowledge foundation enables people to un-learn and to relearn. It enables them, in other words, to become "technologists" who can put knowledge, skills, and tools to work, rather than "craftsmen" who know how to do one specific task one specific way. . . .

14   3. But while knowledge eliminates neither work nor skill, its introduction does constitute a real revolution both in the productivity of work and in the life of the worker.

15   Perhaps its greatest impact lies in changing society from one of predetermined occupations into one of choices for the individual. It is now possible to make one's living, and a good living at that, doing almost anything one wants to do and plying almost any knowledge. This is something new under the sun.

16   Most of mankind through the ages has had no choice at all. Son followed father. The Indian caste system only gave religious sanction to what was the norm for most people. Of course, there was always some mobility, upward and downward; even the caste system in India could not entirely prevent this. But these were the exceptions, the few lucky ones, the occasional highly gifted one, the victim of war and catastrophes, or

the totally improvident who gambled or gave away whatever he inherited. And in a world in which most people eked out a bare subsistence on the land, being a peasant was for most of mankind the one and only occupation.

17   A century ago even the educated man could only make a living through knowledge in a few narrowly circumscribed "professions": clergyman, physician, lawyer, and teacher, plus—the one newcomer—civil servant. Engineers came in at the end of the last century. . . .

18   At the same time, access to education is becoming the birthright of people in advanced societies—and its absence the badge of "class domination." It is the absence of access to education which is now meant when people in the developing countries speak of "colonial oppression" or "neocolonialism." Education a hundred years ago was still a privilege. Around 1850, it first became an opportunity which the educational systems in the developed countries increasingly made available to the gifted and ambitious among the poor and "underprivileged." Within the last twenty or thirty years, access to education has become a right. Nowhere is it yet guaranteed in the Constitution. But it is clearly as important today as any of the rights written into the Bill of Rights. Indeed, when the U.S. Supreme Court outlawed "separate but equal" education for the American Negro and ordered the integration of our schools in 1954, it clearly assumed that the right of access to education was as solemnly embedded in the American Constitution as any of the rights actually guaranteed therein.

19   4. Knowledge opportunities exist primarily in large organizations. Although the shift to knowledge work has made possible large modern organizations, it is the emergence of these organizations—business enterprise, government agency, large university, research laboratory, hospital—that in turn has created the job opportunities for the knowledge worker.

20   The knowledge opportunities of yesterday were largely for independent professionals working on their own. Today's knowledge opportunities are largely for people working within an organization as members of a team, or by themselves. . . .

21   The knowledge worker of today, in other words, is not the successor to the "free professional" of 1750 or 1900. He is the successor to the employee of yesterday, the manual worker, skilled or unskilled.

22   This is very substantial upgrading. But it also creates an unresolved conflict between the tradition of the knowledge worker and his position as an employee. Though the knowledge worker is not a "laborer," and certainly not a "proletarian," he is still an "employee." He is not a "subordinate" in the sense that he can be told what to do; he is paid, on the contrary, for applying his knowledge, exercising his judgment, and taking responsible leadership. Yet he has a "boss"—in fact, he needs to have

a boss to be productive. And the boss is usually not a member of the same discipline but a "manager" whose special competence is to plan, organize, integrate, and measure the work of knowledge people regardless of their discipline or area of specialization. . . .

23   But the knowledge worker sees himself as just another "professional," no different from the lawyer, the teacher, the preacher, the doctor, the government servant of yesterday. He has the same education. He has more income. He has probably greater opportunities as well. He may realize that he depends on the organization for access to income and opportunity, and that without the investment the organization has made—and a high investment at that—there would be no job for him. But he also realizes, and rightly so, that the organization equally depends on him.

24   This hidden conflict between the knowledge worker's view of himself as a "professional" and the social reality in which he is the upgraded and well-paid successor to the skilled worker of yesterday, underlies the disenchantment of so many highly educated young people with the jobs available to them. It explains why they protest so loudly against the "stupidity" of business, of government, of the armed services, and of the universities. They expect to be "intellectuals." And they find that they are just "staff." Because this holds true for organizations altogether and not just for this or that organization, there is no place to flee. If they turn their backs on business and go to the university, they soon find that this, too, is a "machine." If they turn from the university to government service, they find the same situation there. . . .

25   This clash between the expectations in respect to knowledge jobs and their reality will become sharper and clearer with every passing year. It will make the management of knowledge workers increasingly crucial to the performance and achievement of the knowledge society. We will have to learn to manage the knowledge worker both for productivity and for satisfaction, both for achievement and for status. We will have to learn to give the knowledge worker a job big enough to challenge him, and to permit performance as a "professional."

VOCABULARY

gross national product (P1), *sector* (P1), *procuring* (P1), *technologists* (P3), *Gutenberg* (P3), *semiskilled* (P3), *brawn* (P3), *rural* (P4), *embrace* (P4), *linguists* (P7), *pluralist* (P7), *theologians* (P7), *productivity* (P8), *insatiable* (P9), *eminent* (P11), *apprenticeship* (P12), *i.e.* (P12), *plying* (P15), *caste* (P16), *sanction* (P16), *mobility* (P16), *improvident* (P16), *eked out* (P16), *subsistence* (P16), *circumscribed* (P17), *neocolonialism* (P18), *embedded* (P18), *proletarian* (P22)

IDEAS AND AIMS

1. Why is it incorrect, according to Drucker, to classify the knowledge industries as "services"?
2. What are the differences between primary and secondary industries?
3. In what senses has knowledge become productive?
4. What categories of professionals does Drucker include as "information specialists"? Why?
5. List the "fundamentals of the knowledge economy."
6. How is knowledge making apprenticeship obsolete, according to Drucker?
7. What is the difference, according to Drucker, between a "technologist" and a "craftsman"?
8. How is the growth of the knowledge industries related to increased access to education?
9. Why is the knowledge worker a successor to the employee rather than to the free professional?
10. What is the result of the unresolved conflict between the traditions of "the professional" and "the employee"?
11. What is Drucker's solution to this conflict?
12. For the individual entering the job market, what, finally, are the pluses and minuses of the "evolution of the knowledge worker"?

ORGANIZATION AND FORM

1. Cite examples of Drucker's use of comparison and contrast to develop his points throughout the selection.
2. How does Drucker use comparison and contrast to develop P11? To develop P13?
3. In short themes, enumeration or numbering of specific points is usually unnecessary. How or why is it justified (PP10–22) in the selection?
4. List examples of Drucker's use of transitional words and phrases, as well as pronouns, especially at the beginnings of sentences, to make his essay and its paragraphs more coherent. Cite one or two instances, explaining how transition is actually effected from one point to the next through these devices.

WORDS AND STYLE

1. Point out examples of Drucker's concreteness, his use of illustrations, facts, and specifics.
2. List examples of Drucker's use of forceful short sentences. Explain how one or two of these effectively help Drucker get across his point at that particular place in the essay.

3. What effect do all the transition words at or near the beginning of sentences have on the ease of reading the selection? How so?

4. Drucker is fond of parenthetical material and appositives (often punctuated by commas and dashes). List some examples. How do some of these help Drucker explain his ideas in specific instances?

5. In the last sentence of P15 Drucker alludes to Ecclesiastes i.9–10 in the Bible. After looking over i.1–10 and the first two chapters of Ecclesiastes generally, explain how much of a claim Drucker seems to be making at the close of P15.

DISCUSSION AND WRITING

1. Do you think Drucker is correct in saying it is *knowledge*, rather than technology or science, which is the new foundation for work?

2. What are some skills, such as computer programming, that could never be learned through apprenticeship alone?

3. Can you think of a profession that once was learned by apprenticeship? Is it so learned today?

4. Besides Drucker's example of the disenchantment of today's knowledge worker, can you think of other difficulties arising from the conflict between the traditions of the professional and the employee?

5. What are some of the ways modern managers attempt to allow knowledge workers to act as professionals?

6. If you had a choice between going home at 5 P.M. and having more leisure as a typical worker, or taking your work home with you as a "knowledge worker," all as posed by Drucker in P11, which would you choose? Why?

7. How does Drucker's discussion of primary and secondary industries (P6), together with similar comments by Robert Heilbroner in the next essay of this section, in part provide a reply to Russell Baker's droll criticism of a paper-shuffling rather than goods-producing society in the third essay of this section?

WORK AND TECHNOLOGICAL PRIORITIES:
A Historical Perspective

Robert Heilbroner

□

Robert L. Heilbroner was born in New York City in 1919. He was educated at Harvard and at the New School for Social Research, where he has taught economics since 1972. He has also been a practicing economist in government and in business.

Heilbroner's major work, The Worldly Philosophers *(1953; 5th edition, 1980), is an exceptionally well-written, clear, and entertaining account of important economists and economic history. It has been read profitably by three decades of general readers and students in college, where it has been widely adopted as a textbook. He has also written* The Future as History *(1960),* The Making of Economic Society *(1962),* The Limits of American Capitalism *(1966), and* An Inquiry into the Human Prospect *(1975), as well as other texts and many articles. Throughout Heilbroner's work run a knowledge of economic history, particularly the history of American industrialization, and a critical streak he shares with John Kenneth Galbraith and others. In fact, Heilbroner once remarked that Galbraith's* The Affluent Society *was a book he referred to more frequently than any other. (See Section 4, "Careers for the 1990s," for a selection by Galbraith.)*

1 There is good reason why there is so much disagreement about automation. At least two of the reasons are obvious, and I will only state them in

136

passing. One is the fact that we don't have enough figures, numbers, statistics. . . .

2   The second reason is equally apparent. We happen to be in a period in which the forces bearing on the labor market are unusually complex. We are, as you know, at a time when the labor bulge is coming down the pipe, so to speak, as the war babies come of age and take the bread from our mouths. At the same time, we are in a period of technological change. When you find an individual unemployed person, it is not always easy to know whether he is unemployed because the supply and demand situation is out of whack, or because he was bumped and not hired on account of some machine.

3   But there is a third reason why there is disagreement, and this is the one that I want to talk about. This is because there is a very curious lack of interest in the problem. There is a curious aversion to looking at the problem of technology and the market society.

4   I am struck by the fact that the two greatest economists of mature capitalism, Alfred Marshall and Lord Keynes, each wrote about capitalism and explicitly omitted technical change from their formulations. This is an astonishing fact when one considers that of all the phenomena characteristic of this system, the one that is by all odds, by general agreement, the most important is technical change. . . .

Internal Exodus of the Labor Force

5 First, let me call your attention to what I think is the fundamental setting of the employment problem—a setting that has to be explained and that also has to be taken into account in looking at today's and tomorrow's employment problem. This fundamental setting is what can best be described as an enormous internal exodus in the American economy, moving from some kinds of jobs into other kinds of jobs, but in a systematic, not in a haphazard way. Briefly, it is a streaming from the farm through the factory and into the offices. Let me give the magnitudes that this involves.

6   If we start back in the year 1800 and ask ourselves, "Where did people work?" the answer is that the great majority worked in agriculture.

7   Now, there was much less specialization of labor in those days than today, so that a person who was a farmer could very likely also do some manufacturing at home and supply himself with certain services. But nevertheless, there is no doubt that his main contribution to the economy was to raise crops. Roughly speaking, 70 to 80 percent of the people who lived in America in 1800 were essentially farmers. The other 20 or 30 percent were split between two other broad categories of occupations. Some of them—blacksmiths, tanners, printers—handled goods of various

sorts. Some of them—legislators, merchants, clerks—provided services of various sorts. I don't think any figures show how the 20 or 30 percent that weren't essentially farmers were divided between services and goods, but however the division fell, in any event, the proportions in either category were clearly small. . . .

8   Now, finally, we bring the picture up to date and take you down to the present, where the general trend continues. Today, we have but 8 percent of the labor force on the farms, and that includes as we all know, people who are just stuck there. It is effectively 5 or 6 percent who really raise food, the others are just disguised unemployed. About 40 percent, roughly the same percentage (it is really slightly more) is in the goods sector. And there is an enormous increase in the services. Over 50 percent of the Nation's working force push papers.

9   Now, this long secular swing out of agriculture through the factories and into the offices is a phenomenon of the most fundamental force, it seems to me; and it must be, in the first instance, explained, and, in the second instance, made relevant to technical change. That is what I would like to do.

10   When we ask why the exodus took place, what it was that pushed people off the farms and into the factories and then again through the factories and into the offices, the answer is very clearly an interaction of two economic forces, like the famous blades of the scissors in Marshall's description of supply and demand. In this case, however, the two forces are, instead of supply and demand, technology and demand. Behind the shift from agriculture, that is, behind the shift from the farm to the city and from the factory to the city to the office in the city, one of the propelling forces was clearly the introduction of machinery.

Sequence of Technological Introduction

11 There is, in the background of that force, an important characteristic which is not often noted. Machinery was not fed into the American economy, so to speak, at random, haphazardly, but in a certain grand sequence. The sequence was that the first area of occupations where technology lit and did its work was agriculture, and the second area where technology lit and did its work was the goods sector, and the third and last was the service sector. . . .

12   That grand sequence of inventions is not, I think, a mystical or fortuitous occurrence. In a market society we would expect the bulk of men's economic inquisitiveness to be directed to those activities that pay, and the activities that pay would tend to be, on the whole, the activities that occupy men's minds and that, in fact, bulk large in the spectrum of jobs. So that in an agriculturally centered society, we would expect to find inventiveness concerned with agricultural devices; in a society that gradually turns towards manufacturing, we would expect to find more inven-

tion, inventiveness, innovation, and, of course, more investment in those inventions directed towards the varieties of tasks having to do with handling goods. . . .

13   Now, the fact that technology came in this broad sequence—and I don't wish to press that point too hard—was not in itself the sole cause of the great exodus which is at the center of my discussion today. For the exodus would not have taken place had the effects of technology not been met with certain patterns of tastes or demands.

Race Between Technology and Demand

14 When we turn first to agriculture, which was the initial sector of the economy in which the effect of technology became noticeable, we note that between 1800 and 1850—I speak very generally—productivity more or less doubled. Had the demand for food doubled *pari passu*, there would have been no particular reason for farmers not to stay where they were. But, as we all know, the demand for food is very inelastic. Here it became impossible for farmers to exercise the productivity that was theirs by virtue of their machinery and to make a living, or rather, for *all* of them to do so. As a result, they left the farm, or immigrants coming into the country did not go to the land, and stayed in the cities.

15   Between 1800 and 1900, the race between technology and demand on the farms was won by technology at the expense of the farmer, who moved to the city.

16   In the city, something rather different took place.

17   In 1869, which is for my purposes the midpoint of the century, half the motive power furnished in American industry was still provided by the water wheel—we were still at the level of paleotechnic culture. From 1869 to 1900, we saw the first burst of productivity-raising inventions applied on a large scale. So that we see in those years a very considerable growth in the output of goods, as opposed to farm goods. But matching this increase in the growth of goods is a concurrent increase in the demand for those kinds of goods—that is to say, for goods that have been taken from the earth, fabricated, processed, packaged, and transported to the point of sale. So that we find, during this second period, that factory employment—and I use "factory" in a very broad sense to include construction employment and transportation employment—expanded very considerably.

18   Then we enter a curious period from, let's say, 1900 down to the present. This is a period in which extraordinary inventions made their presence felt in the world of manufacturing of goods—not only inventions having to do with lowering costs and with increasing productivity, but inventions having to do with the creation of new kinds of goods, the so-called demand-creating inventions. The years from 1900 to the present were the years that witnessed the birth of such products as the auto-

mobile and the consumer durables, the new fabrics and plastics, airplanes, the modern technology of war, an enormous array in all. Virtually everything we think of as "manufactured goods" was invented and first produced around this period. So that surely this was a time when the demand for goods was stimulated as much as was ever the case in American history. . . .

19   In other words, by 1900 we had moved into the factories as large a percentage of the labor force, give or take a few percentage points, as we would need for the next extraordinary half century of demand creation.

20   Now, where did the rest of the people go? The numbers on the farm, not only proportionately but absolutely, fell all the while after 1900 and, indeed, in recent years, more rapidly than ever. Yet there was this extraordinary stability, this static quality, in the goods-handling sector—not just in manufacturing proper, let me repeat, but in the whole manufacturing, construction, mining, utilities, and transportation complex.

21   Well, we all know where people went. They went into that enormously varied group of occupations we call service occupations.

22   Now, here, too, demand was eager and absorptive, elastic. The most cursory survey of consumer spending shows a long steady swing from the earliest statistics towards spending one's income in these kinds of enjoyments. They correspond, perhaps on a national scale, to the experience of the individual who, at the simplest level of his existence, is forced to spend his subsistence on food; who then turns to the secondary tier of goods, his house, his clothes, and so on; but, when he is partially satisfied with those requirements, turns to the expenditures on services that have always marked the luxury expenditure pattern of the rich. Through history, as we in America have moved towards affluence, we have enjoyed proportionately more services.

23   But the service occupations alone in the grand spectrum of occupations were spared the other blade of the scissors, that is to say, they were spared—anyway, *relatively* spared—the incursion of productivity-enhancing technology.

24   Now let me hasten to say that some extraordinary inventions went into the service area. Automobiles, of course, greatly increased the mobility of the Nation. The telephone, the typewriter, were enormous things. Nevertheless, when you look at all the people who service you, you find vast areas where productivity actually didn't rise and, for all I know, fell. Teaching, for instance. It is very difficult to say that the productivity of a teacher today is significantly greater that it was in 1900. I just got a haircut when I got to the airport. God knows productivity there is lower. A million people work in restaurants today: Waiters, cooks, etc. Their productivity has only marginally improved, if at all. Janitors, sales clerks, file clerks—of the 30 or 35 million people who perform all these kinds of occupations, there are very large numbers whose productivity has scarcely been affected at all.

25   Now, that is, I think, an incontrovertible nutshell sketch of what has happened over the past 150 years. To recapitulate briefly, there has been an introduction of machinery of extraordinary productivity-enhancing effect on the farm and in the secondary echelon of occupations, and a much lesser degree of introduction of machinery into the tertiary sector; and there has been, matching that blade of the scissors, a certain pattern of demand-responsiveness. So far as food has been concerned, demand has been very inelastic; so far as manufactures have been concerned, elastic enough to provide a kind of stable layer of employment; and so far as services have been concerned, considerably elastic.

Technology Entering Service Sector

26 Into that, I believe, incontrovertible description of what has taken place, I now inject a suggestion which is highly controvertible, but which, if true, may go a long way to explaining the furor that surrounds the word "automation" and to providing a kind of perspective for the problems that I think we face.

27   My suggestion is very simply that we have now reached the stage where technology is belatedly making its entrance into the third sector.

28   Now, in terms of the earlier hypothesis that I hold with Professor Schmookler, that invention follows the lure of profit, one would expect the service occupations which now bulk so large in the spectrum, occupy so much of our attention, and drain so much of our costs, to be interesting to work with from a profit-potential point of view.

29   In addition, we have reached a level of technological sophistication which simply makes it possible to do things that begin to duplicate the somewhat more "intellectual" kinds of tasks performed in the third sector, as contrasted, perhaps, with the second and first. But I can't verify, I can only suggest, this invasion by machinery into the third sector. I am forced back to that worst of all economic proofs—my impressions. Impressionism is good enough for art, it is not good enough for economics. But impressions are nevertheless powerful.

30   When I go to the banks and see their extraordinary check-reading equipment, I know what an impact this kind of machinery can have on office employment. But it is not just electronic check-readers that makes me think technology is taking a new turn. Another impression—and I am very well aware that impressions don't prove a point—derives from the bowling alley where my two boys go on Sunday. Last year it had in back of it a little hamburger and milkshake dispensary which was manned by a warmblooded human being. This year he is no longer there; and in his place is a machine that dispenses hamburgers and milkshakes. Vending machinery is very important.

31   In the stores, the drift towards self-help—which doesn't require any technology at all—is nevertheless an innovation, an organizational inno-

vation, which has the same impact as the most highly sophisticated electronic computer. In the offices, the new machinery is everywhere visible, doing "clerk's" or "steno's" work.

32   Now, what I am suggesting is that potentially the most important development going on in the field of technology and its interaction with economics is the introduction of machines into these hitherto sacrosanct or relatively sacrosanct areas of employment.

33   I am not certain that modern automation machinery is more labor-displacing in the factory than old-fashioned machinery. I see no reason *a priori*, and I don't know of any facts *a posteriori*, that would prove to me that $100 worth of automation or $100 worth of electronics hooked up on a lathe will displace any more people than $100 worth of forklift trucks or overhead conveyors. . . .

No Expansive Market Left

34   If it is true that there is this underlying trend of technology into the service occupations, it bears a very important implication for the future. It means that the last sector of the market economy has been, so to speak, preempted by machinery and that there is now no expansive market sector left.

35   Prior to this time, there was always an expansive market sector; going back to the 19th century the goods-handling sector was expansive, and coming into the 20th century the services have been expansive. As people got displaced elsewhere, the very forces of supply and demand in the market place brought them largely into private jobs in the service sector. If it is now true that machines are going to displace more and more people who do service jobs, the question is: Where will they go? . . .

VOCABULARY

curious (P3), *aversion* (P3), *explicitly* (P4), *exodus* (P5), *haphazard* (P5), *magnitudes* (P5), *tanners* (P7), *secular* (P9), *lit* (P11), *mystical* (P12), *fortuitous* (P12), *inquisitiveness* (P12), *productivity* (P14), pari passu (P14), *inelastic* (P14), *paleotechnic* (P17), *concurrent* (P17), *durables* (P18), *array* (P18), *static* (P20), *absorptive* (P22), *cursory* (P22), *subsistence* (P22), *tier* (P22), *expenditures* (P22), *affluence* (P22), *incursion* (P23), *incontrovertible* (P25), *recapitulate* (P25), *echelon* (P25), *tertiary* (P25), *sector* (P25), *furor* (P26), *belatedly* (P27), *dispensary* (P30), *steno* (P31), *hitherto* (P32), *sacrosanct* (P32), a priori (P33), a posteriori (P33), *forklift* (P33), *preempted* (P34)

IDEAS AND AIMS

1. What are the three reasons for the disagreement about automation?
2. How were American workers distributed in the year 1800? Why?
3. What is the current distribution of American workers?
4. What are the forces behind the shift in distribution?
5. Where has productivity increased? Where has it decreased or remained static, according to Heilbroner?
6. What is Heilbroner's argument or line of reasoning in P33? How does it bear on American workers' common fear of automation on the job?

ORGANIZATION AND FORM

1. Where does Heilbroner state his central idea?
2. Heilbroner describes a historical cycle in the essay. How is his description organized? In what order does he present his analysis of the introduction of automation?
3. Where does Heilbroner use transition words to move from one part of the essay to the next, one paragraph to the next, or one part of a paragraph to the next?
4. How does Heilbroner use ordinal numbers to help structure his essay?
5. Where does Heilbroner use one-sentence paragraphs? Are they used effectively? How so?
6. How does P30 function in the essay? What does Heilbroner introduce here? How does this paragraph relate to P29?

WORDS AND STYLE

1. Heilbroner's essay was originally presented as an essay at a seminar. What marks of oral presentation to a listening audience are still left in it?
2. How does Heilbroner use parallelism in the fifth and sixth sentences of P7, the third sentence of P11, and the last sentence of P25?

DISCUSSION AND WRITING

1. Since this essay was written, what changes (if any) have occurred in Americans' attitudes toward "automation" or technology in the workplace?
2. What are "service industries," exactly? Current analyses and forecasts suggest that these are the fastest growing segment of the American economy. How

does this growth accord with Heilbroner's "incontrovertible" historical account of the American economy to the date his essay was published (1966)? How accurate has Heilbroner's prognosis been?

3. Have events and developments since the 1960s proved Heilbroner's "controvertible" hypothesis in PP28–29 correct?

4. If Heilbroner describes the cycles correctly, where will most workers move now that automation equipment is moving into the services sector?

5. Describe some of the "modern automation machinery" introduced in the services sector since the 1960s. Will any affect the job that you are seeking?

6. Can productivity ever be raised in the occupations Heilbroner cites in P24 as unchanged? Why or why not? How?

TAKING STOCK: COMPARING AND CONTRASTING THE SELECTIONS

1. How does what Juanita Kreps says about women in business apply to the examples of female entrepreneurs discussed by Ilene Kantrov in "Women's Business" (Section 6, "Job Opportunities and Other Practical Matters")?

2. How do conditions Kreps describes in her essay bear on the employment of the young in business, as explained by C. Northcote Parkinson in the first paragraph of his essay (Section 9, "The Work Environment")? As explained by Parkinson, how has business defined "young" rather narrowly and unfairly? What large group has been left out of the "young"? What roles are women shown to play in Parkinson's essay?

3. Much of John Kenneth Galbraith's essay deals with education. How do his ideas compare with those of the authors in the section "Work and Education" (especially McCaffrey, Drucker, and Bell)? How do Galbraith's views on education compare or contrast with those of C. Northcote Parkinson (Section 9, "The Work Environment")?

4. In section 6 (PP26–34) of his essay, Galbraith discusses the concepts of wealth and value in our economy—what is really valuable in it, what generates wealth, what the real wealth of our economy is (rather than money). How do his views agree in some important respects with those of Selzer (Section 7, "The Varieties of Work: Professions and Blue Collar"), Berg (Section 1, "Job Choice and Self-Fulfillment"), Fuller (Section 2, "Work and Morality"), and H. D. Thoreau (Section 2), who also discuss the concepts of wealth and value?

5. In what ways do or don't any of Galbraith's points apply equally well to those professions and occupations Juanita Kreps identifies as traditionally associated with women?

6. Review the opening paragraphs of Kreps' essay, which discuss education as it relates and has related to men and women in the work force. Has the concept of education as an "investment," as explained by Galbraith in his essay, been applied to women?

7. In some respects, the views of Russell Baker in his essay are very much at odds with those of Henry David Thoreau (Section 2, "Work and Morality"). The latter, for example, contends that the importance or ennobling effect of a job isn't so much *what* one does or *what* one produces as much as *how* one does it. How do Thoreau's examples show this? How does Baker take a quite different view in his essay, and how does it contrast with Thoreau's?

8. Are the "Careers for the Next Frontier" that Marlys Harris describes in her essay (Section 6, "Job Opportunities and Other Practical Matters") in what Russell Baker would call the "junk-making" line? Explain.

9. Based on PP1–8 of his essay (Section 7, "The Varieties of Work: Professions and Blue Collar"), what would Samuel Johnson reply to Russell Baker's criticism of work in corporate America?

10. How does what Peter Drucker has to say about the "Evolution of the Knowledge Worker," especially in P9 of his essay, bear on the advice given by Marlys Harris (Section 6, "Job Opportunities and Other Practical Matters") and Malcolm Carter (Section 1, "Job Choice and Self-Fulfillment") about promising "careers for the next frontier"?

11. How might PP14–17 of Drucker's essay be used to answer Marlys Harris, who talks in her essay, especially in the beginning, about the overcrowding of the professions and the implications of this on occupational and educational planning?

12. Much of Drucker's essay (particularly PP15–18) focuses on education. How does what Drucker has to say about this area compare with the ideas of the writers in the section "Work and Education," as well as with the views of C. Northcote Parkinson (Section 9, "The Work Environment") and John Kenneth Galbraith?

13. In his essay (particularly PP19–25) Drucker discusses white-collar workers or professionals and their problems. How do Drucker's views on this group compare or contrast with those of Buchwald (Section 6, "Job Opportunities and Other Practical Matters"), Benchley in "From Nine to Five" (Section 8, "Efficiency and Success on the Job"), Parkinson (Section 9, "The Work Environment"), Boroson (Section 1, "Job Choice and Self-Fulfillment"), Berg (Section 1), McCaffrey (Section 3, "Work and Education"), Galbraith, or Baker?

14. How do the ideas of Robert Heilbroner about machines in the workplace and their importance compare or contrast with the ideas of John Kenneth Galbraith on this subject?

15. How do the jobs recommended by Marlys Harris (Section 6, "Job Opportunities and Other Practical Matters") and Malcolm Carter (Section 1, "Job Choice and Self-Fulfillment") accord with the historical shift in job availability described by Heilbroner in his essay?

16. Which essays in "Careers for the 1990s" seem most optimistic or hopeful to you? Which seem gloomiest? Why? Based on your own sense of the American economy (how easily you or friends have found off-campus jobs, what your parents' employment situation is like, etc.) and the essays in this section, are you hopeful or gloomy about your prospects? Explain.

Note: See also the following Discussion and Writing questions: 6 and 7 on John Kenneth Galbraith's essay, 5 on Russell Baker's essay, and 7 on Peter Drucker's essay.

MONEY

OF THE ORIGIN AND USE
OF MONEY

Adam Smith

□

Born in Kirkcaldy, Scotland, and educated at Glasgow University and Oxford University, Adam Smith (1723–1790) held professorships first of logic and then of moral philosophy for thirteen years at Glasgow University. He also gave public lectures on English literature, jurisprudence, and political economy. He abandoned his academic career for a time to become private tutor to a young Duke. The pension from this enabled him to retire for ten years to his home town, where he worked on one of the most influential books of his time and afterwards, Inquiry into the Nature and Causes of the Wealth of Nations *(1776), usually referred to simply as* The Wealth of Nations. *In 1778 Smith was appointed commissioner of customs and moved to Edinburgh, and in 1787 he was elected rector of Glasgow University.*

Smith wrote other books—The Theory of Moral Sentiments *(1759),* Lectures on Rhetoric and Belles Lettres *(1762–1763, published post-humously in 1963), and* Essays on Philosophical Subjects *(1795)—but none was as important as* The Wealth of Nations, *which became the foundation of classical economics and is still a standard textbook. Gathering ideas from others, Smith was so comprehensive and broadly illustrative that his book soon became the authority.*

In this selection Smith's comprehensiveness, illustrative range, and moral inclination (he was, after all, a professor of moral philosophy) are all to be found.

1 When the division of labour has been once thoroughly established, it is but a very small part of a man's wants which the produce of his own labour can supply. He supplies the far greater part of them by exchanging that surplus part of the produce of his own labour, which is over and above his own consumption, for such parts of the produce of other men's labour as he has occasion for. Every man thus lives by exchanging, or becomes in some measure a merchant, and the society itself grows to be what is properly a commercial society.

2 But when the division of labour first began to take place, this power of exchanging must frequently have been very much clogged and embarrassed in its operations. One man, we shall suppose, has more of a certain commodity than he himself has occasion for, while another has less. The former consequently would be glad to dispose of, and the latter to purchase, a part of this superfluity. But if this latter should chance to have nothing that the former stands in need of, no exchange can be made between them. The butcher has more meat in his shop than he himself can consume, and the brewer and the baker would each of them be willing to purchase a part of it. But they have nothing to offer in exchange, except the different productions of their respective trades, and the butcher is already provided with all the bread and beer which he has immediate occasion for. No exchange can, in this case, be made between them. He cannot be their merchant, nor they his customers; and they are all of them thus mutually less serviceable to one another. In order to avoid the inconveniency of such situations, every prudent man in every period of society, after the first establishment of the division of labour, must naturally have endeavoured to manage his affairs in such a manner, as to have at all times by him, besides the peculiar produce of his own industry, a certain quantity of some one commodity or other, such as he imagined few people would be likely to refuse in exchange for the produce of their industry.

3 Many different commodities, it is probable, were successively both thought of and employed for this purpose. In the rude ages of society, cattle are said to have been the common instrument of commerce; and,

though they must have been a most inconvenient one, yet in old times we find things were frequently valued according to the number of cattle which had been given in exchange for them. The armour of Diomede, says Homer, cost only nine oxen; but that of Glaucus cost an hundred oxen. Salt is said to be the common instrument of commerce and exchanges in Abyssinia; a species of shells in some parts of the coast of India; dried cod at Newfoundland; tobacco in Virginia; sugar in some of our West India colonies; hides or dressed leather in some other countries; and there is at this day a village in Scotland where it is not uncommon, I am told, for a workman to carry nails instead of money to the baker's shop or the ale-house.

4   In all countries, however, men seem at last to have been determined by irresistible reasons to give the preference, for this employment, to metals above every other commodity. Metals can not only be kept with as little loss as any other commodity, scarce any thing being less perishable than they are, but they can likewise, without any loss, be divided into any number of parts, as by fusion those parts can easily be reunited again; a quality which no other equally durable commodities possess, and which more than any other quality renders them fit to be the instruments of commerce and circulation. The man who wanted to buy salt, for example, and had nothing but cattle to give in exchange for it, must have been obliged to buy salt to the value of a whole ox, or a whole sheep, at a time. He could seldom buy less than this, because what he was to give for it could seldom be divided without loss; and if he had a mind to buy more, he must, for the same reasons, have been obliged to buy double or triple the quantity, the value, to wit, of two or three oxen, or of two or three sheep. If, on the contrary, instead of sheep or oxen, he had metals to give in exchange for it, he could easily proportion the quantity of the metal to the precise quantity of the commodity which he had immediate occasion for.

5   Different metals have been made use of by different nations for this purpose. Iron was the common instrument of commerce among the anti-ent Spartans; copper among the antient Romans; and gold and silver among all rich and commercial nations.

6   Those metals seem originally to have been made use of for this purpose in rude bars, without any stamp or coinage. Thus we are told by Pliny, upon the authority of Timæus, an antient historian, that, till the time of Servius Tullius, the Romans had no coined money, but made use of unstamped bars of copper, to purchase whatever they had occasion for. These rude bars, therefore, performed at this time the function of money.

7   The use of metals in this rude state was attended with two very considerable inconveniences; first with the trouble of weighing; and, sec-ondly, with that of assaying them. In the precious metals, where a small difference in the quantity makes a great difference in the value, even the business of weighing, with proper exactness, requires at least very accu-

rate weights and scales. The weighing of gold in particular is an operation of some nicety. In the coarser metals, indeed, where a small error would be of little consequence, less accuracy would, no doubt, be necessary. Yet we should find it excessively troublesome, if every time a poor man had occasion either to buy or sell a farthing's worth of goods, he was obliged to weigh the farthing. The operation of assaying is still more difficult, still more tedious, and, unless a part of the metal is fairly melted in the crucible, with proper dissolvents, any conclusion that can be drawn from it, is extremely uncertain. Before the institution of coined money, however, unless they went through this tedious and difficult operation, people must always have been liable to the grossest frauds and impositions, and instead of a pound weight of pure silver, or pure copper, might receive in exchange for their goods, an adulterated composition of the coarsest and cheapest materials, which had, however, in their outward appearance, been made to resemble those metals. To prevent such abuses, to facilitate exchanges, and thereby to encourage all sorts of industry and commerce, it had been found necessary, in all countries that have made any considerable advances towards improvement, to affix a public stamp upon certain quantities of such particular metals, as were in those countries commonly made use of to purchase goods. Hence the origin of coined money, and of those public offices called mints; institutions exactly of the same nature with those of the aulnagers and stampmasters of woollen and linen cloth. All of them are equally meant to ascertain, by means of a public stamp, the quantity and uniform goodness of those different commodities when brought to market.

8   The first public stamps of this kind that were affixed to the current metals, seem in many cases to have been intended to ascertain, what it was both most difficult and most important to ascertain, the goodness or fineness of the metal, and to have resembled the sterling mark which is at present affixed to plate and bars of silver, or the Spanish mark which is sometimes affixed to ingots of gold, and which being struck only upon one side of the piece, and not covering the whole surface, ascertains the fineness, but not the weight of the metal. Abraham weighs to Ephron the four hundred shekels of silver which he had agreed to pay for the field of Machpelah. They are said however to be the current money of the merchant, and yet are received by weight and not by tale, in the same manner as ingots of gold and bars of silver are at present. The revenues of the antient Saxon kings of England are said to have been paid, not in money but in kind, that is, in victuals and provisions of all sorts. William the Conqueror introduced the custom of paying them in money. This money, however, was, for a long time, received at the exchequer, by weight and not by tale.

9   The inconveniency and difficulty of weighing those metals with exactness gave occasion to the institution of coins, of which the stamp,

covering entirely both sides of the piece and sometimes the edges too, was supposed to ascertain not only the fineness, but the weight of the metal. Such coins, therefore, were received by tale as at present, without the trouble of weighing.

10   The denominations of those coins seem originally to have expressed the weight or quantity of metal contained in them. In the time of Servius Tullius, who first coined money at Rome, the Roman As or Pondo contained a Roman pound of good copper. It was divided in the same manner as our Troyes pound, into twelve ounces, each of which contained a real ounce of good copper. The English pound sterling in the time of Edward I., contained a pound, Tower weight, of silver of a known fineness. The Tower pound seems to have been something more than the Roman pound, and something less than the Troyes pound. This last was not introduced into the mint of England till the 18th of Henry VIII. The French livre contained in the time of Charlemagne a pound, Troyes weight, of silver of a known fineness. The fair of Troyes in Champaign was at that time frequented by all the nations of Europe, and the weights and measures of so famous a market were generally known and esteemed. The Scots money pound contained, from the time of Alexander the First to that of Robert Bruce, a pound of silver of the same weight and fineness with the English pound sterling. English, French, and Scots pennies too, contained all of them originally a real pennyweight of silver, the twentieth part of an ounce, and the two-hundred-and-fortieth part of a pound. The shilling too seems originally to have been the denomination of a weight. *When wheat is at twelve shillings the quarter*, says an antient statute of Henry III, *then wastel bread of a farthing shall weigh eleven shillings and four pence.* The proportion, however, between the shilling and either the penny on the one hand, or the pound on the other, seems not to have been so constant and uniform as that between the penny and the pound. During the first race of the kings of France, the French sou or shilling appears upon different occasions to have contained five, twelve, twenty, and forty pennies. Among the antient Saxons a shilling appears at one time to have contained only five pennies, and it is not improbable that it may have been as variable among them as among their neighbours, the antient Franks. From the time of Charlemagne among the French, and from that of William the Conqueror among the English, the proportion between the pound, the shilling, and the penny, seems to have been uniformly the same as at present, though the value of each has been very different. For in every country of the world, I believe, the avarice and injustice of princes and sovereign states, abusing the confidence of their subjects, have by degrees diminished the real quantity of metal, which had been originally contained in their coins. The Roman As, in the latter ages of the Republic, was reduced to the twenty-fourth part of its original value, and, instead of weighing a pound, came to weigh only half an

ounce. The English pound and penny contain at present about a third only; the Scots pound and penny about a thirty-sixth; and the French pound and penny about a sixty-sixth part of their original value. By means of those operations the princes and sovereign states which performed them were enabled, in appearance, to pay their debts and to fulfil their engagements with a smaller quantity of silver than would otherwise have been requisite. It was indeed in appearance only; for their creditors were really defrauded of a part of what was due them. All other debtors in the state were allowed the same privilege, and might pay with the same nominal sum of the new and debased coin whatever they had borrowed in the old. Such operations, therefore, have always proved favourable to the debtor, and ruinous to the creditor, and have sometimes produced a greater and more universal revolution in the fortunes of private persons, than could have been occasioned by a very great public calamity.

11   It is in this manner that money has become in all civilized nations the universal instrument of commerce, by the intervention of which goods of all kinds are bought and sold, or exchanged for one another.

VOCABULARY

wants (P1), *embarrassed* (P2), *superfluity* (P2), *brewer* (P2), *respective* (P2), *prudent* (P2), *endeavoured* (P2), *peculiar* (P2), *successively* (P3), *rude* (P3), *Homer* (P3), *dressed* (P3), *employment* (P4), *durable* (P4), *renders* (P4), *to wit* (P4), *Pliny* (P6), *attended* (P7), *assaying* (P7), *nicety* (P7), *farthing* (P7), *tedious* (P7), *liable* (P7), *grossest* (P7), *impositions* (P7), *adulterated* (P7), *composition* (P7), *facilitate* (P7), *affix* (P7), *offices* (P7), *aulnagers* (officials appointed to check the measurement and quality of woolen goods) (P7), *ascertain* (P7), *current* (P8), *sterling mark* (P8), *ingots* (P8), *struck* (P8), *tale* (P8), *victuals* (P8), *exchequer* (P8), *denomination* (P10), *statute* (P10), *wastel* (P10), *race* (P10), *Franks* (P10), *Charlemagne* (P10), *William the Conqueror* (P10), *avarice* (P10), *defrauded* (P10), *nominal* (P10), *debased* (P10), *calamity* (P10), *intervention* (P11)

IDEAS AND AIMS

1. How does the division of labor lead to a commercial society, according to Smith?

2. Why must cattle have been "a most inconvenient . . . instrument of commerce" (P3)?

3. According to Smith in PP3–4, how did one commodity of exchange give way to another over time? Why did this happen?

4. What metals were used for exchange early in history? How did they differ, according to the kind of country in which the metal was used?

5. Why did the early form of metallic exchange give way to the later form?

6. What two forms of stamps were used on metallic currency, and how did they differ according to what the currency represented?

7. Where and how in P10 does Smith shift from objective or neutral exposition to argument?

8. How does Smith read a gloomy, recurrent moral lesson in the history of currency?

ORGANIZATION AND FORM

1. *Narration* means telling a story in chronological order. A paragraph or more in an essay may also be organized or developed by *cause and effect*. Here, the writer begins with the cause or reason for something and proceeds to explain its effects or results; or, the writer may begin with an effect or result of something and then proceed to explain its causes. Explain how Smith's essay is a blend of narration and cause-and-effect analysis. In what paragraphs may either of these devices of organizing or developing an idea be found?

2. In what paragraphs does Smith use deductive logic (analyzing what consequences must inevitably result from some basic premise or idea) as well as the method of cause-and-effect analysis and paragraph development? How is Smith's logic deductive (what are his premises and what conclusions follow logically from them)?

3. In what paragraphs does the author use illustration and example? Where are these used with special effectiveness, in your opinion?

4. What are the main parts or sections of the essay?

5. Where does Smith use transition words within a paragraph to help bind it up, to give it coherence? Where does he use such words to link one paragraph with another? Explain in one or two instances how these words function to effect such transition.

WORDS AND STYLE

1. Give examples of Smith's effective use of plain and simple words to explain his points or describe events.

2. Smith is fond of litotes, the use of "not" plus an adjective to affirm rather than negate ("I was not unhappy"). What quality or tone does this impart to the essay?

3. Smith frequently uses parenthetical expressions or sentence interrupters, such as "we shall suppose" in P2 and "I am told" in P3. How do these contribute a relaxed effect to Smith's prose style?

4. How are Smith's words slanted in the expressions "all rich and commercial nations" (P5) and "all countries that have made any considerable advances towards improvement" (P7)? How does his word choice reveal bias or value judgment? Toward what, in the examples cited?

DISCUSSION AND WRITING

1. Write an essay in which you apply to today the argumentative point of P10 (about the relation of governments or leaders to diminishing real quantity of metal). Use illustrations and specifics, following Smith as a model.

2. Do you agree or disagree with Smith's contention about the "avarice and injustice of princes and sovereign states, abusing the confidence of their subjects" (P10)? Why or why not? Cite specifics.

3. Research the history of American currency or some particular denomination (penny, nickel, dime, quarter, dollar) and write a combined narration and cause-and-effect analysis similar to Smith's.

THE WAY TO WEALTH— PREFACE TO *POOR RICHARD'S ALMANACK,* 1758

Benjamin Franklin

□

The diverse talents of Benjamin Franklin (1706—1790) are so well known as to be virtually a part of American folklore: he was a printer, publisher, scientist, inventor, statesman (serving in various U.S. political posts as well as foreign ambassador), philosopher, and author of a wide variety of writings. Born in Boston, Franklin was apprenticed at the age of ten in various trades after only two years of schooling, necessitating his self-education, which Franklin undertook through a lifelong habit of attentive reading and study. Franklin's career as one of the great prose writers of his time began with essays done for the newspaper of his brother, to whom he had been apprenticed as a printer. Written when he was only sixteen, these essays, collectively called the Dogood Papers *(1722), show a keen eye, the use of a made-up authorial character (Silence Dogood) rather than Franklin himself, a sprinkling of proverbs, and humor, qualities all to be found in Franklin's almanac, from which this selection is taken. Both his early and later essays were influenced by the prominent eighteenth-century British writers Joseph Addison and Richard Steele.*

Franklin's works, which fill ten volumes in the older standard edition, may be divided into five categories, excluding his justly celebrated Autobiography *(1791; 1868), which doesn't easily fall in any category. His philosophical and religious writing includes* A Dissertation on Liberty and Necessity, Pleasure and Pain *(1725) and* Articles of Belief and Acts of Religion *(1728). His scientific writing includes* Experiments and Observations on Electricity *(1751–1753) and* Physical and Meteorological Observations *(1766). His political writing includes* The Interest of Great Britain Considered with Regard to Her Colonies *(1760),* Cool Thoughts on the Present Situation of Our Public Affairs *(1764), and work (with Thomas Jefferson) on the* Declaration of Independence (1776). *Among his practical writings are* Account of the New Invented Pennsylvania Fireplace *(1744) and* Poor Richard's Almanack *(1733–1758). And among his humorous or satirical writings are* "Advice to a Young Man on the Choice of a Mistress" *(1745),* "Rules by Which a Great Empire May Be Reduced to a Small One" *(1773),* The Ephemera *(1778),* The Morals of Chess *(1779), and* The Dialogue Between Franklin and the Gout *(1780).*

As a moralist, shrewd observer of human affairs, and successful businessman, Franklin in his writings inevitably comments on work and money. He himself is an inspirational model of success in his Autobiography. *Also, he has sound counsel in* Poor Richard's Almanack *as well as in his essay* "Advice to a Young Tradesman" *(1762). The following selection is the preface to the 1758 edition of* Poor Richard's Almanack. *In it you will recognize many sayings that have become standard in our speech and thought.*

Courteous Reader,

1   I have heard that nothing gives an author so great pleasure as to find his works respectfully quoted by other learned authors. This pleasure I have seldom enjoyed; for though I have been, if I may say it without vanity, an eminent author of almanacs annually now a full quarter of a century, my brother authors in the same way, for what reason I know not, have ever been very sparing in their applause; and no other author has taken the least notice of me; so that, did not my writings produce me some solid pudding, the great deficiency of praise would have quite discouraged me.

2   I concluded at length that the people were the best judges of my merit, for they buy my works; and besides, in my rambles where I am not personally known, I have frequently heard one or other of my adages repeated, with "as Poor Richard says" at the end of it. This gave me some satisfaction, as it showed not only that my instructions were regarded, but discovered likewise some respect for my authority; and I own that, to encourage the practice of remembering and repeating those wise sentences, I have sometimes *quoted myself* with great gravity.

3   Judge, then, how much I must have been gratified by an incident I am going to relate to you. I stopped my horse lately where a great number of people were collected at a vendue [sale] of merchant goods. The hour of sale not being come, they were conversing on the badness of the times, and one of the company called to a plain, clean old man with white locks: "Pray, Father Abraham, what think you of the times? Won't these heavy taxes quite ruin the country? How shall we be ever able to pay them? What would you advise us to?" Father Abraham stood up and replied, "If

you'd have my advice, I'll give it you in short, for 'A word to the wise is enough,' and 'Many words won't fill a bushel,' as Poor Richard says." They joined in desiring him to speak his mind, and gathering round him, he proceeded as follows:

4   "Friends," says he, "and neighbors, the taxes are indeed very heavy, and if those laid on by the government were the only ones we had to pay, we might more easily discharge them; but we have many others, and much more grievous to some of us. We are taxed twice as much by our idleness, three times as much by our pride, and four times as much by our folly; and from these taxes the commissioners cannot ease or deliver us by allowing an abatement. However, let us hearken to good advice, and something may be done for us; 'God helps them that help themselves,' as Poor Richard says in his almanac of 1733.

5   "It would be thought a hard government that should tax its people one-tenth part of their time to be employed in its service. But idleness taxes many of us much more, if we reckon all that is spent in absolute sloth, or doing of nothing, with that which is spent in idle employments or amusements that amount to nothing. Sloth, by bringing on diseases, absolutely shortens life. 'Sloth, like rust, consumes faster than labor wears; while the used key is always bright,' as Poor Richard says. 'But dost thou love life? Then do not squander time; for that's the stuff life is made of,' as Poor Richard says. How much more than is necessary do we spend in sleep, forgetting that 'The sleeping fox catches no poultry,' and that 'There will be sleeping enough in the grave,' as Poor Richard says.

6   "'If time be of all things the most precious, wasting time must be,' as Poor Richard says, 'the greatest prodigality'; since, as he elsewhere tells us, 'Lost time is never found again'; and 'What we call time enough always proves little enough.' Let us then up and be doing, and doing to the purpose; so by diligence shall we do more with less perplexity. 'Sloth makes all things difficult, but industry all easy,' as Poor Richard says; and 'He that riseth late must trot all day, and shall scarce overtake his business at night'; while 'Laziness travels so slowly that poverty soon overtakes him,' as we read in Poor Richard, who adds, 'Drive thy business, let not that drive thee'; and 'Early to bed, and early to rise, makes a man healthy, wealthy, and wise.'

7   "So what signifies wishing and hoping for better times? We may make these times better if we bestir ourselves. 'Industry need not wish,' as Poor Richard says, and 'He that lives upon hope will die fasting.' 'There are no gains without pains'; 'Then help, hands, for I have no lands,' or if I have, they are smartly taxed. And, as Poor Richard likewise observes, 'He that hath a trade hath an estate; and he that hath a calling, hath an office of profit and honor'; but then the trade must be worked at, and the calling well followed, or neither the estate nor the office will enable us to pay our taxes. If we are industrious, we shall never starve; for, as Poor Richard says, 'At the workingman's house hunger looks in

but dares not enter.' Nor will the bailiff or the constable enter, for 'Industry pays debts, while despair increaseth them,' says Poor Richard. What though you have found no treasure, nor has any rich relation left you a legacy, 'Diligence is the mother of good luck,' as Poor Richard says, and 'God gives all things to industry.' 'Then plough deep while sluggards sleep, and you shall have corn to sell and keep,' says Poor Dick. Work while it is called today, for you know not how much you may be hindered tomorrow, which makes Poor Richard say, 'One today is worth two tomorrows,' and further, 'Have you somewhat to do tomorrow, do it today.' If you were a servant, would you not be ashamed that a good master should catch you idle? Are you then your own master? 'Be ashamed to catch yourself idle,' as Poor Dick says. When there is so much to be done for yourself, your family, your country, and your gracious king, be up by peep of day; 'Let not the sun look down and say, "Inglorious here he lies."' Handle your tools without mittens; remember that 'The cat in gloves catches no mice,' as Poor Richard says. 'Tis true there is much to be done, and perhaps you are weak-handed; but stick to it steadily, and you will see great effects, for 'Constant dropping wears away stones,' and 'By diligence and patience the mouse ate in two the cable'; and 'Little strokes fell great oaks,' as Poor Richard says in his almanac—the year I cannot just now remember.

8   "Methinks I hear some of you say, 'Must a man afford himself no leisure?' I will tell thee, my friend, what Poor Richard says: 'Employ thy time well, if thou meanest to gain leisure'; and, 'Since thou art not sure of a minute, throw not away an hour.' Leisure is time for doing something useful; this leisure the diligent man will obtain, but the lazy man never; so that, as Poor Richard says, 'A life of leisure and a life of laziness are two things.' Do you imagine that sloth will afford you more comfort than labor? No, for as Poor Richard says, 'Trouble springs from idleness, and grievous toil from needless ease.' 'Many, without labor, would live by their wits only, but they break for want of stock.' Whereas industry gives comfort, and plenty, and respect: 'Fly pleasures, and they'll follow you.' 'The diligent spinner has a large shift'; and, 'Now I have a sheep and a cow, everybody bids me good morrow'; all which is well said by Poor Richard.

9   "But with our industry we must likewise be steady, settled, and careful, and oversee our own affairs with our own eyes, and not trust too much to others; for, as Poor Richard says,

> I never saw an oft-removed tree,
> Nor yet an oft-removed family,
> That throve so well as those that settled be.

And again, 'Three removes is as bad as a fire'; and again, 'Keep thy shop, and thy shop will keep thee'; and again, 'If you would have your business done, go; if not, send.' And again,

He that by the plough would thrive
Himself must either hold or drive.

And again, 'The eye of a master will do more work than his hands'; and again, 'Want of care does us more damage than want of knowledge'; and again, 'Not to oversee workmen is to leave them your purse open.' Trusting too much to others' care is the ruin of many; for, as the almanac says, 'In the affairs of this world men are saved not by faith but by the want of it'; but a man's own care is profitable; for, saith Poor Dick, 'Learning is to the studious, and riches to the careful, as well as power to the bold, and heaven to the virtuous'; and further, 'If you would have a faithful servant and one that you like, serve yourself.' And again, he advises to circumspection and care, even in the smallest matters, because sometimes 'A little neglect may breed great mischief'; adding: 'For want of a nail the shoe was lost; for want of a shoe the horse was lost; and for want of a horse the rider was lost, being overtaken and slain by the enemy; all for want of care about a horseshoe nail.'

10   "So much for industry, my friends, and attention to one's own business; but to these we must add frugality if we would make our industry more certainly successful. A man may, if he knows not how to save as he gets, keep his nose all his life to the grindstone, and die not worth a groat at last. 'A fat kitchen makes a lean will,' as Poor Richard says; and

Many estates are spent in the getting,
Since women for tea forsook spinning and knitting,
And men for punch forsook hewing and splitting.

'If you would be wealthy,' says he in another almanac, 'think of saving as well as of getting: the Indies have not made Spain rich, because her outgoes are greater than her incomes.'

11   "Away then with your expensive follies, and you will not then have so much cause to complain of hard times, heavy taxes, and chargeable families; for, as Poor Dick says,

Women and wine, game and deceit
Make the wealth small and the wants great.

And further, 'What maintains one vice would bring up two children.' You may think, perhaps, that a little tea, or a little punch now and then, diet a little more costly, clothes a little finer, and a little entertainment now and then can be no great matter; but remember what Poor Richard says, 'Many a little makes a mickle'; and further, 'Beware of little expenses; a small leak will sink a great ship'; and again, 'Who dainties love, shall beggars prove'; and moreover, 'Fools make feasts, and wise men eat them.'

12   "Here you are all got together at this vendue of fineries and knick-knacks. You call them goods; but if you do not take care, they will prove evils to some of you. You expect they will be sold cheap, and perhaps they may for less than they cost; but if you have no occasion for them, they must be dear to you. Remember what Poor Richard says, 'Buy what thou hast no need of, and ere long thou shalt sell thy necessaries.' And again, 'At a great pennyworth pause a while.' He means that perhaps the cheapness is apparent only, and not real; or the bargain, by straitening thee in thy business, may do thee more harm than good. For in another place he says, 'Many have been ruined by buying good pennyworths.' Again, Poor Richard says, ''Tis foolish to lay out money in a purchase of repentance'; and yet this folly is practiced every day at vendues for want of minding the almanac. 'Wise men,' as Poor Dick says, 'learn by others' harms, fools scarcely by their own'; but *felix quem faciunt aliena pericula cautum* [fortunate the man who learns caution from the dangers of others]. Many a one, for the sake of finery on the back, have gone with a hungry belly and half starved their families. 'Silks and satins, scarlet and velvets,' as Poor Richard says, 'put out the kitchen fire.'

13   "These are not the necessaries of life; they can scarcely be called the conveniences; and yet, only because they look pretty, how many want to have them! The artificial wants of mankind thus become more numerous than the natural; and, as Poor Dick says, 'For one poor person, there are an hundred indigent.' By these and other extravagancies the genteel are reduced to poverty and forced to borrow of those whom they formerly despised, but who through industry and frugality have maintained their standing; in which case it appears plainly that 'A ploughman on his legs is higher than a gentleman on his knees,' as Poor Richard says. Perhaps they have had a small estate left them, which they knew not the getting of; they think 'tis day and will never be night, that a little to be spent out of so much is not worth minding. 'A child and a fool,' as Poor Richard says, 'imagine twenty shillings and twenty years can never be spent'; but 'Always taking out of the meal tub, and never putting in, soon comes to the bottom'; then as Poor Dick says, 'When the well's dry, they know the worth of water.' But this they might have known before if they had taken his advice. 'If you would know the value of money, go and try to borrow some'; or 'He that goes a borrowing goes a sorrowing'; and indeed so does he that lends to such people, when he goes to get it in again. Poor Dick further advises, and says,

> Fond pride of dress is sure a very curse;
> E'er fancy you consult, consult your purse.

And again, 'Pride is as loud a beggar as want, and a great deal more saucy.' When you have bought one fine thing, you must buy ten more, that your appearance may be all of a piece; but Poor Dick says, "'Tis easier to suppress the first desire than to satisfy all that follow it.' And 'tis as truly folly for the poor to ape the rich as for the frog to swell in order to equal the ox.

> Great estates may venture more,
> But little boats should keep near shore.

'Tis, however, a folly soon punished; for 'Pride that dines on vanity sups on contempt,' as Poor Richard says. And in another place, 'Pride breakfasted with plenty, dined with poverty, and supped with infamy.' And after all, of what use is this pride of appearance, for which so much is risked, so much is suffered? It cannot promote health, or ease pain; it makes no increase of merit in the person; it creates envy, it hastens misfortune.

> What is a butterfly? At best
> He's but a caterpillar drest.
> The gaudy fop's his picture just,

as Poor Richard says.

14   "But what madness must it be to run in debt for these superfluities! We are offered by the terms of this vendue six months' credit; and that perhaps has induced some of us to attend it, because we cannot spare the ready money and hope now to be fine without it. But, ah, think what you do when you run in debt; you give to another power over your liberty! If you cannot pay at the time, you will be ashamed to see your creditor; you will be in fear when you speak to him; you will make poor pitiful sneaking excuses, and by degrees come to lose your veracity, and sink into base downright lying; for, as Poor Richard says, 'The second vice is lying, the first is running in debt.' And again, to the same purpose, 'Lying rides upon debt's back.' Whereas a free-born Englishman ought not to be ashamed or afraid to see or speak to any man living. But poverty often deprives a man of all spirit and virtue; ''Tis hard for an empty bag to stand upright,' as Poor Richard truly says.

15   "What would you think of that prince or that government who should issue an edict forbidding you to dress like a gentleman or a gentlewoman on pain of imprisonment or servitude? Would you not say that you were free, have a right to dress as you please, and that such an edict would be a breach of your privileges, and such a government tyrannical? And yet you are about to put yourself under that tyranny, when you run in debt for such dress! Your creditor has authority at his pleasure to deprive you of your liberty by confining you in jail for life, or to sell you as a servant, if you should not be able to pay him! When you have got your bargain, you may perhaps think little of payment; but 'Creditors,' Poor

Richard tells us, 'have better memories than debtors'; and in another place says, 'Creditors are a superstitious sect, great observers of set days and times.' The day comes round before you are aware, and the demand is made before you are prepared to satisfy it; or, if you bear your debt in mind, the term which at first seemed so long will, as it lessens, appear extremely short. Time will seem to have added wings to his heels as well as shoulders. 'Those have a short Lent,' saith Poor Richard, 'who owe money to be paid at Easter.' Then since, as he says, 'The borrower is a slave to the lender, and the debtor to the creditor,' disdain the chain, preserve your freedom; and maintain your independency. Be industrious and free; be frugal and free. At present, perhaps, you may think yourself in thriving circumstances, and that you can bear a little extravagance without injury; but,

> For age and want, save while you may;
> No morning sun lasts a whole day,

as Poor Richard says. Gain may be temporary and uncertain, but ever while you live expense is constant and certain; and ''Tis easier to build two chimneys than to keep one in fuel,' as Poor Richard says. So, 'Rather go to bed supperless than rise in debt.'

> Get what you can, and what you get hold;
> ''Tis the stone that will turn all your lead into gold,

as Poor Richard says. And when you have got the philosopher's stone, sure you will no longer complain of bad times or the difficulty of paying taxes.

16   "This doctrine, my friends, is reason and wisdom; but after all, do not depend too much upon your own industry, and frugality, and prudence, though excellent things, for they may all be blasted without the blessing of Heaven; and therefore ask that blessing humbly, and be not uncharitable to those that at present seem to want it, but comfort and help them. Remember, Job suffered, and was afterwards prosperous.

17   "And now to conclude, 'Experience keeps a dear school, but fools will learn in no other, and scarce in that'; for it is true, 'We may give advice, but we cannot give conduct,' as Poor Richard says. However, remember this: 'They that won't be counseled can't be helped,' as Poor Richard says; and farther, that 'If you will not hear reason, she'll surely rap your knuckles.'"

18   Thus the old gentleman ended his harangue. The people heard it and approved the doctrine, and immediately practiced the contrary, just as if it had been a common sermon; for the vendue opened, and they began to buy extravagantly, notwithstanding all his cautions and their own fear of taxes. I found the good man had thoroughly studied my

almanacs and digested all I had dropped on these topics during the course of five-and-twenty years. The frequent mention he made of me must have tired anyone else, but my vanity was wonderfully delighted with it, though I was conscious that not a tenth part of the wisdom was my own which he ascribed to me, but rather the gleanings I had made of the sense of all ages and nations. However, I resolved to be the better for the echo of it; and though I had at first determined to buy stuff for a new coat, I went away resolved to wear my old one a little longer. Reader, if thou wilt do the same, thy profit will be as great as mine. I am, as ever, thine to serve thee.

Richard Saunders

VOCABULARY

eminent (P1), *adages* (P2), *discovered* (archaic sense) (P2), *own* (archaic) (P2), *gravity* (P2), *gratified* (P3), *vendue* (P3), *discharge* (P4), *abatement* (P4), *hearken* (P4), *sloth* (P5), *squander* (P5), *prodigality* (P6), *diligence* (P6), *perplexity* (P6), *industry* (P6), *signifies* (P7), *bestir* (P7), *office* (P7), *bailiff* (P7), *constable* (P7), *legacy* (P7), *sluggards* (P7), *peep* (P7), *methinks* (P8), *afford* (P8), *break* (P8), *shift* (P8), *throve* (P9), *removes* (P9), *want* (P9), *circumspection* (P9), *frugality* (P10), *groat* (P10), *mickle* (P11), *dainties* (P11), *knickknacks* (P12), *dear* (P12), *straitening* (P12), *indigent* (P13), *genteel* (P13), *fond* (archaic) (P13), *fancy* (P13), *saucy* (P13), *ape* (P13), *estates* (P13), *sups* (P13), *infamy* (P13), *fop* (P13), *superfluities* (P14), *induced* (P14), *veracity* (P14), *edict* (P15), *servitude* (P15), *breach* (P15), *sect* (P15), *Lent* (P15), *disdain* (P15), *philosopher's stone* (P15), *harangue* (P18), *ascribed* (P18), *gleanings* (P18)

IDEAS AND AIMS

1. How do the first and last paragraphs show that one of Franklin's aims in the essay is satire or irony?

2. Franklin's irony begins in the very first paragraph with Richard Saunders'— Poor Richard's—naiveté about why his "brother authors" who are "in the same way" (i.e., same line of work—almanac makers) have been "very sparing in their applause." What is the reason, that we can see, though Poor Richard can't? What criticism is Franklin making of the writing or almanac business here?

3. What, in Poor Richard's words, made his almanacs worthwhile to him?

4. Why, according to Poor Richard, does he occasionally resort to quoting himself? What good and bad traits in his personality or character does this reveal?

5. According to Father Abraham (P4), how many times are the people taxed? How does Father Abraham broaden the scope of the word "taxed"?

6. How does Father Abraham's recitation of Poor Richard's adages relate to the "multiple taxation" the old man refers to?

7. Why should one not depend completely upon reason and wisdom (P16)? What is "that blessing" referred to in P16?

8. According to Father Abraham, who or what will teach those who ignore these adages?

9. What traits of Poor Richard's character or personality are revealed by his heeding Father Abraham's "harangue" at the conclusion of the essay? How is Franklin endorsing the efficacy of the almanac and the reliability of the almanac maker here?

10. What character or personality traits of the common people are revealed by how they respond to Father Abraham's "harangue"? How is Poor Richard's response used as a foil to theirs?

11. Overall, in light of the crowd's response to the "harangue," what would Franklin's answer be to why more people don't attain wealth?

ORGANIZATION AND FORM

1. How do PP1–3, PP3–17, and P18 form the introduction, body, and conclusion, respectively, of Franklin's piece?

2. Within Father Abraham's "harangue," what paragraphs form the introduction, body, and conclusion, respectively? How do certain of Father Abraham's words clearly delineate these three parts for his audience?

3. What are the several headings and subheadings into which Father Abraham classifies or arranges Poor Richard's sayings? Where does Father Abraham explicitly point to these headings and subheadings?

4. How are Father Abraham's headings organized or sequenced logically in the essay?

5. Within any given paragraph, see if you can find some logic in the arrangement of Father Abraham's collection of Poor Richard's sayings. Are they merely inserted randomly in every paragraph?

WORDS AND STYLE

1. Some of Poor Richard's adages are based on metaphors or similes (comparisons cast in figurative language) such as "Sloth, like rust . . ." (P5). (Look up the technical literary terms in your collegiate dictionary or composition handbook.) List several examples, and choose one or two to explain how they clarify Father Abraham's point.

2. Some of Poor Richard's adages are based on personifications—particularly personification of abstractions—such as "Pride is as loud a beggar as want . . ."

(P13). (Look up these terms in your collegiate dictionary or composition handbook.) List several examples, and choose one or two to explain how they clarify Father Abraham's point.

3. Some of Poor Richard's and Father Abraham's adages are based on punning, such as "you call them goods; but if you do not take care, they will prove evils to some of you" (P12). (Look up "pun" in your collegiate dictionary or composition handbook.) List examples, and choose one or two to explain how they clarify Father Abraham's point.

4. Some of Poor Richard's adages are based on grammar, specifically parallelism ("trouble springs from idleness, and grievous toil from needless ease" [P8]), chiasmus ("drive thy business, let not that drive thee" [P6]), and antithesis ("wise men learn by others' harms, fools scarcely by their own" [P12]). (Look up these terms in your collegiate dictionary or composition handbook.) List examples, and choose one or two to explain how they clarify Father Abraham's point.

5. Point out examples of the use of paradox, rhyme, and miniaturized beast fables in the adages, and analyze how one or two help clarify Father Abraham's point.

6. Where and how does Father Abraham use the interrogative (question) sentence effectively? What other features of his style, apart from the adages he quotes, are highly oratorical (including the use of polysyllabic words)? Cite examples.

DISCUSSION AND WRITING

1. There are no longer any debtors' prisons to fear. Have any other changes occurred that might make any of these adages incorrect? Have any new adages been added to these lists of ways to wealth?

2. Some commentators have made much of the fact that some of these adages contradict each other. Do any of these contradict each other? If so, which ones?

3. Have you ever had an experience that illustrated the truth—or the falsity— of any of Poor Richard's adages?

4. The meaning of some of Poor Richard's adages may be obscure to you. Make a list of the ones you don't understand (noting the paragraph in which they occur) and see if you can collaborate with one or more classmates in puzzling them out.

5. In comparable circumstances, would you behave, or have you behaved, more like the crowd at the auction or Poor Richard, in P18? Why?

6. Using Franklin's writing as a model, concoct some of your own adages about school (" _____ passes tests, but _____ fails them" or "the _____ teacher assigns the _____ paper") or work ("work _____ on Fridays as you _____ Mondays").

THE ALMIGHTY DOLLAR

W. H. Auden

Like writers Henry James and T. S. Eliot, Wystan Hugh Auden (1907–1973) was an Anglo-American, quite evenly divided between the two countries and claimed by each as a major author in its literature. Though born in Britain and educated at Oxford University, Auden emigrated to the United States in 1939 and became a citizen in 1946. Thereafter, he divided his time among America, England, and Continental Europe.

That both the United States and Britain would like to count him among their authors is not surprising, considering his virtuosity. While he is best known for his accomplishment as one of the great twentieth-century poets, he also did exceptional work as playwright, opera librettist, translator, anthologist, critic, and essayist. His main prose works are Education, Today and Tomorrow *(1939),* The Enchafed Flood *(1950),* The Dyer's Hand *(1962),* Selected Essays *(1964),* Secondary Worlds *(1968),* A Certain World: A Commonplace Book *(1970), and* Forewords and Afterwords *(1973).*

From the beginning of his career Auden was a socially and politically committed writer, and some of that kind of concern may be seen in this selection, which has been reprinted from The Dyer's Hand. *As with Henry James, Auden's background in both American and European cultures gives him insight in comparing and contrasting the two.*

1 Political and technological developments are rapidly obliterating all cultural differences and it is possible that, in a not remote future, it will be impossible to distinguish human beings living on one area of the earth's surface from those living on any other, but our different pasts have not yet been completely erased and cultural differences are still perceptible. The most striking difference between an American and a European is the difference in their attitudes towards money. Every European knows, as a matter of historical fact, that in Europe wealth could only be acquired at the expense of other human beings, either by conquering them or by exploiting their labor in factories. Further, even after the Industrial Revolution began, the number of persons who could rise from poverty to wealth was small; the vast majority took it for granted that they would not be much richer nor poorer than their fathers. In consequence, no European associates wealth with personal merit or poverty with personal failure.

2 To a European, money means power, the freedom to do as he likes, which also means that, consciously or unconsciously, he says: "I want to have as much money as possible myself and others to have as little money as possible."

3 In the United States, wealth was also acquired by stealing, but the real exploited victim was not a human being but poor Mother Earth and her creatures who were ruthlessly plundered. It is true that the Indians were expropriated or exterminated, but this was not, as it had always been in Europe, a matter of the conquerer seizing the wealth of the conquered, for the Indian had never realized the potential riches of his country. It is also true that, in the Southern states, men lived on the labor of slaves, but slave labor did not make them fortunes; what made slavery in the South all the more inexcusable was that, in addition to being morally wicked, it didn't even pay off handsomely.

4 Thanks to the natural resources of the country, every American, until quite recently, could reasonably look forward to making more money than his father, so that, if he made less, the fault must be his; he was either lazy or inefficient. What an American values, therefore, is not the possession of money as such, but his power to make it as proof of his manhood; once he has proved himself by making it, it has served its function and can be lost or given away. In no society in history have rich men given away so large a part of their fortunes. A poor American feels guilty at being poor, but less guilty than an American *rentier* who had inherited wealth but is doing nothing to increase it; what can the latter do but take to drink and psychoanalysis?

5 In the Fifth Circle on the Mount of Purgatory, I do not think that many Americans will be found among the Avaricious; but I suspect that

the Prodigals may be almost an American colony. The great vice of Americans is not materialism but a lack of respect for matter.

VOCABULARY

obliterating (P1), *perceptible* (P1), *exploiting* (P1), *Industrial Revolution* (P1), *plundered* (P3), *expropriated* (P3), *exterminated* (P3), *rentier* (P4), *Purgatory* (P5), *Avaricious* (P5), *Prodigals* (P5), *materialism* (P5)

IDEAS AND AIMS

1. What is Auden's central idea? Where is it stated in a thesis sentence?
2. What was the source of European wealth? What was the source of American wealth, according to Auden?
3. What, then, caused the difference in American and European attitudes toward money?
4. What, exactly, is the European attitude toward money?
5. What is the American attitude toward money?
6. Why have wealthy Americans insisted on giving away so much of their wealth?
7. In the final analysis, are Americans really as materialistic, according to Auden, as they have been accused of being? Why or why not?
8. In the last paragraph of his essay Auden could have placed human avarice in Dante's Inferno, where it can also be found, as well as in the Purgatory of Dante's *Divine Comedy*. Why do you suppose he chooses Purgatory for locating avarice and prodigality (the latter can also be found in Dante's Inferno) rather than Inferno? What view of human nature or life might this imply?

ORGANIZATION AND FORM

1. In which paragraphs does Auden discuss Europeans, and in which ones Americans? Which is he more interested in, as suggested by both the relative proportions of space he allots each culture as well as by the title of his essay?
2. Where in the essay does Auden use cause-and-effect analysis? Does he use it well in these instances?
3. How is P3 structured to handle argument and counterargument?
4. In your opinion, is Auden's essay, as an argumentative or persuasive essay, strengthened or weakened in its effect on the reader by the phrasing of his generalizations in the third sentence of P1 ("Every European knows . . .") and the last sentence of the same paragraph ("no European associates . . .")?

5. In what way does the conclusion of Auden's essay represent an extension or development of his central thesis rather than a mere restatement of it?

WORDS AND STYLE

1. Auden uses "slanted" or "charged" words in this essay—that is, words with strong positive or negative connotations or associations. Besides "poor" in "poor Mother Earth" (P3), what other instances can you find, and are they used effectively?
2. How is Auden's wry or ironic tone partly expressed by the matter-of-fact way the first sentence of P3 opens (up to "stealing")? What view of human nature is implied here?
3. How is Auden's wry or ironic tone expressed by the phrasing and sentiment of the last half of the concluding sentence of P3? By the equation created by "and" in "drink and psychoanalysis" in the last sentence of P4?
4. Look up "epigram" and "epigrammatic" in your college desk dictionary. How is the concluding sentence of Auden's essay "epigrammatic"? What does it mean, exactly?
5. How is Auden using the device of allusion in his last paragraph? How does it contribute effectively to the essay?

DISCUSSION AND WRITING

1. In your college library, find Max Weber's *The Protestant Ethic and the Spirit of Capitalism* and R. H. Tawney's *Religion and the Rise of Capitalism*. From reading either or both of these books, what can you say about Auden's generalization in the last sentence of P1?
2. Do you agree with Auden's analysis of American attitudes toward money? Why or why not?
3. Philanthropists who give large sums of money to various causes receive a great deal of attention and publicity. But are most other Americans really as prodigal, in this sense, as Auden claims? Can you provide examples to support your point of view?
4. There is another sense in which "prodigal" means "wasteful," particularly in regard to natural resources, as Auden remarks in P3 and P4. Are American attitudes toward prodigal use of natural resources changing? How or why?
5. In an essay, compare and contrast a friend's or relative's "philosophy of money" with yours, using Auden's essay as a model.

HIGH WAGES
AND OVERWORK

Adam Smith

□

*See the introduction to Adam Smith's "Of the Origin and Use of Money,"
pages 147-48. Like the preceding selection by Smith, this one is taken from his
monumental study* The Wealth of Nations, *published in 1776. This self-
contained excerpt from Chapter viii ("Of the Wages of Labor") of Book I,
shows an eighteenth-century preference for the very long paragraph, which
might be well to call to mind in our age of the opposite extreme, with business
letters or advertisements made up of nothing but cluttered one-sentence paragraphs.*

1 The liberal reward of labour, as it encourages the propagation, so it
increases the industry of the common people. The wages of labour are the
encouragement of industry, which like every other human quality,
improves in proportion to the encouragement it receives. A plentiful subsistence increases the bodily strength of the labourer, and the comfortable hope of bettering his condition, and of ending his days perhaps in
ease and plenty, animates him to exert that strength to the utmost.
Where wages are high, accordingly, we shall always find the workmen
more active, diligent, and expeditious, than where they are low; in
England, for example, than in Scotland; in the neighbourhood of great

towns, than in remote country places. Some workmen, indeed, when they can earn in four days what will maintain them through the week, will be idle the other three. This, however, is by no means the case with the greater part. Workmen, on the contrary, when they are liberally paid by the piece, are very apt to over-work themselves, and to ruin their health and constitution in a few years. A carpenter in London, and in some other places, is not supposed to last in his utmost vigour above eight years. Something of the same kind happens in many other trades, in which the workmen are paid by the piece; as they generally are in manufactures, and even in country labour, wherever wages are higher than ordinary. Almost every class of artificers is subject to some peculiar infirmity occasioned by excessive application to their peculiar species of work. Ramuzzini, an eminent Italian physician, has written a particular book concerning such diseases. We do not reckon our soldiers the most industrious set of people among us. Yet when soldiers have been employed in some particular sorts of work, and liberally paid by the piece, their officers have frequently been obliged to stipulate with the undertaker, that they should not be allowed to earn above a certain sum every day, according to the rate at which they were paid. Till this stipulation was made, mutual emulation and the desire of greater gain, frequently prompted them to over-work themselves, and to hurt their health by excessive labour. Excessive application during four days of the week, is frequently the real cause of the idleness of the other three, so much and so loudly complained of. Great labour, either of mind or body, continued for several days together, is in most men naturally followed by a great desire of relaxation, which, if not restrained by force or by some strong necessity, is almost irresistible. It is the call of nature, which requires to be relieved by some indulgence, sometimes of ease only, but sometimes too of dissipation and diversion. If it is not complied with, the consequences are often dangerous, and sometimes fatal, and such as almost always, sooner or later, bring on the peculiar infirmity of the trade. If masters would always listen to the dictates of reason and humanity, they have frequently occasion rather to moderate, than to animate the application of many of their workmen. It will be found, I believe, in every sort of trade, that the man who works so moderately, as to be able to work constantly, not only preserves his health the longest, but, in the course of the year, executes the greatest quantity of work.

VOCABULARY

propagation, industry, subsistence, comfortable, animates, exert, diligent, expeditious, apt, constitution, vigour, artificers, peculiar, infirmity, particular, stipulate, undertaker, emulation, indulgence, dissipation, diversion, dictates, moderate, application, executes

IDEAS AND AIMS

1. What is the author's attitude toward the working poor?
2. What is the chief disadvantage of pay "by the piece"?
3. What is the relationship between "industry" and high wages?
4. What is the danger of too liberal a wage?
5. What is the author's attitude toward recreation, time off from labor?
6. In the final analysis, why is moderation on the job necessary?
7. Supply the rest of Smith's chain of reasoning: (a) high wages encourage more labor; (b) piecework supplies the greatest possible wage, so it encourages the most labor; (c) the most labor a worker can physically do will cause _____; (d) therefore, _____.
8. How does Smith argue in the selection against both too high *and* too low a wage?

ORGANIZATION AND FORM

1. What are the main parts of the selection?
2. How does Smith use comparison and contrast as a method of analysis and development?
3. Where does Smith argue inductively? (Look up "induction" in your collegiate dictionary or composition handbook.)
4. Where does Smith use cause and effect as a method of analysis and development? Where does he use illustration and example?
5. How does the conclusion of the selection extend or develop the introduction rather than merely repeating or restating it?

WORDS AND STYLE

1. What is the tone of the paragraph? How do Smith's words and style contribute to that tone?
2. How does Smith use parallelism effectively to help express his ideas, as in the first sentence ("as it . . . so it") and fourth sentence ("in England . . . places")? (Look up parallelism in your dictionary or composition handbook.)
3. How does Smith use, in particular, the symmetrical paralleling of pairs, as in "hope of bettering his condition . . . plenty"? How does this affect the tone or emotional quality of his writing?

4. How does Smith use balance in sentences, as in "Great labor . . . relaxation"? How are parallelism and balance, which allow the weighing of one thing with another, in accord with Smith's purpose of weighing one thing with another in this selection? How does all this affect the tone or emotional quality of Smith's writing?

DISCUSSION AND WRITING

1. Contrast the modern view of wages and recreation with the one offered in this selection. In what ways do our ideas differ from those of Adam Smith?

2. How does the currently popular concept of professional "burnout" compare with what Smith was discussing in the eighteenth century? Would Smith's solution to overwork be effective for today's professionals and workers? Why or why not?

3. Do you agree with those whom Smith cites as believing that workers will overwork four days to take off three, or with Smith, who believes that the three-day hiatus following four days of overwork is an inevitable physiological consequence? Cite examples in your answer. Which of these two analyses of workers would you apply to yourself? Why?

THE BIG PUZZLE: Who Makes What and Why?

Frank Trippett

□

A journalist since 1948, Frank Trippett (born in 1926) has served as an editor at both Newsweek *and* Look *magazines, and as a freelance author has published several books and essays. The latter have regularly been appearing in the* Time *essay department, and thence, because of their liveliness and original turns of thought, in essay anthologies. The blend of formal and informal levels of usage in the following selection, plus its citation of facts and authorities, is aimed at the readership of newsmagazines.*

1 Why on earth should Muhammad Ali get $5 million for one night's performance when college professors average only $24,400 a year? Or why should a Johnny Carson be paid a fortune ($3 million-plus a year) while only peanuts, comparatively, go to the workers who happen to keep the TV industry operating? Such questions from typical Americans are familiar. The tone is usually perplexed and often indignant. And no wonder: the pattern of personal income in the U.S. is riddled with wide and often bewildering disparities.

2 These become joltingly clear in any random sampling of typical wages and salaries across the country *(see box)*. They are likely to turn up in any payroll. Persisting differences in wage scales can be catalogued by

race, by sex, by age; striking gaps from region to region are commonplace. It is not hard to understand varying pay for different occupations, but within each trade and profession occur radical differences in earnings that baffle even scholarly experts. Moreover, beyond and above all such helter-skelter inequalities, the nation's overall distribution of income, it seems to many economists, is conspicuously out of whack.

3   Today's income distribution, though lopsided, is not substantially different from what it was at the turn of the century. Every class of Americans is generally better off, but the actual apportioning of the bigger pie has changed little. Today slightly smaller slices go to the bottom and top fifths of the population, while those in the middle get a slightly larger portion. This means, by the latest complete Census Bureau survey of the nation's 56.2 million families, that in 1975 the best-paid fifth (earning $20,487 and up) received 43.4% of all income, while the lowest fifth (earning less than $5,018) got 4.3% of the total.

4   Such is the Big Picture. The main criticism of it is a familiar old blues song: the system favors the well-off and rich while leaving the poor irremediably poor. Arthur Okun, a member of the *Time* Board of Economists, considers the distribution of income and wealth, with its bias against the poor, "invidious and inhumane." Economist Robert Heilbroner of New York City's New School for Social Research protests for the same reason, but also thinks inequalities in the system are so sharp, glaring and pervasive that it is a "perennial puzzle" that a democratic society puts up with it.

5   It is not puzzling that Americans accept inequality as such. Capitalism, after all, requires a hierarchy of unequal rewards as an essential source of the incentives that keep Adam Smith's "invisible hand"—and the economic apparatus—working. Although the nation preaches the ideal of equal opportunity and increasingly tries to practice it, inequality of achievement and reward is embedded in the American scheme and seldom questioned by the public. Says Economics Professor Robert J. Lampman of the University of Wisconsin: "Americans don't really seek any particular degree of income equality." And the public, Lampman adds, is not so much interested in the Big Picture as in "particular differences."

6   The most spectacular of these, when viewed personally and from below, can inspire wonderment and envy. Who could not feel underpaid when contemplating the $1.662 million that Harry J. Gray made last year as chief executive of United Technologies? In the face of such sums, ordinary Americans may ward off envy by remembering that they are also rewarded with "psychic income" (community regard, the feeling of being useful). Yet given the news that Marlon Brando is getting $2.25 million for 12 days of playacting—well, which of the vast hand-to-mouth crowd will not wonder whether psychic income is really preferable to a tax problem?

7   Many Americans are displeased by what certain disparities seem to disclose about social values. To these, prevalent pay differentials, taken as an index of the social soul, seem to prove, for example, that the nation cherishes professional teachers far less than professional athletes. Or, more broadly, that society generally values members who do its most serious work not nearly as much as the actors, clowns and jocks whose task is merely to distract and amuse. But this handy method of social soul searching is not reliable. Far more directly, income differences reflect the operations of the marketplace.

8   The pattern actually takes its shape out of several marketplaces because, in reality, the nation's wages, salaries and other rewards are established not by one system but an arrangement of several. There are different systems for business and industry, for independent professions, for government, for show biz. Each system expresses different values and sets rewards by different standards.

A RANDOM SAMPLE OF PAY

Herewith a random sampling of salaries or other earnings received during 1976 (not including bonuses and other special compensation):

Trial lawyer; Washington, D.C.	$500,000
Chairman, Dow Chemical Co.	$453,000
Basketball star; New York City	$325,000
Publisher, Boston *Globe*	$147,200
Senior vice president, Anheuser-Busch, Inc.	$115,000
Disc jockey; Detroit	$100,000
Flight captain, Boeing 747	$80,000
Anesthesiologist; New York City	$70,000
Charter fishing-boat skipper; Miami	$60,000
U.S. Senator	$57,500
President, United Auto Workers	$43,550
Civilian astronaut	$33,800
Long-haul truck driver	$30,000
History professor, University of Virginia	$30,000
Violinist, Boston Symphony Orchestra	$24,800
Junior high school teacher; Evanston, Ill.	$19,500
Garbage collector; New York City	$16,350
Assembly-line worker, General Motors	$14,860
Assistant professor, Yale University	$14,750
Bus driver; Atlanta	$13,500
Brick mason; Charlottesville, Va.	$12,000
Minister, United Church of Christ; Chicago	$10,500
Textile weaver; Roanoke Rapids, N.C.	$9,980
Sewing-machine operator; New York City	$6,720
Bartender; Seattle	$2,500

9   Consider, say, the big gap between the pay of the Chief Executive of the U.S. ($200,000 plus housing), and the chief executive of General Motors ($950,000, including bonus and stock options). Does it mean that society feels that what is good enough for the nation is not nearly good enough for GM? Hardly. The disparity can be tracked not to some hidden spectrum of social values but to two distinct systems of compensation. In business, pay levels are established by clear criteria toward the equally clear purpose of increasing production and profit; by and large, the system rewards most those most crucial to fulfilling that purpose. On the other hand, in government, which serves perennially disputed purposes—with results beyond measure—the salary scale reflects nothing more precise than the politicians' best guess at the maximum the public will tolerate.

10   The system embracing professionals (independent doctors, lawyers, dentists, engineers) is something else again. Their earnings, though broadly determined by the general marketplace, are also subject to the influences of an intimate psychological marketplace, one in which intangibles of repute and character are bought and sold along with knowledge and service. Some professionals also manipulate their market by limiting their own numbers—in the way that physicians do through their control of professional education and licensing.

11   No system seems as bizarre as that of show biz. Sums paid the big stars appear surreal when compared with other salaries. But the trouble is, such comparisons are specious. For in reimbursing a star, whether of stage, screen or playing field, the entertainment industry is not really paying an employee so much as making a capital appropriation. It is not by chance that in show biz a popular figure is called a hot "property." The star actually is the product to be sold. That the price of such properties has soared is not surprising in a personality-craving society in which the big stars fulfill a public symbolic role once reserved to royalty. The cost of offering the star to the public can be fairly compared only with sums spent by a manufacturer for the development of new merchandise for sale.

12   Each system is marked by its own peculiar inequalities. Those associated with race, sex and age can be counted simply as signs of persisting discrimination. Most regional differences are hangovers from historical divergencies in regional economies. Some disparities, however, simply defy rationalization. M.I.T. Economist Lester Thurow in his book *Generating Inequality* points to extreme variations in income among auto mechanics of roughly equal training and age—along with similarly extreme variations in the earnings of comparable physicians. Why such differences? Nobody has figured it out.

13   The biggest executive salaries, say compensation experts, tend to go to business leaders who, in addition to being crucial to the turning of profit, also demonstrate the capacity to take risks (this even though stu-

dents of corporate gamesmanship say that those at the top often survive by not risking too much along the climb). Certainly the biggest blue-collar pay goes to workers who have most effectively improved their competitive position by organization—and recently blue collars have won ascendancy over poorly organized white collars in average salary. In all systems, the factor of supply and demand is at work as an influence if not an iron law—even in show biz. The great majority of performers earn meager sums, primarily because of the excessive supply of aspirants. For them, as Economics Professor Clair Vickery of the University of California's Institute of Industrial Relations in Berkeley puts it, a performing job is like "buying a ticket in a lottery." It mainly feeds the dream of that legendary Big Break that could bring them the juicy tax problems of a star.

14   In the end, a certain dream underlies the whole scheme of compensation. Its helter-skelter character, after all, is an expression of one overriding national value: the libertarian ideal. It is the intentional absence of central control that produces the unevenness of the final result. The very elasticity that Americans seem to value most produces the disparities that most annoy them: it is at the root of the social and economic mobility that is the very essence of the American scheme.

15   There will continue to be amazement at glaring inequalities, and of course there should be indignation over the plight of the millions of Americans who are either unemployed or existing in poverty. But even if the situation of these worst-off is ameliorated, as it should be, it is likely that the whole system of who makes what and why in America will always seem a puzzle.

VOCABULARY:

perplexed (P1), *indignant* (P1), *disparities* (P1), *conspicuously* (P2), *irremediably* (P4), *invidious* (P4), *pervasive* (P4), *perennial* (P4), *hierarchy* (P5), *incentives* (P5), *psychic* (P6), *prevalent* (P7), *spectrum* (P9), *intangibles* (P10), *repute* (P10), *bizarre* (P11), *specious* (P11), *capital appropriation* (P11), *divergencies* (P12), *gamesmanship* (P13), *ascendancy* (P13), *aspirants* (P13), *libertarian* (P14), *ameliorated* (P15)

IDEAS AND AIMS

1. Which are the causes and which are the effects in Trippett's essay?
2. How many causes does Trippett explore? List them.
3. Besides the existence of different compensation systems, what inequalities exist within these systems? List them.

4. What paradox of cause and effect, particularly relevant to pay inequality, does Trippett claim will make compensation in America remain a puzzle?
5. Overall, would you say that Trippett is in favor of, opposed to, or neutral about the present salary scales in the United States? How can you tell?

ORGANIZATION AND FORM

1. Why does Trippett begin his essay with the particular example he does? How is it a good opening example?
2. Does Trippett's essay begin with cause or with effect? In light of his main point about "who gets what and why," which would be the better choice, and why?
3. Which paragraphs develop the topic of the range of current salaries?
4. Where is the first *specific* instance of a wide disparity in pay? The second?
5. In which paragraph does Trippett begin to explore the causes of these disparities?
6. What sentence in the essay serves to link the sections describing effects and the sections describing their causes?
7. One of the linking devices helping to create coherence in and between paragraphs, repetition of key terms (and synonyms), is much in evidence in this essay. What words are repeated, helping to bind the essay together and bring its central ideas into focus?

WORDS AND STYLE

1. What ideas does the author try to suggest, and how, by capitalizing "Big Picture" (P4) and "Big Break" (P13)?
2. In what ways is Trippett's style a blend of the standard or formal level of usage and the colloquial or informal? Why might Trippett have chosen this style with regard to his specific readers and subject?
3. In what ways is Trippett's style both lively and very concrete (or illustrative)?

DISCUSSION AND WRITING

1. From Trippett's random chart listing occupations and salaries, choose a particular job not discussed in Trippett's essay (e.g., bartender, garbage collector, flight captain) and try to analyze the reasons for the salary and to decide whether the salary is fair.
2. For a particular part-time or full-time job you have now or have had previously, itemize all the tasks and skills involved and discuss whether you think the salary was commensurate with the skills demanded.

3. What disparities in pay are you aware of in your experience? Write an essay in which you explore, as did Trippett in his essay, the possible causes of the disparities.

4. What in P4 of Trippett's essay seems in accord with Adam Smith's ideas in "High Wages and Overwork"? Which author finds more causes for paying high salaries? Which essay is right, in your opinion? Could both authors be correct?

TAKING STOCK: COMPARING AND CONTRASTING THE SELECTIONS

1. Many people have heard the proverb that "money is the root of all evil." Actually, what the author of the New Testament "First Letter of Paul to Timothy" wrote was, "But those who desire to be rich fall into temptation, into a snare, into many senseless and hurtful desires that plunge men into ruin and destruction. For the love of money is the root of all evils; it is through this craving that some have wandered away from the faith and pierced their hearts with many pangs" (vi. 9-10). In contrast to this thought, what benefits does money or the desire for money bring to mankind or society, according to Adam Smith in "Of the Origin and Use of Money," Benjamin Franklin, and W. H. Auden?

2. How might Franklin, as well as Calvin (Section 1, "Job Choice and Self-Fulfillment") and Fuller (Section 2, "Work and Morality"), argue that the possession or acquisition of money is actually a sign of virtue, rather than the opposite?

3. According to Adam Smith, Benjamin Franklin, W. H. Auden, and Frank Trippett, what psychological, social, or political ills for the individual or group may be associated with a money-minded economy?

4. Franklin gives several tips about acquiring and spending money. Which of his ideas do you think would be most helpful to your economic circumstances now? Which in the future, or for your intended care r?

5. In what ways do Trippett and Adam Smith (in "High Wages and Overwork") concur or differ about the ill effects of high salaries or wages?

6. Compare Smith's remark in "High Wages and Overwork" about "mutual emulation" (in the sentence beginning "Till this stipulation was made, mutual emulation . . .") with Hesiod's view in "Two Kinds of Competition" (Section 2, "Work and Morality").

7. Contrast Smith and Hesiod (see the preceding question) with Buchwald in "Before the Ax Falls" (Section 6, "Job Opportunities and Other Practical Matters"), on the benefits or drawbacks of competitiveness in the workplace.

8. Compare what Trippett says in P10 about some professionals manipulating their market by "limiting their own numbers" with facts that
   you can gather from current events sources in the library (considering
   such categories as physicians, lawyers, Ph.D's, teachers, and so on).
   Also, read Joseph Addison's *Spectator* No. 21, available in your college
   library. Which author seems closest to the mark in the mid-1980s or
   1990s? Can Trippett's and Addison's assertions about overcrowding in
   the professions be reconciled?

Note: See also Discussion and Writing question 4 of Smith's "High Wages and
Overwork," and question 4 of Trippett's "The Big Puzzle: Who Makes What and
Why?"

JOB OPPORTUNITIES AND OTHER PRACTICAL MATTERS

HOW TO LAND THE JOB YOU WANT

Davidyne Mayleas

□

Author of a book on second marriages and coauthor of The Hidden Job Market: A System to Beat the System *(1976), Davidyne Mayleas is a free-lance writer. This selection is an article published in* The Reader's Digest, *and it has many of the features of journalism for publications aimed at the mass audience: short paragraphs, arabic numerals to set off sections, and typographical devices like small capitals and italics to set off main headings and subheadings.*

1 Louis Albert, 39, lost his job as an electrical engineer when his firm made extensive cutbacks. He spent two months answering classified ads and visiting employment agencies—with zero results. Albert might still be hunting if a friend, a specialist in the employment field, had not shown him how to be his own job counselor. Albert learned how to research unlisted openings, write a forceful résumé, perform smoothly in an interview, even transform a turndown into a job.

2 Although there seemed to be a shortage of engineering jobs, Albert realized that he still persuaded potential employers to see him. This taught him something—that his naturally outgoing personality might be as great an asset as his engineering degree. When the production head of a small electronics company told him that they did not have an immediate opening, Albert told his interviewer, "You people make a fine product. I think you could use additional sales representation—someone like me who understands and talks electrical engineer's language, and who enjoys selling." The interviewer decided to send Albert to a senior vice president. Albert got a job in sales.

3 You too can be your own counselor if you put the same vigorous effort into *getting* a job as you would into *keeping* one. Follow these three basic rules, developed by placement experts:

4 1. FIND THE HIDDEN JOB MARKET. Classified ads and agency listings reveal only a small percentage of available jobs. Some of the openings that occur through promotions, retirements and reorganization never reach the personnel department. There are three ways to get in touch with this hidden market:

5 *Write a strong résumé with a well-directed cover letter and mail it to the appropriate department manager in the company where you'd like to work.* Don't worry whether there's a current opening. Many managers fill vacancies by reviewing the résumés already in their files. Dennis Mollura, press-relations manager in the public-relations department of American Telephone and Telegraph, says, "In my own case, the company called me months after I sent in my résumé."

6 *Get in touch with people who work in or know the companies that interest you.* Jobs are so often filled through personal referral that Charles R. Lops, executive employment manager of the J.C. Penney Co., says, "Probably our best source for outside people comes from recommendations made by Penney associates themselves."

7 *"Drop in" on the company.* Lillian Reveille, employment manager of Equitable Life Assurance Society of the United States, reports: "A large

percentage of the applicants we see are 'walk-ins'—and we do employ many of these people."

8   2. LOCATE HIDDEN OPENINGS. This step requires energy and determination to make telephone calls, see people, do research, and to keep moving despite turndowns.

9   *Contact anyone who may know of openings,* including relatives, friends, teachers, bank officers, insurance agents—anyone you know in your own or an adjacent field. When the teachers' union and employment agencies produced no teaching openings, Eric Olson, an unemployed high-school math instructor, reviewed his talent and decided that where an analytical math mind was useful, there he'd find a job. He called his insurance agent, who set up an interview with the actuarial department of one of the companies he represented. They hired Olson.

10   It's a good idea to contact not only professional or trade associations in your field, but also your local chamber of commerce and people involved in community activities. After Laura Bailey lost her job as retirement counselor in a bank's personnel department, she found a position in customer relations in another bank. Her contact: a member of the senior-citizens club that Mrs. Bailey ran on a volunteer basis.

11   *Use local or business-school libraries.* Almost every field has its own directory of companies, which provides names, addresses, products and/or services, and lists officers and other executives. Write to the company president or to the executive to whom you'd report. The vice president of personnel at Warner-Lambert Co. says, "When a résumé of someone we could use—now or in the near future—shows up 'cold' in my in-basket, that's luck for both of us."

12   *Consult telephone directories.* Sometimes the telephone company will send you free the telephone directories of various cities. Also, good-sized public libraries often have many city directories. Fred Lewis, a cabinet maker, checked the telephone directories of nine different cities where he knew furniture was manufactured. At the end of five weeks he had a sizable telephone bill, some travel expenses—and ten interviews which resulted in three job offers.

13   3. AFTER YOU FIND THE OPENING, GET THE JOB. The applicants who actually get hired are those who polish these six job-getting skills to perfection.

14   *Compose a better résumé.* A résumé is a self-advertisement, designed to get you an interview. Start by putting yourself in an employer's place. Take stock of your job history and personal achievements. Make an inventory of your skills and accomplishments that might be useful from the employer's standpoint. Choose the most important and describe them in words that stress accomplishments. Avoid such phrases as "my duties included. . ." Use action words like planned, sold, trained, managed.

15   Ask a knowledgeable business friend to review your résumé. Does it stress accomplishment rather than duties? Does it tell an employer what you can do for him? Can it be shortened? (One or two pages should suffice.) Generally, it's not wise to mention salary requirements.

16   *Write a convincing cover letter.* While the résumé may be a copy, the cover letter must be personal. Sy Mann, director of research for Aceto Chemical Co., says: "When I see a mimeographed letter that states, 'Dear Sir, I'm sincerely interested in working for your company,' I wonder, 'How many other companies got this valentine?'" Use the name and title of the person who can give you the interview, and be absolutely certain of accuracy here. Using a wrong title or misspelling a prospective employer's name may route your correspondence directly to an automatic turndown.

17   *Prepare specifically for each interview.* Research the company thoroughly; know its history and competition. Try to grasp the problems of the job you're applying for. For example, a line in an industry journal that a food company was "developing a new geriatric food" convinced one man that he should emphasize his marketing experience with vitamins rather than with frozen foods.

18   You'll increase your edge by anticipating questions the interviewer might raise. Why do you want to work for us? What can you offer us that someone else cannot? Why did you leave your last position? What are your salary requirements?

19   An employer holds an interview to get a clearer picture of your work history and accomplishments, and to look for characteristics he considers valuable. These vary with jobs. Does the position require emphasis on attention to detail or on creativity? Perseverance or aggressiveness? Prior to the interview decide what traits are most in demand. And always send a thank-you note immediately after the interview.

20   *Follow up.* They said you would hear in a week: now it's two. Call them. Don't wait and hope. Hope and act.

21   *Supply additional information.* That's the way Karen Halloway got her job as fashion director with a department store. "After my interview I sensed that the merchandise manager felt I was short on retail experience. So I wrote to him describing the 25 fashion shows I'd staged yearly for the pattern company I'd worked for."

22   *Don't take no for an answer.* Hank Newell called to find out why he had been turned down. The credit manager felt he had insufficient collection experience. Hank thanked him for his time and frankness. The next day, Hank called back saying, "My collection experience is limited, but I don't think I fully emphasized my training in credit checking." They explored this area and found Hank still not qualified. But the credit manager was so impressed with how well Hank took criticism that when

Hank asked him if he could suggest other employers, he did, even going so far as to call one. Probing for leads when an interview or follow-up turns negative is a prime technique for getting personal referrals.

23   The challenge of finding a job, approached in an active, organized, realistic way, can be a valuable personal adventure. You can meet new people, develop new ideas about yourself and your career goals, and improve your skills in dealing with individuals. These in turn can contribute to your long-term job security.

VOCABULARY

adjacent (P9), *actuarial* (P9), *customer relations* (P10), *prospective* (P16), *geriatric* (P17), *perseverance* (P19), *prime* (P22)

IDEAS AND AIMS

1. What is the "hidden job market"? How does this job market differ from the traditional job market?
2. What steps does Mayleas recommend to open the hidden job market?
3. What are the six skills that should help a prospective employee land a job, according to the essay?
4. What is the implicit subsidiary point in P12 about willingness to relocate? How can this point be inferred from this paragraph?
5. Mayleas suggests that a prospective employee should always try to understand an employer's point of view. How does this "help develop new ideas about yourself and your career goals"? Is this true of the examples Mayleas cites in the essay?
6. What lesson about the importance of English courses in school can be learned from the last three sentences of P14?
7. Most people probably think of looking for a job as a job, or chore, itself, rather than some kind of personally beneficial experience. How is it the latter, according to Mayleas?
8. In the second sentence of P23 Mayleas lists various benefits from the job-searching process, which she asserts in the concluding sentence of the essay can contribute to the individual's long-term job security. How, exactly, can these benefits make that contribution?

ORGANIZATION AND FORM

1. Mayleas' essay is organized around the steps in the process used for landing a job. What is the organizing principle or principles of these steps?

2. How do "basic rules" 1 and 2 overlap?

3. What main method of paragraph development does Mayleas use to clarify and validate each step or "rule" she proposes?

4. In most essays, like those by Boroson (Section 1, "Job Choice and Self-Fulfillment") and Harris (Section 6, "Job Opportunities and Other Practical Matters") in this anthology, the reader is informed of the sources of the information about individuals who are cited in the essay as illustrations. Would such brief explanation improve Mayleas' essay? Why or why not?

WORDS AND STYLE

1. Where in P1 and P9 does Mayleas use very colloquial language? Is it effective? Why or why not? Where else in the essay does she use it?

2. Does Mayleas follow her own advice for resumes (P14) about using action words (that is, vivid, specific verbs)? How so? Cite examples.

3. Where does Mayleas use the series sentence effectively, economically listing several items in one sentence?

4. In the second sentence of P15 what precise distinction is Mayleas making between the words "accomplishment" and "duties"?

5. How is Sy Mann's term "valentine" in P16 ironic? How does he think of it as meaning the opposite of what it says (that is, *not* showing "love" or concern)? Why would such a cover letter not show "love" or concern?

6. How is a kind of chiasmus (look up this term in your collegiate dictionary) used meaningfully and effectively in the last two sentences of P20?

DISCUSSION AND WRITING

1. Write an essay listing, explaining, and illustrating the steps in a process you used to land a job.

2. Write an essay listing and explaining the steps in the process of finding a job in the field you hope to enter after college. You may need to consult your college's placement center to develop your essay.

3. Do you think Mayleas' method will work? Write an essay explaining your point of view, discussing Mayleas' method, one step at a time.

4. For an essay or class report, research other articles as well as paperback books giving advice on searching for and landing a job, comparing their advice with Mayleas'.

5. For an essay or class report, research the ever-increasing number of books about writing resumes, and compare their advice with Mayleas'.

BEFORE THE AX FALLS

Art Buchwald

☐

See the introduction to Buchwald's "Confessions of a Roof Seller" in Section 2, "Work and Morality." The following essay exemplifies two other typical devices that Buchwald uses to develop and organize his material: dialogue and little dramatic scenes. These devices also help to enliven and particularize Buchwald's work.

1 As the earnings statements of large companies get gloomier there is more and more pressure on corporation executives to make economies in their firms. Most companies do this first by firing the office boy, then retrenching in the mail room department, and finally cutting the budget on the softball team.

2   But as time goes on and stockholders get unhappier and unhappier, management may have to start making cuts in the upper levels of the company, and even executives are in danger of losing their jobs.

3   How does someone in a large company save his job when all around him are losing theirs? Perhaps I can be of help.

4   The first bit of advice is DO NOT TAKE A VACATION this year. No matter how badly you need one, hang in there, or else this is what could happen:

5   "Maxwell, what are you doing sitting at my desk?"

6   "Oh, Herndon, how was the Cape?"

7   "Fine. Now what are you doing in my office?"

8   "Well, finance decided to merge sales with packaging, and they asked me to take over. I naturally fought the move, but they were adamant. We tried to reach you on the Cape, but they said you were racing in the Hyannis-Nantucket sailboat trials. How did you do?"

9   "I came in third. Now where have I been moved to?"

10   "That's what they were trying to reach you about. They've had to cut across the board. I spoke up for you but. . . ."

11   The second bit of advice is to institute an economy committee, before one is constituted without you. Go into the president and say, "B. J., I'd like to organize a cost-cutting program so we don't get caught like Penn Central with our pants down. What I suggest we do is form a team and go into every department and see how we can eliminate waste. We could report to you within a month, so you'll have something to show the board."

12   If your idea is accepted, you must use great tact in suggesting the elimination of somebody else's job, on the off chance that he might survive and do you in.

13   You could say, "Gentlemen, I think we'd make a mistake if we let Fowler go. It's true his advertising campaign for Fluff was a complete disaster, but we must remember there has been great consumer resistance in toiletries for dogs this year. Fowler is a genius when it comes to advertising, even though he has a tendency to antagonize everyone in the company."

14   If Fowler loses his job, you have the minutes of the meeting to prove that you've defended him.

15   To show that you have the company's interest at heart before your own, announce some economies you're making in your own department. "I'm happy to announce, gentlemen, that I've furloughed two telephone operators and laid off four watchmen in our Wichita warehouse, thus saving the company thirty-three thousand dollars. This cuts my department to the bone, but I believe we can manage with what we've got."

16   The biggest danger during an economy drive is that the company may hire an outside consulting firm to make a private report on which people should be let go.

17   If one comes in the plant, *stop all work you are doing* and spend every waking moment with him. Most consultants know little or nothing about the business they are investigating, and if you can make them look good, they may believe you are necessary to the firm.

18   You can also get even with some old enemies.

19   "Tell me, Herndon, where is Mr. Maxwell?"

20   "Maxwell? I believe he's playing golf. He always plays golf on Wednesday afternoon with his doctor."

VOCABULARY

economies (P1), *retrenching* (P1), *adamant* (P8), *institute* (P11), *constitute* (P11), *tact* (P12), *antagonize* (P13), *furloughed* (P15)

IDEAS AND AIMS

1. What in Buchwald's essay shows that its purpose is primarily humor and satire?
2. What is the irony of the order in which most companies make "economies" (P1)? How does this irony extend to P2 and portray corporations as less than efficient or humane?
3. In the first interchange between Herndon and Maxwell (PP5–10) how is Maxwell's first response to Herndon's question evasive? Why is Maxwell evasive, and what does this suggest about him and the business world? What else in PP5–10 furthers these impressions?
4. How does Buchwald's proposed speech in P13 exemplify the "tact" he calls for in P12?
5. What is the author's opinion of consulting firms?
6. Much about human psychology and its relation to work is implied by the last half of the last sentence in P17, "and if you can make them look good. . . ." What are the logical or psychological connections between "and if you can make them look good" *and* "they may believe you are necessary to the firm"?
7. In PP18–20, what digs does Herndon get in at Maxwell?

ORGANIZATION AND FORM

1. Into what four parts does the essay naturally divide?
2. In what way does the section PP18–20 echo but reverse PP5–10? What is ironic about this reversal?

WORDS AND STYLE

1. How many different words for "firing an employee" are used in this essay? What kinds of synonyms are used in the public speeches the author advises that one make? What kinds are used in Buchwald's direct addresses to the reader? Contrast his private and public attitudes.
2. Why is the advice on vacations in all capital letters (P4)? Why are italics used in P17? Why are italics and not capitals used in P17?

3. How does the near equivalence in sound and meaning of the words "institute" and "constitute" in Buchwald's second bit of advice (P11) help express an important idea of the sentence?
4. How does the language of the speaker in P11 characterize his approach to business?

DISCUSSION AND WRITING

1. What advice would you give someone who is in danger of being fired?
2. Despite the fact that the advice given here is ironic, do you think any of it might be sound? What parts? Why?
3. Is Buchwald wrong to treat such a serious matter in a humorous and ironic way? Why or why not?
4. How does Buchwald's depiction of office politics compare with C. N. Parkinson's in the essay "Crabbed Youth" (Section 9, "The Work Environment")?

WOMEN'S BUSINESS

Ilene Kantrov

☐

Holding a Ph.D. from Tufts University, Ilene Kantrov (born in 1950) has worked as a teacher of freshman writing in college, as a writer and consultant for the Education Development Center, and as a freelance writer. Kantrov's editorial work on the biographical encyclopedia Notable American Women *has obviously provided her with some of the background for our selection, which was written specifically for an essay anthology. The clarity of her prose, variety in the kinds of sentences, and precision in word choice all point to someone who has mastered writing inside and out.*

1 The face of the kindly matron beamed from the pages of newspapers and magazines across the country. The advertising copy promised relief from "falling of the womb and all female weaknesses," touting the product as "the greatest remedy in the world." The year was 1879, and the product was an unproven home remedy called Lydia E. Pinkham's Vegetable Compound. Lydia Pinkham, the woman whose countenance graced the periodical pages, developed the advertising campaign that traded on her benign image.

2   Pinkham brought to her marketing effort the passionate social activism characteristic of many women of her era. Convinced that she

offered more than a mere product, she used her advertising to champion women's rights, temperance, and fiscal reform. One of her cleverest marketing techniques was a Department of Advice. Encouraging women to bypass male physicians to seek guidance from another woman, she dispensed practical suggestions about diet, exercise, and hygiene, along with endorsements of her own medicine.

3   Yet Pinkham did not hesitate to exploit traditional feminine fears— and feminine stereotypes—to market her product. She printed testimonials from women reporting cures not only for a range of physical symptoms, but also for infertility, "nervousness," "hysteria," and even marital discord. According to one early newspaper ad, the murder of a Connecticut clergyman by his wife, whose insanity was "brought on by 16 years of suffering with Female Complaints," could have been prevented by timely administration of the Compound to the afflicted woman.

4   As a result of such bold marketing, the company that Pinkham had founded with her sons earned $200,000 in 1881. Lydia Pinkham herself became something of a folk heroine—the subject of popular songs, jokes, and bawdy verse.

5   Pinkham's introduction of feminine packaging to capitalist enterprise earned her a special place in the annals of American business as well as women's history. It also set a pattern for women entrepreneurs in the following century. The handful of women who emulated Pinkham's success likewise followed her in importing traditional feminine roles into the masculine world of commerce. When feminine ideals collided with the realities of the marketplace, however, the businesswoman often bested the lady.

6   Like Pinkham, her successors consciously exploited their images as women to promote their products. In some cases, the image was that of glamorous socialite: arch-rivals Helena Rubinstein and Elizabeth Arden competed not only in selling cosmetics but also in luring publicity by their marriages to European aristocrats. More often the image cultivated was that of mother or grandmother: following Pinkham in this mold, for example, were Margaret Rudkin, founder of Pepperidge Farm, Inc., and Jennie Grossinger, who ran a resort hotel in upstate New York renowned for its food and entertainment. Grossinger managed to remain the solicitous Jewish grandmother in the eyes of her customers long after she had hired a public relations man and Grossinger's Hotel began serving 150,000 guests a year.

7   Women's businesses tended to grow out of traditional women's skills and catered mainly to women. Lydia Pinkham had collected and administered folk remedies to her family for years before the collapse of her husband's real estate business led her to begin marketing herbal preparations for "female complaints." Margaret Rudkin, faced with a comparable need to supplement her husband's income, also looked close to home.

She reportedly baked her first loaf of additive-free whole wheat bread as part of a special diet for an asthmatic son, and secured her first order from her neighborhood grocer in 1937.

8   To transform a home craft into a thriving business, these female capitalists joined a canny sense of women's tastes with the audacity of a gambler in creating and marketing innovations designed to shape those tastes. In 1909 Elizabeth Arden introduced her first line of makeup, not then widely considered respectable, as "facial treatments." As the beauty market began to expand in the 1920s she kept several steps ahead of demand: introducing, for example, such exotic and vaguely medicinal concoctions as Sensation salve, Arden gland cream, and the Vienna Youth Mask. Applications of the Youth Mask, constructed of papier-mâché and tinfoil, required the customer to be hooked up to a diathermy machine, which applied heat via electric current. Arden assured the women who submitted to the treatment—and paid dearly for the privilege—that they were restoring dead skin tissue.

9   In addition to skin care and cosmetics, Elizabeth Arden salons eventually added hairstyling, ready-made and custom clothes, and advice on nutrition and exercise. Arden herself practiced and advocated yoga, adapting the exercises for the women who frequented her salons and Maine health spa. Competing salon proprietor Helena Rubinstein published a book expounding the benefits of eating raw foods and sold her customers on the diet. In promoting the idea that a beauty salon could provide women with the means to "remake" themselves, inside and out, both women manifested the conviction of American businesswomen from Lydia Pinkham on that they were providing other women with something more than a product.

10   Few of them matched Pinkham in the degree to which she merged her marketing effort with a crusade for economic and social change. But other American women entrepreneurs combined an equally shrewd eye for profit with a passionate belief in their products' social or moral efficacy. Gertrude Muller, who invented the "toidey seat" in 1924 and parlayed it into an entire line of child care products, in 1930 began enclosing in the packages pamphlets she wrote about child raising. Her products, and the literature that accompanied them, embodied a progressive philosophy of child rearing, and one of her booklets was widely distributed by doctors and used by home economics instructors. Of course, none of this free publicity hurt business.

11   A black female capitalist, Annie Turnbo-Malone also cast herself in the role of social activist. Her business was founded at the turn of the century on a hairdressing preparation that, like Lydia Pinkham's Vegetable Compound, was of questionable efficacy. But, again like Pinkham, she developed an innovative marketing strategy—a network of franchised sales agents—and used it both to earn big money and to promote her causes. Turnbo-Malone established a school for training agents in her

"poro" system of hairdressing, named it Poro College, and advertised it as a vehicle for the uplift of her race and a passport to economic independence for women. Her literature also branched out beyond hair care to advocate the benefits of good hygiene, thrift, and other homely virtues.

12   Turnbo-Malone and her sister capitalists genuinely believed in the beneficence of their products and services. If not all of them proclaimed themselves, as Lydia Pinkham did, "Saviour of her Sex," several of them acted the part. And a number turned their profits into good works: Turnbo-Malone, Helena Rubinstein, and Jennie Grossinger, for example, were noted philanthropists as well as executives. They contributed lavishly to hospitals, schools, and cultural organizations.

13   Though they aimed to serve as well as to sell, however, these businesswomen frequently put profit ahead of altruism. Their advertising claims were often extravagant, even misleading. And when regulatory agencies such as the FDA and FTC began to crack down on questionable business practices, female entrepreneurs were as likely to be cited as their male counterparts. Helena Rubinstein, for instance, was forced by the FDA to withdraw some of the medicinal claims she made for her products.

14   The latent conflict between the profit motive and the social service ethic of female entrepreneurs is perhaps best exemplified once again by Lydia Pinkham: a passionate temperance advocate who had no qualms about selling a product that contained sufficient alcohol to make it 40 proof. "Grandma," backed by the Women's Christian Temperance Union, was selling booze.

VOCABULARY

matron (P1), *advertising copy* (P1), *touting* (P1), *countenance* (P1), *benign* (P1), *temperance* (P2), *fiscal* (P2), *bawdy* (P4), *annals* (P5), *entrepreneurs* (P5), *emulated* (P5), *exploited* (P6), *solicitous* (P6), *additive* (P7), *thriving* (P8), *canny* (P8), *audacity* (P8), *concoctions* (P8), *frequented* (P9), *proprietor* (P9), *expounding* (P9), *efficacy* (P10), *parlayed* (P10), *innovative* (P11), *franchised* (P11), *beneficence* (P12), *philanthropists* (P12), *lavishly* (P12), *altruism* (P13), *FDA* (P13), *FTC* (P13), *cited* (P13), *latent* (P14), *ethic* (P14), *exemplified* (P14), *qualms* (P14)

IDEAS AND AIMS

1. What is the central idea of this essay? In what two paragraphs is it most clearly stated?
2. Summarize Lydia Pinkham's business techniques. Do the other examples of "female entrepreneurs" use the same techniques or slightly different ones?

3. According to Kantrov, what two main images have female entrepreneurs cultivated in order to achieve success?

4. Do the other examples of female entrepreneurs—Turnbo-Malone, Rubinstein, Arden, Grossinger—also illustrate Pinkham's conflict between profit and social service? How?

5. How do the examples adduced in P3 show the "exploitation" of "traditional female fears" and "stereotypes"?

6. How does the title of Kantrov's essay contain an ironic play on the expression "women's work"? (Look up the phrase "women's work" in your collegiate dictionary if you are at all uncertain of its meaning.) How would Kantrov and many other women find this expression pejorative and objectionable? How do Kantrov's title and essay take aim at the attitudes and ideas implicit in the phrase "women's work"?

ORGANIZATION AND FORM

1. This essay has what could be called an inductive form, building up to its main thesis from several examples. How can such a form be effective in holding the reader's interest, and how does it work in this particular essay?

2. How does Kantrov's circling back to Pinkham at the end of the essay give the essay a sense of completion or closure? Rather than merely repeating or restating the opening material, how does Kantrov's conclusion add an important new piece of information to the original material of the second sentence of P2? How does this ironically modify the portrait of Pinkham?

3. How does the essay use the cause-and-effect method of analysis and development, moving from effect in the early paragraphs to cause in PP7–8?

4. How does Kantrov's very first sentence grab the reader's attention and pique the reader's interest?

5. What order or meaningful sequence is there in the examples of female entrepreneurs used to build up to Kantrov's thesis?

WORDS AND STYLE

1. What tone does Kantrov use to make her own opinion of these entrepreneurs clear? What specific words in the essay illustrate and convey this tone?

2. How does Kantrov's use of the relatively fancy word "countenance" rather than "face" in P1 help say something about Pinkham's image building?

3. What ironic contrast in connotations does Kantrov exploit between "submitted" and "privilege" in the last sentence of P8 to satirize both entrepreneur and customers?

4. How does Kantrov's use of the relatively fancy word "beneficence" rather than "benefit" in P12 help express or reflect the entrepreneurs' conceptions of them-

selves, their work, and their products? How does the word well accord with the rest of the paragraph?

5. How do the alliteration and sound equivalence of "to serve as well as to sell" (first sentence of P13) help Kantrov express her point about the entrepreneurs here?

6. How is chiasmus (look up this term in your collegiate dictionary) used for irony in the first sentence of P13 ("serve" = a, "sell" = b, "profit" = b, "altruism" = a, to use the formula for chiasmus)?

DISCUSSION AND WRITING

1. Which of Kantrov's examples is her best example of her central idea?

2. Does Kantrov ever indicate that these early female entrepreneurs differed from their male contemporaries? Did they? In what ways?

3. Write an essay about another business field in which there is a "latent conflict between the profit motive and the social service ethic." You might consider such fields as broadcasting, private schools, hospitals, or others. Can profit and social service be balanced in any business?

4. What images have contemporary male entrepreneurs cultivated in order to achieve success (e.g., Lee Iacocca, President of Chrysler, or Bill Blass in the fashion industry)? Are these comparable, contrasting, or both to the female entrepreneurs' images cited in the essay? Using examples and the inductive essay form, write an essay on the topic.

5. How can most of today's advertising campaigns for products be divided along the two main lines as distinguished by Kantrov in P6 (glamorous and sophisticated versus domestic and down-to-earth)? Cite several advertisements from television, magazines, and newspapers in each category, explaining how the product is being marketed in one or the other of these two categories.

6. How does what Kantrov says about successful businesswomen in PP10–13 compare or contrast with Auden's analysis of entrepreneurs in PP4–5 of his essay "The Almighty Dollar" (Section 5, "Money")?

CAREERS FOR THE NEXT FRONTIER

Marlys Harris

□

Written for **Money** *magazine, this essay by Marlys Harris has a journalistic flavor. It has a lively style, beginning with the metaphoric "hook" (what journalists call the opening attention-getter of an article): the pioneers' "frontier" compared to the "frontier" of the new job-seekers in the 1980s and 1990s. Likewise, it has a lively mixture of the levels of usage ("scary" in P3 versus "surmount" and "formidable" in the same paragraph) and vivid adjectives ("hobbled" in P2) and verbs ("stream" in P3). Furthermore, in journalistic style, numbers are printed in Arabic numerals (e.g., in P1 and P3), whereas they would be spelled out in formal, college writing, and paragraphs are often short (three or four sentences) so as not to present eye-wearying blocks of print in the narrow columns of magazines and newspapers. Finally, Harris uses many facts and figures—the illustrations and examples of all good writing—that make journalistic prose not only informative but vigorous as well.*

1 For Americans, the magical word "frontier" has represented an idea, not just a place. The 19th-century newspaper editor who said "Go west, young man" was advocating more than a trek to California. He was telling

young people to get out and push against the known limits, to place their personal stamp on America, to develop the country.

2   The U.S. landscape in 1981 seems to present narrowing vistas rather than beckoning frontiers. The generation now coming of age feels hemmed in by high youth unemployment, continuing inflation, hobbled economic growth, nagging problems with energy and pollution. Nor do young people any longer take it for granted that the U.S. will remain the premier economic and political power.

3   Those developments, which seem so frustrating and even scary, are in fact the new frontier. Careers will stream from the country's efforts to surmount economic barriers as formidable as the mountains and deserts seemed to the pioneers. It may take some psychological reshuffling to see things that way—but then it took settlers in the New World 200 years to stop calling the American West the backcountry.

4   Merely deciding to be a lawyer or a doctor or a corporate manager won't assure anyone of a job, because surpluses in those professions appear imminent. But the country will need doctors who treat the elderly, lawyers who specialize in energy and M.B.A.s who understand data processing. Many of the newest jobs have no established training programs. The trick is to discern the big changes ahead and then figure out where individual abilities and interests fit in.

5   The job market is so amazingly varied that it can absorb almost any skills or talents. Social science and English majors who have had trouble finding a place in a world engrossed in technology may have to market their degrees imaginatively. But even historians, who have seldom found much demand for their services, can apply their discipline to practical problems. Todd Shallat, 26, is taking a Ph.D. in applied history at Carnegie-Mellon. Simultaneously, he has a $29,000 consulting contract from the Army Corps of Engineers to dig out the original purposes of public waterways. His findings will help policymakers decide on future uses of such resources as the Chesapeake and Ohio Canal, an abandoned trade route now treasured by hikers and conservationists.

6   The coming decade seems certain not only to produce brand-new careers but also to give a second life to stagnant ones, change the nature of others and create unlimited possibilities for innovative entrepreneurs. Here is a guide to the job frontiers of the 1980s:

Serving a Changing Population

7 Improvements in diet and medical care have lengthened the average life span of Americans by 10 years since 1940, rapidly altering the demographics of age. The 65-and-over group is growing about twice as fast as the population as a whole. By 1990 there will be about 3 million more people at the high end of the age spectrum—75 and older—than there are today.

8   These "old-olds," more than the "young-olds" (aged 55 to 75), are prone to illness. Geriatricians will be needed to provide comprehensive care for the complex combinations of chronic medical and emotional problems peculiar to the elderly. A study made for the Rand Corp., a California think tank, indicates a need for 8,000 to 9,000 geriatric specialists by 1990 and 20,000 by the turn of the century. Only 600 doctors now practice this specialty. Raymond Cecora, 34, is one of them. As a fellow of the Jewish Institute for Geriatric Care in New Hyde Park, N.Y., he treats elderly patients for physical and emotional problems. His aim: to keep them healthy and active. Social workers, nurses and other medical aides will also find jobs working with the elderly.

9   The improved health of the rest of the population, together with the development of sophisticated diagnostic tests, promises to cut down the time a doctor spends with patients but to increase the need for laboratory technicians and other non-M.D.s who can operate complicated new diagnostic tools. Computer-based equipment—most notably the CAT scanner X-ray machine—will generate a burst of job growth for medical specialists in the 1980s that may even outstrip job creation in data processing, says Charles Bowman, head of the Economic Growth Division of the U.S. Bureau of Labor Statistics.

10   Demographic changes in the workplace will call for new skills and reinforcements in personnel work. One challenge to large employers is a work force augmented by young mothers, semiretired part-timers and two-income couples. Corporations will need plenty of career counselors to make effective use of these people. "As the population changes and technology makes some work obsolete, corporations will have to recruit people for new jobs from their own work force," says Frank Burtnett, director of the American Personnel and Guidance Association. Counselors, usually psychologists or sociologists with advanced degrees in adult counseling, will help employees figure out what their second, third or even fourth careers will be. Zandy Leibowitz, 33, a counseling psychologist, is already engaged in that mission at NASA's Goddard Flight Center in Greenbelt, Md. The development of sophisticated satellite tracking systems has phased out many highly skilled and glamorous jobs in the space program. Miss Leibowitz helps the displaced ground crewmen navigate toward new jobs and careers.

Fueling Planet Earth

11 The goal of U.S. energy independence calls for engineers, engineers and more engineers. "The demand is absolutely staggering for people with training in any energy field, especially petroleum engineers," says Alan Schonberg, president of Management Recruiters International in Cleveland. But as the decade wears on, other engineers will take up the

energy battle on new fronts. Says Van M. Evans of Deutsch Shea & Evans, a New York City recruiting firm for engineers and scientists: "The energy field will be fragmented among a number of efforts—further development of nuclear, solar and geothermal energy and resuscitation of the coal industry." Nuclear engineers have until now worked mostly in research. But despite antinuke protesters, recruiters predict a heavy call for engineers to design commercial reactors and power plants in the next few years.

12   Solar and geothermal energy are still in their infancy, but mechanical engineers in particular will be needed to devise better solar energy systems and to supervise computer analysis of the heating and cooling needs of large buildings. Geothermal engineers figure out ways to tap the natural heat of the earth captured in reservoirs of superheated water thousands of feet underground. The field is so new that most geothermal engineers still work for universities or government and corporate research laboratories. However, an increasing number of oil companies (60 to date) have started exploring for thermal energy sources.

13   More businesses are hiring people who can design systems for conserving energy. Enter a new specialist: the energy manager, or energy policy analyst. In the past he was a glorified janitor who went around turning off lights. Now he is a professional with a background in engineering, architecture and that combination of physics, chemistry, biology and economics called environmental science. He is skilled in cutting energy costs without producing adverse effects on manufacturing processes or the environment. Maggie Clarke, 27, practices those skills for the Power Authority of the State of New York. As a $25,000-a-year energy policy analyst, she searches for new ways to convert anything from wind to garbage into electricity.

14   Even more important than fuel is water. By the year 2000, population growth alone will severely strain the U.S. water supply. With pollution and drought endangering existing water resources, factories will need civil engineers, environmental scientists and hydrologists—people who study the circulation and distribution of water—to discover new supplies, recycle waste water and safely dispose of chemicals that could pollute lakes, streams and groundwater.

15   Water is also supplementing soil as a source of food. Some corporations, chief among them Weyerhaeuser, the forest products company, are experimenting with aquaculture—farming the seas—as a way of satiating the world's hunger. Other companies, such as Control Data, are venturing into hydroponics—intensive growth of plants in water laced with organic nutrients. Although no established paths yet lead to these career fields, Jim Smith, a trends forecaster with SRI International, a research firm in Menlo Park, Calif., predicts that "the '80s will see people with a scientific bent, who never dreamed of going into farming, taking up these new branches of it."

16   The search for energy and other natural resources would seem to narrow opportunities for environmentalists. But even though the Administration is pledged to ease federal antipollution standards, "Reagan won't be able to ignore the toxic waste problem, because our lives depend on solving it," says Van M. Evans, the technology recruiter. He predicts a growing need for toxicologists, who can detect harmful effects of natural and man-made substances on plants, animals and humans. Most toxicologists specialize in pharmacology as undergraduates and then take graduate courses in toxins. For every toxicologist, adds Robert Forney, president of a professional society in the field, there will be a need for three to five skilled technicians and mid-level professionals to conduct lab tests and collect data.

Advancing the Tech Revolution

17 In the 1970s, microelectronics broadened the capabilities of small computers and slashed the costs of storing and manipulating information. In the 1980s, the field will call for armies of systems analysts and programmers. Practically every type of business, from manufacturing to banking, will employ large numbers of them. Systems analysts devise ways for computers to store, classify, shuffle and retrieve information. Programmers tell computers what to do.

18   The Bureau of Labor Statistics estimates that employment of systems analysts will rise from 240,000 today to 400,000 in 1990. Openings for programmers will rise from 341,000 to 500,000. After that, says Betty Vetter of the government's Scientific Manpower Commission, "prefabricated programs that fit into computers like cassettes may level off the need for programmers." In the same period, the number of technicians needed to maintain and repair the complex new equipment should double to around 160,000.

19   Tiny computers supply the brainpower for industrial robots, which are rapidly taking over the drudge work of manufacturing. "People will be needed who can figure out when, how, where and whether it pays to use robots," says Angel Jordan, dean of engineering at Carnegie-Mellon University. "Unfortunately, there's no school that trains people in robotics right now." He suggests an undergraduate degree in engineering and some postgraduate work in computer science—and possibly business training.

20   The rash of new companies pioneering in genetic and biological engineering promises to broaden opportunities in other scientific fields. Some firms are developing antibodies that fight specific diseases without producing nasty side effects. Others are refining medical equipment and diagnostic tests that, for example, can screen a patient for 30 allergies at once. The work calls for molecular biologists and biomedical engineers

with graduate degrees. However, employment in those disciplines won't show a steep rise for another few years.

21   You won't have to be a high-powered scientist to build a career out of the technological revolution. Selling its output will be another growth area. Paul Rosinack, 34, gave up a career as a high school social studies teacher in 1971 to become a salesman of medical instruments. A year ago, Hybritech, a San Diego company specializing in immunological engineering and research, recruited him to direct sales of monoclonal antibodies and other newly developed disease-fighting organisms. Says Alan Schonberg, the Cleveland recruiter: "Anybody with the natural ability to sell can market these sophisticated products after a few weeks of training."

22   Even the hapless English major can fit in—as a technical writer, public relations specialist or advertising copywriter. "There is a dire need for people who can communicate what lasers, microprocessors, genetic devices and other new products do, how they work, how they're assembled and how they're maintained," says Schonberg.

23   Although most Americans are exposed daily to computer output that comes in the form of utility bills and bank statements, many workers don't know much more about using data-processing equipment than they did 10 years ago. The fault is in the educational system. Says Paul Shay, director of the trends forecasting unit at SRI International: "Schools are preparing people to live in the past rather than to use the new computer tools of the future." That may be a plus for teachers, however. Education majors who can master the new technologies will sometimes wind up teaching in schools or colleges—but more often in corporations.

Regaining the Competitive Edge

24 Striving to recapture ground lost in cost and quality to Japanese and German competitors, U.S. firms are looking for people who can help improve worker productivity. So far business school graduates have been getting the jobs. Reports Richard J. Thain, director of placement for the University of Chicago School of Business: "A number of companies want to put M.B.A.s out in the factory where the problems are. Most M.B.A.s don't want to be involved in that kind of dirty work, but if they can raise production, they should have a rosy future with any company." Already on line is Larry Bradner, 30, a Harvard Business School graduate, who always had his eye on the industrial end of business management. At Scientific Atlanta, a communications company, he supervises several hundred workers who manufacture the control boxes that permit TV sets to receive and select cable channels.

25   Also to stimulate productivity, corporations will be hiring lots of psychologists with postgraduate training in motivation, team dynamics and stress management. The assignment: figure out why employees daw-

dle and what changes in company practices and working environment will get them back in gear.

26   Persuading unions to cooperate in speeding up the work will require the services of many more industrial-relations managers. Their skill at negotiating labor contracts will be turned to an even trickier task. Explains Jack Shingleton, director of placement at Michigan State: "Industrial-relations specialists will have to work out complex new agreements between management and unions—called cooperative agreements—that give workers incentives to do well while allowing companies to stay profitable."

27   Executive jobs will grow scarcer. "American management is just too damned fat and top-heavy," says Paul Shay of SRI International, and the baby-boom generation has already filled middle-management ranks to capacity. But Shay and others see places for M.B.A.s with the right skills. Because low productivity is as much a problem in the office as on the assembly line, managers who can design data-processing systems to reduce the office load will have "a direct line to top management in the future," says John Stephens, personnel division chairman of the American Bankers Association.

28   As American companies attempt to manufacture and market more of their products abroad in the next 10 years, they will need cadres of development economists—people with advanced degrees in international aspects of their fields. They can guide companies through the problems of producing and selling in countries with agricultural economies and only small industrial bases. Says Gordon Winston, professor of international economics at Williams College: "Though the number of development economists employed by big corporations is now small, it is bound to increase rapidly."

Servicing the System

29 For the person with an idea—whether in the highly technical realms of electronics, computers or biological engineering, or in the workaday world of corporate housekeeping—entrepreneurship can be one of the best careers in the '80s. Charles Bowman of the Bureau of Labor Statistics predicts that service businesses will be second only to medical technology in job creation during the next decade. As a student at an Ithaca, N.Y. community college, Tony Maione discovered a market for services four years ago when he launched Nightshift, a maintenance company that cleans offices after hours. Back then he had one account and one worker—himself. Today, at 22, he works for 26 businesses and employs 28 people.

30   During the 1970s, inflation put a drag on everyone's hopes for a

better life. However, even though their dollars are worth less in 1981 than in 1970, many families have more real income than ever before. One big reason: wives went to work. Right now, 51% of all married women hold down jobs, up from 41% in 1970. By 1990, 60% of married women are likely to be in the work force.

31   Arising to serve newly monied Americans is the profession of personal financial planning. Its practitioners develop comprehensive investment, tax and estate strategies and sell tax shelters, insurance and mutual fund shares. Financial planners have increased in number from about 2,000 in 1970 to 6,500 today, and demand for their services has been compounding. "The biggest market that's developing is planning for families with annual incomes between $25,000 and $80,000—those who have been bumped into higher tax brackets by inflation and two incomes," says Alan Goldfarb, president of Financial Strategies in Dallas and a board member of the International Association of Financial Planners.

32   Planners come from the ranks of accountants and life insurance agents who have taken courses in tax planning and investment. In the past, most have run their own businesses, but brokerage houses and insurance companies are setting up planning departments to attract new clients and serve the fast-growing demand from corporations that offer their employees financial advisory services as a fringe benefit. "This will create many more new openings for accountants and tax lawyers," says Don Gough, a partner in Sibson & Co., a Princeton, N.J. employee-compensation consulting firm. People in Gough's line of work, who can design fringe-benefit packages and understand the laws regulating them, will probably also be in high demand through the '80s.

33   Busy and separated for long hours during the week, many families are looking for new ways to have fun at home. They're subscribing to cable- and pay-TV networks and adding videotape and videodisc equipment to their home recreation centers. Those new forms of communication should open more jobs for creative people—entertainers, writers, directors, filmmakers, scenery designers and crews of technicians to operate cameras, arrange lighting and perform other behind-the-scenes tasks.

34   The array of careers described here only samples what will be out there by the end of the decade. However, to put almost any kind of talent to work in the '80s will require an understanding of computers and what they can do. "People have to realize that they are going to be information workers," says Paul Shay of SRI. Young people have to abandon any fears they may have of the new technology and learn to use its tools. "Information will be the new source of wealth," says Shay. "The distinction used to be between the haves and the have-nots. In the '80s, it will be the knows and the know-nots."

VOCABULARY

trek (P1), *vistas* (P2), *beckoning* (P2), *hobbled* (P2), *surmount* (P3), *formidable* (P3), *imminent* (P4), *discern* (P4), *engrossed* (P5), *stagnant* (P6), *innovative* (P6), *entrepreneurs* (P6), *demographics* (P7), *prone* (P8), *geriatricians* (P8), *chronic* (P8), *peculiar* (P8), *CAT scanner* (P9), *augmented* (P10), *petroleum* (P11), *geothermal* (P11), *resuscitation* (P11), *reservoirs* (P12), *adverse* (P13), *groundwater* (P14), *satiating* (P15), *organic* (P15), *bent* (P15), *toxic* (P16), *pharmacology* (P16), *toxins* (P16), *prefabricated* (P18), *drudge* (P19), *rash* (P20), *immunological* (P21), *monoclonal* (P21), *hapless* (P22), *dire* (P22), *microprocessors* (P22), *productivity* (P24), *dawdle* (P25), *incentives* (P26), *cadres* (P28), *drag* (P30), *monied* (P31), *mutual fund* (P31), *fringe benefit* (P32), *array* (P34)

IDEAS AND AIMS

1. What is the lesson to be learned from the examples in P4?
2. What trend will enhance career opportunities for those trained in geriatrics?
3. What trends will enhance career opportunities for technicians, engineers, and scientists?
4. What does an energy manager do?
5. What current problems enhance job possibilities for labor relations managers?
6. What are the prospects for would-be executives? Why?

ORGANIZATION AND FORM

1. Where does the central idea of this essay appear?
2. This essay is a list of careers—an "array," as the author calls it. What organizes this list? What are the five main classifications used to organize the careers discussed here?
3. Harris's main method of analysis and development is cause and effect. List examples in the essay of this method of analysis or way of developing paragraphs. What are the causes, in Harris's analysis? What are their effects, in the view of Harris and others?
4. P5, P8, P9, P10, P13, P21, P24, and P29 all share a favorite technique by which Harris develops paragraphs. What is it? How does it work in these paragraphs?
5. How do PP1–6 function as an introduction to the essay?
6. How does the conclusion of the essay in P34 represent an extension or develop-

ment of the introduction and main thesis, rather than a mere repetition and restatement of them?

WORDS AND STYLE

1. How does Harris use the metaphor or analogy of the frontier to effectively bind up PP1–3 of the essay?
2. Point out numerous examples of Harris's mixture of the standard and colloquial levels of usage in her essay.
3. Do you think Harris's terms "old-olds" and young-olds" in P8 are more effective than other or less colloquial terms might be? Why?
4. How does Harris make an amusing but also meaningful pun on "navigate" in the last sentence of P10? How does she make a similar pun on "compounding" in P31?
5. How does Harris use the appositive (look this term up in your collegiate dictionary or composition handbook) to improve the clarity of her essay in the third sentence of P14, second sentence of P15, and third sentence of P16 (which contains an appositive-like adjective clause)?
6. Do you find a favorite sentence structure of Harris's, used in the next-to-last sentence of P8, second sentence of P13, second sentence of P25, and third sentence of P30, to be effective? Why?

DISCUSSION AND WRITING

1. Is there a danger that any of these "hot careers" will be cold by the time you finish school? Why? What can you do to protect yourself for that eventuality?
2. Is your intended career listed here? What are its prospects, and why?
3. What general lesson about career planning can be learned from this essay? What forces created these job possibilities or enhanced possibilities for the existing jobs listed here?
4. What national "agenda items" might affect your intended career? Are there others, not listed by Harris, that are or may become important?
5. Pick up a recent newspaper and glance over the headlines, or check the table of contents in a national newsmagazine. What issues or problems are listed there that might affect career directions for you and your classmates? How might these effects occur?
6. How does the last paragraph of Harris's essay coincide with some of Peter Drucker's points in "Evolution of the Knowledge Worker" (Section 4, "Careers for the 1990s")? How do their comments about professionals and managers compare?

TAKING STOCK: COMPARING AND CONTRASTING
THE SELECTIONS

1. In P3 Mayleas advises the reader to "put the same vigorous effort into *getting* a job as you would into *keeping* one." What similar points are there in Mayleas' advice about landing a job and Buchwald's advice about avoiding "the ax" in "Before the Ax Falls"?

2. In what way does Mayleas' point (in P23 of her essay) about self-development and self-realization from the job search complement the remarks of Thoreau (Section 2, "Work and Morality") about self-development and self-realization in working? Do you agree or disagree with these authors? Why?

3. How do Buchwald's "Before the Ax Falls" and Thoreau's "Getting a Living" (Section 2, "Work and Morality") show a different side to the effects that work may have on human nature? In your opinion, is the good side or bad side of human nature evoked on the job?

4. Compare Buchwald's view of office politics with Thurber's in "How to Adjust Yourself to Your Work" (Section 9, "The Work Environnment") and Parkinson's in "Crabbed Youth" (Section 9).

5. Do Kantrov's businesswomen follow the ethical path in business, as outlined by Fuller (Section 2, "Work and Morality") and Thoreau (Section 2)? Or do they follow the unethical path in business, as depicted in either of Buchwald's essays (Section 2; Section 6, "Job Opportunities and Other Practical Matters") and Clemens' "Jack of All Trades" (Section 8, "Efficiency and Success on the Job")? Or do they combine some of both courses? How so?

6. How does what Juanita Kreps says about women in business in "The Future for Working Women" (Section 4, "Careers for the 1990s") compare with the examples Kantrov discusses in "Women's Business"?

7. What similarities about the varieties of jobs and the assessment of public and corporate needs can you find between Harris's essay and Samuel Johnson's *Adventurer* No. 67, "The City's World of Work" (Section 7, "The Varieties of Work: Professions and Blue Collar")? Though both essays appeared in periodicals, how are the tone and main purpose of each author very different from each other?

8. What are the similarities between Harris's essay and Mayleas' essay? In what essential ways do the authors share the same view about finding a job? Are finding a job and finding a career, ultimately, the same process? Why?

9. Contrast Mayleas' or Harris's very practical view toward choosing a profession with the attitudes of Calvin (Section 1, "Job Choice and

Self-Fulfillment"), Fuller (Section 2, "Work and Morality"), or Thoreau (Section 2).

Note: See also Discussion and Writing question 4 of Buchwald's "Before the Ax Falls," question 6 of Kantrov's "Women's Business," and question 6 of Harris's "Careers for the Next Frontier."

VARIETIES OF WORK: Professions and Blue Collar

THE KNIFE

Richard Selzer

□

Richard Selzer is one of a number of professionals who have bridged the gap between their fields and the general public by way of numerous excellent works of nonfiction prose: this group also includes Carl Sagan (astronomer), Lewis Thomas (biologist, physician), Stephen Jay Gould (biologist), and

Loren Eiseley (paleontologist). Not only have their books and collections of essays appeared in paperback, but their individual essays have also been widely anthologized in texts used in English courses.

Born in Troy, New York, in 1928, the son of a doctor, Selzer was educated at Union College (B.S.), Albany Medical College (M.D.), and Yale University (postdoctoral study). He has been in private practice as a general surgeon since 1960 and also served as a professor of surgery in the medical school at Yale. Selzer early began contributing to several magazines, with essays and stories appearing in Harper's, Esquire, Redbook, Mademoiselle, American Review, *and* Antaeus. *His books are* Rituals of Surgery *(1974), a collection of short stories;* Mortal Lessons: Notes on the Art of Surgery *(1978), a collection of essays, from which this selection is taken;* Confessions of a Knife *(1979); and* Letters to a Young Doctor *(1982).*

1   One holds the knife as one holds the bow of a cello or a tulip—by the stem. Not palmed nor gripped nor grasped, but lightly, with the tips of the fingers. The knife is not for pressing. It is for drawing across the field of skin. Like a slender fish, it waits, at the ready, then, go! It darts, followed by a fine wake of red. The flesh parts, falling away to yellow globules of fat. Even now, after so many times, I still marvel at its power—cold, gleaming, silent. More, I am still struck with a kind of dread that it is I in whose hand the blade travels, that my hand is its vehicle, that yet again this terrible steel-bellied thing and I have conspired for a most unnatural purpose, the laying open of the body of a human being.

2   A stillness settles in my heart and is carried to my hand. It is the quietude of resolve layered over fear. And it is this resolve that lowers us, my knife and me, deeper and deeper into the person beneath. It is an entry into the body that is nothing like a caress; still, it is among the gentlest of acts. Then stroke and stroke again, and we are joined by other instruments, hemostats and forceps, until the wound blooms with strange flowers whose looped handles fall to the sides in steely array.

3   There is sound, the tight click of clamps fixing teeth into severed blood vessels, the snuffle and gargle of the suction machine clearing the field of blood for the next stroke, the litany of monosyllables with which one prays his way down and in: *clamp, sponge, suture, tie, cut.* And there is color. The green of the cloth, the white of the sponges, the red and yellow of the body. Beneath the fat lies the fascia, the tough fibrous sheet encasing the muscles. It must be sliced and the red beef of the muscles separated. Now there are retractors to hold apart the wound. Hands move together, part, weave. We are fully engaged, like children absorbed in a game or the craftsmen of some place like Damascus.

4   Deeper still. The peritoneum, pink and gleaming and membranous, bulges into the wound. It is grasped with forceps, and opened. For the first time we can see into the cavity of the abdomen. Such a primitive place.

One expects to find drawings of buffalo on the walls. The sense of trespassing is keener now, heightened by the world's light illuminating the organs, their secret colors revealed—maroon and salmon and yellow. The vista is sweetly vulnerable at this moment, a kind of welcoming. An arc of the liver shines high and on the right, like a dark sun. It laps over the pink sweep of the stomach, from whose lower border the gauzy omentum is draped, and through which veil one sees, sinuous, slow as just-fed snakes, the indolent coils of the intestine.

5   You turn aside to wash your gloves. It is a ritual cleansing. One enters this temple doubly washed. Here is man as microcosm, representing in all his parts the earth, perhaps the universe.

6   I must confess that the priestliness of my profession has ever been impressed on me. In the beginning there are vows, taken with all solemnity. Then there is the endless harsh novitiate of training, much fatigue, much sacrifice. At last one emerges as celebrant, standing close to the truth lying curtained in the Ark of the body. Not surplice and cassock but mask and gown are your regalia. You hold no chalice, but a knife. There is no wine, no wafer. There are only the facts of blood and flesh.

7   And if the surgeon is like a poet, then the scars you have made on countless bodies are like verses into the fashioning of which you have poured your soul. I think that if years later I were to see the trace from an old incision of mine, I should know it at once, as one recognizes his pet expressions.

8   But mostly you are a traveler in a dangerous country, advancing into the moist and jungly cleft your hands have made. Eyes and ears are shuttered from the land you left behind; mind empties itself of all other thought. You are the root of groping fingers. It is a fine hour for the fingers, their sense of touch so enhanced. The blind must know this feeling. Oh, there is risk everywhere. One goes lightly. The spleen. No! No! Do not touch the spleen that lurks below the left leaf of the diaphragm, a manta ray in a coral cave, its bloody tongue protruding. One poke and it might rupture, exploding with sudden hemorrhage. The filmy omentum must not be torn, the intestine scraped or denuded. The hand finds the liver, palms it, fingers running along its sharp lower edge, admiring. Here are the twin mounds of the kidneys, the apron of the omentum hanging in front of the intestinal coils. One lifts it aside and the fingers dip among the loops, searching, mapping territory, establishing boundaries. Deeper still, and the womb is touched, then held like a small muscular bottle—the womb and its earlike appendages, the ovaries. How they do nestle in the cup of a man's hand, their power all dormant. They are frailty itself.

9   There is a hush in the room. Speech stops. The hands of the others, assistants and nurses, are still. Only the voice of the patient's respiration remains. It is the rhythm of a quiet sea, the sound of waiting. Then you speak, slowly, the terse entries of a Himalayan climber reporting back.

10 "The stomach is okay. Greater curvature clean. No sign of ulcer. Pylorus, duodenum fine. Now comes the gallbladder. No stones. Right kidney, left, all right. Liver . . . uh-oh."

11 Your speech lowers to a whisper, falters, stops for a long, long moment, then picks up again at the end of a sigh that comes through your mask like a last exhalation.

12 "Three big hard ones in the left lobe, one on the right. Metastatic deposits. Bad, bad. Where's the primary? Got to be coming from somewhere."

13 The arm shifts direction and the fingers drop lower and lower into the pelvis—the body impaled now upon the arm of the surgeon to the hilt of the elbow.

14 "Here it is."

15 The voice goes flat, all business now.

16 "Tumor in the sigmoid colon, wrapped all around it, pretty tight. We'll take out a sleeve of the bowel. No colostomy. Not that, anyway. But, God, there's a lot of it down there. Here, you take a feel."

17 You step back from the table, and lean into a sterile basin of water, resting on stiff arms, while the others locate the cancer. . . .

18 What is it, then, this thing, the knife, whose shape is virtually the same as it was three thousand years ago, but now with its head grown detachable? Before steel, it was bronze. Before bronze, stone—then back into unremembered time. Did man invent it or did the knife precede him here, hidden under ages of vegetation and hoofprints, lying in wait to be discovered, picked up, used?

19 The scalpel is in two parts, the handle and the blade. Joined, it is six inches from tip to tip. At one end of the handle is a narrow notched prong upon which the blade is slid, then snapped into place. Without the blade, the handle has a blind, decapitated look. It is helpless as a trussed maniac. But slide on the blade, click it home, and the knife springs instantly to life. It is headed now, edgy, leaping to mount the fingers for the gallop to its feast.

20 Now is the moment from which you have turned aside, from which you have averted your gaze, yet toward which you have been hastened. Now the scalpel sings along the flesh again, its brute run unimpeded by germs or other frictions. It is a slick slide home, a barracuda spurt, a rip of embedded talon. One listens, and almost hears the whine—nasal, high, delivered through that gleaming metallic snout. The flesh splits with its own kind of moan. It is like the penetration of rape.

21 The breasts of women are cut off, arms and legs sliced to the bone to make ready for the saw, eyes freed from sockets, intestines lopped. The hand of the surgeon rebels. Tension boils through his pores, like sweat. The flesh of the patient retaliates with hemorrhage, and the blood chases the knife wherever it is withdrawn.

22   Within the belly a tumor squats, toadish, fungoid. A gray mother and her brood. The only thing it does not do is croak. It too is hacked from its bed as the carnivore knife lips the blood, turning in it in a kind of ecstasy of plenty, a gluttony after the long fast. It is just for this that the knife was created, tempered, heated, its violence beaten into paper-thin force.

23   At last a little thread is passed into the wound and tied. The monstrous booming fury is stilled by a tiny thread. The tempest is silenced. The operation is over. On the table, the knife lies spent, on its side, the bloody meal smear-dried upon its flanks. The knife rests.

24   And waits.

VOCABULARY

wake (P1), *globules* (P1), *quietude* (P2), *resolve* (P2), *hemostats* (P2), *forceps* (P2), *array* (P2), *severed* (P3), *snuffle* (P3), *litany* (P3), *monosyllables* (P3), *suture* (P3), *fibrous* (P3), *peritoneum* (P4), *membranous* (P4), *keener* (P4), *maroon* (P4), *salmon* (P4), *vista* (P4), *arc* (P4), *gauzy* (P4), *omentum* (P4), *sinuous* (P4), *indolent* (P4), *microcosm* (P5), *novitiate* (P6), *celebrant* (P6), *Ark* (P6), *surplice* (P6), *cassock* (P6), *regalia* (P6), *chalice* (P6), *wafer* (P6), *incision* (P7), *cleft* (P8), *spleen* (P8), *diaphragm* (P8), *manta ray* (P8), *hemorrhage* (P8), *denuded* (P8), *appendages* (P8), *dormant* (P8), *frailty* (P8), *terse* (P9), *Himalayan* (P9), *exhalation* (P11), *lobe* (P12), *metastatic* (P12), *tumor* (P16), *colostomy* (P16), *decapitated* (P19), *trussed* (P19), *averted* (P20), *unimpeded* (P20), *talon* (P20), *snout* (P20), *retaliates* (P21), *fungoid* (P22), *brood* (P22), *carnivore* (P22)

IDEAS AND AIMS

1. What is the surgeon's attitude toward the human body?
2. What is the surgeon's attitude toward the knife, as it is described in P1?
3. The last seven paragraphs seem to describe the knife in another way from the opening of the essay. What aspects of the surgeon's original attitude toward the knife are being emphasized in this section?
4. Does a similar transformation occur in the surgeon's attitude toward the act of surgery itself? How does he feel about surgery in P6 and P7? How does he describe surgery in the last section of the essay?
5. Literally, what kind of operation is described in this essay?
6. What are the main aims of Selzer's description of his job? With what attitudes, feelings, or impressions does he want to leave the reader?

ORGANIZATION AND FORM

1. What order is used to arrange the details describing this process?
2. How are PP1–17 and PP18–24 main parts of the essay, as suggested by the break between P17 and P18?
3. How do pronouns function as a device enhancing paragraph coherence (that is, helping the paragraph cohere) in P1 and P2?
4. What is the function in the essay of PP18–19? These paragraphs could have been placed much earlier in the essay. Why does Selzer delay introducing them in the essay until the second half?

WORDS AND STYLE

1. Look at the list of vocabulary words for this essay. From the vocabularies of what professions are these words taken?
2. List the professions to which the surgeon's calling is compared. How are these analogies accurate and applicable? In addition to his profession as surgeon, how in his essay is Selzer like a priest, a poet, and an explorer?
3. This essay is pervaded by figures of speech, especially analogies, metaphors, and similes. Choose several you found vivid or moving, and explain how they help Selzer describe what he wants to more precisely or help him express particular attitudes, feelings, or ideas.
4. One particular figure of speech Selzer uses repeatedly in a pattern is person-ification. (Look up this term in your collegiate dictionary or composition hand-book.) How, and in what paragraphs, does he personify the knife, and what is the cumulative effect of this pattern?
5. How does Selzer use paradox effectively to help express his points in the third sentence of P2, last sentence of P22, and second sentence of P23? (Look up this term in your collegiate dictionary or composition handbook.)
6. What pun does Selzer make on "edgy" in P19? What incisive point does the pun help make?
7. How is the brevity of the concluding one-sentence paragraph of the essay (P24) effective?

DISCUSSION AND WRITING

1. Describe the tools of your vocation or calling, your intended vocation, or your job as a full-time student, as Selzer does, by comparison with other professions' materials.

2. Is there a process—such as surgery, or building bridges, or making fired pots—basic to your chosen field of work? Describe it as Selzer has described his work here.

3. What was your emotional response to Selzer's essay? Why? Was it one that Selzer would have been happy with?

4. Does Selzer's job sharpen or blunt his sensitivity to himself and the world around him? How so? How does his job compare or contrast in this regard to Patrick Fenton's as the latter describes his job in "Confessions of a Working Stiff" later in this section?

THE CITY'S WORLD
OF WORK
(*ADVENTURER* NO. 67)

Samuel Johnson

☐

Born in Lichfield, England, and self-tutored before and after his education at Oxford University—which was interrupted and left incomplete because of his lack of funds—Samuel Johnson (1709–1784) went on to become one of the most learned men of his age and perhaps its most important figure in belles-lettres. The Restoration and eighteenth-century period of British letters was dominated by four writers—John Dryden, Alexander Pope, Jonathan Swift, and Samuel Johnson—all of whom, interestingly, were accomplished in writing both poetry and prose.

Dr. Johnson (he was awarded the honorary LL.D. degree by both Trinity College in Dublin [1765] and Oxford University [1755]), engaged in diverse writing projects, because of the wide range of his mind and his continual need of money. Though he was not a spectacular dramatist in his authorship of Irene *(1749), Johnson's skills as poet, fiction writer, biographer, scholar, lexicographer, literary critic, and essayist shine in his other writings. These include* London: A Poem *(1738);* The Rambler *(1750–1752), a periodical issued twice a week, of whose 208 numbers Johnson wrote 203;* The Adventurer *(1752–1754), a periodical, of whose 140 numbers Johnson wrote 29; and* A Dictionary of the English Language *(1755; 1773), the first great dictionary in English, with some interesting personal definitions (e.g., " 'pension' . . . In England . . . generally understood to mean pay given to a state hireling for treason to his country"). His other notable works are* Rasselas *(1759), a novelette-length fictional tale and travelogue, exploring philosophical issues of human life and happiness;* The Idler *(1758–1760), a periodical, of whose 104 numbers Johnson wrote 92;* The Plays of Shakespeare *(1765; 1773), combining Johnson's skills as textual editor and scholar, as well as literary critic in his introductions to the plays;* A Journey to the Western Isles of Scotland *(1775), a philosophically tinged account of Johnson's tour undertaken with his friend and biographer, James Boswell (author of* The Life of Samuel Johnson *[1791]); and* Lives of the English Poets *(1781), combining biography and criticism.*

Like British author Thomas Carlyle with his "Carlylese," Johnson is famous for a prose style that could be called "Johnsonese." It combines polysyllabic, Latinate words, balance, antithesis, and parallelism, plus compact and weighty generalizations formulated in abstract terms. Johnson's style, many of whose characteristic traits are to be found in this selection (Adventurer No. 67), is a reflection of a mind always weighing things, a mind with an ingrained philosophical and moralizing inclination. A recent scholar has said that Johnson's "writing constantly reveals a process of examining, clarifying, and resolving problems, leading to a powerfully compressed final aphorism in which general truth is revealed" and that his "humanity and sense of the tragic element in human life, together with the inevitability of suffering . . . [suffuse] his reasoning . . . with passion and vivid psychological insights."[1]

Such qualities may be found in this selection, which is a meditation that starts with calling attention to the multiplicity of goods and services in the city and leads to pondering the benefits to producers and to consumers of this panoply. Despite the stereotype of their hostility to trade, Johnson, like many other intellectuals, is fundamentally pro business and strongly endorses its benefits to producer, worker, consumer, and society.

No. 67. Tuesday, 26 June 1753.

Inventas—vitam excoluere per artes.

Virgil, AENEID, VI.663.

They polish life by useful arts.

1 That familiarity produces neglect, has been long observed. The effect of all external objects, however great or splendid, ceases with their novelty: the courtier stands without emotion in the royal presence; the rustic tramples under his foot the beauties of the spring, with little attention to their colour or their fragrance; and the inhabitant of the coast darts his eye upon the immense diffusion of waters, without awe, wonder, or terror.

2   Those who have past much of their lives in this great city, look upon its opulence and its multitudes, its extent and variety, with cold indif-

---

1. W. Ruddick, "Johnson, Samuel," *Webster's New World Companion to English and American Literature,* ed. Arthur Pollard (New York: Popular Library, 1976).

ference; but an inhabitant of the remoter parts of the kingdom is immediately distinguished by a kind of dissipated curiosity, a busy endeavour
to divide his attention amongst a thousand objects, and a wild confusion
of astonishment and alarm.

3   The attention of a new-comer is generally first struck by the multiplicity of cries that stun him in the streets, and the variety of merchandise and manufactures which the shopkeepers expose on every hand; and
he is apt, by unwary bursts of admiration, to excite the merriment and
contempt of those, who mistake the use of their eyes for effects of their
understanding, and confound accidental knowledge with just reasoning.

4   But, surely, these are subjects on which any man may without
reproach employ his meditations: the innumerable occupations, among
which the thousands that swarm in the streets of London are distributed,
may furnish employment to minds of every cast, and capacities of every
degree. He that contemplates the extent of this wonderful city, finds it
difficult to conceive, by what method plenty is maintained in our markets, and how the inhabitants are regularly supplied with the necessaries
of life; but when he examines the shops and warehouses, sees the
immense stores of every kind of merchandise piled up for sale, and runs
over all the manufactures of art and products of nature, which are every
where attracting his eye and soliciting his purse, he will be inclined to
conclude, that such quantities cannot easily be exhausted, and that part
of mankind must soon stand still for want of employment, till the wares
already provided shall be worn out and destroyed.

5   As Socrates was passing through the fair at Athens, and casting his
eyes over the shops and customers, "how many things are here," says he,
"that I do not want!" The same sentiment is every moment rising in the
mind of him that walks the streets of London, however inferior in philosophy to Socrates: he beholds a thousand shops crouded with goods, of
which he can scarcely tell the use, and which, therefore, he is apt to
consider as of no value; and, indeed, many of the arts by which families
are supported, and wealth is heaped together, are of that minute and
superfluous kind, which nothing but experience could evince possible to
be prosecuted with advantage, and which, as the world might easily
want, it could scarcely be expected to encourage.

6   But so it is, that custom, curiosity, or wantonness, supplies every art
with patrons, and finds purchasers for every manufacture; the world is so
adjusted, that not only bread, but riches may be obtained without great
abilities, or arduous performances: the most unskilful hand and
unenlightened mind have sufficient incitements to industry; for he that is
resolutely busy, can scarcely be in want. There is, indeed, no
employment, however despicable, from which a man may not promise
himself more than competence, when he sees thousands and myriads
raised to dignity, by no other merit than that of contributing to supply
their neighbours with the means of sucking smoke through a tube of clay;

and others raising contributions upon those, whose elegance disdains the grossness of smoky luxury, by grinding the same materials into a powder, that may at once gratify and impair the smell.

7   Not only by these popular and modish trifles, but by a thousand unheeded and evanescent kinds of business, are the multitudes of this city preserved from idleness, and consequently from want. In the endless variety of tastes and circumstances that diversify mankind, nothing is so superfluous, but that some one desires it; or so common, but that some one is compelled to buy it. As nothing is useless but because it is in improper hands, what is thrown away by one is gathered up by another; and the refuse of part of mankind furnishes a subordinate class with the materials necessary to their support.

8   When I look round upon those who are thus variously exerting their qualifications, I cannot but admire the secret concatenation of society, that links together the great and the mean, the illustrious and the obscure; and consider with benevolent satisfaction, that no man, unless his body or mind be totally disabled, has need to suffer the mortification of seeing himself useless or burdensome to the community: he that will diligently labour, in whatever occupation, will deserve the sustenance which he obtains, and the protection which he enjoys; and may lie down every night with the pleasing consciousness, of having contributed something to the happiness of life.

9   Contempt and admiration are equally incident to narrow minds: he whose comprehension can take in the whole subordination of mankind, and whose perspicacity can pierce to the real state of things through the thin veils of fortune or of fashion, will discover meanness in the highest stations, and dignity in the meanest; and find that no man can become venerable but by virtue, or contemptible but by wickedness.

10   In the midst of this universal hurry, no man ought to be so little influenced by example, or so void of honest emulation, as to stand a lazy spectator of incessant labour; or please himself with the mean happiness of a drone, while the active swarms are buzzing about him: no man is without some quality, by the due application of which he might deserve well of the world; and whoever he be that has but little in his power, should be in haste to do that little, lest he be confounded with him that can do nothing.

11   By this general concurrence of endeavours, arts of every kind have been so long cultivated, that all the wants of man may be immediately supplied; idleness can scarcely form a wish which she may not gratify by the toil of others, or curiosity dream of a toy which the shops are not ready to afford her.

12   Happiness is enjoyed only in proportion as it is known; and such is the state or folly of man, that it is known only by experience of its contrary; we who have long lived amidst the conveniences of a town immensely populous, have scarce an idea of a place where desire cannot be

gratified by money. In order to have a just sense of this artificial plenty, it is necessary to have passed some time in a distant colony, or those parts of our island which are thinly inhabited: he that has once known how many trades every man in such situations is compelled to exercise, with how much labour the products of nature must be accommodated to human use, how long the loss or defect of any common utensil must be endured, or by what aukward expedients it must be supplied, how far men may wander with money in their hands before any can sell them what they wish to buy, will know how to rate at its proper value the plenty and ease of a great city.

13   But that the happiness of man may still remain imperfect, as wants in this place are easily supplied, new wants likewise are easily created: every man, in surveying the shops of London, sees numberless instruments and conveniences, of which, while he did not know them, he never felt the need; and yet, when use has made them familiar, wonders how life could be supported without them. Thus it comes to pass, that our desires always increase with our possessions; the knowledge that something remains yet unenjoyed, impairs our enjoyment of the good before us.

14   They who have been accustomed to the refinements of science, and multiplications of contrivance, soon lose their confidence in the unassisted powers of nature, forget the paucity of our real necessities, and overlook the easy methods by which they may be supplied. It were a speculation worthy of a philosophical mind, to examine how much is taken away from our native abilities, as well as added to them by artificial expedients. We are so accustomed to give and receive assistance, that each of us singly can do little for himself; and there is scarce any one amongst us, however contracted may be his form of life, who does not enjoy the labour of a thousand artists.

15   But a survey of the various nations that inhabit the earth will inform us, that life may be supported with less assistance, and that the dexterity, which practice enforced by necessity produces, is able to effect much by very scanty means. The nations of Mexico and Peru erected cities and temples without the use of iron; and at this day the rude Indian supplies himself with all the necessaries of life: sent like the rest of mankind naked into the world, as soon as his parents have nursed him up to strength, he is to provide by his own labour for his own support. His first care is to find a sharp flint among the rocks; with this he undertakes to fell the trees of the forest; he shapes his bow, heads his arrows, builds his cottage, and hollows his canoe, and from that time lives in a state of plenty and prosperity; he is sheltered from the storms, he is fortified against beasts of prey, he is enabled to persue the fish of the sea, and the deer of the mountains; and as he does not know, does not envy the happiness of polished nations, where gold can supply the want of fortitude and skill, and he whose laborious ancestors have made him rich, may lie

stretched upon a couch, and see all the treasures of all the elements poured down before him.

16   This picture of a savage life, if it shews how much individuals may perform, shews likewise how much society is to be desired. Though the perseverance and address of the Indian excite our admiration, they nevertheless cannot procure him the conveniences which are enjoyed by the vagrant beggar of a civilized country: he hunts like a wild beast to satisfy his hunger; and when he lies down to rest after a successful chace, cannot pronounce himself secure against the danger of perishing in a few days; he is, perhaps, content with his condition, because he knows not that a better is attainable by man; as he that is born blind does not long for the perception of light, because he cannot conceive the advantages which light would afford him: but hunger, wounds and weariness are real evils, though he believes them equally incident to all his fellow creatures; and when a tempest compels him to lie starving in his hut, he cannot justly be concluded equally happy with those whom art has exempted from the power of chance, and who make the foregoing year provide for the following.

17   To receive and to communicate assistance, constitutes the happiness of human life: man may indeed preserve his existence in solitude, but can enjoy it only in society: the greatest understanding of an individual, doomed to procure food and cloathing for himself, will barely supply him with expedients to keep off death from day to day: but as one of a large community performing only his share of the common business, he gains leisure for intellectual pleasures, and enjoys the happiness of reason and reflection.

VOCABULARY

novelty (P1), *courtier* (P1), *rustic* (P1), *diffusion* (P1), *opulence* (P2), *dissipated* (P2), *multiplicity* (P3), *unwary* (P3), *excite* (P3), *confound* (P3), *reproach* (P4), *cast* (P4), *capacities* (P4), *conceive* (P4), *art* (P4), *want* (P4), *Socrates* (P5), *minute* (P5), *superfluous* (P5), *evince* (P5), *prosecuted* (P5), *wantonness* (P6), *arduous* (P6), *incitements* (P6), *despicable* (P6), *myriads* (P6), *gratify* (P6), *impair* (P6), *modish* (P7), *evanescent* (P7), *diversify* (P7), *refuse* (P7), *concatenation* (P8), *mean* (P8), *illustrious* (P8), *obscure* (P8), *benevolent* (P8), *mortification* (P8), *diligently* (P8), *sustenance* (P8), *incident* (P9), *perspicacity* (P9), *venerable* (P9), *void* (P10), *emulation* (P10), *incessant* (P10), *drone* (P10), *confounded* (P10), *concurrence* (P11), *cultivated* (P11), *toy* (P11), *accommodated* (P12), *contrivance* (P14), *paucity* (P14), *contracted* (P14), *dexterity* (P15), *effect* (P15), *heads* (P15), *fortitude* (P15), *perseverance* (P16), *address* (P16), *procure* (P16), *vagrant* (P16), *conceive* (P16), *afford* (P16), *tempest* (P16), *concluded* (P16), *expedients* (P17)

IDEAS AND AIMS

1. According to Johnson in the essay, what principal benefit does the multiplicity of trades, services, and consumer desires bring to the producer and worker?
2. What principal benefit does the urban consumer receive from living in what economist John Kenneth Galbraith hundreds of years later would call an "affluent society"?
3. What is the relevance of the epigraph to any of the main points of the essay?
4. How does the author illustrate the multiplicity of urban goods and services?
5. What are the author's illustrations of seemingly nonsensical occupations? How are they so?
6. The last example in the essay is the life of the "rude Indian." How do the assertions made in the rest of the essay bear on this final example?
7. Johnson is not usually remembered as having much of a sense of humor. Where in the essay can one find examples of his irony, like that which undercuts the city slickers in P3?

ORGANIZATION AND FORM

1. How do the following paragraphs form main units or blocs in the essay: PP1–4, PP5–10, PP11–14, and PP15–17?
2. In what sense does the concluding paragraph of the essay represent a development of what has gone before rather than a mere restatement?
3. In several places Johnson uses cause and effect as a method of analysis as well as for the development of his paragraphs. Cite examples, identifying what are causes and what are their effects.
4. Johnson's philosophical disposition shows in several very general or abstract topic sentences that at first seem to have little to do with his specific subject of the causes and effects of London's thriving commercial scene—for example, the first two sentences of P1 or the first sentence of P12. How, in fact, are these and other instances tied by Johnson to the main subject and specific points of his essay?
5. How does P9 relate to P8 and P10?
6. Where does Johnson use transitional words to begin paragraphs in order to show their relation to preceding ideas and material?

WORDS AND STYLE

1. How is Johnson's style generally appropriate for the kind of essay he is trying to write, hinted in his word "meditations" (first sentence of P4), his allusion "however inferior in philosophy to Socrates" (second sentence of P5), and his

prefacing remark, "It were a speculation worthy of a philosophical mind" (second sentence of P14)?

2. List examples of that hallmark of Johnson's prose style, the balanced sentence (look up this term in your collegiate dictionary or composition handbook), such as "use . . . understanding; confound . . . reasoning" in the last sentence of P3. Choose one or two instances and explain how this stylistic device helps Johnson express a particular point he is trying to make.

3. List examples of another hallmark of Johnson's prose style, parallelism (look up this term in your collegiate dictionary or composition handbook), such as "the courtier . . . terror" (first sentence of P1) or "its opulence . . . variety" (first sentence of P2). Choose one or two instances and explain how this stylistic device helps Johnson express his particular point.

4. List examples of yet another hallmark of Johnson's prose style, antithesis (look up this term in your collegiate dictionary or composition handbook), such as "nothing is so . . . to buy it" (second sentence of P7). Choose one or two instances and explain how this stylistic device helps Johnson express his particular point.

5. Balance, parallelism, and antithesis (see questions 2–4 above) all may have the effect of weighing one thing with another or against another. Considering what Johnson intends his essay to be (see question 1 above), how are these stylistic elements quite appropriate for it?

6. How do the hallmarks of his prose style enable Johnson to be temperately, though amusingly, ironic or satiric in certain instances (e.g., "use . . . reasoning," cited in question 2)?

7. In P6 how does Johnson's language ("supply . . . clay") function to tease both consumers and producers associated with smoking?

8. In the last portion of the last sentence of P6, Johnson's language obliquely describes the consumers and producers of snuff. How do his periphrasis and paradox here (look up these terms in your collegiate dictionary or composition handbook) tease both consumers and producers?

9. How does his use of personification of abstractions in P11 help Johnson keep the essay from becoming too abstract and dry? How is personification used effectively to convey Johnson's ideas here?

10. Cite and explain Johnson's effective use of metaphor and synecdoche (or metonymy) in the essay. (Look up these terms in your collegiate dictionary or composition handbook.)

DISCUSSION AND WRITING

1. Reread the description of London in P4. Can a modern city be described similarly? Have you had similar reactions upon seeing the vast amount of merchandise and work produced in a modern city? How many things are there that you "do not want"?

2. Do you think the author's idea is true that idleness causes "want" and that therefore employment results in "dignity"? Or is his idea too easy? Do you think all occupations confer dignity of a sort upon the worker?

3. No real examples are provided for the author's assertion in P7. Can you provide examples of the "evanescent" occupations of modern people?

4. Can you provide examples for (or against) the author's point in P8?

5. Do you agree with the author's assertion that happiness is "known only by experience of its contrary" (P12)? Have you ever found it to be true for yourself?

6. Do you agree that "desires increase with our possessions" (P13)? Have you ever found it to be true for yourself or people you have known?

7. Consonant with the eighteenth-century emphasis on the human being as a social animal, Johnson keeps coming back to concern with society and the idea that work benefits society. How does this notion of benefit compare with today's ideas about who benefits from work?

HERE AM I, A WORKER

Studs Terkel

☐

Louis Studs Terkel, born in 1912, was trained as a lawyer at the University of Chicago but quickly turned to a career as a stage actor, then as a host of interview shows on radio and television. Known mainly as a media personality, he wrote short stories, a play, and a history of jazz while also writing a newspaper column, lecturing, narrating films, and engaging in a host of other activities.

But in 1967 Terkel published Division Street: America, *in which he extended the technique of the television interview into the realm of literature. This book, like* Hard Times *(1970) and* Working *(1974), is a collection of interviews with ordinary men and women. Terkel is able to focus his interviews, to create a cumulative effect when the book is finished, yet allowing— even encouraging—each individual interviewed to express his or her own unique views in a unique language. The oral histories Terkel gathers are never dull reading.*

1 In our society (it's the only one I've experienced, so I cannot speak for any other) the razor of necessity cuts close. You must make a buck to survive the day. You must work to make a buck. The job is often a chore, rarely a delight. No matter how demeaning the task, no matter how it dulls the senses or breaks the spirit, one *must* work or else. Lately there has been a

questioning of this "work ethic," especially by the young. Strangely enough, it has touched off profound grievances in others, hitherto silent and anonymous.

2   Unexpected precincts are being heard from in a show of discontent by blue collar and white. Communiqués are alarming concerning absenteeism in auto plants. On the evening bus the tense, pinched faces of young file clerks and elderly secretaries tell us more than we care to know. On the expressways middle-management men pose without grace behind their wheels, as they flee city and job.

3   In all, there is more than a slight ache. And there dangles the impertinent question: Ought there not be another increment, earned though not yet received, to one's daily work—an acknowledgment of a man's *being*?

4   Steve Hamilton is a professional baseball player. At 37 he has come to the end of his career as a major-league pitcher. "I've never been a big star. I've done about as good as I can with the equipment I have. I played with Mickey Mantle and with Willie Mays. People always recognize them. But for someone to recognize me, it really made me feel good. I think everybody gets a kick out of feeling special."

5   Mike Fitzgerald was born the same year as Hamilton. He is a laborer in a steel mill. "I feel like the guys who built the pyramids. Somebody built 'em. Somebody built the Empire State Building, too. There's hard work behind it. I would like to see a building, say The Empire State, with a foot-wide strip from top to bottom and the name of every bricklayer on it, the name of every electrician. So when a guy walked by, he could take his son and say 'See, that's me over there on the 45th floor. I put that steel beam in.' Picasso can point to a painting. I think I've done harder work than Picasso, and what can I point to? Everybody should have something to point to."

6   Sharon Atkins is 24 years old. She's been to college and acridly observes: "The first myth that blew up in my face is that a college education will get you a worthwhile job." For the last two years she's been a receptionist at an advertising agency. "I didn't look at myself as 'just a dumb broad' at the front desk, who took phone calls and messages. I thought I was something else. The office taught me differently."

7   Among her contemporaries there is no such rejection; job and status have no meaning. Blue collar or white, teacher or cabbie, her friends judge her and themselves by their beingness. Nora Watson, a young journalist, recounts a party game, Who Are You? Older people respond with their job titles: "I'm a copy writer," "I'm an accountant." The young say, "I'm me, my name is so-and-so."

8   Harry Stallings, 27, is a spot welder on the assembly line at an auto plant. "They'll give better care to that machine than they will to you. If it breaks down, there's somebody out there to fix it right away. If I break down, I'm just pushed over to the other side till another man takes my

place. The only thing the company has in mind is to keep that line running. A man would be more eager to do a better job if he were given proper respect and the time to do it."

9   You would think that Ralph Grayson, a 25-year-old black, has it made. He supervises twenty people in the audit department of a large bank. Yet he is singularly discontented. "You're like a foreman on an assembly line. Or like a technician sitting in a computer room watching the machinery. It's good for a person who enjoys that kind of job, who can dominate somebody else's life. I'm not too wrapped up in seeing a woman, 50 years old—white, incidentally—get thrown off her job because she can't cut it like the younger ones.

10   "I told management she was a kind and gentle person. They said, 'We're not interested in your personal feelings. Document it up.' They look over my appraisal and say: 'We'll give her about five months to shape up or ship out.'"

11   The hunger persists, obstinately, for pride in a man's work. Conditions may be horrendous, tensions high, and humiliations frequent, yet Paul Dietch finds his small triumphs. He drives his own truck, interstate, as a steel hauler. "Every load is a challenge. I have problems in the morning with heartburn. I can't eat. Once I off-load, the pressure is gone. Then I can eat anything. I accomplished something."

12   Yolanda Leif graphically describes the trials of a waitress in a quality restaurant. They are compounded by her refusal to be demeaned. Yet pride in her skills helps her through the night. "When I put the plate down, you don't hear a sound. When I pick up a glass, I want it to be just right. When someone says, 'How come you're just a waitress?' I say, 'Don't you think you deserve being served by me?'"

13   Peggy Terry has her own sense of pride and beauty. Her jobs have varied with geography, climate, and the ever-felt pinch of circumstance. "What I hated worst was being a waitress, the way you're treated. One guy said, 'You don't have to smile, I'm gonna give you a tip anyway.' I said, 'Keep it, I wasn't smiling for a tip.' Tipping should be done away with. It's like throwing a dog a bone. It makes you feel small."

14   Ballplayer. Laborer. Receptionist. Assembly-line worker. Truck driver. Bank official. Waitress. What with the computer and all manner of automation, add scores of hundreds of new occupations and, thus, new heroes and antiheroes to Walt Whitman's old anthem. The sound, though, is no longer melodious. The desperation is unquiet.

15   Perhaps Nora Watson has put her finger on it. She reflects on her father's work. He was a fundamentalist preacher, with whom she had been profoundly at odds.

16   "Whatever, he was, he was. It was his calling, his vocation. He saw himself as a core resource of the community. He liked his work, even though his family barely survived, because that was what he was sup-

posed to be doing. His work was his life. He himself was not separate and apart from his calling. I think this is what all of us are looking for, a calling, not just a job. Most of us, like the assembly-line worker, have jobs that are too small for our spirit. Jobs are not big enough for people."

17   Does it take another, less competitive, less buck-oriented society to make one match the other?

VOCABULARY

demeaning (P1), *profound* (P1), *precincts* (P2), *communiqués* (P2), *impertinent* (P3), *increment* (P3), *being* (P3), *acridly* (P6), *audit* (P9), *singularly* (P9), *document* (P10), *appraisal* (P10), *persists* (P11), *obstinately* (P11), *horrendous* (P11), *off-load* (P11), *graphically* (P12), *compounded* (P12), *demeaned* (P12), *antiheroes* (P14), *anthem* (P14), *fundamentalist* (P15), *vocation* (P16)

IDEAS AND AIMS

1. Taking points from PP1–3, formulate in one sentence the central ideas of Terkel's essay.
2. Citing examples from the essay (e.g., the question of the closing paragraph), explain how the purpose of Terkel's essay is as much argumentative or persuasive as it is expository.
3. According to Terkel, what is the difference between younger and older workers' views of their jobs?
4. How does Terkel's example of elderly secretaries in P2 and the word "all" in P3 modify Terkel's contrast between younger and older workers?
5. Contrast Yolanda Leif's and Peggy Terry's views on waitress jobs (PP12–13).
6. How does Terkel "establish his credentials," convince us of his expertise and authority about his material, in this essay?

ORGANIZATION AND FORM

1. What are the functions of PP1–3? Of PP14–17?
2. How are PP4–13 organized? What principle has Terkel used to divide the body of his essay into paragraphs?
3. What effect is created by using so many examples? Is Terkel's essay basically inductive or deductive? (Look up these terms in your composition handbook or collegiate dictionary.)

4. What kinds of examples does Terkel use? What are the ages of his interviewees? What other characteristics should the reader look for in the interviewees?

5. How is it an effective idea to end an essay, especially a persuasive essay, with a question, as Terkel does here?

WORDS AND STYLE

1. What examples, indicative of his background in journalistic writing, can you find in the essay of Terkel's short sentences, short paragraphs, and informal style (contractions, colloquial words)?

2. Where in the essay is Terkel's word choice or sentence structure rather elegant, sophisticated, or formal? Why is it important for Terkel to include this stylistic level in his essay, considering his persuasive purpose and main concept, the dignity of workers?

3. How might the pronounced formality of the sentence beginning "Ought there not . . ." in P3 be correlated to or help express the concept in this sentence of human dignity in labor?

4. How would you characterize the language used by Terkel's interviewees? What effects are created by his leaving their grammar and occasional clichés intact?

5. Do you think these are the workers' real names? Why? Why would Terkel use these names rather than more general means of reference, such as "a young steel worker in Chicago" or "a twenty-four-year-old secretary"?

6. What is the meaning of Terkel's metaphor in the first sentence of his essay, "the razor of necessity cuts close"? What ideas or feelings does the metaphor help Terkel convey or evoke that a plainer statement would not do as effectively?

DISCUSSION AND WRITING

1. Do you think jobs in which part of the pay comes in the form of tips are necessarily demeaning jobs? Why or why not?

2. Is it ridiculous for a steelworker to compare his work to the art of Picasso? Why or why not?

3. In P14 Terkel alludes to Walt Whitman's poem "I Hear America Singing." Read this poem and contrast his view of American workers with Terkel's views.

4. Also in P14, in the last sentence, Terkel alludes to Thoreau's famous words in the first section of *Walden*, "Economy": "The mass of men lead lives of quiet desperation. What is called resignation is confirmed desperation. In this pas-

sage, as in his "Getting a Living" (Section 2, "Work and Morality"), Thoreau discusses how one's job and salary may lead to, or away from, self-fulfillment. How do Terkel's views compare with Thoreau's?

5. Compare the views of Fuller (Section 2, "Work and Morality"), Thoreau (Section 2), and Smith's "High Wages and Overwork" (Section 5, "Money") and those of Terkel regarding the impact of money on the issues of work and self-fulfillment.

6. Take your own survey of your classmates, friends, parents, and relatives, based on P7 of Terkel's essay (the Who Are You? game). Do your results correspond to those that Terkel reports?

EINE KLEINE MOTHMUSIK

S. J. Perelman

Reviewing his book Vinegar Puss *(1975), celebrated American author Eudora Welty called S. J. Perelman "a living national treasure," and in 1978 Perelman was the recipient of the first Special Achievement Award of the National Book Awards Committee. Called by one modern critic "an advanced absurdist, much admired by many serious writers," S. J. Perelman will probably be remembered as America's greatest humorist of the late twentieth century.*

Born in Brooklyn, New York, and educated at Brown University, Sidney Joseph Perelman (1904–1979) wrote for college humor magazines and then in 1929 published the first of his 23 books, Dawn Ginsbergh's Revenge, *which, in the words of one scholar, "precipitated a national paroxysm." It also precipitated Perelman to Hollywood, where he was a gagwriter and scriptwriter for some of the early Marx Brothers films. Perelman's work in Hollywood continued intermittently over the years, including contributions to Michael Todd's* Around the World in Eighty Days *(1956), and provided Perelman with plenty of material for his humorous essays. Perelman's leaning toward drama may be seen in the play* One Touch of Venus *(1943), which he coauthored with America's leading comic poet, Ogden Nash; in his own brief-running Broadway play* The Beauty Part, *published in book form in 1963; and in the playlet format of many of his essays.*

From the 1940s on, most of Perelman's essays, which he preferred to call "feuilletons" (a word to be found in your collegiate dictionary), appeared in The New Yorker *magazine, a periodical that publishes high-quality writing. His books, most of which have been published in paperback as well as hard cover, are* Parlor, Bedlam and Bath *(1930),* Strictly from Hunger *(1937),* Look Who's Talking *(1940),* The Dream Department *(1943),* Crazy Like a Fox *(1944),* Keep It Crisp *(1946),* Acres and Pains *(1947),* The Best of S. J. Perelman *(1947),* Westward Ha! *or,* Around the World in Eighty Cliches *(1948),* Listen to the Mocking Bird *(1949),* The Swiss Family Perelman *(1950),* The Ill-Tempered Clavichord *(1953),* Perelman's Home Companion *(1955),* The Road to Miltown, or Under the Spreading Atrophy *(1957),* The Most of S. J. Perelman *(1958),* The Rising Gorge *(1961),* Chicken Inspector No. 23 *(1966),* Baby, It's Cold Inside *(1970),* Eastward Ha! *(1977), and* The Last Laugh *(1981). Note the allusions, puns, and general liveliness of the language in just the titles of Perelman's books.*

Perelman's subjects range from his extensive foreign travels to, domestically, almost everything in American culture, including pieces about business and advertising and hilarious reviews of an awesome spread of specialized trade magazines, brochures, and "house organs." Often, as in this selection, Perelman will take a newspaper item and relate it to his personal experience or expand on it in a whimsical play or narrative. An admirer of novelist and poet James Joyce, one of the great prose stylists of the twentieth century, Perelman in many respects follows the master in his own masterly blend of allusion (note the title of the selection), anglicized foreign terms (couilouirs, jeunesse dore), precise terms for things ("exophthalmic," "bittern," "dottle"), sesquipedalianisms ("peculation," "flocculent"), slang ("sawbuck," "on a toot"), Yiddish ("schmendrick," "shmotta"), puns, and wisecracks. Perelman will often, as in this selection, use for comic, revelatory effect the deliberate interplay of levels of usage, from formal and fancy to colloquial and slang.

This selection has a good deal to suggest about the relations between consumer and businessman and the art of writing argument and persuasion—which all those who are called on to write reports, correspondence, and memoranda at work will have to do.

WAR ON MOTHS BEGINS

1 The moths are beginning to eat. Even if the weather seems cool, this is their season for gluttony. Miss Rose Finkel, manager of Keystone Cleaners at 313 West Fifty-seventh Street, urges that these precautions be taken:

2 All winter clothes should be dry-cleaned, even if no stains are apparent. Moths feast on soiled clothes, and if a garment has been worn several times in the last few months, it should be cleaned.

3 Clean clothes may be kept in the closet in a plastic bag. It is safer, however, to send all woolens to a dry cleaner to put in cold storage.

4 Customers should check to make sure that their clothes are really sent to a cold storage and not hung in the back of the store.—*The Times.*

GAY HEAD,
MARTHA'S VINEYARD, MASS.,
JULY 14

Mr. Stanley Merlin,
Busy Bee Cleaners,
161 Macdougal Street,
New York City

DEAR MR. MERLIN:

5   I heard on the radio this morning before I went for my swim that the heat in New York is catastrophic, but you wouldn't guess it up here. There is a dandy breeze at all times, and the salt-water bathing, as you can imagine, is superlative. Miles of glorious white beach, marvelous breakers, rainbow-colored cliffs—in short, paradise. One feels so rested, so completely purified, that it seems profane to mention anything as sordid as dry cleaning. Still, that's not exactly your problem, is it? I have one that is.

6   Do you, by chance, remember a tan gabardine suit I sent in to be pressed three or four years ago? It's a very expensive garment, made of that changeable, shimmering material they call solari cloth. The reverse side is a reddish color, like cayenne pepper; during the British occupation of India, as you doubtless know, it was widely used for officers' dress uniforms. Anyway, I'm a trifle concerned lest moths get into the closet where I left it in our apartment. The suit isn't really stained, mind you; there's just a faint smudge of lychee syrup on the right sleeve, about the size of your pinkie, that I got in a Chinese restaurant last winter. (I identify it only to help you expunge it without too much friction. I mean, it's a pretty costly garment, and the nap could be damaged if some boob started rubbing it with pumice or whatever.)

7   Will you, hence, arrange to have your delivery boy pick up the suit at my flat any time next Thursday morning after nine-fifteen? He'll have to show before ten-twenty, since the maid leaves on the dot and would certainly split a gusset if she had to sit around a hot apartment waiting for a delivery boy. (You know how they are, Mr. Merlin.) Tell the boy to be sure and take the right suit; it's hanging next to one made of covert cloth with diagonal flap pockets, and as the Venetian blinds are drawn, he could easily make a mistake in the dark. Flotilla, the maid, is new, so I think I'd better explain which closet to look in. It's in the hall, on his right when he stands facing the bedroom windows. If he stands facing the other way, naturally it's on his left. The main thing, tell him, is not to get rattled and look in the closet *opposite*, because there may be a gabardine suit in there, without pockets, but that isn't the one I have reference to.

8   Should Flotilla have gone, the visiting super will admit your boy to the flat if he arrives before eleven; otherwise, he is to press our landlord's bell (Coopersmith), in the next building, and ask them for the key. They

can't very well give it to him, as they're in Amalfi, but they have a Yugoslav woman dusting for them, a highly intelligent person, to whom he can explain the situation. This woman speaks English.

9   After the suit is dry-cleaned—which, I repeat, is not essential if you'll only brush the stain with a little moist flannel—make certain that it goes into cold storage at once. I read a piece in the newspaper recently that upset me. It quoted a prominent lady in your profession, a Miss Rose Finkel, to the effect that some dry cleaners have been known to hang such orders in the back of their store. You and I have had such a long, cordial relationship, Mr. Merlin, that I realize you'd never do anything so unethical, but I just thought I'd underscore it.

10   Incidentally, and since I know what the temperature in your shop must be these days, let me pass on a couple of hot-weather tips. Eat lots of curries—the spicier the better—and try to take at least a three-hour siesta in the middle of the day. I learned this trick in India, where Old Sol can be a cruel taskmaster indeed. That's also the place, you'll recall, where solari cloth used to get a big play in officers' dress uniforms. Wears like iron, if you don't abuse it. With every good wish,

Yours sincerely,
S. J. PERELMAN

NEW YORK CITY,
JULY 22

DEAR MR. PEARLMAN:

11   I got your letter of instructions spelling everything out, and was happy to hear what a glorious vacation you are enjoying in that paradise. I only hope you will be careful to not run any fishhooks in your hand, or step in the undertow, or sunburn your body so badly you lay in the hospital. These troubles I personally don't have. I am a poor man with a wife and family to support, not like some people with stocks and bonds that they can sit in a resort all summer and look down their nose on the rest of humanity. Also my pressing machine was out of commission two days and we are shorthanded. Except for this, everything is peaches and cream.

12   I sent the boy over like you told me on Thursday. There was no sign of the maid, but for your information he found a note under the door saying she has quit. She says you need a bulldozer, not a servant, and the pay is so small she can do better on relief. Your landlady, by the way, is back from Amalfi, because some of the tenants, she didn't name names, are slow with the rent. She let the boy in the apartment, and while he was finding your red suit she checked over the icebox and the stove, which she claims are very greasy. (I am not criticizing your housekeeping, only reporting what she said.) She also examined the mail in the bureau drawers to see if the post office was forwarding your bills, urgent telegrams, etc.

13   I don't believe in telling a man his own business. Mine is dry cleaning, yours I don't know what, but you're deceiving yourself about this
Indian outfit you gave us. It was one big stain from top to bottom. Maybe
you leaned up against the stove or the icebox? (Just kidding.) The plant
used every kind of solvent they had on it—benzine, naphtha, turpentine,
even lighter fluid—and knocked out the spots, all right, but I warn you
beforehand, there are a few brownish rings. The lining was shot to begin
with, so that will be no surprise to you; according to the label, you had the
suit since 1944. If you want us to replace same, I can supply a first-class,
all-satin quarter lining for $91.50, workmanship included. Finally, but-
tons. Some of my beatnik customers wear the jacket open and don't need
them. For a conservative man like yourself, I would advise spending
another eight dollars.

14   As regards your worry about hiding cold-storage articles in the back
of my store, I am not now nor have I ever been a chiseler, and I defy you to
prove different. Every season like clockwork, I get one crackpot who
expects me to be Santa Claus and haul his clothing up to the North Pole
or someplace. My motto is live and let live, which it certainly is not this
Rose Finkel's to go around destroying people's confidence in their dry
cleaner. Who is she, anyway? I had one of these experts working for me
already, in 1951, that nearly put me in the hands of the receivers. She
told a good customer of ours, an artist who brought in some hand-painted
ties to be rainproofed, to save his money and throw them in the Harlem
River. To a client that showed her a dinner dress with a smear on the
waist, she recommends the woman should go buy a bib. I am surprised
that you, a high-school graduate, a man that pretends to be intelligent,
would listen to such poison. But in this business you meet all kinds.
Regards to the Mrs.

Yours truly,
S. MERLIN

GAY HEAD, MASS.,
JULY 25

DEAR MR. MERLIN:

15   While I'm altogether sympathetic to your plight and fully aware
that your shop's an inferno at the moment—I myself am wearing an
imported cashmere sweater as I write—I must say you misinterpreted my
letter. My only motive in relaying Miss Stricture's finkels (excuse me, the
strictures of Miss Finkel) on the subject of proper cold storage was concern for a favorite garment. I was not accusing you of duplicity, and I
refuse to share the opinion, widespread among persons who deal with
them frequently, that most dry cleaners are crooks. It is understandably
somewhat off-putting to hear that my suit arrived at your establishment

in ruinous condition, and, to be devastatingly candid, I wonder whether your boy may not have collided with a soup kitchen in transit. But each of us must answer to his own conscience, Mr. Merlin, and I am ready, if less than overjoyed, to regard yours as immaculate.

16   Answering your question about Miss Finkel's identity, I have never laid eyes on her, needless to say, though reason dictates that if a distinguished newspaper like the *Times* publishes her counsel, she must be an authority. Furthermore, if the practice of withholding clothes from cold storage were uncommon, why would she have broached the subject at all? No, my friend, it is both useless and ungenerous of you to attempt to undermine Miss Finkel. From the way you lashed out at her, I deduce that she touched you on the raw, in a most vulnerable area of our relationship, and that brings me to the core of this communication.

17   Nowhere in your letter is there any direct assertion that you *did* send my valuable solari suit to storage, or, correlatively, that you are *not* hiding it in the back of the store. I treasure my peace of mind too much to sit up here gnawed by anxiety. I must therefore demand from you a categorical statement by return airmail special delivery. Is this garment in your possession or not? Unless a definite answer is forthcoming within forty-eight hours, I shall be forced to take action.

Yours truly,

S. J. PERELMAN

NEW YORK CITY,

JULY 27

DEAR MR. PERLEMAN:

18   If all you can do with yourself in a summer place is hang indoors and write me love letters about Rose Finkel, I must say I have pity on you. Rose Finkel, Rose Finkel—why don't you marry this woman that you are so crazy about her. Then she could clean your suits at home and stick them in the icebox—after she cleans that, too. What do you want from me? Sometimes I think I am walking around in a dream.

19   Look, I will do anything you say. Should I parcel-post the suit to you so you can examine it under a microscope for holes? Should I board up my store, give the help a week free vacation in the mountains, and bring it to you personally in my Cadillac? I tell you once, twice, a million times—it went to cold storage. I didn't send it myself; I gave orders to my assistant, which she has been in my employ eleven years. From her I have no secrets, and you neither. She told me about some of the mail she found in your pants.

20   It is quite warm here today, but we are keeping busy and don't notice. My tailor collapsed last night with heat prostration, so I am han-

dling alterations, pressing, ticketing, and hiding customers' property in the back of the store. Also looking up psychiatrists in the Yellow Pages.

Yours truly,

S. MERLIN

GAY HEAD, MASS.,
JULY 29

DEAR MR. MERLIN:

21   My gravest doubts are at last confirmed: You are unable to say unequivocally, without tergiversating, that you *saw* my suit put into cold storage. Knowing full well that the apparel was irreplaceable, now that the British Raj has been supplanted—knowing that it was the keystone of my entire wardrobe, the *sine qua non* of sartorial taste—you deliberately entrusted it to your creature, a cat's-paw who you admit rifles my pockets as a matter of routine. Your airy disavowal of your responsibility, therefore, leaves me with but one alternative. By this same post, I am delegating a close friend of mine, Irving Wiesel, to visit your place of business and ferret out the truth. You can lay your cards on the table with Wiesel or not, as you see fit. When he finishes with you, you will have neither cards nor table.

22   It would be plainly superfluous, at this crucial stage in our association, to hark back to such petty and characteristic vandalism as your penchant for jabbing pins into my rainwear, pressing buttons halfway through lapels, and the like. If I pass over these details now, however, do not yield to exultation. I shall expatiate at length in the proper surroundings; viz., in court. Wishing you every success in your next vocation,

Yours truly,

S. J. PERELMAN

NEW YORK CITY
AUGUST 5

DEAR MR. PERLMAN:

23   I hope you received by now from my radiologist the two X-rays; he printed your name with white ink on the ulcer so you should be satisfied that you, and you alone, murdered me. I wanted him to print also "Here lies an honest man that he slaved for years like a dog, schlepped through rain and snow to put bread in his children's mouths, and see what gratitude a customer gave him," but he said there wasn't room. Are you satisfied now, you Cossack you? Even my *radiologist* is on your side.

24   You didn't need to tell me in advance that Wiesel was a friend of yours; it was stamped all over him the minute he walked in the store. Walked? He was staggering from the highballs you and your bohemian cronies bathe in. No how-do-you-do, explanations, nothing. Ran like a hooligan to the back and turned the whole stock upside down, pulled

everything off the racks. I wouldn't mind he wrecked a filing system it cost me hundreds of dollars to install. Before I could grab the man, he makes a beeline for the dressing room. So put yourself for a second in someone else's shoes. A young, refined matron from Boston, first time in the Village, is waiting for her dress to be spot-cleaned, quietly loafing through *Harper's Bazaar*. Suddenly a roughneck, for all she knows a plainclothesman, a junkie, tears aside the curtain. Your delegate Wiesel.

25   I am not going to soil myself by calling you names, you are a sick man and besides on vacation, so will make you a proposition. You owe me for cleaning the suit, the destruction you caused in my racks, medical advice, and general aggravation. I owe you for the suit, which you might as well know is kaput. The cold-storage people called me this morning. It seems like all the brownish rings in the material fell out and they will not assume responsibility for a sieve. This evens up everything between us, and I trust that on your return I will have the privilege of serving you and family as in years past. All work guaranteed, invisible weaving our specialty. Please remember me to your lovely wife.

Sincerely yours,
Stanley Merlin

VOCABULARY

gluttony (P1), *woolens* (P3), *superlative* (P5), *breakers* (P5), *profane* (P5), *sordid* (P5), *gabardine* (P6), *cayenne* (P6), *dress uniforms* (P6), *lychee* (P6), *expunge* (P6), *garment* (P6), *nap* (P6), *pumice* (P6), *flat* (P7), *gusset* (P7), *covert cloth* (P7), *rattled* (P7), *super* (P8), *cordial* (P9), *underscore* (P9), *curries* (P10), *siesta* (P10), *Sol* (P10), *taskmaster* (P10), *undertow* (P11), *relief* (P12), *solvent* (P13), *benzine* (P13), *naphtha* (P13), *beatnik* (P13), *chiseler* (P14), *receivers* (P14), *inferno* (P15), *cashmere* (P15), *strictures* (P15), *duplicity* (P15), *off-putting* (P15), *devastatingly* (P15), *candid* (P15), *soup kitchen* (P15), *immaculate* (P15), *counsel* (P16), *broached* (P16), *correlatively* (P17), *categorical* (P17), *prostration* (P20), *gravest* (P21), *unequivocally* (P21), *tergiversating* (P21), *Raj* (P21), *supplanted* (P21), *keystone* (P21), *sine qua non* (P21), *sartorial* (P21), *cat's-paw* (P21), *rifles* (P21), *airy* (P21), *disavowal* (P21), *post* (P21), *superfluous* (P22), *penchant* (P22), *exultation* (P22), *expatiate* (P22), *viz.* (P22), *vocation* (P22), *schlepped* (P23), *Cossack* (P23), *highballs* (P24), *bohemian* (P24), *cronies* (P24), *hooligan* (P24), *beeline* (P24), *matron* (P24), *kaput* (P25), *sieve* (P25)

IDEAS AND AIMS

1. What evidence from the essay suggests that one of Perelman's chief aims is to amuse or satirize?

2. Both Perelman's and Merlin's letters are essentially argumentative or persuasive. Each writer tries to get his correspondent to do something or change his mind about something. Cite specifics that exemplify this argumentative or persuasive nature of the letters.

3. How do several specifics of the opening and closing paragraphs of Perelman's first letter (P5, P10) undermine the chances of success of the whole letter by causing an initial unfavorable reaction in its addressee? How does the first paragraph of Merlin's reply (P11) indeed verify that Merlin *has* responded unfavorably to Perelman's ill-considered paragraphs? What is wrong with P5 and P10 in a basic way for the purpose of persuasion or getting someone to do something?

4. In the first paragraph of his reply (P11), how does Merlin requite the first and last paragraphs of Perelman's first letter (P5, P10)?

5. What several jibes does Perelman get in at landlords and landladies in P12, including Merlin's remarks about the mail?

6. How does the fourth sentence of P13 contradict the sixth sentence of P12? What mood does this suggest in Merlin? Does he have a good reason?

7. How does Merlin's response in P14 show that Perelman's gambit in P9 is another miscalculation?

8. Is Perelman's inference or deduction in the last sentence of P16 correct? What might this show about his perception?

9. How does the second sentence of P20 contradict the first sentence, and how does this favorably portray Merlin as a businessman?

10. What is the implication of the last sentence of P20? How does this sentence hark back to the last sentence of P18?

11. How does Merlin misinterpret his radiologist's chirographical refusal in P23? What does this reveal about Merlin's psychological state and its effect on his perception of people around him?

12. What does the concluding part of Merlin's final letter (the last three sentences of P25) suggest about doing or staying in business?

13. What point does the whole essay make about the role of trust in a business relationship?

14. How are consumers and businessmen satirized in the essay? In what way does Perelman mock the consumer more than the businessman?

ORGANIZATION AND FORM

1. Overall, what letters between the two correspondents form the beginning of Perelman's essay, which the middle, and which the end? How so?

2. How is there a progressive change in the attitudes and emotions of the two writers in their letters?

3. How do some of the individual letters have a distinct beginning (or introduction), middle (or body), and end (or conclusion)? Cite examples.

4. What implicit connections can you find between letters, or allusions in a letter to an earlier one, such as the reference to the icebox in P18, pointing to P12 and P13? How is the example cited in this question funny and also psychologically revealing?

5. How do the concluding sentences of Merlin's last letter bring the relationship between the two writers full circle? Why is this funny? What does it suggest about the seriousness of storms in human relationships or about business dealings?

WORDS AND STYLE

1. How do Perelman's word choice and sentence structure characterize his education, social class, and so on in his letters? Cite examples. Where does he use highfalutin language inappropriately?

2. How do Stanley Merlin's word choice and sentence structure characterize his education, social class, and so on? Cite examples.

3. How does the motif in Perelman's essays of people misspelling his name appear in this essay? What does it help suggest about the relationship between customer and firm? How does it undercut the fourth sentence of P9 and the sixth sentence of P25?

4. A hallmark of Perelman's prose style is ubiquitous punning. What are the puns (and the ideas they help suggest or character traits they help reveal) on the name of the maid, Flotilla in P8 (look up "flotilla" in your collegiate dictionary)? On "immaculate" in P15 (especially considering the preceding sentence in P15 as well as Merlin's occupation)? On the last name of Perelman's "delegate," Wiesel (pronounced "WEE-sill") in P21 (look up "ferret" in your collegiate dictionary)? On "soil" in P25, considering the occupation of the user of the word?

5. How does another hallmark of Perelman's prose, the deliberate comic interplay of levels of usage (fancy versus colloquial words), appear in the last two sentences of P6? What other examples can you find?

6. How do the last sentence and complimentary close of the two correspondents' letters change during the course of their business dealing? How are their emotional states revealed at each change in these two epistolary elements?

7. How can we tell from the last sentence of P11 and the fourth item in his series in the second sentence of P20 that Merlin has a wizard sense of irony?

8. How does Perelman use the rhetorical device of apophasis or paraleipsis in P9 and P22? Why is this device useful for argument? Does it work for Perelman the consumer?

9. What in his language makes the concluding sentences of Merlin's last letter sound like a commercial or advertisement? How might this relate to question 12 of Ideas and Aims, and question 5 of Organization and Form?

10. The title of Perelman's essay alludes to and is a comically fitting alteration of the title of Mozart's serenade *Eine kleine Nachtmusik* (K. 525), "A Little

Night-Music." How is the discordant correspondence between Perelman and Merlin anything but harmonious and serene? In what ways *does* their correspondence resemble the classical sonata musical form and the Mozart piece? For example, how does it have three or four distinct, almost musical "movements": a symmetrical, upbeat ("allegro") opening and closing, resolving the tension of the middle part; and recall of or allusion to melodies, phrases, or motifs already heard?

DISCUSSION AND WRITING

1. In your personal experience, are consumers or businesses more often at fault in business dealings? Is "the customer always right"?
2. Have you or has anyone you know been guilty, like Perelman, of disregarding Mayleas' advice in P14, third sentence, of her essay "How to Land the Job You Want" (Section 6, "Job Opportunities and Other Practical Matters")?
3. Are Perelman and Merlin even, at the end of the essay? Why or why not?
4. Write a letter in which you try to get a client, business prospect, or company to do something for you. Be as persuasive as you can, avoiding Perelman's (intentionally ironic) mistakes.

CONFESSIONS
OF A WORKING STIFF

Patrick Fenton

☐

When this essay appeared in 1975, Patrick Fenton was 31 years old and had worked as a cargo handler at Seaboard Airlines in New York for seven years. Published in New York *magazine, the essay has the qualities of good journalistic, magazine writing: it uses in general a relatively simple level of words; it varies in style and word choice from the colloquial to the formal; it uses many vivid details and some very expressive figures of speech.*

Though he is unenthusiastic about his airline job, Fenton's talent and enthusiasm for writing clearly show in his essay. Indeed, in a recent letter to the editors of this book he enthusiastically volunteered to write his own introduction to the selection, which has been appreciatively reprinted in many essay anthologies. In that same letter Mr. Fenton disclosed that he had jettisoned his cargo-handling job in favor of working in the New York State court system. From the following essay, the reader will understand the motives behind this jurisprudence.

1 The Big Ben is hammering out its 5:45 alarm in the half-dark of another Tuesday morning. If I'm lucky, my car down in the street will kick over for me. I don't want to think about that now; all I want to do is roll over into the warm covers that hug my wife. I can hear the wind as it whistles up and down the sides of the building. Tuesday is always the worst day—

it's the day the drudgery, boredom, and fatigue start all over again. I'm off from work on Sunday and Monday, so Tuesday is my blue Monday.

2   I make my living humping cargo for Seaboard World Airlines, one of the big international airlines at Kennedy Airport. They handle strictly all cargo. I was once told that one of the Rockefellers is the major stockholder for the airline, but I don't really think about that too much. I don't get paid to think. The big thing is to beat that race with the time clock every morning of your life so the airline will be happy. The worst thing a man could ever do is to make suggestions about building a better airline. They pay people $40,000 a year to come up with better ideas. It doesn't matter that these ideas never work; it's just that they get nervous when a guy from South Brooklyn or Ozone Park acts like he actually has a brain.

3   I throw a Myadec high-potency vitamin into my mouth to ward off one of the ten colds I get every year from humping mailbags out in the cold rain at Kennedy. A huge DC-8 stretch jet waits impatiently for the 8,000 pounds of mail that I will soon feed its empty belly. I wash the Myadec down with some orange juice and grab a brown bag filled with bologna and cheese. Inside the lunch bag there is sometimes a silly note from my wife that says, "I Love You—Guess Who?" It is all that keeps me going to a job that I hate.

4   I've been going there for seven years now and my job is still the same. It's weary work that makes a man feel used up and worn out. You push and you pull all day long with your back. You tie down pallets loaded with thousands of pounds of freight. You fill igloo-shaped containers with hundreds of boxes that all look the same. If you're assigned to work the warehouse, it's really your hard luck. This is the job all the men hate most. You stack box upon box until the pallet resembles the exact shape of the inside of the plane. You get the same monotonous feeling an adult gets when he plays with a child's blocks. When you finish one pallet, you find another and start the whole dull process over again.

5   The airline pays me $192 a week for this. After they take out taxes and $5.81 for the pension, I go home with $142. Once a month they take out $10 for term life insurance, and $5.50 for union dues. The week they take out the life insurance is always the worst: I go home with $132. My job will never change. I will fill up the same igloos with the same boxes for the next 34 years of my life, I will hump the same mailbags into the belly of the plane, and push the same 8,000-pound pallets with my back. I will have to do this until I'm 65 years old. Then I'll be free, if I don't die of a heart attack before that, and the airline will let me retire.

6   In winter the warehouse is cold and damp. There is no heat. The large steel doors that line the warehouse walls stay open most of the day. In the cold months, wind, rain and snow blow across the floor. In the summer the warehouse becomes an oven. Dust and sand from the run-

ways mix with the toxic fumes of fork lifts, leaving a dry, stale taste in your mouth. The high windows above the doors are covered with a thick, black dirt that kills the sun. The men work in shadows with the constant roar of jet engines blowing dangerously in their ears.

7   Working the warehouse is a tedious job that leaves a man's mind empty. If he's smart he will spend his days wool-gathering. He will think about pretty girls that he once knew, or some other daydream of warm, dry places where you never had a chill. The worst thing he can do is to think about his problems. If he starts to think about how he is going to pay the mortgage on the $30,000 home that he can't afford, it will bring him down. He will wonder why he comes to the cargo airline every morning of his life, and even on Christmas Day. He will start to wonder why he has to listen to the deafening sound of the jets as they rev up their engines. He will wonder why he crawls on his hands and knees, breaking his back a little bit more every day.

8   To keep his kids in that great place in the country in the summer, that great place far away from Brooklyn and the South Bronx, he must work every hour of overtime that the airline offers him. If he never turns down an hour, if he works some 600 hours over, he can make about $15,000. To do this he must turn against himself, he must pray that the phone rings in the middle of the night, even though it's snowing out and he doesn't feel like working. He must hump cargo late into the night, eat meatball heroes for supper, drink coffee that starts to taste like oil, and then hope that his car starts when it's time to go home. If he gets sick— well, he better not think about that.

9   All over Long Island, Ozone Park, Brooklyn, and as far away as the Bronx, men stir in the early morning hours as a new day begins. Every morning is the same as the last. Some of the men drink beer for breakfast instead of coffee. Way out in Bay Shore a cargoman snaps open a can of Budweiser. It's 6 A.M., and he covers the top of the can with his thumb in order to keep down the loud hiss as the beer escapes. He doesn't want to awaken his children as they dream away the morning in the next room. Soon he will swing his Pinto wagon up onto the crowded Long Island Expressway and start the long ride to the job. As he slips the car out of the driveway he tucks another can of beer between his legs.

10   All the men have something in common: they hate the work they are doing and they drink a little too much. They come to work only to punch a timecard that has their last name on it. At the end of the week they will pick up a paycheck with their last name on it. They will never receive a bonus for a job well done, or even a party. At Christmastime a card from the president of the airline will arrive at each one of their houses. It will say Merry Christmas and have the president's name printed at the bottom of it. They know that the airline will be there long

after they are dead. Nothing stops it. It runs non-stop, without sleep, through Christmas Day, New Year's Eve, Martin Luther King's birthday, even the deaths of Presidents.

11   It's seven in the morning and the day shift is starting to drift in. Huge tractors are backing up to the big-mouth doors of the warehouse. Cattle trucks bring tons of beef to feed its insatiable appetite for cargo. Smoke-covered trailers with refrigerated units packed deep with green peppers sit with their diesel engines idling. Names like White, Mack, and Kenworth are welded to the front of their radiators, which hiss and moan from the overload. The men walk through the factory-type gates of the parking lot with their heads bowed, oblivious of the shuddering diesels that await them.

12   Once inside the warehouse they gather in groups of threes and fours like prisoners in an exercise yard. They stand in front of the two time clocks that hang below a window in the manager's office. They smoke and cough in the early morning hour as they await their work assignments. The manager, a nervous-looking man with a stomach that is starting to push out at his belt, walks out with the pink work sheets in his hand.

13   Eddie, a young Irishman with a mustache, has just bolted in through the door. The manager has his timecard in his hand, holding it so no one else can hit Eddie in. Eddie is four minutes late by the time clock. His name will now go down in the timekeeper's ledger. The manager hands the card to him with a "you'll be up in the office if you don't straighten out" look. Eddie takes the card, hits it in, and slowly takes his place with the rest of the men. He has been out till four in the morning drinking beer in the bars of Ozone Park; the time clock and the manager could blow up, for all he cares. "Jesus," he says to no one in particular, "I hope to Christ they don't put me in the warehouse this morning."

14   Over in another group, Kelly, a tall man wearing a navy knit hat, talks to the men. "You know, I almost didn't make it in this morning. I passed this green VW on the Belt Parkway. The girl driving it was singing. Jesus, I thought to myself, it must be great going somewhere at 6:30 in the morning that makes you want to sing." Kelly is smiling as he talks. "I often think, why the hell don't you keep on going, Kelly? Don't get off at the cargo exit, stay on. Go anywhere, even if it's only Brooklyn. Christ, if I was a single man I think I would do just that. Some morning I'd pass this damn place by and drive as far away as Riverhead. I don't know what I'd do when I got there—maybe I'd pick up a pound of beefsteak tomatoes from one of those roadside stands or something."

15   The men laugh at Kelly but they know he is serious. "I feel the same way sometimes," the man next to him says. "I find myself daydreaming a lot lately; this place drives you to that. I get up in the morning and I just don't want to come to work. I get sick when I hit that parking lot. If it

wasn't for the kids and the house I'd quit." The men then talk about how hard it is to get work on "the outside." They mention "outside" as if they were in a prison.

16   Each morning there is an Army-type roll call from the leads. The leads are foremen who must keep the men moving; if they don't, it could mean their jobs. At one time they had power over the men but as time went by the company took away their little bit of authority. They also lost the deep interest, even enjoyment, for the hard work they once did. As the cargo airline grew, it beat this out of them, leaving only apathy. The ramp area is located in the backyard of the warehouse. This is where the huge jets park to unload their 70,000-pound payloads. A crew of men fall in behind the ramp lead as he mopes out of the warehouse. His long face shows the hopelessness of another day.

17   A brutal rain has started to beat down on the oil-covered concrete of the ramp as the 306 screeches in off the runway. Its engines scream as they spit off sheets of rain and oil. Two of the men cover their ears as they run to put up a ladder to the front of the plane. The airline will give them ear covers only if they pay for half of them. A lot of the men never buy them. If they want, the airline will give them two little plugs free. The plugs don't work and hurt the inside of the ears.

18   The men will spend the rest of the day in the rain. Some of them will set up conveyor belts and trucks to unload the thousands of pounds of cargo that sit in the deep belly of the plane. Then they will feed the awkward bird until it is full and ready to fly again. They will crawl on their hands and knees in its belly, counting and humping hundreds of mailbags. The rest of the men will work up topside on the plane, pushing 8,000-pound pallets with their backs. Like Egyptians building a pyramid, they will pull and push until the pallet finally gives in and moves like a massive stone sliding through sand. They don't complain too much; they know that when the airline comes up with a better system some of them will go.

19   The old-timers at the airline can't understand why the younger men stay on. They know what the cargo airline can do to a man. It can work him hard but make him lazy at the same time. The work comes in spurts. Sometimes a man will be pushed for three hours of sweat, other times he will just stand around bored. It's not the hard work that breaks a man at the airline, it's the boredom of doing the same job over and over again.

20   At the end of the day the men start to move in off the ramp. The rain is still beating down at their backs but they move slowly. Their faces are red and raw from the rain-soaked wind that has been snapping at them for eight hours. The harsh wind moves in from the direction of the city. From the ramp you can see the Manhattan skyline, gray- and blue-looking, as it peeks up from the west wall of the warehouse. There is nothing

to block the winter weather as it rolls in like a storm across a prairie. They head down to the locker room, heads bowed, like a football team that never wins.

21 With the workday almost over, the men move between the narrow, gray rows of lockers. Up on the dirty walls that surround the lockers someone has written a couple of four-letter words. There is no wit to the words; they just say the usual. As they strip off their wet gear the men seem to come alive.

22 "Hey, Arnie! You want to stay four hours? They're asking for over-time down in Export," one of the men yells over the lockers.

23 Arnie is sitting about four rows over, taking off his heavy winter clothing. He thinks about this for a second and yells back, "What will we be doing?"

24 "Working the meat trailer." This means that Arnie will be humping huge sides of beef off rows of hooks for four hours. Blood will drip down onto his clothes as he struggles to the front of the trailer. Like most of the men, he needs the extra money, and knows that he should stay. He has Master Charge, Korvettes, Times Square Stores, and Abraham & Straus to pay.

25 "Nah, I'm not staying tonight. Not if it's working the meat trailer. Don wanted to stop for a few beers at The Owl; maybe I'll stay tomorrow night."

26 It's four o'clock in the afternoon now—the men have twelve minutes to go before they punch out. The airline has stopped for a few seconds as the men change shifts. Supervisors move frantically across the floor push-ing the fresh lot of new men who have just started to come in. They hand out work sheets and yell orders: "Jack, get your men into their rain gear. Put three men in the bellies to finish off the 300 flight. Get someone on the pepper trailers, they've been here all morning."

27 The morning shift stands around the time clock with three minutes to go. Someone says that Kevin Delahunty has just been appointed to the Fire Department. Kevin, a young Irishman from Ozone Park, has been working the cargo airline for six years. Like most of the men, he has hated every minute of it. The men are openly proud of him as they reach out to shake his hand. Kevin has found a job on "the outside." "Ah, you'll be leaving soon," he tells Pat. "I never thought I'd get out of here either, but you'll see, you're going to make it."

28 The manager moves through the crowd handing out timecards and stops when he comes to Kevin. Someone told him Kevin is leaving. "Is that right, Delahunty? Well I guess we won't expect you in tomorrow, will we? Going to become a fireman eh? That means you'll be jumping out of windows like a crazy man. Don't act like you did around here," he adds as he walks back to his office.

29   The time clock hits 4:12 and the men pour out of the warehouse. Kevin will never be back, but the rest of them will return in the morning to grind out another eight hours. Some of them will head straight home to the bills, screaming children, and a wife who tries to understand them. They'll have a Schaefer or two, then they'll settle down to a night of television.

30   Some of them will start to fill up the cargo bars that surround Kennedy Airport. They will head to places like Gaylor's on Rockaway Boulevard or The Dew Drop Inn down near Farmers Boulevard. They will drink deep glasses of whiskey and cold mugs of Budweiser. The Dew Drop has a honky-tonk mood of the Old West to it. The barmaid moves around like a modern-day Katie Elder. Like Brandy, she's a fine girl, but she can out-curse any cargoman. She wears a low-cut blouse that reveals most of her breasts. The jukebox will beat out some Country & Western as she says, "Ah, hell, you played my song." The cargomen will hoot and holler as she substitutes some of her own obscene lyrics.

31   They will drink late into the night, forgetting time clocks, Master Charge, First National City, Korvettes, mortgages, cars that don't start, and jet engines that hurt their ears. They will forget about damp, cold warehouses, winters that get longer and colder every year, minutes that drift by like hours, supervisors that harass, and the thought of growing old on a job they hate. At midnight they will fall dangerously into their cars and make their way up onto the Southern State Parkway. As they ride into the dark night of Long Island they will forget it all until 5:45 the next morning—when the Big Ben will start up the whole grind all over again.

VOCABULARY

drudgery (P1), *blue Monday* (P1), *humping* (P2), *stretch jet* (P3), *pallets* (P4), *toxic* (P6), *fork lifts* (P6), *tedious* (P7), *wool-gathering* (P7), *rev up* (P7), *heroes* (P8), *insatiable* (P11), *oblivious* (P11), *beefsteak tomatoes* (P14), *apathy* (P16), *mopes* (P16), *harass* (P31)

IDEAS AND AIMS

1. A single thesis statement expressing Fenton's main ideas is implicit rather than explicit in the essay. Formulate the main points in a single thesis statement.

2. Which aspect of a cargo loader's job is the worst, according to Fenton?

THE WAREHOUSE

3. According to Fenton, why do he and the other cargo loaders stay at this job? Are you surprised by this? *TO PAY THE BILLS & WORK ON OUTSIDE IS HARD TO GET*

4. In the last sentence of P8, Fenton leaves his thought implicit. *Why* doesn't the worker want to think about getting sick? *NO PAY & POSSIBLY LOSE YOUR JOB*

5. Why does Fenton stress that the company paycheck has only a last name on it (P10)? How is the treatment of names similarly revealing in PP27–28, where Fenton and the workers use one name while the manager uses another one for Kevin Delahunty? *TO SHOW COMPANYS HARD IMPERSONAL CHARACTE THEY SHOW A PERSONAL FEELING*

6. What is suggested by Fenton's descriptive detail of the men walking through the gates "with . . . heads bowed" (P11)? How is this point reinforced by the last sentence of P20? *THERE APATHY TOWARD JOB. SHOWS A DEFEATED ATTITUDE*

7. What seems to be the workers' attitude toward "the outside" (P15, P27)? Why? *A BETTER PLACE BUT PRACTICALLY IMPOSSIBLE TO GET*

8. What does Fenton's illustrative detail about company policy on ear protectors (P17) suggest about the company, its relation to the men, and the men themselves? *DO ONLY WHAT LAW REQUIRES WITH NO CARE FOR MENS WELL BEING*

9. Why don't the cargo loaders hope the airline will invent an easier way to load planes? What collision of values in the workers is shown here? *LOSS OF JOBS*

10. What are the workers' attitudes toward supervisors and managers? Cite evidence from the essay to support your observations. *DISLIKE HARASSMEN BUT HAVE SLIGHT UNS*

11. Is the overall aim of Fenton's essay strictly neutral, objective description or exposition? Cite evidence to support your answer.

ORGANIZATION AND FORM

1. How does Fenton organize his essay principally by time—that is, chronologically? Give examples of how parts of the essay are pulled together in this manner.

2. Besides time or chronology, Fenton also uses description and illustration as a method of development and organization. How do PP4–8, for example, depart from strict chronological sequence, and what method of development do they use to help Fenton get across his points?

3. How do repetition and parallelism bind up P7, that is, make it more coherent?

4. In PP14–15 Fenton introduces a somewhat different method of developing his ideas. What is it? How do these paragraphs function?

5. Fenton's reference to Big Ben (an inexpensive windup alarm clock, named after the famous London timepiece) and the time of his awakening in the last paragraph link it directly with the first paragraph. What form or shape does this help to give the essay? How is this form or shape related to any of Fenton's main points about the job or the workers' feelings and attitudes toward it?

WORDS AND STYLE

1. How does Fenton's use of the venerable slang term for a worker in his title ("working stiff") have extra meaning in this essay, gathering several of Fenton's main points about his job?

2. An important element of Fenton's style is repetition of certain key words and metaphors. How does Fenton's repeated phrase to describe his job, "humping cargo," capture what he feels about it? Where does he use this phrase? How does it differ from some synonym like "loading cargo"?

3. Fenton often uses concrete words and terms with vivid effectiveness, rather than more general or abstract words. For example, instead of "they'll have a beer," what does Fenton write in P29? How is his concreteness more effective than generality here? Find and discuss similar examples.

4. One pattern of repeated metaphors, similes, and comparisons in the essay has to do with feeding. It starts in P3 (first three sentences), when the author describes his breakfast and also speaks of feeding something else besides himself. How does Fenton's meal ironically contrast with that of the "creature" he feeds, and what is implied thereby? How do the second and third sentences of P11 and the third sentence of P18 tie in with this pattern? How does Fenton's favorite, repeated term for the plane's cargo hold, "belly," tie in with the pattern? What other instances of this pattern can you find in the essay (e.g., Fenton's description of the taste of food on the job)?

5. Another pattern of repeated metaphors, similes, and comparisons in the essay begins with the last sentence of P5 in Fenton's peculiar phrasing about retirement: "the airline will let me retire." By contrast to some such phrasing as "I'll retire from the airline," what does Fenton seem to be getting at here? How does it relate to the simile in the first sentence of P12, in the last sentence of P15, and in the next to last sentence of P18?

6. Fenton uses figures of speech and comparisons very effectively to describe and explain more clearly in several instances other than those cited in questions 4 and 5. Choose one or more of the following, and discuss how Fenton's point is expressed through his word choice: the ninth sentence of P4, next-to-last sentence of P6, second sentence of P7 (think about the contrast to Fenton's work environment), fifth sentence of P11 (the personification), next to last sentence of P20, last sentence of P20, fifth sentence of P30, third sentence of P31 ("fall").

7. What is the overall tone of the essay? How do Fenton's words and style, as suggested in the preceding questions of this section, create or express that tone?

DISCUSSION AND WRITING

1. Describe a typical day at a job you've held (or try to imagine a typical day at a job that interests you). Use an organization like Fenton's, beginning with the

first moments of work and following through to the evening. Try to provide details that will sustain one mood or tone throughout the essay.

2. What things can be done to improve the working conditions of workers like these cargo loaders? Refer to your reading, and describe how innovations made in recent years might apply to a specific situation like the one Fenton describes.

3. What do you personally think is the worst aspect of a cargo handler's job? Do you agree with Fenton's ranking?

4. This essay was written in 1975. What details may have changed since then?

5. Have you ever held a boring or disheartening job over a long period (some might include being a full-time student in this category)? What was boring or disheartening about it? How did you adjust or cope?

TAKING STOCK: COMPARING AND CONTRASTING THE SELECTIONS

1. In what ways does Selzer's view of his profession contain many of the ideas about work enumerated in earlier essays in this anthology, such as those by Fuller (Section 2, "Work and Morality"), Calvin (Section 1, "Job Choice and Self-Fulfillment"), or Thoreau (Section 2)?

2. Compare or contrast what Eric Hoffer says about the benefits of dull work in his essay about that subject (Section 1, "Job Choice and Self-Fulfillment"), with what effects his exciting work seems to have had on Richard Selzer in "The Knife."

3. Are Samuel Johnson and Calvin (Section 1, "Job Choice and Self-Fulfillment") or Fuller (Section 2, "Work and Morality") presenting similar ideas about the dignity of work? Does Johnson's notion of the benefit of work—and the recipients of that benefit—differ from the notions of any of these other writers? How so?

4. What similarities in thought about the varieties of jobs and the assessment of public and corporate needs can you find between Samuel Johnson's essay and Harris's essay (Section 6, "Job Opportunities and Other Practical Matters")? Though both articles appeared in periodicals, how are the tone, style, and main purpose of each author different?

5. What do you think Calvin or Fuller would have to say to the workers interviewed by Terkel?

6. What would Samuel Johnson's reaction be to the complaints of the workers interviewed by Terkel?

7. What are some essential differences between the workers in Terkel's essay and workers in professions that can be celebrated, as Selzer celebrates the profession of surgery?

8. Contrast the dry cleaner's relationship to or attitude toward the materials of his profession, according to Perelman, with the surgeon's relationship to or attitude toward his, as suggested by Selzer.

9. Both S. J. Perelman and Russell Baker (Section 4, "Careers for the 1990s") have fun at the expense of dry cleaners and corporate executives, respectively, though presumably neither author engaged in those lines of work. Try to imagine a dry cleaner writing about his own profession. Write an essay, using ideas from Perelman and other authors in "Varieties of Work: Professions and Blue Collar" (or other sections of this book), about "the good dry cleaner" or the virtues of this occupation. Argue that others should choose this worthy line of work.

10. Perelman and Fenton point to actual physical conditions of the work space. What will (or might) these be on your job? How would they compare with the conditions described by Perelman and Fenton? What are the attractions or drawbacks of the physical conditions of a job that you've held (including the occupation of full-time student) or the job that you hope to have?

11. How do the attitudes toward work in Fenton's essay compare with those of the workers interviewed by Terkel? How do these attitudes compare or contrast with those of authors—such as Franklin (Section 5, "Money"), Calvin (Section 1, "Job Choice and Self-Fulfillment"), and Fuller (Section 2, "Work and Morality")—who extol the virtues of work?

12. Contrast Fenton's attitude toward "dull work" (to use Eric Hoffer's term) with the attitude of Hoffer in his essay "Dull Work" (Section 1, "Job Choice and Self-Fulfillment").

Note: See also the following Discussion and Writing questions: question 4 of Selzer's "The Knife," 4 and 5 of Terkel's "Here Am I, A Worker," and questions 2 and 5 of Perelman's "Eine Kleine Mothmusik."

EFFICIENCY AND SUCCESS ON THE JOB

JACK OF ALL TRADES

Samuel Langhorne Clemens

Samuel Langhorne Clemens (1835–1910), whose pseudonym is Mark Twain, is one of the great lights of late nineteenth-century American literature. He is perhaps best known for his fiction, often humorous and satirical, exemplified by such novels as The Adventures of Tom Sawyer *(1876),* The Prince and the Pauper *(1882),* The Adventures of Huckleberry Finn *(1884),* A Connecticut Yankee in King Arthur's Court *(1889), and* The Tragedy of Pudd'nhead Wilson *(1894). Among his numerous stories and sketches are "The Cele-brated Jumping Frog of Calaveras County," "The Man That Corrupted*

Hadleyburg," "The £1,000,000 Bank Note," "Was It Heaven? Or Hell?," and
"The Mysterious Stranger."

Unfortunately, his fame as a novelist and short story writer has often
unjustly overshadowed the mastery of Clemens—who was also an essayist,
journalist, and lecturer—in nonfiction prose. His pungent style and comic
sense pervade his essays, travelogues, and autobiographical works, which
include The Innocents Abroad (1869), Roughing It (1872), A Tramp Abroad
(1880), Life on the Mississippi (1883), What Is Man? (1906), Is Shakespeare
Dead? (1909), and the posthumously compiled The Autobiography of Mark
Twain (1959) and The Complete Essays of Mark Twain (1963). The following excerpt is from one of Clemens' funniest books, Roughing It, which
uproariously chronicles Clemens' real-life lively doings in Nevada, California, and Hawaii. In Chapter 41, immediately preceding this selection (Chapter 42 of the book), Twain recounts how he and his friend Calvin Higbie
found and then lost a fabulously rich mining claim in Nevada—undermin-
ing Twain's grand letters home and plans for a European vacation, among
other things.

1   What to do next?

2   It was a momentous question. I had gone out into the world to shift
for myself, at the age of thirteen (for my father had endorsed for friends;
and although he left us a sumptuous legacy of pride in his fine Virginian
stock and its national distinction, I presently found that I could not live
on that alone without occasional bread to wash it down with). I had
gained a livelihood in various vocations, but had not dazzled anybody
with my successes; still the list was before me, and the amplest liberty in
the matter of choosing, provided I wanted to work—which I did not, after
being so wealthy. I had once been a grocery clerk, for one day, but had
consumed so much sugar in that time that I was relieved from further
duty by the proprietor; said he wanted me outside, so that he could have
my custom. I had studied law an entire week, and then given it up
because it was so prosy and tiresome. I had engaged briefly in the study of
blacksmithing, but wasted so much time trying to fix the bellows so that
it would blow itself, that the master turned me adrift in disgrace, and told
me I would come to no good. I had been a bookseller's clerk for a while,
but the customers bothered me so much I could not read with any comfort,
and so the proprietor gave me a furlough and forgot to put a limit to it. I
had clerked in a drugstore part of a summer, but my prescriptions were
unlucky, and we appeared to sell more stomach pumps than soda water.
So I had to go. I had made of myself a tolerable printer, under the impression that I would be another Franklin someday, but somehow had missed
the connection thus far. There was no berth open in the Esmeralda
Union, and besides I had always been such a slow compositor that I
looked with envy upon the achievements of apprentices of two years'

standing; and when I took a "take," foremen were in the habit of suggesting that it would be wanted "sometime during the year." I was a good average St. Louis and New Orleans pilot and by no means ashamed of my abilities in that line; wages were two hundred and fifty dollars a month and no board to pay, and I did long to stand behind a wheel again and never roam any more—but I had been making such an ass of myself lately in grandiloquent letters home about my blind lead and my European excursion that I did what many and many a poor disappointed miner had done before; said "It is all over with me now, and I will never go back home to be pitied—and snubbed." I had been a private secretary, a silver miner, and a silver-mill operative, and amounted to less than nothing in each, and now—

3   What to do next?

4   I yielded to Higbie's appeals and consented to try the mining once more. We climbed far up on the mountainside and went to work on a little rubbishy claim of ours that had a shaft on it eight feet deep. Higbie descended into it and worked bravely with his pick till he had loosened up a deal of rock and dirt and then I went down with a long-handled shovel (the most awkward invention yet contrived by man) to throw it out. You must brace the shovel forward with the side of your knee till it is full, and then, with a skillful toss, throw it backward over your left shoulder. I made the toss, and landed the mess just on the edge of the shaft and it all came back on my head and down the back of my neck. I never said a word, but climbed out and walked home. I inwardly resolved that I would starve before I would make a target of myself and shoot rubbish at it with a long-handled shovel. I sat down, in the cabin, and gave myself up to solid misery—so to speak. Now in pleasanter days I had amused myself with writing letters to the chief paper of the Territory, the Virginia *Daily Territorial Enterprise*, and had always been surprised when they appeared in print. My good opinion of the editors had steadily declined; for it seemed to me that they might have found something better to fill up with than my literature. I had found a letter in the post office as I came home from the hillside, and finally I opened it. Eureka! (I never did know what Eureka meant, but it seems to be as proper a word to heave in as any when no other that sounds pretty offers.) It was a deliberate offer to me of Twenty-Five Dollars a week to come up to Virginia and be city editor of the *Enterprise*.

5   I would have challenged the publisher in the "blind lead" days—I wanted to fall down and worship him, now. Twenty-Five Dollars a week—it looked like bloated luxury—a fortune, a sinful and lavish waste of money. But my transports cooled when I thought of my inexperience and consequent unfitness for the position—and straightway, on top of this, my long array of failures rose up before me. Yet if I refused this place I must presently become dependent upon somebody for my bread, a

thing necessarily distasteful to a man who had never experienced such a humiliation since he was thirteen years old. Not much to be proud of, since it is so common—but then it was all I had to *be* proud of. So I was scared into being city editor. I would have declined, otherwise. Necessity is the mother of "taking chances." I do not doubt that if, at that time, I had been offered a salary to translate the Talmud from the original Hebrew, I would have accepted—albeit with diffidence and some misgivings—and thrown as much variety into it as I could for the money.

6   I went up to Virginia and entered upon my new vocation. I was a rusty-looking city editor, I am free to confess—coatless, slouch hat, blue woolen shirt, pantaloons stuffed into boot tops, whiskered half down to the waist, and the universal navy revolver slung to my belt. But I secured a more Christian costume and discarded the revolver. I had never had occasion to kill anybody, nor ever felt a desire to do so, but had worn the thing in deference to popular sentiment, and in order that I might not, by its absence, be offensively conspicuous and a subject of remark. But the other editors, and all the printers, carried revolvers. I asked the chief editor and proprietor (Mr. Goodman, I will call him, since it describes him as well as any name could do) for some instructions with regard to my duties, and he told me to go all over town and ask all sorts of people all sorts of questions, make notes of the information gained, and write them out for publication. And he added:

7   "Never say 'We learn' so-and-so, or 'It is reported,' or 'It is rumored,' or 'We understand' so-and-so, but go to headquarters and get the absolute facts, and then speak out and say 'It *is* so-and-so.' Otherwise, people will not put confidence in your news. Unassailable certainty is the thing that gives a newspaper the firmest and most valuable reputation."

8   It was the whole thing in a nutshell; and to this day when I find a reporter commencing his article with "We understand," I gather a suspicion that he has not taken as much pains to inform himself as he ought to have done. I moralize well, but I did not always practice well when I was a city editor; I let fancy get the upper hand of fact too often when there was a dearth of news. I can never forget my first day's experience as a reporter. I wandered about town questioning everybody, boring everybody, and finding out that nobody knew anything. At the end of five hours my notebook was still barren. I spoke to Mr. Goodman. He said:

9   "Dan used to make a good thing out of the hay wagons in a dry time when there were no fires or inquests. Are there no hay wagons in from the Truckee? If there are, you might speak of the renewed activity and all that sort of thing, in the hay business, you know. It isn't sensational or exciting, but it fills up and looks businesslike."

10   I canvassed the city again and found one wretched old hay truck dragging in from the country. But I made affluent use of it. I multiplied it by sixteen, brought it into town from sixteen different directions, made

sixteen separate items out of it, and got up such another sweat about hay as Virginia City had never seen in the world before.

11   This was encouraging. Two nonpareil columns had to be filled, and I was getting along. Presently, when things began to look dismal again, a desperado killed a man in a saloon and joy returned once more. I never was so glad over any mere trifle before in my life. I said to the murderer:

12   "Sir, you are a stranger to me, but you have done me a kindness this day which I can never forget. If whole years of gratitude can be to you any slight compensation, they shall be yours. I was in trouble and you have relieved me nobly and at a time when all seemed dark and drear. Count me your friend from this time forth, for I am not a man to forget a favor."

13   If I did not really say that to him I at least felt a sort of itching desire to do it. I wrote up the murder with a hungry attention to details, and when it was finished experienced but one regret—namely, that they had not hanged my benefactor on the spot, so that I could work him up too.

14   Next I discovered some emigrant wagons going into camp on the plaza and found that they had lately come through the hostile Indian country and had fared rather roughly. I made the best of the item that the circumstances permitted, and felt that if I were not confined within rigid limits by the presence of the reporters of the other papers I could add particulars that would make the article much more interesting. However, I found one wagon that was going on to California, and made some judicious inquiries of the proprietor. When I learned, through his short and surly answers to my cross-questioning, that he was certainly going on and would not be in the city next day to make trouble, I got ahead of the other papers, for I took down his list of names and added his party to the killed and wounded. Having more scope here, I put this wagon through an Indian fight that to this day has no parallel in history.

15   My two columns were filled. When I read them over in the morning I felt that I had found my legitimate occupation at last. I reasoned within myself that news, and stirring news, too, was what a paper needed, and I felt that I was peculiarly endowed with the ability to furnish it. Mr. Goodman said that I was as good a reporter as Dan. I desired no higher commendation. With encouragement like that, I felt that I could take my pen and murder all the emigrants on the plains if need be and the interests of the paper demanded it.

VOCABULARY

momentous (P2), *endorsed for* (P2), *sumptuous* (P2), *amplest* (P2), *custom* (P2), *prosy* (P2), *furlough* (P2), *berth* (P2), *compositor* (P2), *"take"* (P2), *pilot* (P2), *grandiloquent* (P2), *blind lead* (P2), *excursion* (P2), *deal* (P4),

Eureka (P4), *bloated* (P5), *transports* (P5), *array* (P5), *Talmud* (P5), *albeit* (P5), *diffidence* (P5), *rusty* (P6), *slouch hat* (P6), *pantaloons* (P6), *deference* (P6), *conspicuous* (P6), *unassailable* (P7), *moralize* (P8), *fancy* (P8), *dearth* (P8), *canvassed* (P10), *affluent* (P10), *nonpareil* (P11), *drear* (P12), *benefactor* (P13), *emigrant* (P14), *fared* (P14), *judicious* (P14), *surly* (P14), *scope* (P14)

IDEAS AND AIMS

1. Why does Twain quit mining?
2. Why is the offer from the *Enterprise* unexpected?
3. What is the real reason Twain accepts the editorship?
4. Describe Twain's ideas of reporting "facts." How do his ideas point to his more famous choice of profession?
5. Why does Twain refer to the desperado as his "benefactor"?
6. Why is the chief editor's advice to Twain ironic?
7. Is Twain's position *really* that of an editor?
8. What personality traits does Twain imply that he has in P2, and how do they relate to how successful he is at the various jobs he talks about?
9. What personality traits does Twain reveal about himself in P5 and following, and how do they relate to how successful he is at his job?
10. What evidence is there that Twain's purposes in this chapter are to amuse and satirize as well as to inform?
11. What comments does Twain imply (and how does he imply them) about the reliability and motives of reporters or journalists?

ORGANIZATION AND FORM

1. In what way or ways might PP1–3, PP4–5, and PP6–15 be seen as the principal organizational units or blocks in this selection?
2. Where can you find pronouns used for transition in and between paragraphs in Twain's chapter?
3. In what ways might the organization of PP1–3 be described as circular, and how might this circularity in any way help express Twain's feelings or situation at this point in his life?
4. How does the repetition of his question in P1 and P3, bracketing as it does all of the content of P2, help in some sense to convey Twain's mood or state of mind at the opening of this chapter?
5. How is parallelism used as a main device to create paragraph coherence in P2?
6. What is the main organizational method or principle of PP4–15?

WORDS AND STYLE

1. What instances can you find of Twain's use of hyperbole and understatement? (Look up these terms in your collegiate dictionary.) How do these help express something about Twain's personality, his attitudes about himself or work or other people or life?

2. What instances can you find of Twain's mixture of sentence lengths (long and short)? How might any of these suggest some specific point in the place where it is used?

3. What instances can you find of antithesis in Twain's chapter? (Look up this term in your collegiate dictionary or composition handbook.) How might repeated antitheses help to convey both Twain's humor as well as his attitudes toward his own life and the world around him?

4. Through his word choice, how does Twain create humor in "bread to wash it down with" (second sentence of P2) and "affluent" (P10)?

5. In P2 how does the parallelism of the sentences, from the fourth one on ("I had . . . but," "I was . . . but"), help Twain to describe his life at this point?

6. How does Twain's use of the dash rather cleverly and humorously suggest something about his honesty in enumerating his emotional responses in the following sentence from P2: "It is all over with me now, and I will never go back home to be pitied—and snubbed"? As suggested by the dash, which action would bother Twain more? Why?

7. Besides the instance mentioned in the preceding question, what other expressive ways does Twain use the dash in P2, P5, P6, and P13?

DISCUSSION AND WRITING

1. Write an essay listing, as Twain does at the beginning of this selection, your past jobs or professions. What did you learn from each one? Why did you move on to the next?

2. Have you held a job that was particularly difficult to learn, as Twain's newspaper job was? Describe the way you learned to handle that job.

3. What led you to your current choice of major or your current job? Try to list the reasons as clearly and succinctly as Twain does.

4. In what ways have your personality traits ever proved to be singularly appropriate or inappropriate to some job you have held?

5. Have you or a friend ever found some humorous side to losing a job or not getting it done? How so?

6. Do you think in the interest of success that it may be acceptable to act as Twain did to "become as good a reporter as Dan" (P15)? Would you act, or have you acted analogously?

7. John Calvin in his essay (Section 1, "Job Choice and Self-Fulfillment") seems to assume and to suggest that finding one's right occupation is relatively easy and straightforward. Contrast Clemens' "Jack of All Trades" on this point. Which author is closer to the truth in your view? Provide specific examples for support.

HOW TO GET THINGS DONE

Robert Benchley

□

James Thurber, considered by many scholars today to be America's greatest twentieth-century humorist, himself had a different choice for this honor. As he explained in a letter to Katharine and E. B. White: "Mrs. T[rimingham] has . . . all of Benchley (which I have reread in toto). There is no doubt that Benchley is our No. 1 humorist. He has simply said everything."* Advertising writer, editor, star of fifty short subject films (one of which, "How to Sleep" [1935], won an Academy Award), and author of sixteen books collecting his essays, Robert Benchley (1889–1945) was one of the foremost writers of humorous nonfiction, theater reviews, and book reviews from the 1920s to the mid-1940s, publishing in many of the leading newspapers and magazines of the time. Among his books—note the whimsicality of several of their titles— are 20,000 Leagues Under the Sea, or David Copperfield *(1928),* The Treasurer's Report, and Other Aspects of Community Singing *(1930),* No Poems: Or Around the World Backwards and Sideways *(1932),* From Bed to Worse: Or Comforting Thoughts About the Bison *(1934),* My Ten Years in a Quandary and How They Grew *(1936),* Benchley Roundup *(1954), and* Benchley Lost and Found *(1970). Benchley, together with Thurber, was a member of the Algonquin Round Table, a group of some of the most celebrated American writers of the era; and the tradition of fame continues in the*

*Printed in Burton Bernstein's *Thurber: A Biography* (New York: Ballantine Books, 1976), p. 364.

family with Peter Benchley, Robert Benchley's grandson, author of the best-selling Jaws, The Deep, *and* Island.

Despite his jocularity about his procrastination in the following humorous piece written for the New York Tribune *in 1930, Benchley did manage to write well over 500 essays (about one every two weeks for twenty years), as well as letters and movie scripts.*

1   A great many people have come up to me and asked me how I manage to get so much work done and still keep looking so dissipated. My answer is "Don't you wish you knew?" and a pretty good answer it is, too, when you consider that nine times out of ten I didn't hear the original question.

2   But the fact remains that hundreds of thousands of people throughout the country are wondering how I have time to do all my painting, engineering, writing and philanthropic work when, according to the rotogravure sections and society notes I spend all my time riding to hounds, going to fancy-dress balls disguised as Louis XIV or spelling out GREETINGS TO CALIFORNIA in formation with three thousand Los Angeles school children. "All work and all play," they say.

3   The secret of my incredible energy and efficiency in getting work done is a simple one. I have based it very deliberately on a well-known psychological principle and have refined it so that it is now almost *too* refined. I shall have to begin coarsening it up again pretty soon.

4   The psychological principle is this: anyone can do any amount of work, provided it isn't the work he is *supposed* to be doing at that moment.

5   Let us see how this works out in practice. Let us say that I have five things which have to be done before the end of the week: (1) a basketful of letters to be answered, some of them dating from October, 1928, (2) some bookshelves to be put up and arranged with books (3) a hair-cut to get (4) a pile of scientific magazines to go through and clip (I am collecting all references to tropical fish that I can find, with the idea of some day buying myself one) and (5) an article to write for this paper.

6   *Now.* With these five tasks staring me in the face on Monday morning, it is little wonder that I go right back to bed as soon as I have had breakfast, in order to store up health and strength for the almost super-human expenditure of energy that is to come. *Mens sana in corpore sano* is my motto, and, not even to be funny, am I going to make believe that I don't know what the Latin means. I feel that the least that I can do is to treat my body right when it has to supply fuel for an insatiable mind like mine.

7   As I lie in bed on Monday morning storing up strength, I make out a schedule. "What do I have to do first?" I ask myself. Well, those letters

really should be answered and the pile of scientific magazines should be clipped. And here is where my secret process comes in. Instead of putting them first on the list of things which have to be done, I put them last. I practice a little deception on myself and say, "First you must write that article for the newspaper." I even say this out loud (being careful that nobody hears me, otherwise they would *keep* me in bed) and try to fool myself into really believing that I must do the article that day and that the other things can wait. I sometimes go so far in this self-deception as to make out a list in pencil, with "No. 1. Newspaper article" underlined in red. (The underlining in red is rather difficult, as there is never a red pencil on the table beside the bed, unless I have taken one to bed with me on Sunday night.)

8   Then, when everything is lined up, I bound out of bed and have lunch. I find that a good, heavy lunch, with some sort of glutinous dessert, is good preparation for the day's work as it keeps one from getting nervous and excitable. We workers must keep cool and calm, otherwise we would just throw away our time in jumping about and fidgeting.

9   I then seat myself at my desk with my typewriter before me, and sharpen five pencils. (The sharp pencils are for poking holes in the desk-blotter, and a pencil has to be pretty sharp to do that. I find that I can't get more than six holes out of one pencil.) Following this I say to myself (again out loud, if it is practical), "Now, old man! Get at this article!"

10   Gradually the scheme begins to work. My eye catches the pile of magazines, which I have artfully placed on a nearby table beforehand. I write my name and address at the top of the sheet of paper in the typewriter and then sink back. The magazines being within reach (also part of the plot) I look to see if anyone is watching me and get one off the top of the pile. Hello, what's this! In the very first one is an article by Dr. William Beebe, illustrated by horrifying photographs! Pushing my chair away from my desk, I am soon hard at work clipping.

11   One of the interesting things about the *Argyopelius*, or "Silver Hatchet" fish, I find, is that it has eyes in its wrists. I would have been sufficiently surprised just to find out that a fish had wrists, but to learn that it has eyes in them is a discovery so astounding that I am hardly able to cut out the picture. What a lot one learns simply by thumbing through the illustrated weeklies! It is hard work, though, and many a weaker spirit would give it up half-done, but when there is something else of "more importance" to be finished (you see, I still keep up the deception, letting myself go on thinking that the newspaper article is of more importance) no work is too hard or too onerous to keep one busy.

12   Thus, before the afternoon is half over, I have gone through the scientific magazine and have a neat pile of clippings (including one of a Viper Fish which I wish you could see. You would die laughing). Then it is back to the grind of the newspaper article.

13   This time I get as far as the title, which I write down with considerable satisfaction until I find that I have misspelled one word terribly, so that the whole sheet of paper has to come out and a fresh one be inserted. As I am doing this, my eye catches the basket of letters.

14   Now, if there is one thing that I hate to do (and there is, you may be sure) it is to write letters. But somehow, with the magazine article before me waiting to be done, I am seized with an epistolary fervor that amounts to a craving, and I slyly sneak the first of the unanswered letters out of the basket. I figure out in my mind that I will get more into the swing of writing the article if I practice a little on a few letters. This first one, anyway, I really must answer. True, it is from a friend in Antwerp asking me to look him up when I am in Europe in the summer of 1929, so he can't actually be watching the incoming boats for an answer, but I owe something to politeness after all. So instead of putting a fresh sheet of copy-paper into the typewriter, I slip in one of my handsome bits of personal stationery and dash off a note to my friend in Antwerp. Then, being well in the letter-writing mood, I clean up the entire batch. I feel a little guilty about the article, but the pile of freshly stamped envelopes and the neat bundle of clippings on tropical fish do much to salve my conscience. Tomorrow I will do the article, and no fooling this time, either.

15   When tomorrow comes I am up with one of the older and more sluggish larks. A fresh sheet of copy-paper in the machine, and my name and address neatly printed at the top, and all before eleven A.M.! "A human dynamo" is the name I think up for myself. I have decided to write something about snake-charming and am already more than satisfied with the title "These Snake-Charming People." But, in order to write about snake-charming, one has to know a little about its history, and where should one go to find history but to a book? Maybe in that pile of books in the corner is one on snake-charming! Nobody could point the finger of scorn at me if I went over to those books for the avowed purpose of research work for the matter at hand. No writer could be supposed to carry all that information in his head.

16   So, with a perfectly clear conscience, I leave my desk for a few minutes and begin glancing over the titles of the books. Of course, it is difficult to find any book, much less one on snake-charming, in a pile which has been standing in the corner for weeks. What really is needed is for them to be on a shelf where their titles will be visible at a glance. And there is the shelf, standing beside the pile of books! It seems almost like a divine command written in the sky: "If you want to finish that article, first put up the shelf and arrange the books on it!" Nothing could be clearer or more logical.

17   In order to put up the shelf, the laws of physics have decreed that there must be nails, a hammer and some sort of brackets to hold it up on

the wall. You can't just wet a shelf with your tongue and stick it up. And, as there are no nails or brackets in the house (or, if there are, they are probably hidden somewhere) the next thing to do is put on my hat and go out to buy them. Much as it disturbs me to put off the actual start of the article, I feel that I am doing only what is in the line of duty to put on my hat and go out to buy nails and brackets. And, as I put on my hat, I realize to my chagrin that I need a hair-cut badly. I can kill two birds with one stone, or at least with two, and stop in at the barber's on the way back. I will feel all the more like writing after a turn in the fresh air. Any doctor would tell me that.

18   So in a few hours I return, spick and span and smelling of lilac, bearing nails, brackets, the evening papers and some crackers and peanut butter. Then it's ho! for a quick snack and a glance through the evening papers (there might be something in them which would alter what I was going to write about snake-charming) and in no time at all the shelf is up, slightly crooked but up, and the books are arranged in a neat row in alphabetical order and all ready for almost instantaneous reference. There does not happen to be one on snake-charming among them, but there is a very interesting one containing some Hogarth prints and one which will bear even closer inspection dealing with the growth of the Motion Picture, illustrated with "stills" from famous productions. A really remarkable industry, the motion pictures. I might want to write an article on it sometime. Not today, probably, for it is six o'clock and there is still the one on snake-charming to finish up first. Tomorrow morning sharp! Yes, *sir!*

19   And so, you see, in two days I have done four of the things I had to do, simply by making believe that it was the fifth that I *must* do. And the next day, I fix up something else, like taking down the bookshelf and putting it somewhere else, that I *have* to do, and then I get the fifth one done.

20   The only trouble is that, at this rate, I will soon run out of things to do, and will be forced to get at that newspaper article the first thing Monday morning.

VOCABULARY

dissipated (P1), *philanthropic* (P2), *rotogravure* (P2), *expenditure* (P6), mens sana in corpore sano (P6), *insatiable* (P6), *glutinous* (P8), *desk-blotter* (P9), *weeklies* (P11), *onerous* (P11), *epistolary* (P14), *fervor* (P14), *Antwerp* (P14), *salve* (P14), *dynamo* (P15), *avowed* (P15), *chagrin* (P17), *Hogarth* (P18)

IDEAS AND AIMS

1. What sentence in the essay enunciates Benchley's thesis?
2. How do we know that Benchley's chief aims in this essay are to amuse the reader as well as to gently mock himself and procrastinators?
3. What are some of the serious ideas about efficiency and work that Benchley's essay may imply?
4. What is the essential "self-deception" that makes Benchley's "secret process" work for him?
5. What shortcomings or defects in his personality does Benchley humorously reveal in the essay?
6. Despite its obviously being meant as humorous, would a system like Benchley's work for most people? Some people? Why or why not?
7. Is such "self-deception" as Benchley describes really possible? Why? How?
8. What logic can you find for the order of the items Benchley lists in P5? For instance, for what reasons (in light of the whole essay) might he have put the fifth item last?
9. What may Benchley be suggesting about how the proper selection of a goal affects its accomplishment in PP15–16?

ORGANIZATION AND FORM

1. Benchley is considered a master of non sequitur humor. Find and explain examples of non sequiturs in PP1–3, P6, and P11.
2. Benchley's essay has a very well-articulated beginning or introduction, middle, and end or conclusion. What paragraphs are allotted to each, and how are they demarcated?
3. How does Benchley follow or not follow in the rest of the essay the order of the items he enumerates in P5? How does this comment on the orderliness of his procedure or process?
4. What transitional words, in which paragraphs, does Benchley use to link one paragraph with another? How do they help suggest the elapse of time during the process he describes?
5. Where does Benchley use repetition of key words to link one paragraph with another?

WORDS AND STYLE

1. Find and list examples of Benchley's choice of words from the formal, standard, and informal levels of usage. Which level predominates in the essay, and how is it appropriate to Benchley's intended audience?

2. How does his mixture of his levels of usage (see question 1) help portray what sort of person Benchley is? Explain what sort of person Benchley appears to be, as suggested by various examples of his word choice.

3. What are some of the effects, individually and collectively, of Benchley's use of italics in P4, P6 (first word), P7, P18, and P19?

4. What are examples of Benchley's exaggeration, and what things does it convey in the essay?

5. How does Benchley repeatedly use parentheses or parenthetical expressions for ironic or humorous qualification of particular points? Cite examples.

DISCUSSION AND WRITING

1. Do you make lists of things to do, as Benchley does, and do you have the same sort of trouble getting them done?

2. How do you decide in what order to put items on your list of things to do? If you have such a list now, explain what the order of the items is or how you would put them in an explainable order.

3. What would be a better, more logical order for the items on Benchley's list? How so?

4. Do you have a system for "getting things done"? How does it compare with Benchley's?

5. How might there be something to be said for not tackling the most difficult task on a list either head on or exclusively *at first*?

6. What would be the reaction of Richard Saunders or Father Abraham in Benjamin Franklin's "The Way to Wealth" (Section 5, "Money") to Benchley's views and conduct? What adages would they quote and wish to apply from Poor Richard, relating to Benchley and his essay?

FROM NINE TO FIVE

Robert Benchley

□

For notes on Benchley's life and work, see the introduction to Benchley's essay "How to Get Things Done," which immediately precedes this selection. Because "From Nine to Five" is based on shrewd observation of human behavior, the essay is as applicable today as it was when it was first published more than forty years ago.

1 One of the necessary qualifications of an efficient businessman in these days of industrial literature seems to be the ability to write, in clear and idiomatic English, a thousand-word story on how efficient he is and how he got that way. A glance through any one of our more racy commercial magazines will serve nicely to illustrate my point, for it was after glancing through one of them only five minutes ago that the point suggested itself to me.

2 "What Is Making Our Business Grow"; "My $10,000 System of Carbon-Copy Hunting"; "Making the Turnover Turn In"; "If I Can Make My Pencil Sharpenings Work, Why Can't You?" "Getting Sales Out of Sahara," etc., are some of the intriguing titles which catch the eye of the student of world affairs as he thumbs over the business magazines on the newsstands before buying his newspaper. It seems as if the entire busi-

ness world were devoting its working hours to the creation of a school of introspective literature.

3   But the trouble with these writers is that they are all successful. There is too much sameness to their stuff. They have their little troubles at first, it is true, such as lack of co-ordination in the central typing department, or congestion of office boys in the room where the water cooler is situated; but sooner or later you may be perfectly sure that Right will triumph and that the young salesman will bring in the order that puts the firm back on its feet again. They seem to have no imagination, these writers of business confessions. What the art needs is some Strindberg of Commerce to put down on paper the sordid facts of Life as they really are, and to show, in bitter words of cynical realism, that ink erasers are not always segregated or vouchers always all that they should be, and that, behind the happy exterior of many a mahogany railing, all is not so gosh-darned right with the world after all.

4   Now, without setting myself up as a Strindberg, I would like to start the ball rolling toward a more realistic school of business literature by setting down in my rough, impulsive way a few of the items in the account of "How We Make Our Business Lose $100,000 a Year."

5   All that I ask in the way of equipment is an illustration showing a square-jawed, clean-cut American businessman sitting at a desk and shaking his finger at another man, very obviously the head of the sales department because it says so under the picture, who is standing with his thumbs in the armholes of his waistcoat, gnawing at a big, black cigar, and looking out through the window at the smokestacks of the works. With this picture as a starter, and a chart or two, I can build up a very decent business story around them.

6   In the first place let me say that what we have done in our business any firm can do in theirs. It is not that we have any extraordinary talents along organization lines. We simply have taken the lessons learned in everyday trading, have tabulated them, and filed them in triplicate. Then we have forgotten them.

7   I can best give an idea of the secret of our mediocrity as a business organization by outlining a typical day in our offices. I do this in no spirit of boasting, but simply to show these thousands of systematized businessmen who are devoting themselves to literature that somewhere in all this miasma of success there shines a ray of inefficiency, giving promise of the day that is to come.

8   The first part of the morning in our establishment is devoted to the mail. This starts the day off right, for it gives everyone something to do, which is, I have found, a big factor in keeping the place looking busy.

9   Personally I am not what is known as a "snappy" dictator. It makes me nervous to have a stenographer sitting there waiting for me to say something so that she can pounce on it and tear it into hieroglyphics. I feel that, mentally, she is checking me up with other men who have

dictated to her, and that I am being placed in Class 5a, along with the licensed pilots and mental defectives, and the more I think of it the more incoherent I become. If exact and detailed notes were to be preserved of one of my dictated letters, mental processes, and all, they might read something like this:

10   "Good morning, Miss Kettle . . . Take a letter, please . . . to the Nipco Drop Forge and Tool Company, Schenectady . . . S-c-h-e-c—er— well, Schenectady; you know how to spell that, I guess, Miss Kettle, ha! ha! . . . Nipco Drop Forge and Tool Company, Schenectady, New York . . . Gentlemen—er (business of touching finger tips and looking at the ceiling meditatively)—Your favor of the 17th inst. at hand, and in reply would state that—er (I should have thought this letter out before beginning to dictate and decided just what it *is* that we desire to state in reply)—and in reply would state that—er . . . our Mr. Mellish reports that—er . . . where is that letter from Mr. Mellish, Miss Kettle? . . . The one about the castings. . . . Oh, never mind, I guess I can remember what he said . . . Let's see, where were we? . . . Oh, yes, that our Mr. Mellish reports that he shaw the sipment—I mean *saw* the *shipment*—what's the matter with me? (this girl must think that I'm a perfect fool) . . . that he shaw the sipment in question on the platform of the station at Miller's Falls, and that it—er . . . ah . . . ooom . . . (I'll have this girl asleep in her chair in a minute. I'll bet that she goes and tells the other girls that she has just taken a letter from a man with the mind of an eight-year-old boy). . . . We could, therefore, comma . . . what's the matter? . . . Oh, I didn't finish that other sentence, I guess. . . . Let's see, how did it go? . . . Oh, yes . . . and that I, or rather *it* was in good shape . . . er, cross that out, please (this girl is simply wasting her time here. I could spell this out with alphabet blocks quicker and let her copy it) . . . and that it was in excellent shape at that shape—er . . . or rather, at that *time* . . . er . . . period. New paragraph.

11   "We are, comma, therefore, comma, unable to . . . hello, Mr. Watterly, be right with you in half a second. . . . I'll finish this later, Miss Kettle . . . thank you."

12   When the mail is disposed of we have what is known as Memorandum Hour. During this period everyone sends memoranda to everyone else. If you happen to have nothing in particular about which to dictate a memorandum, you dictate a memorandum to someone, saying that you have nothing to suggest or report. This gives a stimulating exchange of ideas, and also helps to use up the blue memorandum blanks which have been printed at some expense for just that purpose.

13   As an example of how this system works, I will give a typical instance of its procedure. My partner, let us say, comes in and sits down at the desk opposite me. I observe that his scarfpin is working its way out from his tie. I call a stenographer and say: "Take a memo to Mr. MacFurdle, please. *In re* Loosened Scarfpin. You are losing your scarfpin."

14   As soon as she has typed this it is given to Mr. MacFurdle's secretary, and a carbon copy is put in the files. Mr. MacFurdle, on receiving my memo, adjusts his scarfpin and calls his secretary.

15   "A memo to Mr. Benchley, please. *In re* Tightened Scarfpin. Thank you. I have given the matter my attention."

16   As soon as I have received a copy of this typewritten reply to my memorandum we nod pleasantly to each other and go on with our work. In all, not more than half an hour has been consumed, and we have a complete record of the negotiations in our files in case any question should ever arise concerning them. In case *no* question should ever arise, we still have the complete record. So we can't lose—unless you want to call that half hour a loss.

17   It is then almost lunchtime. A quick glance at a pile of carbons of mill reports which have but little significance to me owing to the fact that the figures are illegible (it being a fifth-string carbon); a rapid survey of the matter submitted for my O.K., most of which I dislike to take the responsibility for and therefore pass on to Mr. Houghtelling for his O.K.; a short tussle in the washroom with the liquid-soap container which contains no liquid soap, and a thorough drying of the hands on my hand-kerchief, the paper towels having given out early in the morning, and I am ready to go to lunch with a man from the Eureka Novelty Company who wants to sell us a central paste-supply system (whereby all the office paste is kept in one large vat in the storeroom, individual brushfuls being taken out only on requisitions O.K.'d by the head of the department).

18   Both being practical businessmen, we spend only two hours at lunch. And, both being practical businessmen, we know all the subtleties of selling. It is a well-known fact that personality plays a big role in the so-called "selling game" (one of a series of American games, among which are "the newspaper game," "the advertising game," "the cloak-and-suit game," "the ladies' mackintosh and overshoe game," "the seedless-raisin-and-dried-fruit game," etc.), and so Mr. Ganz of the Eureka Novelty Company spends the first hour and three-quarters developing his "personality appeal." All through the tomato bisque aux croutons and the roast prime ribs of beef, dish gravy, he puts into practice the principles enunciated in books on Selling, by means of which the subject at hand is deferred in a subtle manner until the salesman has had a chance to impress his prospect with his geniality and his smile (an attractive smile has been known to sell a carload of 1897-style derbies, according to authorities on The Smile in Selling), his knowledge of baseball, his rich fund of stories, and his general aversion to getting down to the disagreeable reason for his call.

19   The only trouble with this system is that I have done the same thing myself so many times that I know just what his next line is going to be, and can figure out pretty accurately at each stage of his conversation just when he is going to shift to one position nearer the thing he has to sell. I

know that he has not the slightest interest in my entertainment other than the sale of a Eureka Central Paste-Supply System, and he knows that I know it, and so we spend an hour and three-quarters fooling the waiter into thinking that we are engaged in disinterested camaraderie.

20   For fifteen minutes we talk business, and I agree to take the matter up with the directors at the next meeting, holding the mental reservation that a central paste-supply system will be installed in our plant only over my dead body.

21   This takes us until two-thirty, and I have to hurry back to a conference. We have two kinds of "conference." One is that to which the office boy refers when he tells the applicant for a job that Mr. Blevitch is "in conference." This means that Mr. Blevitch is in good health and reading the paper, but otherwise unoccupied. The other kind of "conference" is bona fide in so far as it implies that three or four men are talking together in one room, and don't want to be disturbed.

22   This conference is on, let us say, the subject of Window Cards for display advertising: shall they be triangular or diamond shaped?

23   There are four of us present, and we all begin by biting off the ends of four cigars. Watterly has a pile of samples of window cards of various shapes, which he hangs, with a great deal of trouble, on the wall, and which are not referred to again. He also has a few ideas on Window Card Psychology.

24   "It seems to me," he leads off, "that we have here a very important question. On it may depend the success of our Middle Western sales. The problem as I see it is this: what will be the reaction on the retina of the eye of a prospective customer made by the sight of a diamond-shaped card hanging in a window? It is a well-known fact in applied psychology that when you take the average man into a darkened room, loosen his collar, and shout "Diamonds!" at him suddenly, his mental reaction is one in which the ideas of Wealth, Value, Richness, etc., predominate. Now, it stands to reason that the visual reaction from seeing a diamond-shaped card in the window will . . ."

25   "Excuse me a moment, George." says MacFurdle, who has absorbed some pointers on Distribution from a book entitled *The World Salesman*, "I don't think that it is so important to get after the psychology of the thing first as it is to outline thoroughly the Theory of Zone Apportionment on which we are going to work. If we could make up a chart, showing in red ink the types of retail stores and in green ink the types of jobber establishments, in this district, then we could get at the window display from that angle and tackle the psychology later, if at all. Now, on such a chart I would try to show the zones of Purchasing Power, and from these could be deduced . . ."

26   "Just a minute, Harry," Inglesby interrupts, "let me butt in for half a second. That chart system is all very well when you are selling goods

with which the public is already familiar through association with other brands, but with ours it is different. We have got to estimate the Consumer Demand first in terms of dollar-and-a-quarter units, and build our selling organization up around that. Now, if I know anything about human nature at all—and I think I do, after being in the malleable-iron game for fifteen years—the people in this section of the country represent an entirely different trade current than . . ."

27   At this point I offer a few remarks on one of my pet hobbies, the influence of the Gulf Stream on Regional Commerce, and then we all say again the same things that we said before, after which we say them again, the pitch of the conversation growing higher at each repetition of views and the room becoming more and more filled with cigar smoke. Our final decision is to have a conference tomorrow afternoon, before which each one is to "think the matter over and report his reactions."

28   This brings the day to a close. There has been nothing remarkable in it, as the reader will be the first one to admit. And yet it shows the secret of whatever we have not accomplished in the past year in our business.

29   And it also shows why we practical businessmen have so little sympathy with a visionary, impractical arrangement like this League of Nations. President Wilson was all right in his way, but he was too academic. What we practical men in America want is deeds, not words.

VOCABULARY

idiomatic (P1), *Sahara* (P2), *introspective* (P2), *Strindberg* (P3), *sordid* (P3), *cynical* (3), *vouchers* (P3), *waistcoat* (P5), *works* (P5), *mediocrity* (P7), *miasma* (P7), *hieroglyphics* (P9), *drop forge* (P10), *favor* (P10), *inst.* (P10), *In re* (P13), *tussle* (P17), *mackintosh* (P18), *bisque* (P18), *enunciated* (P18), *geniality* (P18), *derbies* (P18), *aversion* (P18), *camaraderie* (P19), *bona fide* (P21), *jobber* (P25), *malleable* (P26), *Gulf Stream* (P27), *League of Nations* (P29)

IDEAS AND AIMS

1. According to his introduction, what has inspired Benchley to describe his daily routine?

2. Is Benchley serious about his purpose? If he is satirizing business operations to show their inefficiency, what must his *real* purpose be?

3. Which sentence comes closest to enunciating Benchley's overall thesis in the essay? How so?

4. What, exactly, does Benchley mean by the last sentence of P2? What defect or defects is he teasing the business world about here?

5. In PP3–4, what does Benchley criticize about business writing?

6. What lessons about business and human nature can be learned from Benchley's description of his experience in dictating letters?

7. What lessons about business and human nature can be learned from Benchley's description of what he calls the "Memorandum Hour"?

8. How practical is the central-paste supply system (P17 and following) Benchley describes? In what ways is it similar to almost every other detail Benchley provides to describe his working day?

9. Many of the scenes or situations in Benchley's essay concern communication: the dictation of memoranda, the business lunch, the conference. What characterizes these communications? What do they have in common? What does Benchley seem to be saying about communication on the job?

ORGANIZATION AND FORM

1. How does Benchley organize his humorous look at the operation of an inefficient business? What key transition words referring to time reveal the principle of his organization? In what paragraphs are these key words to be found?

2. What paragraphs of the essay form an introduction, and how do they do so? What paragraphs of the essay form the body of the essay, and how do they do so? What paragraphs form the conclusion of the essay, and how do they do so?

3. What transitional words and key repeated terms does Benchley use as linking devices in the openings of P6, P8, P13, P19, P21, P27, and P28?

WORDS AND STYLE

1. Throughout the essay, what examples can you find of Benchley's verbal irony (words where the meaning is really the opposite of what they say on the surface)? Explain in a few instances how Benchley really means the opposite of what his words apparently say.

2. How does Benchley use very concrete, pictorial words to convey his meaning in his phrase "realism, that ink erasers are not always segregated" (P3)? in his sentence "behind the happy exterior of many a mahogany railing, all is not . . . right" (P3)?

3. Why, and how, has Benchley reversed what the metaphors "miasma" and "shines a ray" should each apply to in P7?

4. In what way does the second sentence of P8 contain a redundancy, and how is this redundancy funny? What serious criticism might Benchley be making here if the redundancy mainly depends on the word "looking"?

5. In light of PP9–11, how are the words "disposed of" in the first sentence of P12 ironic?

DISCUSSION AND WRITING

1. Is irony a good technique to use in communicating ideas? Why or why not? When or in what circumstances?

2. Do you agree with Benchley about business writing or business textbooks? Why or why not?

3. Describe a typical day at school or a typical day at work. You may want to adopt an ironic tone similar to Benchley's, or you may prefer a more straightforward narration. In either case, provide as many examples of your daily routine as possible.

4. Reverse Benchley's technique in this essay, which describes how *not* to get things done. From his situations, can you deduce positive rules which describe efficient ways to plan and complete work? Do such rules work as well for students as they do for office workers?

5. The last paragraph of Benchley's essay points to the cherished American truism "If only such and such were run like a *business!*" Have businesses, large and small, always been practical, efficient, and sound in their management and operation? Using current reference sources and books in the library, investigate this topic for a class report. Some likely choices to explore might be the automobile, steel, airline, or aircraft-manufacturing industries.

OF DISPATCH

Francis Bacon

□

A Renaissance man both in period and in temperament, Francis Bacon (1561–1626) earned distinction as a jurist, statesman, philosopher, amateur scientist, and essayist. After being educated at Cambridge University and then Gray's Inn (one of the principal law schools of the time), Bacon went on to a career in law and politics, eventually becoming Lord Chancellor and holding other high offices in the British government. When he discusses human nature or principles of management in his essays, he thus speaks with the authority of a man experienced in practical affairs.

Of his mainly prose works, including letters, which fill fourteen volumes in the standard collected edition, the chief (written in Latin or English) are Essays *(in English) (1597; 1612; 1625),* The Advancement of Learning *(in English) (1605),* On the Wisdom of the Ancients *(in Latin) (1609),* Novum Organum *(in Latin) (1620),* The History of the Reign of King Henry VII *(in English) (1622),* On the Advancement of Learning *(in Latin) (1623),* Sylva Sylvarum: Or a Natural History *(in English) (1627), and* The New Atlantis *(in English) (1627). Bacon could be considered the founding father of the English essay, since he is one of the earliest and most masterly essayists in English, adopting the form under the influence of its originator, Michel de Montaigne, a contemporary who also coined the word "essay." (See the essay by Montaigne in Section 2, "Work and Morality.") The various specimens in Bacon's* Essays, *from which this selection has been taken, are distinguished by their brevity, pithiness, and use of vivid illustrations through concrete instances and various figures of speech. In addition to this selection, other brief and penetrating discussions of conducting business and handling money may be found in Bacon's* Essays: *"Of Innovations," "Of Riches," "Of Fortune," "Of Usury," and "Of Negociating" (Bacon's spelling).*

1 Affected dispatch is one of the most dangerous things to business that can be. It is like that which the physicians call *predigestion*, or hasty digestion; which is sure to fill the body full of crudities and secret seeds of diseases. Therefore measure not dispatch by the times of sitting, but by the advancement of the business. And as in races it is not the large stride or high lift that makes the speed; so in business, the keeping close to the matter, and not taking of it too much at once, procureth dispatch. It is the care of some only to come off speedily for the time; or to contrive some false periods of business, because they may seem men of dispatch. But it is one thing to abbreviate by contracting, another by cutting off. And business so handled at several sittings or meetings goeth commonly backward and forward in an unsteady manner. I knew a wise man that had it for a by-word, when he saw men hasten to a conclusion, *Stay a little, that we may make an end the sooner.*

2 On the other side, true dispatch is a rich thing. For time is the measure of business, as money is of wares; and business is bought at a dear hand where there is small dispatch. The Spartans and Spaniards have been noted to be of small dispatch; *Mi venga la muerte de Spagna; Let my death come from Spain*; for then it will be sure to be long in coming.

3 Give good hearing to those that give the first information in business; and rather direct them in the beginning, than interrupt them in the continuance of their speeches; for he that is put out of his own order will go forward and backward, and be more tedious while he waits upon his memory, than he could have been if he had gone on in his own course. But sometimes it is seen that the moderator is more troublesome than the actor.

4 Iterations are commonly loss of time. But there is no such gain of time as to iterate often the state of the question; for it chaseth away many a frivolous speech as it is coming forth. Long and curious speeches are as fit for dispatch, as a robe or mantle with a long train is for race. Prefaces and passages, and excusations, and other speeches of reference to the person, are great wastes of time; and though they seem to proceed of modesty, they are bravery. Yet beware of being too material when there is any impediment or obstruction in men's wills; for pre-occupation of mind ever requireth preface of speech; like a fomentation to make the unguent enter.

5   Above all things, order, and distribution, and singling out of parts, is the life of dispatch; so as the distribution be not too subtle: for he that doth not divide will never enter well into business; and he that divideth too much will never come out of it clearly. To choose time is to save time; and an unseasonable motion is but beating the air. There be three parts of business; the preparation, the debate or examination, and the perfection. Whereof, if you look for dispatch, let the middle only be the work of many, and the first and last the work of few. The proceeding upon somewhat conceived in writing doth for the most part facilitate dispatch: for though it should be wholly rejected, yet that negative is more pregnant of direction than an indefinite; as ashes are more generative than dust.

VOCABULARY

affected (P1), *dispatch* (P1), *crudities* (P1), *procure* (P1), *contrive* (P1), *abbreviate* (P1), *contracting* (P1), *by-word* (P1), *wares* (P2), *dear* (P2), *Spartans* (P2), *Tedious* (P3), *iterations* (P4), *frivolous* (P4), *curious* (archaic sense) (P4), *bravery* (archaic sense) (P4), *impediment* (P4), *obstruction* (P4), *fomentation* (P4), *unguent* (P4), *unseasonable* (P5), *perfection* (archaic sense) (P5), *somewhat* (archaic sense) (P5), *facilitate* (P5), *generative* (P5)

IDEAS AND AIMS

1. What does Bacon mean by the word "dispatch"? What modern term or terms could you substitute for it? What evidence from the essay would back up your translation?
2. What are the author's rules for achieving real dispatch? Try to isolate each piece of advice and restate it in your own words.
3. What is the author's advice to a listener at any kind of business conference?
4. What is the author's advice to speakers at any kind of business conference?

ORGANIZATION AND FORM

1. The first and second paragraphs contrast real and pretended dispatch. Does this comparison extend throughout the rest of the essay? Where or how?
2. What are the subjects of PP3–5? How does this section link itself to P1 and P2?
3. How might Bacon's opening of the essay with a discussion of "affected dispatch" be an effective way of treating the whole subject?
4. Where, and in what instances, does Bacon use division into parts or classification into categories in his discussion of "dispatch"?

5. Cite examples of Bacon's inclination for opening sentences with coordinate conjunctions and transition words. Explain in a few instances how these help bind up particular paragraphs or parts of the essay.

6. How does the conclusion of Bacon's essay represent an extension or development of his introduction, rather than a mere repetition or restatement?

WORDS AND STYLE

1. The author uses an analogy, a comparison (technically, a simile), in the essay when he states that "Long and curious speeches are as fit for dispatch, as a robe or mantle with a long train is for race" (P4). How is this an effective way to make his point?

2. What other analogies are used in the essay, and how do they help Bacon clarify his meaning in each instance?

3. While Bacon treats his subject at a general and abstract level, with general and abstract words in places, how and where does he balance this abstractness with vivid, concrete, and specific words or illustrations?

4. What components of his prose make Bacon's style seem so sententious, that is, packed with wisdom?

5. Bacon is fond of balanced and antithetical sentences, often set up by the words "rather . . . than," "more . . . than," or ". . ., but. . . ." How do these constructions lend themselves to the thoughtful tone of the essay or to its purpose of comparing the wrong way of doing something with the right way?

6. How does the word "rich" that Bacon uses in the first sentence of P2 apply in more than one sense in the context in which it is used? (Consult your college desk dictionary for the many possible meanings of the word.) Why is it an especially appropriate word to use, given Bacon's subject?

7. In Bacon's last analogy in the essay (technically, a simile), the rejection of a written plan is compared to ashes, while a vague response to an unwritten plan is compared to dust. Why is the image of ashes particularly apt in suggesting the negation of the written plan? Why, in the physical world, are ashes more "generative" than dust? And why should a "negative" response to a definite, written plan be more "pregnant of direction" or "generative" than an "indefinite" response to an oral plan?

DISCUSSION AND WRITING

1. Can you remember an incident that illustrates the rules for speakers and writers given in this essay? Have you ever faced an "impediment or obstruction in men's wills" that made your audience hostile? How did you deal with this situation?

2. The style of this essay is to present its subject in rather general, even abstract, terms. Provide some examples of "real dispatch" or "affected dispatch" from your own work or school experience.

3. The "case history" of a matter treated with dispatch in P5 is particularly general. Give a good concrete example of a business or organization problem (at work, school, or home), and show how it was or wasn't treated with the methods the author recommends.

4. As an optional part of any of the foregoing projects, try to work in analogies or comparisons of the kind that Bacon uses in order to better and more vividly explain your points to your reader.

5. Which of Bacon's ideas seem particularly correct or right to you? Why? Which, if any, of his ideas appear no longer valid or not as valid as they once were?

NOW THAT I'M ORGANIZED

E. B. White

□

Although he has written poetry, most recently gathered in Poems *and* Sketches *(1981), as well as short stories, E. B. White (1899—1985), an important and influential American writer and editor, is known primarily for his style manual, (Strunk and White,* The Elements of Style*), used by generations of students, his children's books (Stuart Little [1945] and* Charlotte's Web *[1952]), and especially his critical and humorous essays, collected in such books as* Quo Vadimus? or, The Case for the Bicycle *(1939),* One Man's Meat *(1942),* Here Is New York *(1949),* The Second Tree from the Corner *(1954), and* The Points of My Compass *(1962). One could do worse than to try to aim for the crystal clarity of White's pellucid prose style, or (despite all his remarks about his troubles in the following selection) for White's productivity—hundreds of essays and more than fifteen books.*

1 It will be a week come tomorrow that Miss Nulty looked up from her dictation and said: "You have no work-organizer on your desk, have you, Mr. White?"

2 Seven crowded days have intervened. I can hardly believe that at this time last week I did not even know what a work-organizer was.

3   "You see," said Miss Nulty, returning from the stock room with a package under her arm, "now instead of having your papers strewn all over your desk, you place them in this organizer under the proper headings, where you can always find them quick." Then, seeing my embarrassment, she considerately left the room, and I was alone with my work-organizer.

4   I lit a cigarette. The new article was brown, and very cleverly constructed—a sort of flat paper file, with twelve flaps, each flap fitted with a small isinglass frame in which the person whose work was to be organized could insert a "heading" or "classification." It did not take me long to realize that the first step would be to organize the organizer.

5   Cutting the little strips of paper for the frames took quite a while and was light, pleasant work. Thinking up headings, however, did not come so easily. I decided to devote the first compartment to Beazley & Hoke, to whom we sell most of our harness snaps, and with whom, for that reason, I have a great deal of correspondence. I lettered the name on one of the strips of paper and inserted it in the first frame. It showed up well, although my capital B was never anything to go around telling people about. The second flap I called "Letters to Answer."

6   Next it occurred to me that there should be one compartment in my organizer given over to matters that demanded immediate attention. I wrote out "Matters Demanding Immediate Attention"—but it was too long to fit the little isinglass frame, and didn't have quite the right sound anyway. I tried shortening it to "Immediate Attention Things" and then to "Right Away Papers," but neither of these seemed to have the authentic tone. By this time the strain of trying to invent headings was making me a little bit sick, and I had to leave my desk for a moment and get a drink of water. It worried me to be showing signs of nerves—here it was eleven o'clock, my desk piled high, and no work done. Still, I thought, once I get this organizer going I certainly will be able to tear through this stuff.

7   When I returned from the water-cooler I settled on the word "Quick" as the best heading for the third compartment. Just before inserting it, another thought came to me, and I took my pen and added an exclamation point, making it "Quick!" It looked fine.

8   Before another hour was over I had reserved a compartment for Mr. Higgins, one for "Unimportant," one for "To Think About," one called "Yes or No?" (in which I decided to put matters which might come to me for my opinion, although there are not many of these), and then I remembered that after all it was Miss Nulty who had got the work-organizer for me and the least I could do to show my appreciation would be to name one of the compartments for her.

9   I called the ninth "Personal," the tenth "Loose Papers," and then, with two compartments still unnamed, my imagination refused to budge.

This bothered me, for I decided that there would be no vacant compartments in a desk file of mine. For a time I didn't know but that I would have to close my desk and go home and lie down there for a while.

10 Finally, despairing, I named one of the flaps "Cigarette Coupons" and destroyed the twelfth (and last) one by ripping out the flap and throwing it away.

11 It was now past one o'clock, and I went to lunch.

12 How clearly the events of that day stand out in my memory! I recall perfectly picking up the menu at the restaurant and seeing, instead of items of food, a bill which read like this:

BEAZLEY & HOKE
LETTERS TO ANSWER
QUICK!
MR. HIGGINS
UNIMPORTANT
TO THINK ABOUT
YES OR NO?
MISS NULTY
PERSONAL
LOOSE PAPERS
CIGARETTE COUPONS

13 "Beef stew," I told the waiter—but I could do no more than pick at it. On my way back to the office I bought a pack of cigarettes. A few moments later, when I thought no one was looking, I slid the coupons in the right compartment and felt a whole lot of relief at having taken the first step toward filling up the organizer. Still, even with that as a starter, the task proved to be only in its infancy.

14 All afternoon things got steadily worse. Almost every paper on my desk seemed to admit of more than one classification, and I have never been able to make quick decisions. Here, for example, was a letter from Mr. Hoke. First I pushed it tentatively under "Beazley & Hoke," only to withdraw it hurriedly and put it under "Letters to Answer." There again I wasn't sure of myself. I remembered that it was probably a pretty urgent letter and therefore should be under "Quick!" I made that change. Unfortunately, in filing it, I happened to glance at it and saw how very urgent it really was. It was so urgent that it should have been acknowledged by phone at ten o'clock in the morning, and here it was three in the afternoon and the letter just being filed under "Quick!" Heaven knew when I would get round to looking under "Quick!" For an instant I wavered and was tempted to tend to the letter directly; but I knew how fatal to any work-organizer system it would be were I to start acting that way.

I was thoroughly frightened, now. It was no longer possible for me to remain seated; the phone rang intermittently, the distribution boy appeared at intervals with new memoranda and letters, and I saw only too clearly that I was not even holding my own—the desk was littered worse than when I started. In my panicky condition I went about picking up pieces of paper, with a vague garbled expression on my face—picking them up, laying them down again, and all the while walking slowly round and round my desk. I was ten minutes trying to decide whether to put a circular letter from my university's endowment fund under "Unimportant" or "To Think About." That's how bad I was. At four o'clock, echoes from my inactive, distraught state began to be heard. The first was an inquiry from the office of our first vice-president, wanting to know why I hadn't sent a confirmation of Beazley & Hoke's order of even date for five thousand harness snaps. After twenty minutes' frantic search I found the order under "Loose Papers," refiled it under "Quick!" and sent back a memorandum to the vice-president, saying: "Everything in good time."

15   When the news of the second echo arrived, I was in the reception-room, lying on the couch, the blood pumping in my head. Miss Nulty brought me the tidings. It seems that in one of the letters on my desk there had been a P.S., stating that Mr. Beazley himself would be in New York on Thursday, and would our Mr. Higgins care to see him for lunch and possibly for a little golf? "Don't you know that is very important?" asked Miss Nulty, trying to speak gently.

16   "Yes," I replied, wearily, "where did you find it?"

17   "In the bottom of your work-organizer," she replied, "in amongst a couple of cigarette coupons!"

18   Well, as I say, seven crowded days have intervened since I got my work-organizer. On the whole it has been a happy period. Things have gradually smoothed out, and I am glad to say that it still takes me the entire day, from nine to five, to organize my work, with the gratifying result that I never have to do any.

VOCABULARY

intervened (P2), *isinglass* (P4), *authentic tone* (P6), *to admit of* (P14), *tentatively* (P14), *intermittently* (P14), *garbled expression* (P14), *circular letter* (P14), *endowment fund* (P14), *distraught* (P14), *confirmation* (P14)

IDEAS AND AIMS

1. How might White's ideas about the relationship between organization and efficiency be summed up, judging from his narrative?

2. Why was White embarrassed, as he mentions in passing in P3?

3. Why does his addition of the exclamation point to his category "Quick" please him so (P7)? In what ways does it turn out to be ironic?

4. In what ways are White's categories for his work-organizer good or bad according to the logical principles of classification?

5. What things can be learned about White's—and the average person's—thinking or personality from the underlying reasons he destroys the final compartment of his work-organizer?

6. Why can White "no more than pick" (P13) at his beef stew at the restaurant? What can we learn about efficiency from this?

7. Why would it be "fatal to any work-organizer system" for White to start acting the way he says he's tempted to in P14? In light of how things turn out, what might White's true point be here?

8. What does White's action of "walking slowly round and round" his desk in P14 reveal about his state of mind at this point? In the next sentence of that paragraph, what pun, referring to White's physical activity, may there be on the word designating the kind of letter White says he received about his university's endowment?

9. Why does White's inability to decide between the two classifications for the university endowment fund letter show, as he says in P14, how bad his mental state was?

ORGANIZATION AND FORM

1. What sentence comes closest to being White's thesis statement?

2. In what ways does White tie together his introduction and conclusion without merely repeating or restating himself?

3. What is the general principle by which White's essay is organized, and how does it ironically contrast with the organizing principle of his work-organizer?

4. How much time do the actual events of the essay take, and how do we know?

5. What transition words and phrases link the events in the essay?

WORDS AND STYLE

1. What are the two main levels of usage in the essay, and how do they characterize White as well as help us sympathize with him and his dilemma?

2. Which paragraph of the essay is the longest, and how is its length appropriate?

DISCUSSION AND WRITING

1. Has anything like White's experience with his work-organizer ever happened to you? How did you react, and what did you learn?

2. In what ways, overall, are White's points about being organized valid or invalid in your opinion?

3. What kinds of compartments would you make in a work-organizer for your job as a student? For your part-time or full-time job off campus?

4. Write an essay describing your attempt to learn a new job or to learn a new procedure.

5. In the second sentence of P14, White hits on the crux of the problem in one's attempting to classify any group of people or things. Try to classify students, workmates, or acquaintances into mutually exclusive categories, and then explain how some individuals would fit into more than one of these categories.

6. How does White's essay vividly illustrate the truth of the first sentence in P5 of Bacon's "Of Dispatch," the essay that immediately precedes "Now That I'm Organized"?

TAKING STOCK: COMPARING AND CONTRASTING THE SELECTIONS

1. What serious ideas about efficiency in work are implied in Samuel Clemens' "Jack of All Trades"? How do these ideas compare or contrast with those of Benchley in either of his essays?

2. Contrast the elements of Clemens' concept of what could be called "The Good Reporter" with those of Thomas Fuller's "The Good Merchant" (Section 2, "Work and Morality"). For instance, Fuller's merchant works mainly to benefit others—the state. Whom is Clemens really working for when he strives to succeed?

3. Both Benchley's "How to Get Things Done" and E. B. White's "Now That I'm Organized" deal with priorities—ranking items in some particular order of importance. Compare or contrast the two essays on this topic.

4. Both Benchley in "How to Get Things Done" and Clemens in "Jack of All Trades" focus on the occupation of writing. What satiric points do they make about this job or its practitioners?

5. How might Benchley's "From Nine to Five" and Fenton's "Confessions of a Working Stiff" (Section 7, "The Varieties of Work: Professions and Blue Collar") be considered comic and tragic versions, respectively, of routine on the job? Compare and contrast the role of routine in Benchley's and Fenton's jobs. How is routine related to efficiency or inefficiency in both instances?

6. After considering the material in question 5 above, speculate about what part routine plays in your job as a student or what part it will play in the occupation you plan to engage in after your schooling.

7. How does Benchley's depiction of sales and salesmen in PP17–20 of "From Nine to Five" compare or contrast with Buchwald's portrayal

of them in "Confessions of a Roof Seller" (Section 6, "Job Opportunities and Other Practical Matters") and George Ade's in "The Fable of the Divided Concern That Was Reunited Under a New Management" (Section 9, "The Work Environment")? How do these views square with yours on this subject?

8. Discuss how the contrast between "real dispatch" and "affected dispatch" in Bacon's essay may be applied to Samuel Clemens' "Jack of All Trades."

9. Discuss how the contrast between "real dispatch" and "affected dispatch" in Bacon's essay may be applied to either or both of Robert Benchley's essays.

10. Using E. B. White's essay as an example, adapt Bacon's concepts in "Of Dispatch" to explain the contrast between "real organization" and "affected organization." What, in your opinion, could one say are the essential distinctions between these categories?

11. Robert Benchley, E. B. White, James Thurber, as well as many other humorists (several of them represented in this book) often gently mock humanity's foolish and idealistic overlooking of the irrational element in human beings and daily affairs. Correspondingly, they mock our overconfidence in the power of intellect and will to accomplish all things. In what ways can these concepts be seen to occur in E. B. White's essay? In the essays by Benchley, Thurber, and other humorists in this book?

Note: See also Discussion and Writing question 7 of Clemens' "Jack of All Trades," question 6 of Robert Benchley's "How to Get Things Done," question 6 of Benchley's "From Nine to Five," question 6 of E. B. White's "Now That I'm Organized," and question 8 of George Ade's "The Fable of the Divided Concern That Was Reunited Under a New Management (Section 9, "The Work Environment").

THE WORK ENVIRONMENT

HOW TO ADJUST YOURSELF TO YOUR WORK

James Thurber

□

Probably a majority of students enter college having read James Thurber's humorous story "The Secret Life of Walter Mitty" in high school. Many more will read the story in college. This popularity is justified, for in the story Thurber captures in a humorous way some of the central problems and anxieties of living in the modern urban world, as well as describing the psychological state of the individual who is put upon. No wonder "walter mitty" has become a word in the English language, listed in the unabridged Webster's Third New International Dictionary.

Born in Ohio and educated at Ohio State University, Thurber (1894–1961) went on to a career first as a journalist in Columbus, Ohio; Paris; and New York, and then as a cartoonist and writer for the New Yorker *magazine. Most of his books collect the diversity of his output: essays, reminiscences, sketches, stories, fables, and parables. He also collaborated on a play entitled* The Male Animal *(1940), which was made into a film, and several children's books that may be profitably read by adults:* Many Moons *(1943),* The Great Quillow *(1944),* The White Deer *(1945),* The 13 Clocks *(1950), and* The Wonderful O *(1957).*

Other books by the author considered by some scholars to be America's greatest twentieth-century humorous writer are Is Sex Necessary? *(1929), a satire of pseudo-scientific sex manuals, written in collaboration with E. B. White (see the preceding section for an essay by White);* The Owl in the Attic and Other Perplexities *(1931);* The Seal in the Bedroom and Other Predicaments *(1932);* My Life and Hard Times *(1933), reminiscences of his childhood and very eccentric family;* The Middle-Aged Man on the Flying Trapeze *(1935);* Let Your Mind Alone! *(1937), from which this selection is taken, a satire of self-help and pop psychology books;* Fables for Our Time and Famous Poems Illustrated *(1940);* My World—and Welcome to It *(1942);* Men, Women, and Dogs *(1943);* The Thurber Carnival *(1945), an omnibus collection and the best place to begin reading Thurber;* The Beast in Me and Other Animals *(1948);* The Thurber Album *(1952);* Thurber Country *(1953);* Thurber's Dogs *(1955);* Further Fables for Our Time *(1956);* Alarms and Diversions *(1957);* The Years with Ross *(1959), a memoir of Thurber's editor at the* New Yorker; Lanterns and Lances *(1961); and* Credos and Curios *(1962).*

The titles of these books, most of them still in print and available in paperback, reveal Thurber's twin preoccupations with dogs and animals (his and the modern urbanite's mixed feelings of affection for and fear of the animal kingdom) and with the essential ingredients of unpredictability and complexity in life and human nature ("perplexities," "predicaments"). Too often, as Thurber and his friend Robert Benchley suggest (see the preceding section for essays by Benchley), there is a tendency to ignore or forget the latter—especially in self-help books.

1 I find that the inspirational books are frequently disposed to touch, with pontifical cheerfulness or owlish mysticism, on the problem of how to get along in the business world, how to adjust yourself to your employer and to your fellow-worker. It seems to me that in this field the trainers of the mind, both lady and gentleman, are at their unhappiest. Let us examine, in this our fourth lesson, what Mrs. Dorothea Brande, who is reputedly changing the lives of almost as many people as the Oxford Group, has to say on the subject. She presents the case of a man (she calls him "you") who is on the executive end of an enterprise and feels he should be on the planning end. "In that case," she writes, "your problem is to bring your

talents to the attention of your superior officers with as little crowding and bustling as possible. Learn to write clear, short, definite memoranda and present them to your immediate superior until you are perfectly certain that he will never act upon them. In no other circumstances are you justified in going over his head." Very well, let us start from Mrs. Brande's so-called point of justification in going over your superior's head, and see what happens.

2   Let us suppose that you have presented your favorite memoranda to your immediate superior, Mr. Sutphen, twice and nothing has happened. You are still not perfectly certain that he will never act upon them. To be sure, he has implied, or perhaps even said in so many words, that he never will, but you think that maybe you have always caught him at the wrong moment. So you get up your memoranda a third time. Mr. Sutphen, glancing at your paper and noting that it is that same old plan for tearing out the west wall, or speeding up the out-of-town truck deliveries, or substituting colored lights for bells, is pretty well convinced that all you do in your working hours is write out memoranda. He figures that you are probably suffering from a mild form of monomania and determines to dispense with your services if you submit any memoranda again. After waiting a week and hearing nothing from Mr. Sutphen, you decide, in accordance with Mrs. Brande's suggestion, to go over his head and take the matter up with Mr. Leffley. In doing so, you will not be stringing along with me. I advise you not to go over Mr. Sutphen's head to Mr. Leffley; I advise you to quit writing memoranda and get to work.

3   The Mr. Leffleys of this country have enough to do the way it is, or think they have, and they do not like to have you come to them with matters which should be taken up with the Mr. Sutphens. They are paying the Mr. Sutphens to keep you and your memoranda from suddenly bobbing up in front of them. In the first place, if you accost the Mr. Leffleys personally, you become somebody else in the organization whose name and occupation they are supposed to know. Already they know who too many people are. In the second place, the Mr. Leffleys do not like to encounter unexpected memoranda. It gives them a suspicion that there is a looseness somewhere; it destroys their confidence that things are going all right; it shakes their faith in the Mr. Sutphens—and in the Mr. Bairds, the Mr. Crowfuts, and the old Miss Bendleys who are supposed to see that every memorandum has been filed away, or is being acted on. I know of one young man who was always sending to his particular Mr. Leffley, over Mr. Sutphen's head, memoranda done up in limp-leather covers and tied with ribbon, this to show that he was not only clear, short, and definite, but neat. Mr. Leffley did not even glance between the leather covers; he simply told Miss Bendley to turn the thing over to Mr. Sutphen, who had already seen it. The young man was let go and is now a process-server. Keep, I say, your clear, short, and definite memoranda to

yourself. If Mr. Sutphen has said no, he means no. If he has taken no action, no action is going to be taken. People who are all the time submitting memoranda are put down as jealous, disgruntled, and vaguely dangerous. Employers do not want them around. Sooner or later Mr. Sutphen, or Mr. Leffley himself, sees to it that a printed slip, clear, short, and definite, is put in their pay envelopes.

4   My own experience, and the experience of many of my friends, in dealing with superiors has covered a wide range of crucial situations of which these success writers appear to be oblivious and for which they therefore have no recommended course of action (which is probably just as well). I am reminded of the case of Mr. Russell Soames, a friend of mine, who worked for a man whom we shall call Mr. B. J. Winfall. This Winfall, some five or six years ago, in the days when Capone was at large and wholesale shootings were common in Chicago, called Soames into his office and said, "Soames, I'm going out to Chicago on that Weltmer deal and I want you to go along with me." "All right, Mr. Winfall," said Soames. They went to Chicago and had been there only four or five hours when they were calling each other Russell and B. J. and fighting for the check at the bar. On the third day, B. J. called Russell into his bedroom (B. J. had not left his bedroom in thirty-six hours) and said, "Russell, before we go back to New York, I want to see a dive, a hideout, a joint. I want to see these gangsters in their haunts. I want to see them in action, by God, if they ever get into action. I think most of it is newspaper talk. Your average gangster is a yellow cur." B. J. poured himself another drink from a bottle on his bedside table and repeated, "A yellow cur." Drink, as you see, made B. J. pugnacious (he had already gone through his amorous phase). Russell Soames tried to argue his chief out of this perilous plan, but failed. When Russell would not contact the right parties to arrange for B. J.'s little expedition, B. J. contacted them himself, and finally got hold of a man who knew a man who could get them into a regular hangout of gorillas and finger men.

5   Along about midnight of the fourth day in Chicago, B. J. Winfall was ready to set out for the dive. He wore a cap, which covered his bald spot, and he had somehow got hold of a cheap ill-fitting suit, an ensemble which he was pleased to believe gave him the effect of a hardboiled fellow; as a matter of fact, his nose glasses, his pink jowls, and his paunch betrayed him instantly for what he was, a sedentary businessman. Soames strove to dissuade his boss, even in the taxi on their way to the tough spot, but Winfall pooh-poohed him. "Pooh pooh, Russell," he snarled out of the corner of his mouth, unfamiliarly. "These kind of men are rats." He had brought a flask with him and drank copiously from it. "Rats," he said, "of the first order. The first order, Russell, my boy." Soames kept repeating that he felt B. J. was underating the dangerousness of the Chicago gangster and begged him to be on his good

behavior when they got to the joint, if only for the sake of B. J.'s wife and children and his (Russell's) old mother. He exacted a reluctant promise that B. J. would behave himself, but he was by no means easy in his mind when their taxi finally stopped in front of a low, dark building in a far, dark street. "Leave it to me, Russell, my boy," said B. J. as they got out of the cab. "Leave it to me." Their driver refused to wait, and Russell, who paid him off, was just in time to restrain his employer from beating on the door of the place with both fists. Russell himself knocked, timidly. A thin Italian with deadly eyes opened the door a few inches, Russell mentioned a name, falteringly, and the man admitted them.

6   As Russell described it to me later, it was a dingy, smoky place with a rough bar across the back attended by a liver-faced barman with a dirty rag thrown over one shoulder, and only one eye. Leaning on the bar and sitting at tables were a lot of small tough-faced men. They all looked up sullenly when Russell and B. J. walked in. Russell felt that there was a movement of hands in pockets. Smiling amiably, blinking nervously, Russell took his companion's arm, but the latter broke away, strode to the bar, and shouted for whiskey. The bartender fixed his one eye on B. J. with the glowering, steady gaze Jack Dempsey used to give his opponents in the ring. He took his time slamming glasses and a bottle down on the bar. B. J. filled a glass, tossed it off, turned heavily, and faced the roomful of men. "I'm Two-Gun Winfall from New York City!" he shouted. "Anybody *want* anything?"

7   By the most cringing, obsequious explanations and apologies, Russell Soames managed to get himself and his boss out of the place alive. The secret of accomplishing such a feat as he accomplished that night is not to be found in any of the inspirational books. Not a single one of their impressive bits of advice would get you anywhere. Take Mrs. Brande's now famous italicized exhortation, *"Act as if it were impossible to fail."* Wasn't B. J. Winfall doing exactly that? And was that any way to act in this particular situation? It was not. It was Russell Soames' craven apologies, his abject humility, his (as he told me later) tearful admission that he and B. J. were just drunken bums with broken hearts, that got them out of there alive. The success writers would never suggest, or even tolerate, any such behavior. If Russell Soames had followed their bright, hard rules of general conduct, he would be in his grave today and B. J. Winfall's wife would be a widow.

8   If Mrs. Brande is not, as in the case of the memoranda-writer, suggesting a relationship with a superior which I believe we have demonstrated to be dangerous and unworkable (and missing altogether the important problem of how to handle one's employer in his more difficult moments), she is dwelling mystically on the simple and realistic subject of how to deal with one's fellow-workers. Thus, in embroidering the theme that imagination can help you with your fellow-workers, she

writes, "When you have seen this, you can work out a code for yourself which will remove many of the irritations and dissatisfactions of your daily work. Have you ever been amused and enlightened by seeing a familiar room from the top of the stepladder; or, in mirrors set at angles to each other, seen yourself as objectively for a second or two as anybody else in the room? It is that effect you should strive for in imagination." Here again I cannot hold with the dear lady. The nature of imagination, as she describes it, would merely terrify the average man. The idea of bringing such a distorted viewpoint of himself into his relation with his fellow-workers would twist his personality laboriously out of shape and, in the end, appall his fellow-workers. Men who catch an unfamiliar view of a room from the top of a stepladder are neither amused nor enlightened; they have a quick, gasping moment of vertigo which turns rapidly into plain terror. No man likes to see a familiar thing at an unfamiliar angle, or in an unfamiliar light, and this goes, above all things, for his own face. The glimpses that men get of themselves in mirrors set at angles to each other upset them for days. Frequently they shave in the dark for weeks thereafter. To ask a man to steadily contemplate this thing he has seen fleetingly in a mirror and to figure it as dealing with his fellow-workers day by day is to ask him to abandon his own character and to step into another, which he both disowns and dislikes. Split personality could easily result, leading to at least fifteen of the thirty-three "varieties of obliquity" which Mr. David Seabury lists in his "How to Worry Successfully," among them Cursory Enumeration, Distortion of Focus, Nervous Hesitation (superinduced by Ambivalence), Pseudo-Practicality, Divergency, Retardation, Emotionalized Compilation, Negative Dramatization, Rigidism, Secondary Adaptation, False Externalization, Non-Validation, Closure, and Circular Brooding.

9   I don't know why I am reminded at this point of my Aunt Kate Obetz, but I am. She was a woman without any imaginative la-di-da, without any working code save that of direct action, who ran a large dairy farm near Sugar Grove, Ohio, after her husband's death, and ran it successfully. One day something went wrong with the cream separator, and one of her hands came to her and said nobody on the farm could fix it. Should they send to town for a man? "No!" shouted my Aunt Kate. "I'll fix it myself!" Shouldering her way past a number of dairy workers, farm hands and members of her family, she grasped the cream separator and began monkeying with it. In a short time she had reduced it to even more pieces than it had been in when she took hold of it. She couldn't fix it. She was just making things worse. At length, she turned on the onlookers and bawled, "Why doesn't somebody take this goddam thing away from me?" Here was a woman as far out of the tradition of inspirationalist conduct as she could well be. She admitted failure; she had no code for removing irritations and dissatisfactions; she viewed herself as in a single mirror,

directly; she lost her temper; she swore in the presence of subordinates; she confessed complete surrender in the face of a difficult problem; she didn't think of herself as a room seen from the top of a stepladder. And yet her workmen and her family continued to love and respect her. Somebody finally took the cream separator away from her; somehow it was fixed. Her failure did not show up in my aunt's character; she was always the same as ever.

10   For true guidance and sound advice in the business world we find, I think, that the success books are not the place to look, which is pretty much what I thought we would find all along.

VOCABULARY

pontifical (P1), *owlish* (P1), *mysticism* (P1), *unhappiest* (P1), *reputedly* (P1), *Oxford Group* (P1), *bustling* (P1), *monomania* (P2), *accost* (P3), *process-server* (P3), *disgruntled* (P3), *oblivious* (P4), *Capone* (P4), *wholesale* (P4), *dive* (P4), *joint* (P4), *cur* (P4), *pugnacious* (P4), *amorous* (P4), *gorillas* (P4), *finger men* (P4), *ensemble* (P5), *jowls* (P5), *paunch* (P5), *sedentary* (P5), *dissuade* (P5), *copiously* (P5), *exacted* (P5), *falteringly* (P5), *dingy* (P6), *sullenly* (P6), *amiably* (P6), *glowering* (P6), *Jack Dempsey* (P6), *obsequious* (P7), *exhortation* (P7), *craven* (P7), *abject* (P7), *embroidering* (P8), *appall* (P8), *vertigo* (P8), *obliquity* (P8), *cursory* (P8), *superinduced* (P8), *ambivalence* (P8)

IDEAS AND AIMS

1. How can we tell from the essay that one of Thurber's main aims is to amuse or satirize as well as inform?
2. Who is Mrs. Brande? What are "the inspirational books" Thurber refers to?
3. What *overall* criticisms does Thurber make of self-help books in business and psychology?
4. Why are people fired who constantly go over their supervisors' heads, according to Thurber?
5. What joke about and comment on management does Thurber make in his remark "Already they know who too many people are" (P3)?
6. In P4 what is the main criticism Thurber makes of self-help books? How does his following example support, in a humorous nonsequitur way, this criticism?
7. In what way does Winfall's behavior off the job stem from his managerial position *on* the job? What sort of superior is Winfall? (In P4 why hasn't Winfall left his hotel room in 36 hours, and what is comically or ironically revealed through his settling in? What do we learn about Winfall's personality from his penchant for repetition in PP4–5?)

8. What is the implication of Russell's observation "that there was a movement of hands in pockets" (P6)?
9. What joke does Thurber make about the language of psychology and the social sciences at the end of P8? Use examples in your explanation.
10. How does the essay show the all-important link between human nature and business?

ORGANIZATION AND FORM

1. What are the main parts of the essay?
2. How does Thurber make use of narration or narrative incidents for illustration and example? In what paragraphs does he do so?
3. How is the transition that opens P9 humorous? What more serious transition could be used instead?
4. How is Thurber's final example in P9 a very moving one, appropriate for a conclusion of the essay?

WORDS AND STYLE

1. How does Thurber's constant reference to various self-proclaimed self-help authorities contribute to the tone of his essay?
2. How does Thurber use effective interplay between the standard and colloquial levels of usage in the last three sentences of P2? How does he use it in the contrast between the last sentence of P8 and the first sentence of P9?
3. In addition to the examples cited in question 2, where else does Thurber use colloquialism or slang effectively to help make a point or describe someone's personality more clearly?
4. How are many of the names that Thurber makes up for his illustrations humorous or ironic?
5. What is the joke, as well as irony, in the word "unfamiliarly" in "he snarled out of the corner of his mouth, unfamiliarly" (P5)?
6. How do the words in the last sentence of P3 ironically echo those of a preceding sentence in the paragraph? How does this repetition suggest cause and effect?
7. Where does Thurber use repetition of a word in a sentence effectively? Cite one or two examples and explain how the repetition helps Thurber express his point.

DISCUSSION AND WRITING

1. Who are some of the modern "success writers"? What is their advice on adjusting yourself to your work? Contrast their advice and Thurber's.

2. Take a bit of modern commonplace advice, such as might be found in one of the modern "success writers." Try to write an ironic story, as Thurber has done, illustrating how the advice is bad advice.

3. Do you agree with Thurber's counsel about not going over your immediate supervisor's head? Have you or have acquaintances of yours ever done this? What was the result? What are recent instances in government agencies where this has happened, as reported in newspapers and on television? What were the results?

4. Compare Thurber's mockery of writers on business with Robert Benchley's in "From Nine to Five" (Section 8, "Efficiency and Success on the Job"). What essential elements of human nature and daily life do these success writers overlook, in the opinion of these two humorists? Do you agree that these elements of human nature and daily life *are* essential? How important are they at school or in business? Cite several examples in your answer.

JAPANESE AND AMERICAN WORKERS: Two Casts of Mind

William Ouchi

□

William Ouchi, like Peter Drucker, is a business expert. (See Drucker's essays in Section 3, "Work and Education," and Section 4, "Careers for the 1990s.") Born in 1943, Ouchi has both an M.B.A. from Stanford University and a doctorate in business administration from the University of Chicago. He is both a prominent business consultant, who has worked for Fortune 500 companies, and a professor in the Graduate School of Management at U.C.L.A. This selection, a classic example of comparison and contrast, is from his book Theory Z: How American Business Can Meet the Japanese Challenge *(1981), which has been a bestseller in hardcover and paperback editions. Ouchi's is one of several recent books by various authors studying the reasons for the phenomenal success of Japanese businesses and exploring what lessons can be learned by American business.*

Basically, Ouchi in his book distinguishes three different types of business organization: Type A (American, profit-motivated, and inattentive to its workers), Type J (the Japanese organization), and Type Z (American with the best elements of the Japanese adapted to it). Ouchi seems to have chosen the letter Z to contrast strongly the two American forms: the title of Chapter 5 is "Going from A to Z—the Steps"; that of Chapter 6 is "Going from A to Z— Blueprints for a Philosophy." Perhaps, also, his "Z" term is related to his assertion that the "Z approach to management . . . [is] that involved workers are the key to increased productivity." Ouchi traces the concept of employing workers for their lifetime to small clusters of Japanese firms called Zaibatsu *(significantly, the word begins with a* Z*).*

In the preface to his book Ouchi explains that he resisted publishing a "college textbook or a slick but, in my view, insubstantial quickie." Although he has published articles in scholarly business journals, Ouchi prefers a middle path in his writing here, between the technical and slick. On one hand, he has footnotes, a bibliography, solid concepts, and history; on the other, he uses illustrative headings to sections (in magazine style) and relatively uncomplicated sentences.

(PP1–9 of this selection are from Chapter 2 of Theory Z, *while PP10–15 are from Chapter 3.)*

Collective Values

1 Perhaps the most difficult aspect of the Japanese for Westerners to comprehend is the strong orientation to collective values, particularly a collective sense of responsibility. Let me illustrate with an anecdote about a visit to a new factory in Japan owned and operated by an American electronics company. The American company, a particularly creative firm, frequently attracts attention within the business community for its novel approaches to planning, organizational design, and management systems. As a consequence of this corporate style, the parent company determined to make a thorough study of Japanese workers and to design a plant that would combine the best of East and West. In their study they discovered that Japanese firms almost never make use of individual work incentives, such as piecework or even individual performance appraisal tied to salary increases. They concluded that rewarding individual achievement and individual ability is always a good thing.

2   In the final assembly area of their new plant long lines of young Japanese women wired together electronic products on a piece-rate system: the more you wired, the more you got paid. About two months after opening, the head foreladies approached the plant manager. "Honorable plant manager," they said humbly as they bowed, "we are embarrassed to be so forward, but we must speak to you because all of the girls have threatened to quit work this Friday." (To have this happen, of course, would be a great disaster for all concerned.) "Why," they wanted to know, "can't our plant have the same compensation system as other Japanese companies? When you hire a new girl, her starting wage should be fixed by her age. An eighteen-year-old should be paid more than a sixteen-year-old. Every year on her birthday, she should receive an automatic increase in pay. The idea that any one of us can be more productive than another must be wrong, because none of us in final assembly could make

a thing unless all of the other people in the plant had done their jobs right first. To single one person out as being more productive is wrong and is also personally humiliating to us." The company changed its compensation system to the Japanese model.

3   Another American company in Japan had installed a suggestion system much as we have in the United States. Individual workers were encouraged to place suggestions to improve productivity into special boxes. For an accepted idea the individual received a bonus amounting to some fraction of the productivity savings realized from his or her suggestion. After a period of six months, not a single suggestion had been submitted. The American managers were puzzled. They had heard many stories of the inventiveness, the commitment, and the loyalty of Japanese workers, yet not one suggestion to improve productivity had appeared.

The managers approached some of the workers and asked why the suggestion system had not been used. The answer: "No one can come up with a work improvement idea alone. We work together, and any ideas that one of us may have are actually developed by watching others and talking to others. If one of us was singled out for being responsible for such an idea, it would embarrass all of us." The company changed to a group suggestion system, in which workers collectively submitted suggestions. Bonuses were paid to groups which would save bonus money until the end of the year for a party at a restaurant or, if there was enough money, for family vacations together. The suggestions and productivity improvements rained down on the plant.

5   One can interpret these examples in two quite different ways. Perhaps the Japanese commitment to collective values is an anachronism that does not fit with modern industrialism but brings economic success despite that collectivism. Collectivism seems to be inimical to the kind of maverick creativity exemplified in Benjamin Franklin, Thomas Edison, and John D. Rockefeller. Collectivism does not seem to provide the individual incentive to excel which has made a great success of American enterprise. Entirely apart from its economic effects, collectivism implies a loss of individuality, a loss of the freedom to be different, to hold fundamentally different values from others.

6   The second interpretation of the examples is that the Japanese collectivism is economically efficient. It causes people to work well together and to encourage one another to better efforts. Industrial life requires interdependence of one person on another. But a less obvious but far-reaching implication of the Japanese collectivism for economic performance has to do with accountability.

7   In the Japanese mind, collectivism is neither a corporate or individual goal to strive for nor a slogan to pursue. Rather, the nature of things operates so that nothing of consequence occurs as a result of individual

effort. Everything important in life happens as a result of teamwork or collective effort. Therefore, to attempt to assign individual credit or blame to results is unfounded. A Japanese professor of accounting, a brilliant scholar trained at Carnegie-Mellon University who teaches now in Tokyo, remarked that the status of accounting systems in Japanese industry is primitive compared to those in the United States. Profit centers, transfer prices, and computerized information systems are barely known even in the largest Japanese companies, whereas they are a commonplace in even small United States organizations. Though not at all surprised at the difference in accounting systems, I was not at all sure that the Japanese were primitive. In fact, I thought their system a good deal more efficient than ours.

8   Most American companies have basically two accounting systems. One system summarizes the overall financial state to inform stockholders, bankers, and other outsiders. That system is not of interest here. The other system, called the managerial or cost accounting system, exists for an entirely different reason. It measures in detail all of the particulars of transactions between departments, divisions, and key individuals in the organization, for the purpose of untangling the interdependencies between people. When, for example, two departments share one truck for deliveries, the cost accounting system charges each department for part of the cost of maintaining the truck and driver, so that at the end of the year, the performance of each department can be individually assessed, and the better department's manager can receive a larger raise. Of course, all of this information processing costs money, and furthermore may lead to arguments between the departments over whether the costs charged to each are fair.

9   In a Japanese company a short-run assessment of individual performance is not wanted, so the company can save the considerable expense of collecting and processing all of that information. Companies still keep track of which department uses a truck how often and for what purposes, but like-minded people can interpret some simple numbers for themselves and adjust their behavior accordingly. Those insisting upon clear and precise measurement for the purpose of advancing individual interests must have an elaborate information system. Industrial life, however, is essentially integrated and interdependent. No one builds an automobile alone, no one carries through a banking transaction alone. In a sense the Japanese value of collectivism fits naturally into an industrial setting, whereas the Western individualism provides constant conflicts. The image that comes to mind is of Chaplin's silent film "Modern Times" in which the apparently insignificant hero played by Chaplin successfully fights against the unfeeling machinery of industry. Modern industrial life can be aggravating, even hostile, or natural: all depends on the fit between our culture and our technology.

A Difference of Tradition

10   The *shinkansen* or "bullet train" speeds across the rural areas of Japan giving a quick view of cluster after cluster of farmhouses surrounded by rice paddies. This particular pattern did not develop purely by chance, but as a consequence of the technology peculiar to the growing of rice, the staple of Japanese diet. The growing of rice requires the construction and maintenance of an irrigation system, something that takes many hands to build. More importantly, the planting and the harvesting of rice can only be done efficiently with the cooperation of twenty or more people. The "bottom line" is that a single family working alone cannot produce enough rice to survive, but a dozen families working together can produce a surplus. Thus the Japanese have had to develop the capacity to work together in harmony, no matter what the forces of disagreement or social disintegration, in order to survive.

11   Japan is a nation built entirely on the tips of giant, suboceanic volcanoes. Little of the land is flat and suitable for agriculture. Terraced hillsides make use of every available square foot of arable land. Small homes built very close together further conserve the land. Japan also suffers from natural disasters such as earthquakes and hurricanes. Traditionally homes are made of light construction materials, so a house falling down during a disaster will not crush its occupants and also can be quickly and inexpensively rebuilt. During the feudal period until the Meiji restoration of 1868, each feudal lord sought to restrain his subjects from moving from one village to the next for fear that a neighboring lord might amass enough peasants with which to produce a large agricultural surplus, hire an army and pose a threat. Apparently bridges were not commonly built across rivers and streams until the late nineteenth century, since bridges increased mobility between villages.

12   Taken all together, this characteristic style of living paints the picture of a nation of people who are homogeneous with respect to race, history, language, religion, and culture. For centuries and generations these people have lived in the same village next door to the same neighbors. Living in close proximity and in dwellings which gave very little privacy, the Japanese survived through their capacity to work together in harmony. In this situation, it was inevitable that the one most central social value which emerged, the one value without which the society could not continue, was that an individual does not matter.

13   To the Western soul this is a chilling picture of society. Subordinating individual tastes to the harmony of the group and knowing that individual needs can never take precedence over the interests of all is repellent to the Western citizen. But a frequent theme of Western philosophers and sociologists is that individual freedom exists only when

people willingly subordinate their self-interests to the social interest. A society composed entirely of self-interested individuals is a society in which each person is at war with the other, a society which has no freedom. This issue, constantly at the heart of understanding society, comes up in every century, and in every society, whether the writer be Plato, Hobbes, or B. F. Skinner. The question of understanding which contemporary institutions lie at the heart of the conflict between automatism and totalitarianism remains. In some ages, the kinship group, the central social institution, mediated between these opposing forces to preserve the balance in which freedom was realized; in other times the church or the government was most critical. Perhaps our present age puts the work organization as the central institution.

14   In order to complete the comparison of Japanese and American living situations, consider flight over the United States. Looking out of the windows high over the state of Kansas, we see a pattern of a single farmhouse surrounded by fields, followed by another single homestead surrounded by fields. In the early 1800s in the state of Kansas there were no automobiles. Your nearest neighbor was perhaps two miles distant; the winters were long, and the snow was deep. Inevitably, the central social values were self-reliance and independence. Those were the realities of that place and age that children had to learn to value.

15   The key to the industrial revolution was discovering that non-human forms of energy substituted for human forms could increase the wealth of a nation beyond anyone's wildest dreams. But there was a catch. To realize this great wealth, non-human energy needed huge complexes called factories with hundreds, even thousands of workers collected into one factory. Moreover, several factories in one central place made the generation of energy more efficient. Almost overnight, the Western world was transformed from a rural and agricultural country to an urban and industrial state. Our technological advance seems to no longer fit our social structure: in a sense, the Japanese can better cope with modern industrialism. While Americans still busily protect our rather extreme form of individualism, the Japanese hold their individualism in check and emphasize cooperation.

VOCABULARY

collective (P1), *anecdote* (P1), *novel* (P1), *incentives* (P1), *piecework* (P1), *appraisal* (P1), *compensation* (P2), *productivity* (P3), *anachronism* (P5), *inimical* (P5), *maverick* (P5), *accountability* (P6), *integrated* (P9), *rural* (P10), *terraced* (P11), *arable* (P11), *feudal* (P11), *amass* (P11), *homogeneous* (P12), *subordinating* (P13), *repellent* (P13), *Plato* (P13), *[Thomas] Hobbes* (P13), *B. F. Skinner* (P13), *automatism* (P13), *totalitarianism* (P13), *kinship group* (P13), *mediated* (P13)

IDEAS AND AIMS

1. What are the American and Japanese views of the individual in society?
2. How does each society's view of the individual affect the way businesses function in that society, according to Ouchi?
3. Specifically, why do Japanese workers feel humiliated by work incentives that reward performance?
4. Why were Japanese workers humiliated by the suggestion system described by Ouchi?
5. According to Ouchi, what are the advantages and disadvantages of Japanese collectivism?
6. What is the relationship between Japan's history, particularly its agricultural history, and the Japanese view of the individual?
7. What is the relationship between America's history and the American view of the individual?
8. How do Japanese and American accounting systems reflect the contrasting points of view of collectivism and individualism?
9. How is there an argumentative or persuasive overtone to this basically expository selection?

ORGANIZATION AND FORM

1. How may PP1–6, PP7–9, PP10–15 be viewed as the main parts or sections of the essay?
2. How does Ouchi use narration in the introduction of the essay to help explain and clarify his subject? In what paragraphs, specifically, does he use this method? What word does he use in P1 that directly refers to this narrative method?
3. Where does Ouchi use comparison and contrast as a method of analysis and development within a single paragraph? Where does he use it to develop a section of the essay, balancing one paragraph or more against another one or more?
4. Where does Ouchi use cause and effect as a method of analysis and development?
5. How is the first sentence of P14 clearly marked off as transitional?

WORDS AND STYLE

1. How are Ouchi's words "busily" and "rather extreme form of individualism" (P15) slanted? What side do they suggest he is on? How?
2. What other examples of Ouchi's point of view favoring one country can you find? What ironic reversal of nationalistic roles is there in P7?

3. Citing examples from his language, explain what kind of audience you think Ouchi is writing for. How does his prose style differ from that of fellow economist Juanita Kreps (Section 4, "Careers for the 1990s")?

4. In the third sentence of P15 Ouchi could have chosen any one of a number of synonyms for his verbal designating the collecting of workers in a factory—e.g., *gathered, congregated, assembled, clustered, aggregated, accumulated.* In light of his key repeated term for the central feature of Japan's social system—used in P5, P6, P7, and P9—why is the verbal Ouchi chooses in P15 especially appropriate and significant? How does it help reinforce his point about why Japan's society seems especially well adapted to the modern industrial age?

5. What exactly do Ouchi's words "non-human forms of energy substituted for human forms" (first sentence of P15) mean? What are "non-human forms of energy"? What are "human forms [of energy]"? How does the first apply to the United States, the second to Japan?

DISCUSSION AND WRITING

1. Do you think Japanese management and accounting systems would work in American businesses with American workers? Why?

2. Ouchi does not explain or develop the topic of American individualism as fully as he develops the topic of Japanese collectivism. Write an essay explaining the origins, causes, characteristics, and manifestations of American individualism as you see it. If possible, use comparison and contrast to help develop some of your points.

3. Both England's and America's manufacturing and economies prospered during the Industrial Revolution, from its onset in the nineteenth century, through the time of Henry Ford, to now. Why should individualism *now* be inappropriate to the Industrial Revolution, as Ouchi suggests in P15?

4. What observations by Ouchi on the Japanese worker might be used as, adapted to, or transformed into advice for young managers in American companies?

5. How does what the company learned in the case history in PP1–2 compare with what Adam Smith said in 1776 about piecework in "High Wages and Overwork" (pages 170-71)?

6. At the library or a bookstore look through some other books that have appeared on Japanese management—for example, *The Book of Five Rings* or *The Art of Japanese Management.* How do these works compare with Ouchi's in their views or style of presentation?

CRABBED YOUTH

C. Northcote Parkinson

☐

Probably the two most celebrated, incisive, and humorous "laws" applicable to the business world in the last two decades are "Parkinson's Law" and "the Peter Principle." (The latter was formulated by Laurence J. Peter in The Peter Principle: *Each individual's final promotion is to a job or level where he or she is incompetent; every individual winds up at his own level of incompetence.) "Parkinson's Law" was formulated by C. Northcote Parkinson in his book* Parkinson's Law and Other Studies in Administration *(1957): "Work expands so as to fill the time available for its completion."*

Parkinson (born in 1909) has enunciated several "laws" in a series of books that are marked by clear, graceful, and compact prose style, and by amusing and penetrating insights into business, finance, and human behavior generally. These books, most of them available in paperback editions, are Parkinson's Law *(1957),* The Law and the Profits *(1960),* In-Laws and Outlaws *(1962),* Mrs. Parkinson's Law, and Other Studies in Domestic Science *(1968),* The Law of Delay: Interviews and Outerviews *(1971), and* Parkinson: The Law *(1980). But these titles are only a fraction of Parkinson's output, which totals more than forty books.*

Born in Durham, England, Parkinson was educated at Cambridge University (B.A.) and King's College in London (Ph.D.). He has taught history at universities in the United States, Britain, and Malaya, and several of his books deal with naval and military history, as well as economic history. He has also published novels and a biography.

Parkinson's knowledge of the workings of bureaucracy in the military as well as civilian sectors of the population and his expertise in military history contribute toward his unsurpassed analysis of this crucial development of organizations in the modern world, which employ some of us and affect all of us. Other Parkinson's laws include "Expenditure rises to meet income" (Parkinson's Second Law), "the number of people in any working group tends to increase regardless of the amount of work to be done" (part of Parkinson's science of "comitology"—the study of committees), and "heat produced by pressure expands to fill the mind available, from which it can pass only to a cooler mind" (Mrs. Parkinson's Law).

1 Is this an age of opportunity for the young? The stories we hear would suggest that it is. There are companies which recruit young men for preference and give them managerial responsibility at the age of 28–34, sometimes with as little as five years of experience in the business. Is it generally true that youth is being given a chance? There are at least three reasons for thinking that it may be so. First of all, there was a low birth rate for much of the period from 1925 to 1945, the result of trade depression and war. Productive people thus tend to be outnumbered by schoolchildren and pensioners and should retain a scarcity value until about 1980. In the second place there has been a disproportionate growth on the managerial as opposed to the manual side of industry. Supervisory staff which formed perhaps 7% of the working population in 1900 amounts now to 11% or more. In the third place, the mere existence of recruiting firms would seem to indicate a shortage of talent. Instead of young men scheming to attract the attention of employers, it is the employers who are trying to attract the attention of the young men. Their advertisements are large, urgent and costly and they are obviously prepared for a high failure rate among the staff they can thus attract. One way to have met the shortage would have been to employ women instead but the actual practice has been different, for the women in managerial positions number only one per cent of the working population and this percentage has remained unaltered since 1900.

2   The trend in favour of youth is, in many ways, all to the good. The middle-aged among us can look back, very often, on years of frustration. We can remember, many of us, the old men who refused to retire, the years we spent upon trivial routine, the feeling perhaps that our promotion (when it came) was all too late in the day. We can recall the appointments made of men who were at once inexperienced and elderly, men who had spent their first years filing away documents, their middle period in taking the minutes at committee meetings, their early maturity in answering routine correspondence and now, when old, were given a responsibility for which they were totally unfitted. In politics we have

had occasion to deplore the same trend, with statesmen of many countries cluttering the political scene with the deadweight of their obsolescence.

3   One looks back, by contrast, to the heroes of an earlier period; to men who commanded warships or regiments at the age of nineteen or twenty, to one, even who became Prime Minister at the age of twenty-four. These examples inspire but we should remember that men of this sort left school a great deal earlier and usually married (if at all) a great deal later. A general aged 32 might have had ten years' experience in active command. How preferable he is to a general aged 55 who had had no useful experience of any kind! For youth at the helm there is much to be said. As an ideal, however, it is difficult to achieve in a country where people tend to spend so long a period attending courses of instruction. To combine youth with experience implies an earlier start than many people achieve, and it often happens that a prolonged education can prove a decisive handicap. There are young men today who have made a million before they are 25. This sort of success depends, as a rule, on having left school at fifteen without distinction and without regret. Others attempting to do the same end, admittedly, in prison. The fact remains, however, that the self-made millionaire (unlike the well-paid executive) must usually start life in a slum.

4   Take the case of an imaginary young business man, A, who is appointed to a responsible position at the age of 28. Let us suppose that he married at the age of 23, graduated well from the business school at 24 and joined the company soon afterwards. Regarded as promising from the outset, he was moved rapidly round the organisation and given a spell, latterly, as assistant to the Managing Director. Now, at 28 (the father of three children) he is made Sales Manager. Should he prove a success there is every likelihood of his being appointed manager of the company's new Zed Plant at Runcorn. His assistants in the sales department are B (aged 51), C (aged 43) and D (aged 37); all three rejected as candidates for the post he occupies. A's immediate problem is to gain the loyalty of B, C and D, ensuring that the sales graph will at once justify his appointment and ensure his further promotion. A has somehow to convince these older men that he knows best. Still more to the point, however, he must first convince himself. For the chief danger to A lies in his own sense of insecurity. Should he feel ignorant as compared with his immediate staff, he will reveal the fact in one of two ways. He will either seek popularity by making concessions and promises, or else he will assert himself by petty acts of tyranny. Other symptoms of instability may appear daily on the notice board—typewritten warnings which should have been delivered verbally (if at all) and directives which are classifiable as needless or futile. Where A does feel sufficiently secure it is because his aim is to better the company and not merely himself. If his chief concern is for the shareholders, clients and employees, he can point to further achieve-

ments in which B, C and D can share the credit. He cannot expect them to join in furthering his personal ambition, if that is his main concern, for they have no reason to prefer his interest to their own. The appeal must be to something that is beyond them all; some object in the light of which all animosities must be laid aside.

5   If carefully chosen in the first place the majority of those given responsible positions before the age of 35 should justify their promotion. But this policy, like any other, has its drawbacks as well as its advantages. Should it become known that the company's policy is to promote men aged 30–35, all men aged 37 or more will know that they have been passed over and are no longer being considered. This realisation can be extremely bad for morale. Men who do not actually resign may still lose interest in their work. Others may feel embittered and may express themselves accordingly.

6   The trouble with men in this category is that the wife's disappointment may be fatal to the husband's further usefulness: B's wife will resent having to treat A's wife with a certain deference; A's wife not only being younger but prettier. Poor C's wife will be as restive but D's wife will be the most dissatisfied of the three. For D, remember is *almost* young enough to be still in the running. What is the difference, after all, between 35 and 37, especially if your birthday comes late in the year? Even when young men are preferred, there is good reason to reserve some higher positions for older men. Granted that some must be disappointed to the end, they should still be allowed to know that they have a chance. A last retiring post of Director (Maintenance) might be kept as reward for long service. It would cost little to secure loyalty thus over the previous decade.

7   Another point to remember is that men promoted to responsible positions at the age of 30–35 may remain in the company for another 30–35 years. Provided that the industry is growing and developing fast, there will be new appointments for them as the years go by. But what if business should slacken? All the responsible positions will be filled, in that case, by men aged (say) 40–45. For the next generation of young men there is no hope of a senior vacancy. Ten years later the same group of crabbed youth holds the field and no man of destiny has joined the company for the last decade. Ten years after that the company's senior executives arrive almost simultaneously at their retiring age. They retire over a five-year period and there is nobody to replace them. This is, of course, an exaggerated picture, for the board would have taken some action to prevent such a crisis. But the risk of youth at the helm is obvious. It could mean blocking all promotion for the youth of the next generation. It may create a dull period when everyone seems elderly, followed by a crisis (in 1995) when there seems to be nobody at all.

8   Time is the cure for youth and the brightest young men of 1970 will be the more experienced and cautious men of 1984. In a period of reces-

sion, incidentally, it may be experience and caution that you want. But there is another danger against which we need to be on our guard. For the men we promote at the age of 30 tend to be too much alike. They have started with a technical training designed to make up for their inexperience. They have the language of the computer on their lips and their lives are programmed to the same pattern. They are not only graduates of the business school but are often from the *same* business school: pupils of the same professors in economics, cybernetics and automation. It is an initial advantage that they can understand each other. It is an ultimate drawback that they may all give the same advice. The boardroom table could be surrounded, eventually, by men whose outlook is too stereotyped. Instead of studying the current problem from different angles (financial, technical, commercial, political, sociological and legal) they may all see it in exactly the same light. Their memories may all go back to the same lectures delivered in the same room and to the same examinations taken so successfully at the same time. Here again there is a risk of exaggeration but companies do exist in which people have been trained to think alike. The immediate convenience of this may bring with it an ultimate penalty.

9   We talk too much these days of the subjects which should be studied at school or college or on the course in business method. It is not the subjects which matter so much as the sense of ignorance, the eagerness to inquire, the method of study and the habit of thought. Education is something which should perpetuate itself and lead to further study of different problems. With side interests and the pursuit of casual information people with widely ranging tastes will diverge from each other. They will end with a valuable diversity of opinion, provided only that they begin with a capacity to develop. Men of the highest distinction usually turn out to be well-informed, not merely in the details of their own careers but in many other directions as well.

10   There are reasons, then, for doubting whether the early promotion of the young would benefit every endeavour at every time. Where the endeavour is new and where the field is just beginning to develop, there may be good reason to choose the young. But to make early promotion a general rule would be neither feasible nor wise. It would merely create a log-jam in the years to come.

VOCABULARY

pensioners (P1), *disproportionate* (P1), *manual* (P1), *obsolescence* (P2), *helm* (P3), *spell* (P4), *latterly* (P4), *zed* (P4), *concessions* (P4), *petty* (P4), *instability* (P4), *futile* (P4), *animosities* (P4), *morale* (P5), *deference* (P6), *restive* (P6), *crabbed* (P7), *destiny* (P7), *recession* (P8), *cybernetics* (P8), *stereotyped* (P8), *diverge* (P9), *diversity* (P9), *feasible* (P10)

IDEAS AND AIMS

1. How is Parkinson's overall aim of the essay partly humor, or irony? Cite and discuss examples, such as the author's offhanded reference to women at the close of P1 (ironically undercutting the business world) or his humorous points in discussing spouses' effects on middle-level managers in P6.
2. What are the three reasons for the growth in opportunities for the young?
3. What, according to the author, were the previous expectations of career advancement for young people?
4. How did the elderly managers' previous jobs, as outlined in the fourth sentence of P2, not prepare them for top management? Explain how their job in each "period" was unhelpful for such preparation.
5. In what sense may a prolonged education prove to be a handicap, according to Parkinson?
6. What is the central idea being illustrated by the case history in P4?
7. How does Parkinson's irony glimmer in his suggestion of what post should be reserved for long service in a company (next-to-last sentence of P6)?
8. What are the disadvantages of early promotion?

ORGANIZATION AND FORM

1. Parkinson's essay has the classical organization of an argument: first the con side (the opposing view) is given, and then the pro side (the side, point, or position that the author is advocating). What paragraphs are allotted to the con (promotion of youth) side? Which to the pro (arguing against the early promotion of youth) side?
2. How does P3 function as a transition from con to pro sides?
3. What are the main parts or blocs of paragraphs within Parkinson's overall section devoted to the pro side? What idea or focus makes each of these blocs a unit?
4. In what paragraphs does Parkinson make use of illustrations or extended examples?
5. How does Parkinson use cause-and-effect analysis and development in P4? Where else does he use cause and effect?
6. In what paragraph does Parkinson state his central thesis most clearly? How does this impart to his essay a sense of inductive form (see the questions on Organization and Form for Ilene Kantrov's "Women's Business" in Section 6, "Job Opportunities and Other Practical Matters")?
7. List examples of Parkinson's use of transition words and pronouns to effect greater continuity or coherence within and between paragraphs. Choose one or two instances and explain how Parkinson's transitional devices make that part of the essay flow more smoothly.

WORDS AND STYLE

1. Explain the irony and exact application of the title of the essay.
2. How does the author use series sentences effectively in P1 and P2?
3. What is the effect of the author's use of the first person plural pronoun in P2? Why might it make the reader not so lightly dismiss Parkinson's later argument against promotion of the young?
4. What implications, humorous and serious, about youth does Parkinson convey by the word "cure" in his opening sentence of P8, "Time is the cure for youth . . ."?
5. How does the parallelism of the fifth through seventh sentences of P8 help Parkinson express the point he is making about uniformity, in this paragraph? (Look up "parallelism" in your composition handbook.)
6. What point or idea does Parkinson's repetition of the word "same" make in the third from the last sentence of P8?
7. How is balanced antithesis used for ironic effect in the last sentence of P8 (the second and third words versus the eleventh and twelfth of the sentence)? (Look up "balance" and "antithesis" in your collegiate dictionary or composition handbook.)
8. What is the meaning of Parkinson's phrase "sense of ignorance" in the second sentence of P9?

DISCUSSION AND WRITING

1. Is the author's worry in P8 contradicted by his remarks in P9? Are people from the same schools necessarily going to think alike? Is there a difference between British schools and universities and American schools and universities in this respect?
2. Do you agree with the author that youth should not be promoted or rewarded too quickly? Why or why not? What are your own expectations in your career?
3. Can you write an essay in which you argue the opposite position, that age and experience should not be rewarded? Can almost all of the points the author raises in this essay also be said of older workers?
4. Do you agree or disagree with Parkinson's contention in the last sentence of P3 about the best candidates for self-made millionaires? Research the topic in the library for supporting examples.
5. Compare Parkinson's analysis of a spouse's effect on someone in business with that of George Ade in PP14–16 of "The Fable of the Divided Concern That Was Reunited Under a New Management" (the next essay in this section). Do you agree or disagree with these authors' assessments? Offer supporting evidence and examples in your answer.

THE FABLE OF THE DIVIDED CONCERN THAT WAS REUNITED UNDER A NEW MANAGEMENT

George Ade

□

George Ade (1866–1944) was born in Indiana and educated at Purdue University. His origins in America's heartland served him in good stead, for he became one of the first great masters of the American vernacular (the British called him "the Shakespeare of slang") and one of the shrewdest observers of the American scene. Short story writer, dramatist (two of his plays, The County Chairman, 1903, and The College Widow, 1904, are still performed), journalist, and essayist, Ade fashioned his skills to become a humorist winning the highest praise from such distinguished writers as H. L. Mencken, William Dean Howells, and S. J. Perelman. From his berth on the Chicago Morning News, in 1898 Ade began publishing a "fable in slang" once a week and continued for a decade. These acute, ironic explorations of American customs, manners, and institutions were collected in Fables in Slang (1900), More Fables (1900), Forty Modern Fables (1901), Ade's Fables (1914), and Hand-Made Fables (1920), among other books of essays, stories, and plays. Ade's fables, frequently used by President Franklin Roosevelt to make points to his cabinet, are distinguished for their use of colloquial English and individualistic use of capitalization, besides their mordant wit.

While the following "fable" is dated in some respects (we now use the word "salesman" or "sales representative" rather than "drummer," for example), its observations on business and human nature remain as true as ever. In the most convenient collection of his work, The America of George Ade: Fables, Short Stories, Essays, edited by Jean Shepherd, are to be found

1 Once upon a Time there was a Firm doing Business under the Name of Hailfellow and Grouch.

2 They had a large Retail Establishment, upon entering which the Customer was greeted by the mingled Odors of Kerosene, Roasted Coffee, Leather, Herkimer County Cheese, Navy Plug, Dried Apples, and petrified Codfish. In the good old Summer-Time it was not necessary to go into the Store in order to get the complicated Aroma. Farmers driving by could come very near guessing what Hailfellow and Grouch carried in Stock.

3 The Firm did a Nice Business and used to split quite a Piece of Money every January 1st. But neither one was satisfied. Each felt that he was entitled to at least two-thirds of the Net Profits.

4 Mr. Hailfellow was the Hand-Shaker for the Outfit. His Long Suit was to know everybody and call him by his front Name. On every pleasant Day he stood in front of the fragrant Emporium, in his Shirt Sleeves, holding a public Levee.

5 He was a quiet Josher and knew a lot of good Jokes that he had once heard in a Minstrel Show at Columbus, Ohio, and that made him very strong with the Country Trade.

6 Furthermore, he was a good Mixer. He belonged to the K. P.'s and the Odd Fellows and a few others, so that about four Nights out of the week he would fill his Pockets with mild Smokers, usually neglecting to make out a Ticket, and then he would pike for the Lodge-Room and let his Partner and the Boy with the Pink Shirt attend to the Store.

7 If there was an Auction Sale or a Baseball Game or a Circus anywhere within a Radius of twenty Miles, then Mr. Hailfellow would put on his Dark Suit and stand-up Collar and drive over, just to get his Mind off his Business. In one Way and another he managed to keep his Mind off of Business about seven-eighths of the Time.

8 Sometimes, when he was around the Store, and there was a Saturday Rush, he would have to wait on a few Customers, but he was a shine Salesman because he never could make out what the Cost-Mark meant.

9 Mr. Grouch, the Partner, possessed a Good Head for Business, but he had the Social Disposition of a Coffin-Trimmer. While Hailfellow would be up and down the Street, kidding the local Population and making himself well liked, Grouch would be in the back end of the Store straightening out the Books and figuring Discounts.

10 Grouch was at the Store by 7 o'clock every Morning, keeping Tab, for fear that some one who was No Good would get his Name on the Books.

11   Hailfellow would land in about 9:30 and open the Day by reading the Morning Paper through from the Weather Bulletin in front to the Testimonials on the last Page. After which he was ready to go out and plant himself on a Salt-Barrel and discuss the Issues of the Day.

12   Grouch had only one Day off in Four Years, and then he had to attend the Funeral of a Relative. So that when he did get a Vacation there was not much Enjoyment in it.

13   There was no denying his Industry, but no one liked him. He seemed to have some kind of an inward Grudge against every one who came in to buy a Bill of Goods. If a Customer remarked that it was a Nice Day, he didn't seem to believe it. The Trade would not have stuck at all, had it not been for Hailfellow, who had a way of giving Stick Candy to the Kids and beautiful Colored Pictures, advertising Breakfast Foods, to the Women Folks.

14   Each Partner naturally believed that he was getting the Short End of the Arrangement. They would go home and tell their Troubles to the Wives. Mrs. Hailfellow went around to Sewing Societies and Missionary Meetings telling how Mr. Hailfellow had to put up with a lot and was really the one who brought all the Trade to the Store.

15   Mrs. Grouch loved to let all her Friends know that her Husband slaved like a Dog while the Partner soldiered, but, just the same, always came in on the cut-up of the Profits.

16   When the Wives begin to take part in a Business Row, the Dissolution Notice is about Due.

17   Hailfellow and Grouch agreed to disagree. Hailfellow took his Share and opened a New Place across the Street, with a Gilt Sign and nickel-plated Show-Cases.

18   Almost immediately it was the most popular Joint in Town. At Times there were as many as ten Men sitting around the Stove swapping Fish Stories. Hailfellow employed a couple of Clerks who knew more about a Cash Register than the Man that invented it.

19   He issued Pass-Books to all those who cared for his Jokes. The Drummers would jump several Towns in order to get to him in a Hurry, because, if Hailfellow liked a Drummer, he would order a thousand gross of Lamp Chimneys rather than appear cold and unsociable. In a short time he had a Magnificent Stock, but he could not remember exactly how much it cost him. So he sold Goods at whatever seemed to be Reasonable and the Farmers drove long distances so as to give him their Trade.

20   In the meantime Grouch was reaping the sure Reward of one who is not kind to his Fellow-Man. People did not care to patronize one whose Conversation consisted very largely of Grunts, and why should they do so when they could go right across the Street and buy Stuff below Cost, and a Joke given away with every Purchase?

21 Grouch began to lose Money and the Rent ate up his Invested Capital. At last the Jobbers closed in on him and asked the Sheriff to step in, and the Sheriff said he would do so as soon as he got through closing up the Hailfellow Matter.

22 Mr. Hailfellow had done a rushing Business. He owed nearly every Wholesale House west of New York, and in addition to laying up the most remarkable mess of Junk ever seen under one Roof, he had collected the Autograph Signatures of all the Paupers in the County. Four Experts worked for a Month trying to find out where he stood, and at last they figured out Fourteen Cents on the Dollar.

23 It is always pleasant to record a Reconciliation. After all their Differences and Misunderstandings, Hailfellow and Grouch came together and resumed Friendly Relations.

24 Both are employed by a New Concern which bought up the Bankrupt Stocks.

25 Grouch is keeping the Books at not very much per Month, and Hailfellow receives exactly the same Salary for standing around the front Doorway and glad-handing the Yaps.

26 Which proves that it is impossible for a Business Man to side-step his Destiny.

Moral: *Pick out the Other Kind for a Partner.*

VOCABULARY

hailfellow (P1), *Navy Plug* (P2), *petrified* (P2), *emporium* (P4), *levee* (P4), *josher* (P5), *K.P.'s* (P6), *Odd Fellows* (P6), *stand-up collar* (P7), *disposition* (P9), *industry* (P13), *soldiered* (P15), *dissolution* (P16), *gilt* (P17), *passbooks* (P19), *drummer* (P19), *gross (P19)*, *unsociable* (P19), *patronize* (P20), *jobbers* (P21), *paupers* (P22), *reconciliation* (P23), *yaps* (P25)

IDEAS AND AIMS

1. What main ideas or points of Ade's piece are summarized in his moral?
2. What strengths and weaknesses as a businessman does Hailfellow have? How is his name appropriate to his temperament?
3. What strengths and weaknesses as a businessman does Grouch have? How is his name appropriate to his temperament?
4. How do the outcomes of the partners' careers follow inevitably from their characters?

5. What negative effects may spouses have on business or business relationships, as depicted by Ade?

6. How are customers portrayed uncomplimentarily by Ade?

7. How can we tell from Ade's essay-fable that one of its main aims is to amuse or satirize? Cite several examples or details from the fable in your answer.

ORGANIZATION AND FORM

1. A fable is a story, necessarily told as a narrative, in chronological order. What other pattern or patterns of organization can you find used in this piece?

2. How does Ade's piece naturally divide into two parts, PP1–13 and PP14–26?

3. In what paragraphs does Ade handle comparison and contrast of Hailfellow and Grouch? Is his method to compare them in the same paragraph, one paragraph against another paragraph, or some combination?

4. How does the opening sentence of P23 playfully mislead the reader, setting up an ironic turn in the concluding three paragraphs of the piece?

WORDS AND STYLE

1. Pick out some instances of Ade's colloquialisms (remember that the book containing the essay appeared in 1902) and explain how they help Ade show something about Hailfellow, Grouch, or doing business in America's heartland.

2. What tone is created by the use of phrases like "Long Suit" (P4) and "front Name" (P4)?

3. How does Ade's use of capitals contribute to the fairy tale or fable quality of his piece?

4. How does Ade's use of capitals contribute to the humor of his piece generally and in any particular instances?

5. In what way is Ade's phrase "complicated Aroma" in P2 a euphemism? How is this euphemism both amusing and ironic?

6. How are Ade's words ironic in "sure Reward" (P20), "rushing Business" (P22), and "Autograph Signatures" (P22)?

DISCUSSION AND WRITING

1. Who profited from the partners' difficulties? What is Ade showing about business here?

2. There are actually two morals to the fable, one in the labeled moral and the other in the last sentence of the body of the fable. Explain them both in your own words. Are the morals actually proven by the events in the fable?

3. In the last analysis, according to Ade, what does business success or failure depend upon?

4. How true do you think the "moral" of Ade's piece is for business? Might it be true in other areas of life as well?

5. Write an essay based on Ade's narrative, detailing what traits and attributes a successful retail businessman ought to have.

6. Try to compose a "fable," using capitals and colloquialisms in the manner of Ade, that reveals some folly of human behavior at work, school, or home.

7. In an essay, compare and contrast two friends, relatives, acquaintances, or teachers who fall in the Hailfellow and Grouch categories. Be sure to use plenty of concrete details, following Ade as a model (e.g., the gilt sign and nickel-plated showcases of Hailfellow's store in P17).

8. Compare Ade's view of a spouse's effect on someone in business (PP14–16) with Parkinson's analysis in P6 of his essay (the selection immediately preceding Ade's piece).

TAKING STOCK: COMPARING AND CONTRASTING THE SELECTIONS

1. Draw an extended contrast between the poor boss or manager as presented in Thurber's "How to Adjust Yourself to Your Work" and the good boss or manager as presented in John L. McCaffrey's "What Corporation Presidents Think About at Night" (Section 3, "Work and Education"). Don't overlook Mr. McCaffrey himself as an exemplar.

2. What similarities or differences are there in the depiction of office politics in the essays by Art Buchwald (Section 6, "Job Opportunities and Other Practical Matters"), Robert Benchley ("From Nine to Five" in the preceding section), and James Thurber?

3. Apply the ideas and views in William Ouchi's "Japanese and American Workers: Two Casts of Mind" to the workers, management, and corporation as these are presented in Patrick Fenton's "Confessions of a Working Stiff" (Section 7, "The Varieties of Work: Professions and Blue Collar"). Does the corporation in Fenton's essay concern itself with relating, through middle management (or directly, from higher up), with its employees? Is it concerned with helping its employees better communicate or get along with each other? Explain your answer.

4. Applying some of Ouchi's concepts in "Japanese and American Workers" (see also our introduction to the essay), would you say that John L. McCaffrey (Section 3, "Work and Education") is more a Type A or a Type Z corporation president? Is his corporation more a Type A or a Type Z company? How so?

5. How can the concept of what Greek author Hesiod calls "strife" in "Two Kinds of Competition" (Section 2, "Work and Morality") be seen operating in the way Americans, in Ouchi's essay, run or want to run business (e.g., the incentive system in PP1–2, the cost accounting system in PP8–9)? Compare and contrast Hesiod's and Ouchi's views of "strife" (competition), particularly, in Ouchi's essay, "strife" within the corporation.

6. How would the advice of C. Northcote Parkinson to a young manager, which may be inferred from his essay, differ from the advice of James Thurber? On what points of advice, if any, would these authors concur?

7. Compare and contrast Parkinson's remarks on the interrelationships between education and business (P3, P9) with the views of the dry cleaner in P14 of Perelman's essay (Section 7, "The Varieties of Work: Professions and Blue Collar"), those of any of the authors in the section "Work and Education," or with Peter Drucker's in "Evolution of the Knowledge Worker" (Section 4, "Careers for the 1990s").

8. Much of Parkinson's essay is about what the Greek author Hesiod in our selection from his work (Section 2, "Work and Morality") would call "strife." Is this "strife" (competition) as described in Parkinson's essay (between old and young, between 35-year-olds and 37-year-olds, and between Mrs. A and Mrs. B, Mrs. C, and Mrs. D) the good thing that it is in Hesiod's view? Why or why not?

9. With questions 5 and 8 in mind, combine Ouchi's and Parkinson's views on "strife" within the corporation. How do these views compare or contrast with Hesiod's?

10. How do the selections by Ade, Thurber, and Parkinson all concur on the need for businesses to take account of the foibles of human nature? Do you agree with these authors' assessments of the importance of considering human folly in running a company successfully?

11. How does the stated moral of Ade's fable in some sense coincide with Parkinson's main point about diversity in PP8–9 of his essay? How does Benchley's depiction of his office's afternoon business conference in "From Nine to Five" (Section 8, "Efficiency and Success on the Job") contradict this view?

Note: See also question 10 of the Taking Stock questions in the "Efficiency and Success on the Job" section. In addition, see Discussion and Writing question 4 for Thurber's essay; Words and Style question 3 as well as Discussion and Writing question 5 for Ouchi's essay; and Organization and Form question 6 as well as Discussion and Writing question 5 for Parkinson's essay.

ALTERNATE RHETORICAL TABLE OF CONTENTS

ALPHABETICAL
TABLE OF CONTENTS
AND INDEX
TO RHETORICAL PATTERNS

CREDITS